CAMBRIDGE LIB

Maritime Exploration

This series includes accounts, by eye-witnesses and contemporaries, of voyages by Europeans to the Americas, Asia, Australasia and the Pacific during the colonial period. Driven by the military and commercial interests of powers including Britain, France and the Netherlands, particularly the East India Companies, these expeditions brought back a wealth of information on climate, natural resources, topography, and distant civilisations. Their detailed observations provide fascinating historical data for climatologists, ecologists and anthropologists, and the accounts of the mariners' experiences on their long and dangerous voyages are full of human interest.

The Principal Navigations, Voyages, Traffiques and Discoveries of the English Nation

Richard Hakluyt (1552?–1616) was fascinated from his earliest years by stories of strange lands and voyages of exploration. A priest by profession, he was also an indefatigable editor and translator of geographical accounts, and a propagandist for English expeditions to claim new lands, especially in the Americas. His most famous work was first published in 1589, and expanded in 1598–1600: reissued here is the twelve-volume edition prepared by the Scottish firm of James MacLehose and Sons and first published between 1903 and 1905, which included introductory essays and notes. Hakluyt's subjects range from transcriptions of personal accounts and 'ruttiers' (descriptive charts of voyages) to patriotic attacks against rival nations (especially Spain). Volume 1 contains Hakluyt's 'Epistles Dedicatory' and letters to the reader, followed by accounts of voyages to the 'north and northeast quarters'.

Cambridge University Press has long been a pioneer in the reissuing of out-of-print titles from its own backlist, producing digital reprints of books that are still sought after by scholars and students but could not be reprinted economically using traditional technology. The Cambridge Library Collection extends this activity to a wider range of books which are still of importance to researchers and professionals, either for the source material they contain, or as landmarks in the history of their academic discipline.

Drawing from the world-renowned collections in the Cambridge University Library and other partner libraries, and guided by the advice of experts in each subject area, Cambridge University Press is using state-of-the-art scanning machines in its own Printing House to capture the content of each book selected for inclusion. The files are processed to give a consistently clear, crisp image, and the books finished to the high quality standard for which the Press is recognised around the world. The latest print-on-demand technology ensures that the books will remain available indefinitely, and that orders for single or multiple copies can quickly be supplied.

The Cambridge Library Collection brings back to life books of enduring scholarly value (including out-of-copyright works originally issued by other publishers) across a wide range of disciplines in the humanities and social sciences and in science and technology.

The Principal Navigations, Voyages, Traffiques and Discoveries of the English Nation

VOLUME 1

RICHARD HAKLUYT

CAMBRIDGE
UNIVERSITY PRESS

CAMBRIDGE
UNIVERSITY PRESS

University Printing House, Cambridge, CB2 8BS, United Kingdom

Published in the United States of America by Cambridge University Press, New York

Cambridge University Press is part of the University of Cambridge.

It furthers the University's mission by disseminating knowledge in the pursuit of education, learning and research at the highest international levels of excellence.

www.cambridge.org
Information on this title: www.cambridge.org/9781108071291

© in this compilation Cambridge University Press 2014

This edition first published 1903
This digitally printed version 2014

ISBN 978-1-108-07129-1 Paperback

The Principal
Navigations Voyages Traffiques and Discoveries of the English Nation

In Twelve Volumes

Volume I

GLASGOW

PRINTED AT THE UNIVERSITY PRESS BY
ROBERT MACLEHOSE AND COMPANY FOR
JAMES MACLEHOSE AND SONS, PUBLISHERS
TO THE UNIVERSITY OF GLASGOW

MACMILLAN AND CO. LTD.   LONDON
THE MACMILLAN CO.   NEW YORK
SIMPKIN, HAMILTON AND CO. LONDON
MACMILLAN AND BOWES   CAMBRIDGE
DOUGLAS AND FOULIS   EDINBURGH

MCMIII

ELIZABETA D. G. ANGLIÆ.FRANCIÆ.HIBERNIÆ.ET VERGINIÆ
REGINA CHRISTIANAE FIDEI VNICVM PROPVGNACVLVM.

Immortalis honos Regum, cui non tulit ætas
Vlla prior, veniens nec feret vlla parem,
Sospite quo nunquam terras habitare Britannas
Desinet alma Quies, Iustitia atque Fides:

Queis ipsa tantum superent reliqua omnia regna,
Quantum tu maior Regibus es reliquis,
Viue precor felix tanti in moderamine regni,
Dum tibi Rex Regum cælica regna paret.

In honorem serenissimae suæ Maiestatis hanc effigiem fieri curabat Ioannes Whitnellius Belga. Anno 1596.

The Principal Navigations Voyages Traffiques & Discoveries of the English Nation

Made by Sea or Over-land to the Remote and Farthest Distant Quarters of the Earth at any time within the compasse of these 1600 Yeeres

By
RICHARD HAKLUYT
Preacher, and sometime Student of Christ-Church in Oxford

VOLUME I

Glasgow
James MacLehose and Sons
Publishers to the University
MCMIII

THE TABLE

THE TABLE

THE TABLE

THE TABLE

THE TABLE

A Catalogue of the Voyages—*Continued.*

ILLUSTRATIONS

ILLUSTRATIONS

PUBLISHERS' NOTE

THE first edition of 'The Principall Navigations,
Voiages and Discoveries of the English nation, made
by Sea or ouer Land, to the most remote and farthest
distant Quarters of the earth at any time within the
compasse of these 1500. yeeres. . . . By Richard Hakluyt
Master of Artes, and Student sometime of Christ-
Church in Oxford' was 'imprinted at London by
George Bishop and Ralph Newberie, Deputies to
Christopher Barker, Printer to the Queenes most
excellent Maiestie' in the year 1589, in one
volume foolscap folio. Some copies of this first edition
contain a cancel of pp. 491-501, substituting for 'The
Ambassage of Sir Hierome Bowes to the Emperour of
Moscouie 1583' a different account entitled 'A briefe
discourse of the voyage of Sir Ierome Bowes knight, her
Maiesties ambassador to the Emperour of Muscouia, in
the yeere 1582 : and printed this second time, according
to the true copie I receiued of a gentleman that went
in the same voyage, for the correction of the errours
in the former impression.' It was, of course, this
amended account which appeared in the second edition,
but for the purposes of comparison the original account
will be printed as an appendix in the third volume.

PUBLISHERS' NOTE

A second edition of 'The Principall Navigations' revised and enlarged, and with the voyages now stated as having been made 'within the compasse of these 1600. yeeres' was 'imprinted at London by George Bishop, Ralph Newberie and Robert Barker' in the years 1598, 1599, and 1600, in three volumes foolscap folio.

The title page of the first volume of the second edition originally contained a reference to 'the famous victorie atchieued at the citie of Cadiz, 1596,' but after the disgrace of the Earl of Essex this title page was cancelled in many copies, and a new one, bearing the date 1599, without any reference to the Cadiz expedition was substituted. This reprinted title-page states the contents of the Second Volume as well as of the First. The text of 'the briefe and true report' of the expedition occupying pp. 607-619 was at the same time cut out, but in many copies has been replaced by a modern reprint occupying one page more.

Facsimiles of the title page of the first edition and of the three title pages of the second edition are reproduced here ; and the dedication and preface to the first edition are also included.

The text of this edition is an exact reprint of that of 1598-1600 with the following exceptions :—the letters i, j, u, and v are used according to modern custom ; contracted forms such as m̄ for 'mm,' n̄ for 'nn,' ū for 'um,' q; for 'que' have been extended, and obvious printers' errors have been corrected. The punctuation of the second edition has been followed throughout. At the suggestion of Professor Skeat references to the volumes and pages of the original text have been inserted in the margin.

PUBLISHERS' NOTE

Professor Walter Raleigh's Essay on the Life and Work of Hakluyt and a full Index to the whole text, will be included in the twelfth volume.

The Publishers desire to express their indebtedness to Mr. Basil H. Soulsby, Superintendent of the Map Room, British Museum, and Secretary of the Hakluyt Society, for his assistance in the selection of maps and illustrations.

All the maps, plans, and charts in this edition are from contemporary sources, and have been reproduced in exact facsimile with the view of illustrating the state of cartography in Hakluyt's time.

GLASGOW,
September, 1903.

Dedications & Prefaces

THE EPISTLE DEDICATORIE IN THE
FIRST EDITION, 1589.

To the Right Honorable Sir Francis Walsingham
Knight, Principall Secretarie to her Majestie,
Chancellor of the Duchie of Lancaster, and
one of her Majesties most honourable Privie
Councell.

IGHT Honorable, I do remember that
being a youth, and one of her Majesties
scholars at Westminster that fruitfull nur-
serie, it was my happe to visit the chamber
of M. Richard Hakluyt my cosin, a Gentleman of the Middle Temple, well knowen
unto you, at a time when I found lying
open upon his boord certeine bookes of Cosmographie,
with an universall Mappe : he seeing me somewhat
curious in the view therof, began to instruct my ignorance,
by shewing me the division of the earth into three parts
after the olde account, and then according to the latter,
& better distribution, into more : he pointed with his
wand to all the knowen Seas, Gulfs, Bayes, Straights,
Capes, Rivers, Empires, Kingdomes, Dukedomes, and
Territories of ech part, with declaration also of their
speciall commodities, & particular wants, which by the
benefit of traffike, & entercourse of merchants, are plentifully supplied. From the Mappe he brought me to the
Bible, and turning to the 107 Psalme, directed mee to the
23 & 24 verses, where I read, that they which go downe
to the sea in ships, and occupy by the great waters, they
see the works of the Lord, and his woonders in the deepe,

I   xvii   *b*

THE EPISTLE DEDICATORIE

&c. Which words of the Prophet together with my cousins discourse (things of high and rare delight to my yong nature) tooke in me so deepe an impression, that I constantly resolved, if ever I were preferred to the University, where better time, and more convenient place might be ministred for these studies, I would by Gods assistance prosecute that knowledge and kinde of literature, the doores whereof (after a sort) were so happily opened before me.

According to which my resolution, when, not long after, I was removed to Christ-church in Oxford, my exercises of duety first performed, I fell to my intended course, and by degrees read over whatsoever printed or written discoveries and voyages I found extant either in the Greeke, Latine, Italian, Spanish, Portugall, French, or English languages, and in my publike lectures was the first, that produced and shewed both the olde imperfectly composed, and the new lately reformed Mappes, Globes, Spheares, and other instruments of this Art for demonstration in the common schooles, to the singular pleasure, and generall contentment of my auditory. In continuance of time, and by reason principally of my insight in this study, I grew familiarly acquainted with the chiefest Captaines at sea, the greatest Merchants, and the best Mariners of our nation : by which meanes having gotten somewhat more then common knowledge, I passed at length the narrow seas into France with sir Edward Stafford, her Majesties carefull and discreet Ligier, where during my five yeeres abroad with him in his dangerous and chargeable residencie in her Highnes service, I both heard in speech, and read in books other nations miraculously extolled for their discoveries and notable enterprises by sea, but the English of all others for their sluggish security, and continuall neglect of the like attempts especially in so long and happy a time of peace, either ignominiously reported, or exceedingly condemned : which singular opportunity, if some other people our neighbors had beene blessed with, their protestations are often and vehement, they would farre otherwise have used. And that the trueth and evidence heerof may better appeare, these are the very words of Popiliniere in his booke called L'Admiral de France, and printed at Paris. Fol. 73. pag. 1, 2. The occasion of his speech is the commendation of the Rhodians, who being (as we are) Islanders, were excellent in navigation, whereupon he woondereth much that the English should not surpasse in that qualitie, in this sort : Ce qui m'a fait autresfois rechercher les occasions, qui empeschent, que les Anglois, qui ont d'esprit, de moyens, & valeur assez, pour s'aquerir un grand honneur parmi tous les Chrestiens, ne se font plus valoir sur l'element qui leur est, & doit estre plus naturel qu'à autres peuples : qui leur doivent ceder en la structure, accommodement & police de navires : comme j'ay veu en plusieurs endroits parmi eux. Thus both hearing, and reading the obloquie of our nation, and finding few or none of our owne men able to replie heerin : and further, not seeing any man to have care to recommend to the world, the industrious labors, and painefull travels of our countrey men : for stopping the mouthes of the reprochers, my selfe being the last winter returned from France with the honorable the Lady Sheffield, for her passing good behavior highly esteemed in all the French court, determined notwithstanding all difficulties, to undertake the burden of that worke wherin all others pretended either ignorance, or lacke of leasure, or want of sufficient argument, whereas (to speake truely) the huge toile, and the small profit to insue, were the chiefe causes of the refusall. I call the worke a burden, in consideration that these voyages lay so dispersed, scattered, and hidden in severall hucksters hands, that I now woonder at my selfe, to see how I was able to endure the delayes, curiosity, and backwardnesse of many from whom I was to receive my originals : so that I have just cause to make that complaint of the maliciousnes of divers in our time, which Plinie made of the men of his age : At nos elaborata iis abscondere atque supprimere cupimus, & fraudare vitam etiam alienis bonis, &c.

Plinius. lib. 25. cap. 1. Naturalis historiæ.

THE EPISTLE DEDICATORIE

To harpe no longer upon this string, & to speake a word of that just commendation which our nation doe indeed deserve : it can not be denied, but as in all former ages, they have bene men full of activity, stirrers abroad, and searchers of the remote parts of the world, so in this most famous and peerlesse governement of her most excellent Majesty, her subjects through the speciall assistance, and blessing of God, in searching the most opposite corners and quarters of the world, and to speake plainly, in compassing the vaste globe of the earth more then once, have excelled all the nations and people of the earth. For, which of the kings of this land before her Majesty, had theyr banners ever seene in the Caspian sea? which of them hath ever dealt with the Emperor of Persia, as her Majesty hath done, and obteined for her merchants large & loving privileges? who ever saw before this regiment, an English Ligier in the stately porch of the Grand Signor at Constantinople? who ever found English Consuls & Agents at Tripolis in Syria, at Aleppo, at Babylon, at Balsara, and which is more, who ever heard of Englishman at Goa before now? what English shippes did heeretofore ever anker in the mighty river of Plate? passe and repasse the unpassable (in former opinion) straight of Magellan, range along the coast of Chili, Peru, and all the backside of Nova Hispania, further then any Christian ever passed, travers the mighty bredth of the South sea, land upon the Luzones in despight of the enemy, enter into alliance, amity, and traffike with the princes of the Moluccaes, & the Isle of Java, double the famous Cape of Bona Speranza, arive at the Isle of Santa Helena, & last of al returne home most richly laden with the commodities of China, as the subjects of this now florishing monarchy have done? Lucius Florus in the very end of his historie de gestis Romanorum recordeth as a wonderfull miracle, that the Seres, (which I take to be the people of Cathay, or China) sent Ambassadors to Rome, to intreate frindship, as moved with the fame of the majesty of the Romane

Empire. And have not we as good cause to admire, that the Kings of the Moluccaes, and Java major, have desired the favour of her majestie, and the commerce & traffike of her people? Is it not as strange that the borne naturalles of Japan, and the Philippinaes are here to be seene, agreeing with our climate, speaking our language, and informing us of the state of their Easterne habitations? For mine owne part, I take it as a pledge of Gods further favour both unto us and them : to them especially, unto whose doores I doubt not in time shalbe by us caried the incomparable treasure of the trueth of Christianity, and of the Gospell, while we use and exercise common trade with their marchants. I must confesse to have read in the excellent history intituled Origines of Joannes Goropius, a testimonie of king Henrie the viii. a prince of noble memory, whose intention was once, if death had not prevented him, to have done some singular thing in this case : whose words speaking of his dealing to that end with himselfe, he being a stranger, & his history rare, I thought good in this place verbatim to record : Ante *Joannis* viginti & plus eo annos ab Henrico Knevetto Equite *Goropii* Anglo nomine Regis Henrici arram accepi, qua con- *originum lib.* venerat, Regio sumptu me totam Asiam, quoad Turcorum *5. pag.* 494. & Persarum Regum commendationes, & legationes ad- mitterentur, peragraturum. Ab his enim duobus Asiæ principibus facile se impetraturum sperabat, ut non solùm tutò mihi per ipsorum fines liceret ire, sed ut com- mendatione etiam ipsorum ad confinia quoque daretur penetrare. Sumptus quidem non exiguus erat futurus, sed tanta erat principi cognoscendi aviditas, ut nullis pecuniis ad hoc iter necessariis se diceret parsurum. O Dignum Regia Majestate animum, O me fœlicem, si Deus non antè & Knevettum & Regem abstulisset, quàm reversus ab hac peregrinatione fuissem, &c. But as the purpose of David the king to builde a house and temple to God was accepted, although Salomon performed it : so I make no question, but that the zeale in this matter of the aforesaid most renowmed prince may seeme

THE EPISTLE DEDICATORIE

no lesse worthy (in his kinde) of acceptation, although reserved for the person of our Salomon her gratious Majesty, whome I feare not to pronounce to have received the same Heroicall spirit, and most honorable disposition, as an inheritance from her famous father.

Now wheras I have alwayes noted your wisdome to have had a speciall care of the honor of her Majesty, the good reputation of our country, & the advancing of navigation, the very walles of this our Island, as the oracle *Plutarch in* is reported to have spoken of the sea forces of Athens : *the life of* and whereas I acknowledge in all dutifull sort how *Themistocles.* honorably both by your letter and speech I have bene animated in this and other my travels, I see my selfe bound to make presentment of this worke to your selfe, as the fruits of your owne incouragements, & the manifestation both of my unfained service to my prince and country, and of my particular duty to your honour : which I have done with the lesse suspition either of not satisfying the world, or of not answering your owne expectation, in that according to your order, it hath passed the sight, and partly also the censure of the learned phisitian M. Doctor James, a man many wayes very notably qualified.

And thus beseeching God, the giver of all true honor & wisdome to increase both these blessings in you, with continuance of health, strength, happinesse, and whatsoever good thing els your selfe can wish, I humbly take my leave. London the 17 of November.

Your honors most humble alwayes to be
commanded RICHARD HAKLUYT.

Richard Hakluyt to the favourable Reader.

 Have thought it very requisite for thy further instruction and direction in this historie (Good Reader) to acquaint thee brieflie with the Methode and order which I have used in the whole course thereof : and by the way also to let thee understand by whose friendly aide in this my travell I have bene furthered : acknowledging that ancient speach to be no lesse true then ingenious, that the offence is great, Non agnoscere per quos profeceris, not to speake of them by whom a man in his indevours is assisted.

Concerning my proceeding therefore in this present worke, it hath bene this. Whatsoever testimonie I have found in any authour of authoritie appertaining to my argument, either stranger or naturall, I have recorded the same word for word, with his particular name and page of booke where it is extant. If the same were not reduced into our common language, I have first expressed it in the same termes wherein it is originally written, whether it were a Latine, Italian, Spanish or Portingall discourse, or whatsoever els, and thereunto in the next roome have annexed the signification and translation of the wordes in English. And to the ende that those men which were the paynefull and personall travellers might reape that good opinion and just commendation which they have deserved, and further, that every man might answere for himselfe, justifie his reports, and stand accountable for his owne doings, I have referred every voyage to his Author, which both in person hath performed, and in writing hath left the same : for I am not ignorant of Ptolomies assertion, that Peregrinationis historia, and not those wearie volumes bearing the titles of universall Cosmographie which some men that I could name have published as their owne, beyng in deed most untruly and unprofitablie ramassed and hurled together, is that which must bring us to the certayne and full discoverie of the world.

Moreover, I meddle in this worke with the Navigations onely of our owne nation : And albeit I alleage in a few places (as the matter and occasion required) some strangers as witnesses of the things done, yet are they none but such as either faythfully remember, or sufficiently confirme the travels of our owne people : of whom (to speake trueth) I have received more light in some respects, then all our owne Historians could affoord me in this case, Bale, Foxe, and Eden onely excepted.

And it is a thing withall principally to be considered, that I stand not upon any action perfourmed neere home, nor in any part of Europe commonly frequented by our shipping, as for example : Not upon that victorious exploit not long since atchieved in our narow Seas agaynst that monstrous Spanish army under the valiant and provident conduct of the right honourable the lord Charles Howard high Admirall of England : Not upon the good services of our two woorthie Generals in their late Portugall expedition : Not upon the two most fortunate attempts of our famous Chieftaine Sir Frauncis Drake, the one in the Baie of Cales upon a great part of the enimies chiefest shippes, the other neere the Islands upon the great Carrack of the East India, the first (though peradventure not the last) of that imployment, that ever discharged Molucca spices in English portes : these (albeit singular and happy voyages of our renowmed countrymen) I omit, as things distinct and without the compasse of my prescribed limites, beyng

THE PRINCIPALL

NAVIGATIONS,VOIA-
GES AND DISCOVERIES OF THE
Englifh nation,made by Sea or ouer Land,

to the moſt remote and fartheſt diſtant Quarters of
the earth at any time within the compaſſe
of theſe 1500. yeeres: Deuided into three
feuerall parts,according to the pofitions of the Regions wherun-
to they were directed.

The firſt,conteining the perſonall trauels of the Englifh vnto *Iudæa,Syria,A-rabia*,the riuer *Euphrates,Babylon,Balſara*, the *Perſian* Gulfe, *Ormuz, Chaul, Goa,India,*and many Iſlands adioyning to the South parts of *Aſia*: toge-ther with the like vnto *Egypt*, the chiefeſt ports and places of *Africa* with-in and without the Streight of *Gibraltar,* and about the famous Promon-torie of *Buona Eſperanʒa.*

The ſecond,comprehending the worthy difcoueries of the Englifh towards the North and Northeaſt by Sea,as of *Lapland, Scrikfinia, Corelia*, the Baie of *S.Nicholas*,the Iſles of *Colgoieue, Vaigats,* and *Noua Zembla* toward the great riuer *Ob,*with the mightie Empire of *Ruſſia*, the *Caſpian* Sea,*Georgia, Armenia,Media,Perſia,Boghar* in *Bactria,*& diuers kingdoms of *Tartaria.*

The third and laſt,including the Englifh valiant attempts in ſearching al-moſt all the corners of the vaſte and new world of *America*, from 73.de-grees of Northerly latitude Southward,to *Meta Incognita,Newfoundland,* the maine of *Virginia*, the point of *Florida*,the Baie of *Mexico*, all the In-land of *Noua Hiſpania*, the coaſt of *Terra firma, Braſill*, the riuer of *Plate*,to the Streight of *Magellan:* and through it,and from it in the South Sea to *Chili, Peru, Xaliſco,* the Gulfe of *California, Noua Albion* vpon the backſide of *Canada*, further then euer any Chriſtian hitherto hath pierced.

Whereunto is added the laſt moſt renowmed Englifh Nauigation,
round about the whole Globe of the Earth.

By *Richard Hakluyt Maſter of Artes, and Student ſometime*
of Chriſt-church in Oxford.

Imprinted at London by GEORGE BISHOP
and RALPH NEWBERIE, Deputies to
CHRISTOPHER BARKER, Printer to the
Queenes moſt excellent Maieſtie.

1589.

TO THE FAVOURABLE READER

neither of remote length and spaciousnesse, neither of search and discoverie of strange coasts, the chiefe subject of this my labour.

Thus much in brevitie shall serve thee for the generall order. Particularlie I have disposed and digested the whole worke into 3. partes, or as it were Classes, not without my reasons. In the first I have martialled all our voyages of any moment that have bene performed to the South and Southeast parts of the world, by which I chiefly meane that part of Asia which is neerest, and of the rest hithermost towards us : For I find that the oldest travels as well of the ancient Britains, as of the English, were ordinarie to Judea which is in Asia, termed by them the Holy land, principally for devotions sake according to the time, although I read in Joseph Bengorion a very authenticall Hebrew author, a testimonie of the passing of 20000. Britains valiant souldiours, to the siege and fearefull sacking of Jerusalem under the conduct of Vespasian and Titus the Romane Emperour, a thing in deed of all the rest most ancient. But of latter dayes I see our men have pierced further into the East, have passed downe the mightie river Euphrates, have sayled from Balsara through the Persian gulfe to the Citie of Ormuz, and from thence to Chaul and Goa in the East India, which passages written by the parties themselves are herein to be read. To these I have added the Navigations of the English made for the parts of Africa, and either within or without the streights of Gibraltar : within, to Constantinople in Romania, to Alexandria, and Cayro in Egypt, to Tunez, to Goletta, to Malta, to Algier, and to Tripolis in Barbary : without, to Santa Cruz, to Asafi, to the Citie of Marocco, to the River of Senega, to the Isles of Cape Verde, to Guinea, to Benyn, and round about the dreadfull Cape of Bona Speranza, as far as Goa.

The north, and Northeasterne voyages of our nation I have produced in the second place, because our accesse to those quarters of the world is later and not so auncient as the former : and yet some of our travailes that way be of

more antiquitie by many hundred yeeres, then those that
have bene made to the westerne coastes of America.
Under this title thou shalt first finde the old northerne
Navigations of our Brittish Kings, as of Arthur, of Malgo,
of Edgar Pacificus the Saxon Monarch, with that also of
Nicholaus de Linna under the north pole: next to them
in consequence, the discoveries of the bay of Saint
Nicholas, of Colgoieve, of Pechora, of the Isles of Vaigats,
of Nova Zembla, and of the Sea eastwards towardes the
river of Ob: after this, the opening by sea of the great
Dukedome, and Empire of Russia, with the notable and
strange journey of Master Jenkinson to Boghar in Bactria.
Whereunto thou maist adde sixe of our voyages eleven
hundred verstes up against the streame of Dwina to the
towne of Vologhda: thence one hundred, and fourescore
verstes by land to Yeraslave standing upon the mighty
river of Volga: there hence above two thousand and five
hundred versts downe the streame to the ancient marte
Towne of Astracan, and so to the manifolde mouthes of
Volga, and from thence also by ship over the Caspian sea
into Media, and further then that also with Camels unto
Georgia, Armenia, Hyrcania, Gillan, and the cheefest
Cities of the Empire of Persia: wherein the Companie of
Moscovie Marchants to the perpetuall honor of their
Citie, and societie, have performed more then any one,
yea then all the nations of Europe besides: which thing
is also acknowledged by the most learned Cosmographers,
and Historiographers of Christendome, with whose honorable testimonies of the action, not many for number, but
sufficient for authoritie I have concluded this second part.

Touching the westerne Navigations, and travailes of
ours, they succeede naturallie in the third and last roome,
forasmuch as in order and course those coastes, and
quarters came last of all to our knowledge and experience.
Herein thou shalt reade the attempt by Sea of the sonne
of one of the Princes of Northwales, in sayling and
searching towards the west more then 400. yeeres since:
the offer made by Christopher Columbus that renowned

TO THE FAVOURABLE READER

Genouoys to the most sage Prince of noble memorie King Henrie the 7. with his prompt and cheerefull acceptation thereof, and the occasion whereupon it became fruitlesse, and at that time of no great effect to this kingdome: then followe the letters Patentes of the foresaid noble Prince given to John Cabot a Venetian and his 3. sonnes, to discover & conquer in his name, and under his Banners unknowen Regions: who with that royall incouragement & contribution of the king himselfe, and some assistance in charges of English Marchants departed ‖ with 5. sailes from the Port of Bristoll accompained with *Robert* 300. Englishmen, and first of any Christians found out *Fabian.* that mightie and large tract of lande and Sea, from the circle Arcticke as farre as Florida, as appeareth in the discourse thereof. The triumphant raigne of King Henry the 8. yelded some prosecution of this discoverie: for the 3. voyages performed, and the 4. intended for all Asia by his Majesties selfe, do approove and confirme the same. Then in processe of yeeres ariseth the first English trade to Brasill, the first passing of some of our nation in the ordinarie Spanish fleetes to the west Indies, and the huge Citie of Mexico in Nova Hispania. Then immediatlye ensue 3. voyages made by M. John Hawkins now Knight, then Esquire, to Hispaniola, and the gulfe of Mexico: upon which depende sixe verie excellent discourses of our men, whereof some for 15. or 16. whole yeeres inhabited in New Spaine, and ranged the whole Countrie, wherein are disclosed the cheefest secretes of the west India, which may in time turne to our no smal advantage. The next leaves thou turnest, do yeelde thee the first valiant enterprise of Sir Francis Drake upon Nombre de Dios, the mules laden with treasure which he surprised, and the house called the Cruzes, which his fire consumed: and therewith is joyned an action more venterous then happie of John Oxnam of Plimmouth written, and confessed by a Spanyard, which with his companie passed over the streight Istme of Darien, and building certaine pinnesses on the west shoare, was the first Englishman that entered the South sea. To passe over Master Frobisher and his actions, which I have also newly though briefely printed, and as it were revived, whatsoever Master John Davis hath performed in continuing that discovery, which Master Frobisher began for the northwest passage, I have faithfully at large communicated it with thee, that so the great good hope, & singular probabilities & almost certaintie therof, which by his industry have risen, may be knówen generally of all men, that some may yet still prosecute so noble an action. Sir Humfrey Gilbert, that couragious Knight, and very expert in the mysteries of Navigation amongst the rest is not forgotten : his learned reasons & arguments for the proofe of the passage before named, together with his last more commendable resolution then fortunate successe, are here both to be read. The continuance of the historie, produceth the beginnings, and proceedings of the two English Colonies planted in Virginia at the charges of sir Walter Raleigh, whose entrance upon those newe inhabitations had bene happie, if it had ben as seruiously followed, as it was cheerefully undertaken. I could not omit in this parte the two voyages made not long since to the Southwest, whereof I thinke the Spanyard hath had some knowledge, and felt some blowes : the one of Master Edward Fenton, and his consort Master Luke Warde : the other of Master Robert Withrington, and his hardie consort Master Christopher Lister as farre as 44. degrees of southerly latitude, set out at the direction and charge of the right honorable the Earle of Cumberland, both which in divers respectes may yelde both profite and pleasure to the reader, being carefully perused.

For the conclusion of all, the memorable voyage of Master Thomas Candish into the South sea, and from thence about the globe of the earth doth satisfie mee, and I doubt not but will fully content thee : which as in time it is later then that of Sir Frauncis Drake, so in relation of the Philippinaes, Japan, China, and the Isle of S. Helena it is more particular, and exact : and therfore the want of

TO THE FAVOURABLE READER

the first made by Sir Frauncis Drake will be the lesse:
wherein I must confesse to have taken more then ordinarie paines, meaning to have inserted it in this worke:
but being of late (contrary to my expectation) seriously
delt withall, not to anticipate or prevent another mans
paines and charge in drawing all the services of that
worthie Knight into one volume, I have yeelded unto
those my freindes which pressed me in the matter, refer-
ring the further knowledge of his proceedinges, to those
intended discourses.

Now for the other part of my promise, I must crave
thy further patience frendly reader, and some longer
suspence from the worke it selfe, in acquainting thee with
those vertuous gentlemen, and others which partly for
their private affection to my selfe, but chiefely for their
devotion to the furtherance of this my travaile, have
yelded me their severall good assistances: for I accompt
him unworthy of future favours, that is not thankefull for
former benefites. In respect of a generall incouragement
in this laborious travaile, it were grosse ingratitude in mee
to forget, and wilfull maliciousnes not to confesse that
man, whose onely name doth carrie with it sufficient
estimation and love, and that is Master Edward Dier, of
whom I will speake thus much in few wordes, that both
my selfe and my intentions herein by his frendly meanes
have bene made knowne to those, who in sundrie particulars have much steeded me. More specially in my
first part, Master Richard Staper Marchant of London,
hath furnished me with divers thinges touching the trade
of Turkie, and other places in the East. Master William
Burrowgh, Clarke of her Majesties navie, and Master
Anthonie Jenkinson, both gentlemen of great experience,
and observations in the north Regions, have much
pleasured me in the second part. In the third and last
besides myne owne extreeme travaile in the histories of
the Spanyards, my cheefest light hath bene received from
Sir John Hawkins, Sir Walter Raleigh, and my kinseman
Master Richard Hakluyt of the middle Temple.

RICHARD HAKLUYT

And whereas in the course of this history often mention is made of many beastes, birds, fishes, serpents, plants, fruits, hearbes, rootes, apparell, armour, boates, and such other rare and strange curiosities, which wise men take great pleasure to reade of, but much more contentment to see: herein I my selfe to my singuler delight have bene as it were ravished in beholding all the premisses gathered together with no small cost, and preserved with no litle diligence, in the excellent Cabinets of my very worshipfull and learned friends M. Richard Garthe, one of the Clearkes of the pettie Bags, and M. William Cope Gentleman Ussier to the right Honourable and most prudent Counseller (the Seneca of our common wealth,) the Lord Burleigh, high Treasourer of England.

Nowe, because peradventure it would bee expected as necessarie, that the descriptions of so many parts of the world would farre more easily be conceived of the Readers, by adding Geographicall, and Hydrographicall tables thereunto, thou art by the way to be admonished that I have contented my selfe with inserting into the worke one of the best generall mappes of the world onely, untill the comming out of a very large and most *The excellent* exact terrestriall Globe, collected and reformed according *newe Globe of* to the newest, secretest, and latest discoveries, both *M. Mulli-* Spanish, Portugall, and English, composed by M. *neux.* Emmerie Mollineux of Lambeth, a rare Gentleman in his profession, being therein for divers yeeres, greatly supported by the purse and liberalitie of the worshipfull marchant M. William Sanderson.

This being the summe of those things which I thought good to admonish thee of (good Reader) it remaineth that thou take the profite and pleasure of the worke: which
I wish to bee as great to thee, as my paines and labour
have bene in bringing these rawe fruits unto
this ripenesse, and in reducing these
loose papers into this order.
Farewell.

To the right honorable my singular good Lord, the
Lord Charles Howard, Erle of Notingham,
Baron of Effingham, Knight of the noble
Order of the Garter, Lord high Admirall of
England, Ireland, and Wales, &c. one of her
Majesties most honourable privie Counsell.

Ight Honourable and my very good Lord,
after I had long since published in Print
many Navigations and Discoveries of
Strangers in divers languages, as well
here at London, as in the citie of Paris,
during my five yeeres abode in France,
with the woorthie Knight Sir Edward
Stafford your brother in lawe, her Majesties most prudent
and carefull Ambassador ligier with the French King:
and had waded on still farther and farther in the sweet
studie of the historie of Cosmographie, I began at length
to conceive, that with diligent observation, some thing
might be gathered which might commend our nation
for their high courage and singular activitie in the Search
and Discoverie of the most unknowen quarters of the
world. Howbeit, seeing no man to step forth to undertake the recording of so many memorable actions, but
every man to folow his private affaires: the ardent love
of my countrey devoured all difficulties, and as it were
with a sharpe goad provoked me and thrust me forward
into this most troublesome and painfull action. And
after great charges and infinite cares, after many watchings,

toiles, and travels, and wearying out of my weake body;
at length I have collected three severall Volumes of
the English Navigations, Traffiques, and Discoveries,
to strange, remote, and farre distant countreys. Which
worke of mine I have not included within the compasse
of things onely done in these latter dayes, as though
litle or nothing woorthie of memorie had bene performed
in former ages; but mounting aloft by the space of
many hundred yeeres, have brought to light many very
rare and worthy monuments, which long have lien
miserably scattered in mustie corners, & retchlesly
hidden in mistie darkenesse, and were very like for the
greatest part to have bene buried in perpetuall oblivion.
The first Volume of this worke I have thus for the
present brought to light, reserving the other two untill
the next Spring, when by Gods grace they shall come
to the Presse. In the meane season bethinking my
selfe of some munificent and bountifull Patrone, I called
to mind your honorable Lordship, who both in regard
of my particular obligation, and also in respect of the
subject and matter, might justly chalenge the Patronage
thereof. For first I remembred how much I was bound,
and how deeply indebted for my yongest brother
Edmund Hackluyt, to whom for the space of foure
whole yeeres your Lordship committed the government
and instruction of that honorable yong noble man,
your sonne & heire apparant, the lord William
Howard, of whose high spirit and wonderful toward-
linesse full many a time hath he boasted unto me.
Secondly, the bounden duetie which I owe to your
most deare sister the lady Sheffield, my singular good
lady & honorable mistresse, admonished me to be mind-
full of the renoumed familie of the Howards. Thirdly,
when I found in the first Patent graunted by Queene
Marie to the Moscovie companie, that my lord your
father being then lord high Admirall of England, was
one of the first favourers and furtherers, with his
purse and countenance, of the strange and wonderfull

THE

PRINCIPAL NAVI-

GATIONS, VOIAGES,

TRAFFIQVES AND DISCO-

ueries of the Englifh Nation, made by Sea
or ouer-land , to the remote and fartheft di-
ftant quarters of the Earth, at any time within
the compaffe of thefe 1500. yeeres: Deuided
into three feuerall Volumes, according to the
pofitions of the Regions, whereunto
they were directed.

This firft Volume containing the woorthy Difcoueries,
&c. of the Englifh toward the North and Northeaft by fea,
as of *Lapland,Scrikfinia,Corelia,*the Baie of S. *Nicolas,* the Ifles of *Colgoieue, Vaigatz,* and *Noua Zembla,* toward the great riuer *Ob,*
with the mighty Empire of *Ruſsia,*the *Caſpian* fea, *Georgia, Armenia, Media, Perſia, Boghar* in *Bactria,*
and diuers kingdoms of *Tartaria:*

Together with many notable monuments and teftimo-
nies of the ancient forren trades, and of the warrelike and
other fhipping of this realme of *England* in former ages.

VVhereunto is annexed alfo a briefe Commentarie of the true
ftate of *Ifland ,* and of the Northren Seas and
lands fituate that way.

And laftly, the memorable defeate of the Spaniſh huge
Armada, Anno 1588. and the famous victorie
atchieued at the citie of *Cadiz,* 1596.
are defcribed.

By RICHARD HAKLVYT *Mafter of*
Artes, and fometime Student of Chrift-
Church in Oxford.

Imprinted at London by GEORGE
BISHOP, RALPH NEWBERIE
and ROBERT BARKER.
1598.

The material originally positioned here is too large for reproduction in this
reissue. A PDF can be downloaded from the web address given on page iv
of this book, by clicking on 'Resources Available'.

TO LORD CHARLES HOWARD

Discoverie of Russia, the chiefe contents of this present Volume, then I remembred the sage saying of sweet Isocrates, That sonnes ought not onely to be inheriters of their fathers substance, but also of their commendable vertues and honours. But what speake I of your ancestors honors (which to say the trueth, are very great, and such as our Chronicles have notably blazoned) when as your owne Heroicall actions from time to time have shewed themselves so admirable, as no antiquitie hath affoorded greater, and the future times will not in haste (I thinke) performe the like. To come to some particulars, when the Emperors sister, the spouse of Spaine, with a Fleete of an 130. sailes, stoutly and proudly passed the narow Seas, your Lordship accompanied with ten ships onely of her Majesties Navie Roiall, environed their Fleet in most strange and warrelike sort, enforced them to stoope gallant, and to vaile their bonets for the Queene of England, and made them perfectly to understand that olde speach of the prince of Poets;

> Non illi imperium pelagi sævúmque tridentem,
> sed tibi sorte datum.

Yet after they had acknowledged their dutie, your lordship on her Majesties behalfe conducted her safely through our English chanell, and performed all good offices of honor and humanitie to that forren Princesse. At that time all England beholding your most honorable cariage of your selfe in that so weightie service, began to cast an extraordinarie eie upon your lordship, and deeply to conceive that singular hope which since by your most worthie & wonderfull service, your L hath more then fully satisfied. I meane (among others) that glorious, triumphant, and thrise-happy victory atchieved against that huge and haultie Spanish Armada (which is notably described in the ende of this volume) wherein being chiefe and sole Commander under her sacred and roiall Majestie, your noble government and worthy

THE EPISTLE DEDICATORIE

behavior, your high wisedom, discretion and happinesse, accompanied with the heavenly blessing of the Almightie, are shewed most evidently to have bene such, as all posteritie and succeeding ages shall never cease to sing and resound your infinite prayse and eternall commendations. As for the late renoumed expedition and honorable voyage unto Cadiz, the vanquishing of part of the king of Spaines Armada, the destruction of the rich West Indian Fleete, the chasing of so many brave and gallant Gallies, the miraculous winning, sacking, and burning of that almost impregnable citie of Cadiz, the surprising of the towne of Faraon upon the coast of Portugal, and other rare appendances of that enterprise, because they be hereafter so judicially set downe, by a very grave and learned Gentleman, which was an eye witnesse in all that action, I referre your good L. to his faithfull report, wherein I trust (as much as in him lay) he hath wittingly deprived no man of his right. Upon these and other the like considerations, I thought it fit and very convenient to commend with all humilitie and reverence this first part of our English Voiages & Discoveries unto your Honors favourable censure and patronage.

And here by the way most humbly craving pardon, and alwayes submitting my poore opinion to your Lordships most deep and percing insight, especially in this matter, as being the father and principall favourer of the English Navigation, I trust it shall not be impertinent in passing by, to point at the meanes of breeding up of skilfull Sea-men and Mariners in this Realme. Sithence your Lordship is not ignorant, that ships are to litle purpose without skilfull Sea-men; and since Sea-men are not bred up to perfection of skill in much lesse time (as it is said) then in the time of two prentiships; and since no kinde of men of any profession in the common wealth passe their yeres in so great and continuall hazard of life; and since of so many, so few grow to gray heires: how needfull it is, that by way of Lectures and such like instructions, these ought to have a better education, then hitherto they have had; all wise men may easily judge. When I call to minde, how many noble ships have bene lost, how many worthy persons have bene drenched in the sea, and how greatly this Realme hath bene impoverished by losse of great Ordinance and other rich commodities through the ignorance of our Sea-men, I have greatly wished there were a Lecture of Navigation read in this Citie, for the banishing of our former grosse ignorance in Marine causes, and for the increase and generall multi-plying of the sea-knowledge in this age, wherein God hath raised so generall a desire in the youth of this Realme to discover all parts of the face of the earth, to this Realme in former ages not knowen. And, that it may appeare that this is no vaine fancie nor devise of mine, it may please your Lordship to understand, that the late Emperour Charles the fift, considering the rawnesse of his Sea-men, and the manifolde shipwracks which they susteyned in passing and repassing betweene Spaine and the West Indies, with an high reach and great foresight, established not onely a Pilote Major, for the examination of such as sought to take charge of ships in that voyage, but also founded a notable Lecture of the Art of Naviga-tion, which is read to this day in the Contractation house at Sivil. The readers of which Lecture have not only carefully taught and instructed the Spanish Mariners by word of mouth, but also have published sundry exact and worthy treatises concerning Marine causes, for the direction and incouragement of posteritie. The learned works of three of which readers, namely of Alonso de Chavez, of Hieronymo de Chavez, and of Roderigo Zamorano came long ago very happily to my hands, together with the straight and severe examining of all such Masters as desire to take charge for the West Indies. Which when I first read and duely considered, it seemed to mee so excellent and so exact a course, as I greatly wished, that I might be so happy as to see the like order established here with us. This matter, as it seemeth, tooke no light impression in the royall brest of that most renowmed and victorious prince King Henry the eight of famous memory ; who for the increase of knowledge in his Sea-men, with princely liberalitie erected three severall Guilds or brotherhoods, the one at Deptford here upon the Thames, the other at Kingston upon Hull, and the third at Newcastle upon Tine: which last was established in the 28. yeere of his reigne. The chiefe motives which induced his princely wisedome hereunto, himselfe expresseth in maner following. Ut magistri, marinarii, gubernatores, & alii officiarii navium, juventutem suam in exercitatione gubernationis navium transigentes, mutilati, aut aliquo alio casu in paupertatem collapsi, aliquod relevamen ad eorum sustentationem habeant, quo non solùm illi reficiantur, verùmetiam alii juvenes moveantur & instigentur ad eandem artem exercendam, ratione cujus, doctiores & aptiores fiant navibus & aliis vasis nostris & aliorum quorumcúnque in Mare gubernandis & manutenendis, tam pacis, quàm belli tempore, cum opus postulet, &c. To descend a litle lower, king Edward the sixt that prince of peerelesse hope, with the advise of his sage and prudent Counsaile, before he entred into the Northeasterne discovery, advanced the worthy and excellent Sebastian Cabota to be grand Pilot of England, allowing him a most bountifull pension of 166.li. vi.s. viii.d. by the yeere during his life, as appeareth in his Letters Patents which are to be seene in the third part of my worke. And if God had granted him longer life, I doubt not but as he delt most royally in establishing that office of Pilote Major (which not long after to the great hinderance of this Common wealth was miserably turned to other private uses) so his princely Majestie would have shewed himselfe no nigard in erecting, in imitation of Spaine, the like profitable Lecture of the Art of Navigation. And surely when I considered of late the memorable bountie of sir Thomas Gresham, who being but a

TO LORD CHARLES HOWARD

Merchant hath founded so many chargeable Lectures, and
some of them also which are Mathematicall, tending to
the advancement of Marine causes; I nothing doubted of
your Lordships forwardnes in settling and establishing of
this Lecture; but rather when your Lordship shall see
the noble and rare effects thereof, you will be heartily sory
that all this while it hath not bene erected. As therefore
our skill in Navigation hath hitherto bene very much
bettered and increased under the Admiraltie of your
Lordship; so if this one thing be added thereunto,
together with severe and straight discipline, I doubt not
but with Gods good blessing it will shortly grow to the
hiest pitch and top of all perfection: which whensoever it
shall come to passe, I assure my selfe it will turne to the
infinite wealth and honour of our Countrey, to the prosperous and speedy discoverie of many rich lands and
territories of heathens and gentiles as yet unknowen, to
the honest employment of many thousands of our idle
people, to the great comfort and rejoycing of our friends,
to the terror, daunting and confusion of our foes. To
ende this matter, let mee now I beseech you speake unto
your Lordship, as in times past the elder Scipio spake to
Cornelius Scipio Africanus: Quò sis, Africane, alacrior ad
tutandam Rempublicam, sic habeto: Omnibus, qui
patriam conservaverint, adjuverint, auxerint, certum esse
in cœlo, ac definitum locum, ubi beati ævo sempiterno
fruantur. It remaineth therefore, that as your Lordship
from time to time under her most gracious and excellent
Majestie, have shewed your selfe a valiant protectour, a
carefull conserver, and an happy enlarger of the honour
and reputation of your Countrey; so at length you may
enjoy those celestial blessings, which are prepared to such
as tread your steps, and seeke to aspire to such divine and
heroical vertues. And even here I surcease, wishing all
temporal and spirituall blessings of the life present and
that which is to come to be powred out in most ample
measure, not onely upon your honourable Lordship, the
noble and vertuous Lady your bedfellow, and those two

THE EPISTLE DEDICATORIE

rare jewels, your generous off-springs, but also upon all the rest wheresoever of that your noble and renowmed family. From London the 7. day of this present October 1598.

Your honours most humble alwayes
to be commanded :

Richard Hakluyt Preacher.

A preface to the Reader as touching the principall Voyages and discourses in this first part.

Aving for the benefit and honour of my
Countrey zealously bestowed so many
yeres, so much traveile and cost, to bring
Antiquities smothered and buried in darke
silence, to light, and to preserve certaine
memorable exploits of late yeeres by our
English nation atchieved, from the greedy
and devouring jawes of oblivion : to gather likewise, and as
it were to incorporate into one body the torne and scattered
limmes of our ancient and late Navigations by Sea, our
voyages by land, and traffiques of merchandise by both :
and having (so much as in me lieth) restored ech particular member, being before displaced, to their true joynts
and ligaments ; I meane, by the helpe of Geographie and
Chronologie (which I may call the Sunne and the Moone,
the right eye and the left of all history) referred ech
particular relation to the due time and place : I do this
second time (friendly Reader, if not to satisfie, yet at
least for the present to allay and hold in suspense thine
expectation) presume to offer unto thy view this first part
of my threefold discourse. For the bringing of which
into this homely and rough-hewen shape, which here thou
seest ; what restlesse nights, what painefull dayes, what
heat, what cold I have indured ; how many long &
chargeable journeys I have traveiled ; how many famous
libraries I have searched into ; what varietie of ancient

PREFACE TO THE

and moderne writers I have perused; what a number
of old records, patents, privileges, letters, &c. I have
redeemed from obscuritie and perishing; into how manifold acquaintance I have entred; what expenses I have not
spared; and yet what faire opportunities of private gaine,
preferment, and ease I have neglected; albeit thy selfe
canst hardly imagine, yet I by daily experience do finde
& feele, and some of my entier friends can sufficiently
testifie. Howbeit (as I told thee at the first) the honour
and benefit of this Common weale wherein I live and
breathe, hath made all difficulties seeme easie, all paines
and industrie pleasant, and all expenses of light value and
moment unto me.

For (to conteine my selfe onely within the bounds of
this present discourse, and in the midst thereof to begin)
wil it not in all posteritie be as great a renowme unto our
English nation, to have bene the first discoverers of a Sea
beyond the North cape (never certainly knowen before)
and of a convenient passage into the huge Empire of
Russia by the bay of S. Nicolas and the river of Duina;
as for the Portugales to have found a Sea beyond the Cape
of Buona Esperanza, and so consequently a passage by
Sea into the East Indies; or for the Italians and Spaniards
to have discovered unknowen landes so many hundred
leagues Westward and Southwestward of the streits of
Gibraltar, & of the pillers of Hercules? Be it granted
that the renowmed Portugale Vasques de Gama traversed
the maine Ocean Southward of Africke: Did not Richard
Chanceler and his mates performe the like Northward of
Europe? Suppose that Columbus that noble and high-
spirited Genuois escried unknowen landes to the Westward
of Europe and Africke: Did not the valiant English
knight sir Hugh Willoughby; did not the famous Pilots
Stephen Burrough, Arthur Pet, and Charles Jackman
accoast Nova Zembla, Colgoieve, and Vaigatz to the North
of Europe and Asia? Howbeit you will say perhaps, not
with the like golden successe, not with such deductions of
Colonies, nor attaining of conquests. True it is, that our

SECOND EDITION 1598

successe hath not bene correspondent unto theirs: yet in this our attempt the uncertaintie of finding was farre greater, and the difficultie and danger of searching was no whit lesse. For hath not Herodotus (a man for his time, most skilfull and judicial in Cosmographie, who writ above 2000. yeeres ago) in his 4. booke called Melpomene, signi-fied unto the Portugales in plaine termes; that Africa, except the small Isthmus betwèen the Arabian gulfe and the Mediterran sea, was on all sides environed with the Ocean? And for the further confirmation thereof, doth he not make mention of one Neco an Ægyptian King, who (for trials sake) sent a fleet of Phœnicians downe the Red sea; who setting forth in Autumne and sailing Southward till they had the Sunne at noonetide upon their sterbourd (that is to say, having crossed the Æquinoctial and the Southerne tropique) after a long Navigation, directed their course to the North, and in the space of 3. yeeres envi-roned all Africk, passing home through the Gaditan streites, and arriving in Ægypt? And doth not ‖ Plinie ‖ *Lib. 2. nat.* tel them, that noble Hanno, in the flourishing time and *hist. cap. 67.* estate of Carthage, sailed from Gades in Spaine to the coast of Arabia fœlix, and put downe his whole journall in writing? Doth he not make mention, that in the time of Augustus Cæsar, the wracke of certaine Spanish ships was found floating in the Arabian gulfe? And, not to be over-tedious in alleaging of testimonies, doth not Strabo in the 2. booke of his Geography, together with Cornelius Nepos and Plinie in the place beforenamed, agree all in one, that one Eudoxus fleeing from king Lathyrus, and valing downe the Arabian bay, sailed along, doubled the Southern point of Africk, and at length arrived at Gades? And what should I speake of the Spaniards? Was not divine ‖ Plato (who lived so many ages ago, and plainely ‖ *In Timæo.* described their West Indies under the name of Atlantis) was not he (I say) instead of a Cosmographer unto them? Were not those Carthaginians mentioned by Aristotle lib. ‖ de admirabil. auscult. their forerunners? And had they ‖περὶ θαυμα-σίων ἀκουσμά-not Columbus to stirre them up, and pricke them forward των.

xli

unto their Westerne discoveries; yea, to be their chiefe
loads-man and Pilot? Sithens therefore these two worthy
Nations had those bright lampes of learning (I meane the
most ancient and best Philosophers, Historiographers and
Geographers) to shewe them light; and the load-starre of
experience (to wit those great exploits and voyages layed
up in store and recorded) whereby to shape their course:
what great attempt might they not presume to undertake?
But alas our English nation, at the first setting foorth for
their Northeasterne discovery, were either altogether destitute of such cleare lights and inducements, or if they
had any inkling at all, it was as misty as they found the
Northren seas, and so obscure and ambiguous, that it was
meet rather to deterre them, then to give them encouragement.

But besides the foresaid uncertaintie, into what dangers
and difficulties they plunged themselves, Animus memi-
nisse horret, I tremble to recount. For first they were to
expose themselves unto the rigour of the sterne and un-
couth Northren seas, and to make triall of the swelling
waves and boistrous winds which there commonly do
surge and blow: then were they to saile by the ragged and
perilous coast of Norway, to frequent the unhaunted
shoares of Finmark, to double the dreadfull and misty
North cape, to beare with Willoughbies land, to run along
within kenning of the Countreys of Lapland and Corelia,
and as it were to open and unlocke the seven-fold mouth
of Duina. Moreover, in their Northeasterly Navigations,
upon the seas and by the coasts of Condora, Colgoieve,
Petzora, Joughoria, Samoedia, Nova Zembla, &c. and
their passing and returne through the streits of Vaigatz,
unto what drifts of snow and mountaines of yce even in
June, July, and August, unto what hideous overfals, uncer-
taine currents, darke mistes and fogs, and divers other
fearefull inconveniences they were subject and in danger
of, I wish you rather to learne out of the voyages of sir
Hugh Willoughbie, Stephen Burrough, Arthur Pet and
the rest, then to expect in this place an endlesse catalogue

thereof. And here by the way I cannot but highly commend the great industry and magnanimity of the Hollanders, who within these few yeeres have discovered to 78. yea (as themselves affirme) to 81. degrees of Northerly latitude: yet with this proviso; that our English nation led them the dance, brake the yce before them, and gave them good leave to light their candle at our torch. But nowe it is high time for us to weigh our ancre, to hoise up our sailes, to get cleare of these boistrous, frosty, and misty seas, and with all speede to direct our course for the milde, lightsome, temperate, and warme Atlantick Ocean, over which the Spaniards and Portugales have made so many pleasant prosperous and golden voyages. And albeit I cannot deny, that both of them in their East and West Indian Navigations have indured many tempests, dangers and shipwracks: yet this dare I boldly affirme; first that a great number of them have satisfied their fame-thirsty and gold-thirsty mindes with that reputation and wealth, which made all perils and misadventures seeme tolerable unto them; and secondly, that their first attempts (which in this comparison I doe onely stand upon) were no whit more difficult and dangerous, then ours to the Northeast. For admit that the way was much longer, yet was it never barred with yce, mist, or darknes, but was at all seasons of the yeere open and Navigable; yea and that for the most part with fortunate and fit gales of winde. Moreover they had no forren prince to intercept or molest them, but their owne Townes, Islands, and maine lands to succour them. The Spaniards had the Canary Isles: and so had the Portugales the Isles of the Açores, of Porto santo, of Madera, of Cape verd, the castle of Mina, the fruitfull and profitable Isle of S. Thomas, being all of them conveniently situated, and well fraught with commodities. And had they not continuall and yerely trade in some one part or other of Africa, for getting of slaves, for sugar, for Elephants teeth, graines, silver, gold, and other precious wares, which served as allurements to draw them on by little and litle, and as proppes to stay them from giving over their attempts? But nowe let us leave them and returne home unto our selves.

In this first Volume (friendly Reader) besides our Northeasterne Discoveries by sea, and the memorable voyage of M. Christopher Hodson, and M. William Burrough, Anno 1570. to the Narve, wherein with merchants ships onely, they tooke five strong and warrelike ships of the Freebooters, which lay within the sound of Denmark of purpose to intercept our English Fleete: besides all these (I say) thou maiest find here recorded, to the lasting honor of our nation, all their long and dangerous voyages for the advauncing of traffique by river and by land to all parts of the huge and wide Empire of Russia: as namely Richard Chanceler his first fortunate arrivall at Newnox, his passing up the river of Dwina to the citie of Vologda for the space of 1100. versts, and from thence to Yaruslave, Rostove, Peraslave, and so to the famous citie of Mosco, being 1500. versts travell in all. Moreover, here thou hast his voiage penned by himselfe (which I hold to be very authentical, & for the which I do acknowledge my selfe beholding unto the excellent Librarie of the right honorable my lord Lumley) wherein he describeth in part the state of Russia, the maners of the people and their religion, the magnificence of the Court, the majestie, power, and riches of the Emperour, and the gracious entertainment of himselfe. But if he being the first man, and not having so perfect intelligence as they that came after him, doeth not fullie satisfie your expectation in describing the foresayd countrey and people; I then referre you to Clement Adams his relation next following, to M. Jenkinsons discourse as touching that argument, to the smooth verses of M. George Turbervile, and to a learned and excellent discourse set downe, pag. 475. of this volume, and the pages following. Unto all which (if you please) you may adde Richard Johnsons strange report of the Samoeds, pag. 283. But to returne to our voyages performed within the bounds of Russia, I suppose (among the rest) that difficult journey of Southam and Sparke, from Colmogro and S. Nicholas Baie, up the great river of Onega, and so by other rivers and lakes to the citie of Novogrod velica upon the West frontier of Russia, to be right woorthy of observation ; as likewise that of Thomas Alcock from Mosco to Smolensko, and thence to Tirwill in Polonia, pag. 304. & that also of M. Hierome Horsey from Mosco to Vobsko, and so through Liefland to Riga, thence by the chiefe townes of Prussia and Pomerland to Rostok, and so to Hamburg, Breme, Emden, &c. Neither hath our nation bene contented onely throughly to search into all parts of the Inland, and to view the Northren, Southerne, and Westerne frontiers, but also by the rivers of Moscua, Occa and Volga, to visite Cazan and Astracan, the farthest Easterne and Southeasterne bounds of that huge Empire. And yet not containing themselves within all that maine circumference, they have adventured their persons, shippes, and goods, homewards and outwards, foureteene times over the unknowen and dangerous Caspian sea ; that valiant, wise, and personable gentleman M. Anthonie Jenkinson being their first ring-leader : who in Anno 1558. sailing from Astracan towards the East shore of the Caspian sea, and there arriving at the port of Mangusla, travelled thence by Urgence and Shelisur, and by the rivers of Oxus and Ardok, 40. dayes journey over desert and wast countreys, to Boghar a principall citie of Bactria, being there & by the way friendly entertained, dismissed, and safely conducted by certaine Tartarian kings and Murses. Then have you a second Navigation of his performance to the South shore of the foresayd Caspian sea, together with his landing at Derbent, his arrivall at Shabran, his proceeding unto Shamaky, the great curtesie vouchsafed on him by Obdolowcan king of Hircan, his journey after of 30. dayes Southward, by Yavate, Ardouil, and other townes and cities to Casben, being as then the seate imperiall of Shaugh Thamas the great Sophy of Persia, with divers other notable accidents in his going foorth, in his abode there, and in his returne

PREFACE TO THE

home. Immediately after you have set downe in five
severall voiages the successe of M. Jenkinsons laudable
and well-begun enterprise, under the foresayd Shaugh
Thamas, under Shally Murzey the new king of Hircan,
and lastly our traffique with Osman Basha the great
Turkes lieutenant at Derbent. Moreover, as in M.
Jenkinsons travel to Boghar the Tartars, with their
territories, habitations, maner of living, apparell, food,
armour, &c. are most lively represented unto you : so
likewise in the sixe Persian Journals you may here and
there observe the state of that countrey, of the great
Shaugh and of his subjects, together with their religion,
lawes, customes, & maner of government, their coines,
weights and measures, the distances of places, the temperature of the climate and region, and the natural commodities and discommodities of the same.

Furthermore in this first Volume, all the Ambassages
and Negotiations from her Majestie to the Russian
Emperor, or from him unto her Majestie, seemed by
good right to chalenge their due places of Record. As
namely, first that of M. Randolph, 1568. then the
emploiment of M. Jenkinson 1571. thirdly, Sir Jerome
Bowes his honorable commission and ambassage 1582.
and last of all the Ambassage of M. Doct. Fletcher 1588.
Neither do we forget the Emperours first Ambassador
Osep Napea, his arrivall in Scotland, his most honourable
entertainment and abode in England, and his dismission
into Russeland. In the second place we doe make
mention of Stephen Tuerdico, and Pheodata Pogorella ;
thirdly, of Andrea Savin ; and lastly, of Pheodor
Andrewich Phisemski. And to be briefe, I have not
omitted the Commissions, Letters, Privileges, Instructions,
Observations, or any other Particulars which might serve
both in this age, and with all posteritie, either for
presidents in such like princely and weightie actions to
bee imitated, or as woorthy monuments in no wise to bee
buried in silence. Finally, that nothing should be wanting
which might adde any grace or shew of perfection unto

this discourse of Russia ; I have prefixed before the beginning thereof, the petigree and genealogie of the Russian Emperors and Dukes, gathered out of their owne Chronicles by a Polonian, containing in briefe many notable antiquities and much knowledge of those partes : as likewise about the conclusion, I have signified in the branch of a letter, the last Emperour Pheodor Ivanowich his death, and the inauguration of Boris Pheodorowich unto the Empire.

But that no man should imagine that our forren trades of merchandise have bene comprised within some few yeeres, or at least wise have not bene of any long continuance ; let us now withdraw our selves from our affaires in Russia, and ascending somewhat higher, let us take a sleight survey of our traffiques and negotiations in former ages. First therefore the Reader may have recourse unto the 124 page of this Volume, & there with great delight and admiration, consider out of the judicial Historiographer Cornelius Tacitus, that the Citie of London fifteene hundred yeeres agoe in the time of Nero the Emperour, was most famous for multitude of merchants and concourse of people. In the pages folowing he may learne out of Venerable Beda, that almost 900. yeeres past, in the time of the Saxons, the said citie of London was multorum emporium populorum, a Mart-towne for many nations. There he may behold, out of William of Malmesburie, a league concluded betweene the most renoumed and victorious Germane Emperour Carolus Magnus, and the Saxon king Offa, together with the sayd Charles his patronage and protection granted unto all English merchants which in those dayes frequented his dominions. There may hee plainly see in an auncient testimonie translated out of the Saxon tongue, how our merchants were often woont for traffiques sake, so many hundred yeeres since, to crosse the wide Seas, and how their industry in so doing was recompensed. Yea, there mayest thou observe (friendly Reader) what privileges the Danish king Canutus obtained at Rome of Pope John, of

Conradus the Emperour, and of king Rudolphus for our
English merchants Adventurers of those times.   Then if
you shall thinke good to descend unto the times and ages
succeeding the conquest, there may you partly see what
our state of merchandise was in the time of king Stephen
and of his predecessor, and how the Citie of Bristol (which
may seeme somewhat strange) was then greatly resorted
unto with ships from Norway and from Ireland.   There
may you see the friendly league betweene king Henry the
second, and the famous Germane Emperour Friderick
Barbarossa, and the gracious authorizing of both their
merchants to traffique in either of their dominions.   And
what need I to put you in mind of king John his
favourable safe-conduct, whereby all forren merchants
were to have the same privileges here in England, which
our English merchants enjoied abroad in their severall
countreys.   Or what should I signifie unto you the
entercourse of league and of other curtesies betweene
king Henry the third, and Haquinus king of Norway;
and likewise of the free trade of merchandise between
their subjects: or tell you what favours the citizens of
Colen, of Lubek, and of all the Hansetownes obtained of
king Edward the first ; or to what high endes and purposes the generall, large, and stately Charter concerning
all outlandish merchants whatsoever was by the same
prince most graciously published ?   You are of your
owne industry sufficiently able to conceive of the letters
& negotiations which passed between K. Edward the 2.
& Haquinus the Noruagian king ; of our English
merchants and their goods detained upon arrest at
Bergen in Norway ; and also of the first ordination of
a Staple, or of one onely setled Mart-towne for the
uttering of English woolls & woollen fells, instituted
by the sayd K. Edward last before named.   All which
(Reader) being throughly considered, I referre you then
to the Ambassages, Letters, Traffiques, and prohibition
of Traffiques, concluding and repealing of leagues,
damages,   reprisals,   arrests,   complaints,   supplications,

compositions and restitutions which happened in the time of king Richard the 2. and king Henry the 4. between the said kings and their subjects on the one partie; and Conradus de Zolner, Conradus de Jungingen, and Ulricus de Jungingen, three of the great masters of Prussia, and their subjects, with the common societie of the Hans-townes on the other partie. In all which discourse you may note very many memorable things; as namely first the wise, discreet, and cautelous dealing of the Ambassadors and Commissioners of both parts, then the wealth of the foresaid nations, and their manifold and most usuall kinds of wares uttered in those dayes, as likewise the qualitie, burthen, and strength of their shipping, the number of their Mariners, the maner of their combates at sea, the number and names of the English townes which traded that way, with the particular places as well upon the coast of Norway, as every where within the sound of Denmark which they frequented; together with the inveterate malice and craftie crueltie of the Hanse. And because the name, office, and dignitie of the masters generall, or great Masters of Prussia would otherwise have bene utterly darke and unknowen to the greater part of Readers, I have set downe immediatly before the first Prussian ambassage, pagina 144 a briefe and orderly Catalogue of them all, contayning the first originall and institution of themselves and of their whole knightly order and brotherhood, with the increase of revenues and wealth which befell them afterward in Italy and Germany and the great conquests which they atchieved upon the infidels of Prussia, Samogitia, Curland, Liefland, Lituania, &c. also their decay and finall overthrow, partly by the revolt of divers Townes and Castles under their jurisdiction, and partly by the meanes of their next mightie neighbour the King of Poland.

After all these, out of 2. branches of 2. ancient statutes, is partly shewed our trade and the successe thereof with divers forren Nations in the time of K. Henry the sixt.

Then followeth the true processe of English policie, I meane that excellent and pithy treatise de politia conservativa maris : which I cannot to any thing more fitly compare, then to the Emperour of Russia his palace called the golden Castle, and described by Richard Chanceller pag. 238. of this volume : whereof albeit the outward apparance was but homely and no whit correspondent to the name, yet was it within so beautified and adorned with the Emperour his majesticall presence, with the honourable and great assembly of his rich-attired Peers and Senatours, with an invaluable and huge masse of gold and silver plate, & with other princely magnificence; that well might the eyes of the beholders be dazeled, and their cogitations astonished thereat. For indeed the exteriour habit of this our English politician, to wit, the harsh and unaffected stile of his substantiall verses and the olde dialect of his wordes is such; as the first may seeme to have bene whistled of Pans oaten pipe, and the second to have proceeded from the mother of Evander : but take you off his utmost weed, and beholde the comelinesse, beautie, and riches which lie hid within his inward sense and sentence; and you shall finde (I wisse) so much true and sound policy, so much delightfull and pertinent history, so many lively descriptions of the shipping and wares in his time of all the nations almost in Christendome, and such a subtile discovery of outlandish merchants fraud, and of the sophistication of their wares ; that needes you must acknowledge, that more matter and substance could in no wise be comprised in so little a roome. And notwithstanding (as I said) his stile be unpolished, and his phrases somewhat out of use; yet, so neere as the written copies would give me leave, I have most religiously without alteration observed the same : thinking it farre more convenient that himselfe should speake, then that I should bee his spokesman ; and that the Readers should enjoy his true verses, then mine or any other mans fained prose.

SECOND EDITION 1598

Next after the conclusion of the last mentioned discourse, the Reader may in some sort take a vieu of our state of merchandise under K. Edward the fourth, as likewise of the establishing of an English company in the Netherlands, and of all the discreet provisoes, just ordinations, & gratious privileges conteined in the large Charter which was granted for the same purpose.

Now besides our voyages and trades of late yeeres to the North and Northeast regions of the world, and our ancient traffique also to those parts; I have not bene unmindefull (so farre as the histories of England and of other Countreys would give me direction) to place in the fore-front of this booke those forren conquests, exploits, and travels of our English nation, which have bene atchieved of old. Where in the first place (as I am credibly informed out of Galfridus Monumetensis, and out of M. Lambert his Αρχαιονομία) I have published unto the world the noble actes of Arthur and Malgo two British Kings. Then followeth in the Saxons time K. Edwin his conquest of Man and Anglesey, and the expedition of Bertus into Ireland. Next succeedeth Octher making relation of his doings, and describing the North Countreys, unto his soveraigne Lord K. Ecfrid. After whom Wolstans Navigation within the Sound of Denmark is mentioned, the voyage of the yong Princes Edmund and Edward into Sweden and Hungarie is recorded, as likewise the mariage of Harald his daughter unto the Russian duke Jeruslaus. Neither is that Englishman forgotten, who was forced to traveile with the cruel Tartars into their Countrey, and from thence to beare them company into Hungary and Poland. And because those Northeasterne Regions beyond Volga, by reason of the huge deserts, the colde climate, and the barbarous incivilitie of the people there inhabiting, were never yet throughly traveiled by any of our Nation, nor sufficiently knowen unto us; I have here annexed unto the said Englishmans traveile, the rare & memorable

li

journals of 2. Friers, who were some of the first
Christians that travailed farthest that way, and brought
home most particular intelligence & knowledge of all
things which they had seene. These Friers were sent
as Ambassadours unto the savage Tartars (who had
as then wasted and overrunne a great part of Asia,
and had pierced farre into Europe with fire and sword)
to mitigate their fury, and to offer the glad tidings of
the Gospel unto them. The former, namely Johannes
de Plano Carpini (whose journey, because he road sixe
moneths poste directly beyond Boristhenes, did, I thinke,
both for length and difficultie farre surpasse that of
Alexander the great, unto the river of Indus) was in the
yeere 1246. sent with the authoritie and commission of
a Legate from Pope Innocentius the fourth : who
passed through more garisons of the Tartars, and
wandered over more vast, barren, and cold deserts,
then (I suppose) an army of an hundred thousand good
souldiers could have done. The other, to wit, William
de Rubricis, was 1253. by the way of Constantinople,
of the Euxin sea, and of Taurica Chersonesus imployed
in an ambassage from Lewis the French King (waging
warre as then against the Saracens in the Holy land)
unto one Sartach a great duke of the Tartars, which
Sartach sent him forthwith unto his father Baatu, and
from Baatu he was conducted over many large territories
unto the Court of Mangu-Can their Emperour. Both
of them have so well played their parts, in declaring
what befell them before they came at the Tartars, what
a terrible and unmanerly welcomming they had at their
first arrivall, what cold intertainment they felt in traveiling towards the great Can, and what slender cheere they
found at his Court; that they seeme no lesse worthy of
praise then of pitie. But in describing of the Tartars
Countrey, and of the Regions adjacent, in setting downe
the base and sillie beginnings of that huge and over-
spreading Empire, in registring their manifolde warres
and bloody conquests, in making relation of their hords

and mooveable Townes, as likewise of their food, apparell
and armour, and in setting downe their unmercifull
lawes, their fond superstitions, their bestiall lives, their
vicious maners, their slavish subjection to their owne
superiours, and their disdainfull and brutish inhumanitie
unto strangers, they deserve most exceeding and high
commendation. Howbeit if any man shall object that
they have certaine incredible relations: I answere, first,
that many true things may to the ignorant seeme incredible. But suppose there be some particulars which
hardly will be credited; yet thus much I will boldly
say for the Friers, that those particulars are but few,
and that they doe not avouch them under their owne
names, but from the report of others. Yet farther,
imagine that they did avouch them, were they not to
be pardoned as well as Herodotus, Strabo, Plutarch,
Plinie, Solinus, yea & a great many of our new principall
writers, whose names you may see about the end of
this Preface; every one of which hath reported more
strange things then the Friers between them both?
Nay, there is not any history in the world (the most
Holy writ excepted) whereof we are precisely bound to
beleeve ech word and syllable. Moreover sithens these
two journals are so rare, that Mercator and Ortelius (as
their letters unto me do testifie) were many yeeres
very inquisitive, and could not for all that attaine unto
them; and sithens they have bene of so great accompt
with those two famous Cosmographers, that according
to some fragments of them they have described in their
Mappes a great part of those Northeastern Regions;
sith also that these two relations containe in some respect
more exact history of those unknowen parts, then all
the ancient and newe writers that ever I could set mine
eyes on : I thought it good, if the translation should
chance to swerve in ought from the originals (both for
the preservation of the originals themselves, and the
satisfying of the Reader) to put them downe word for
word in that homely stile wherein they were first

penned. And for these two rare jewels, as likewise for many other extraordinary courtesies, I must here acknowledge my selfe most deepely bounden unto the right reverend, grave, and learned Prelate, my very good lord the Bishop of Chichester, and L. high Almner unto her Majestie; by whose friendship and meanes I had free accesse unto the right honor. my L. Lumley his stately library, and was permitted to copy out of ancient manuscripts, these two journals and some others also.

After these Friers (though not in the next place) foloweth a testimonie of Gerardus Mercator, and another of M. Dee, concerning one Nicholas de Linna an English Franciscan Frier.

Then succeedeth the long journey of Henry Earle of Derbie, and afterward king of England into Prussia & Lithuania, with a briefe remembrance of his valiant exploits against the Infidels there; as namely, that with the help of certaine his Associates, he vanquished the king of Letto his armie, put the sayd king to flight, tooke and slew divers of his captains, advanced his English colours upon the wall of Vilna, & made the citie it selfe to yeeld. Then mention is made also of Tho. of Woodstock his travel into Pruis, and of his returne home. And lastly, our old English father Ennius, I meane, the learned, wittie, and profound Geffrey Chaucer, under the person of his knight, doeth full judicially and like a cunning Cosmographer, make report of the long voiages and woorthy exploits of our English Nobles, Knights, & Gentlemen, to the Northren, and to other partes of the world in his dayes.

Neither have we comprehended in this Volume, onely our Trades and Voiages both new and old; but also have scattered here and there (as the circumstance of times would give us leave) certaine fragments concerning the beginnings, antiquities, and grouth of the classical and warrelike shipping of this Island: as namely, first of the great navie of that victorious Saxon prince king Edgar, mentioned by Florentius Wigorniensis, Roger Hoveden, Rainulph of Chester, Matthew of Westminster, Flores historiarum, & in the libel of English policie, pag. 202. and 203. of this present volume. Of which Authors some affirme the sayd Fleet to have consisted of 4800. others of 4000. some others of 3600. ships : howbeit (if I may presume to gloze upon the text) I verily thinke that they were not comparable, either for burthen, strength, building, or nimble stirrage unto the ships of later times, and specially of this age. But howsoever it be, they all agree in this, that by meanes of the sayd huge Fleet he was a most puissant prince; yea, and some of them affirme together with William of Malmesbury, that he was not onely soveraigne lord of all the British seas, and of the whole Isle of Britaine it selfe, but also that he brought under his yoke of subjection, most of the Isles and some of the maine lands adjacent. And for that most of our Navigators at this time bee (for want of trade and practise that way) either utterly ignorant, or but meanely skilfull, in the true state of the Seas, Shoulds, and Islands, lying between the North part of Ireland and of Scotland ; I have for their better en-couragement (if any weightie action shall hereafter chance to drawe them into those quarters) translated into English a briefe treatise called, A Chronicle of the Kings of Man. Wherein they may behold as well the tragical and dolefull historie of those parts, for the space almost of 300. yeeres, as also the most ordinarie and accustomed navigations, through those very seas, and amidst those Northwesterne Isles called the Hebrides, so many hundred yeeres agoe. For they shall there read, that even then (when men were but rude in sea-causes in regard of the great knowledge which we now have) first Godredus Crovan with a whole Fleet of ships, throughly haunted some places in that sea : secondly, that one Ingemundus setting saile out of Norway, arrived upon the Isle of Lewis : then, that

Magnus the king of Norway came into the same seas with 160. sailes, and having subdued the Orkney Isles in his way, passed on in like conquering maner, directing his course (as it should seeme) even through the very midst, and on all sides of the Hebrides, who sailing thence to Man, conquered it also, proceeding afterward as farre as Anglesey; and lastly crossing over from the Isle of Man to the East part of Ireland. Yea, there they shall read of Godredus the sonne of Olavus his voiage to the king of Norway, of his expedition with 80. ships against Sumerledus, of Sumerled his expedition with 53. ships against him; of Godred his flight and second journey into Norway; of Sumerled his second arrival with 160. shippes at Rhinfrin upon the coast of Man, and of many other such combates, assaults, & voyages which were performed onely upon those seas & Islands. And for the bringing of this woorthy monument to light, we doe owe great thanks unto the judiciall and famous Antiquarie M. Camden. But sithens we are entred into a discourse of the ancient warrelike shipping of this land, the Reader shall give me leave to borow one principall note out of this litle historie, before I quite take my leave thereof: and that is in few words, that K. John passed into Ireland with a Fleet of 500. sailes; so great were our sea-forces even in his time. Neither did our shipping for the warres first begin to flourish with king John, but long before his dayes in the reign of K. Edward the Confessor, of William the Conqueror, of William Rufus and the rest, there were divers men of warre which did valiant service at sea, and for their paines were roially rewarded. All this and more then this you may see recorded, pag. 17. out of the learned Gentleman M. Lambert his Perambulation of Kent; namely, the antiquitie of the Kentish Cinque ports, which of the sea-townes they were, how they were infranchised, what gracious privileges and high prerogatives were by divers kings vouchsafed upon them, and what services they were tied unto in regard thereof; to wit, how many ships, how many souldiers, mariners, Garsons, and for how many dayes each of them, and all of them were to furnish for the kings use; and lastly, what great exploits they performed under the conduct of Hubert of Burrough, as likewise against the Welshmen, upon 200. French ships, and under the commaund of captaine Henry Pay. Then have you, pag. 117. the franke and bountifull Charter granted by king Edward the first, upon the foresayd Cinque portes: & next thereunto a Roll of the mightie fleet of seven hundred ships which K. Edward the third had with him unto the siege of Caleis: out of which Roll (before I proceed any further) let me give you a double observation. First, that these ships, according to the number of the mariners which were in all 14151. persons, seeme to have bene of great burthen; and secondly, that Yarmouth an haven towne in Northfolke (which I much wonder at) set foorth almost twise as many ships and mariners, as either the king did at his owne costs and charges, or as any one citie or towne in England besides. Howbeit Tho. Walsingham maketh plaine and evident mention of a farre greater Fleete of the same king; namely, of 1100. shippes lying before Sandwich, being all of them sufficiently well furnished. Moreover, the Reader may behold, pag. 186. a notable testimonie of the mightie ships of that valiant prince king Henry the 5. who (when after his great victory at Agincourt the Frenchmen to recover Harflew had hired certaine Spanish and Italian ships and forces, & had united their owne strength unto them) sent his brother John duke of Bedford to encounter them, who bidding them battell, got the victory, taking some of their ships, and sinking others, and putting the residue to dishonorable flight. Likewise comming the next yeere with stronger powers, and being then also overcome, they were glad to conclude a perpetuall league with K. Henry; & propter eorum naves (saieth mine Author) that is, for the resistance of their ships, the sayd king caused such huge ships to be built, quales non erant in mundo, as the like were not to be found in the whole world besides.

But to leave our ancient shipping, and descend unto later times; I thinke that never was any nation blessed of JEHOVAH, with a more glorious and wonderfull victory upon the Seas, then our vanquishing of the dreadfull Spanish Armada, 1588. But why should I presume to call it our vanquishing; when as the greatest part of them escaped us, and were onely by Gods out-stretched arme overwhelmed in the Seas, dashed in pieces against the Rockes, and made fearefull spectacles and examples of his judgements unto all Christendome? An excellent discourse whereof, as likewise of the honourable expedition under two of the most noble and valiant peeres of this Realme, I meane, the renoumed Erle of Essex, and the right honorable the lord Charles Howard, lord high Admirall of England, made 1596. unto the strong citie of Cadiz, I have set downe as a double epiphonema to conclude this my first volume withall. Both of which, albeit they ought of right to have bene placed among the Southerne voyages of our nation: yet partly to satisfie the importunitie of some of my special friends, and partly, not longer to deprive the diligent Reader of two such woorthy and long-expected discourses; I have made bold to straine a litle curtesie with that methode which I first propounded unto my selfe.

And here had I almost forgotten to put the Reader in mind of that learned and Philosophical treatise of the true state of Iseland, and so consequently of the Northren Seas & regions lying that way: wherein a great number of none of the meanest Historiographers and Cosmographers of later times, as namely, Munster, Gemma Frisius, Zieglerus, Krantzius, Saxo Grammaticus, Olaus Magnus, Peucerus and others, are by evident arguments convinced of manifold errors: that is to say, as touching the true situation and Northerly latitude of that Island, and of the distance thereof from other places; touching the length of dayes in Sommer and of nights in Winter, of the temperature of the land and sea, of the time and maner of the congealing, continuance, and thawing of the Ice in those Seas, of the first Discoverie and inhabiting of that Island, of the first planting of Christianitie there, as likewise of the continuall flaming of mountains, strange qualities of fountains, of hel-mouth, and of purgatorie which those authors have fondly written and imagined to be there. All which treatise ought to bee the more acceptable; first in that it hath brought sound trueth with it; and secondly, in that it commeth from that farre Northren climate which most men would suppose could not affoord any one so learned a Patrone for it selfe.

And thus (friendly Reader) thou seest the briefe summe and scope of all my labours for the commonwealths sake, and thy sake, bestowed upon this first Volume: which if thou shalt as thankefully accept, as I have willingly and freely imparted with thee, I shall bee the better encouraged speedily to acquaint thee with those rare, delightfull and profitable histories, which I purpose (God willing) to publish concerning the Southerne and Westerne partes of the World.

Postscriptum.

Not knowing any other place so convenient, I am here to advertise the friendly Reader of certaine faultes escaped in the printing of this booke, and to request him that in the Page 54. and in the last line save two, hee would in stead of Kine, read Swine, and he shall thereby avoid a great contradiction: likewise pag. 187. that hee would unto the ende of the second verse of the Prologue to the English Policy, make supply of the word Rest, which is there wanting: also pag. 221. lin. 29. for woorthinesse read woorthies, &c. Other faults (if there bee any) are (I doubt not) easily corrigible.

Εἰς Ἀποδημίας Βρεττανῶν
Πόνημα Ριχάρδου τοῦ Ἀκλυΐτου,

Ὕγων ὁ Βροχθωνὸς.

Ὅσσοι γαῖαν ἔχουσι βροτοὶ ἑνὸς ἐκπέφυασι
    ὡς ἄλληλα ὁρᾶν ἔθνεσι χάρμα φύσει.
Ὃς δὲ θ᾽ ἀλίπλαγκτος μετεκίαθεν ἔθνεα πλεῖστα,
    ὅικοι μιμνάζουσ᾽ ἀξιάγαστος ἔφυ.
Ἔξοχα Βρεττανοὶ δ᾽, ἄλλων σχισθέντες ἔρανται,
    ἴδμεναι ἀλλοθρόων φῦλα πολυσπερέα.
Ἰνδοὺς ἑσπερίους καὶ ἑώους, Αἰθίοπάς τε,
    καὶ Μόσχους, καὶ πάντ᾽ ἐσχατόωντα γένη.
Τούτων δ᾽ ὅια μάλιστα κλυτὰ, κλυτός Ἀκλυΐτος
    γράψεν ἀριφραδέως, μνῆμ᾽ ἀεὶ ἐσσόμενον.

In navales RICHARDI HAKLUYTI Commentarios.

ANglia magnarum fœcunda puerpera rerum,
    sive solum spectes nobile, sive salum;
Quæ quantum sumptis se nobilitaverit armis,
    sive domi gessit prælia, sive foris;
Multorum celebrant matura volumina: tantæ
    Insula materiem parvula laudis alit.
At se in quot, qualésque, & quando effuderit oras.
    -qua fidit ignotum pervia classis iter,
Solius Hakluyti decus est, prædivite penna
    ostendisse suis civibus ausa mari.

PANEGYRICK VERSES

Quæcunque idcirco celeri gens Anglica navi,
   Oceani tristes spernere doctaminas,
A prima generísque & gentis origine gessit,
   qua via per fluctus ulla patere potest,
Sive decus, laudémque secuta, ut & hostibus alas
   demeret, atque suis læta pararet opes:
Hoc opus Hakluyti; cui debet patria multum,
   cui multum, patriæ quisquis amicus erit.
Qua re námque magis se nostra Britannia jactat,
   quàm quod sit præter cætera classe potens?
Quam prius obsessam tenebris sic liberat, ut nunc
   quisque sciat, quàm sit nobile classis opus.
Quam si Dædalicè utemur, surgemus in altum,
   sin autem Icaricè, quod voret, æquor habet.

RICH. MULCASTER.

Ejusdem in eundem.

QUi gravi primus cecinit camœna
  Aureum vellus, procerésque Græcos,
quos sibi adjunxit comites Jäson
                Vectus in Argo
Nave, quam primùm secuisse fluctus
prædicant salsos, sibi comparavit
Inde non unquam moritura magnæ
                præmia famæ.
Tanta si merces calamum secuta
Unicæ navis referentis acta,
Quanta Richardum manet Hakluytum
                gloria? cujus
Penna descripsit freta mille, mille
Insulæ nostræ celeres carinas,
Quæ per immensi loca pervolarunt
                omnia mundi.
Senties gratam patriam, tuæque
Laudis æternùm memorem, & laboris:
Quæ tua cura, calamóque totum
                ibit in orbem:

PANEGYRICK VERSES

Quam doces omni studio fovere
Nauticum robur, validámque classem.
Hac luet quisquis violentus Anglos
                       usserit hostis.

In eximium opus R. HAKLUYTI de Anglorum ad
disjunctissimas regiones navigationibus GULIELMI
CAMDENI Hexastichon.

ANglia quæ penitùs toto discluditur orbe,
   Angulus orbis erat, parvus & orbis erat.
Nunc cùm sepositos alios detexerit orbes,
   Maximus orbis honos, Orbis & orbis erit.
At quid Haklute tibi monstranti hæc debeat orbis?
   Laus tua, crede mihi, non erit orbe minor.

Di Marc' Antonio Pigafeta Gentilhuomo Vicentino.

IGnota mi starei, con poco honore
   Sepolta nell' oscure, antiche carte,
   S'alcun de figli miei con spesa & arte
   Non havesse hor scoperto il mio splendore.
Ramusio pria pieno d' ardente amore
   Manifesto le mie piu riche parte,
   Che son lá dove il Maragnon diparte,
   E dove il Negro allaga, e'l Gange scorre,
Hakluyto poi senza verun risguardo
   Di fatica o di danno accolt' hà insieme,
   Ciò c' hà potuto haver da typhi Inglesi.
Onde vedrassie dove bella sguardo,
   E la Dwina agghiaccia, e l' Obi freme,
   Et altri membri miei non ben palesi.

To the Right Honorable Sir Robert Cecil Knight, principall Secretarie to her Majestie, master of the Court of Wardes and Liveries, and one of her Majesties most honourable privie Counsell.

Ight honorable, having newly finished a Treatise of the long Voyages of our Nation made into the Levant within the Streight of Gibraltar, & from thence overland to the South and Southeast parts of the world, all circumstances considered, I found none to whom I thought it fitter to bee presented then to your selfe : wherein having begun at the highest Antiquities of this realme under the government of the Romans; next under the Saxons; and thirdly since the conquest under the Normans, I have continued the histories unto these our dayes. The time of the Romans affoordeth small matter. But after that they were called hence by forren invasions of their Empire, and the Saxons by degrees became lords in this Iland, and shortly after received the Christian faith, they did not onely travell to Rome, but passed further unto Jerusalem, and therewith not contented, Sigelmus bishop of Shireburne in Dorcetshire caried the almes of king Alfred even to the Sepulcher of S. Thomas in India, (which place at this day is called Maliapor) and brought from thence most fragrant spices, and rich jewels into England : which jewels, as William of Malmesburie in two sundry treatises writeth, were remaining in the afore-

THE EPISTLE DEDICATORIE

sayd Cathedrall Church to be seene even in his time. And this most memorable voyage into India is not onely mentioned by the aforesayd Malmesburie, but also by Florentius Wigorniensis, a grave and woorthy Author which lived before him, and by many others since, and even by M. Foxe in his first volume of his Acts and Monuments in the life of king Alfred. To omit divers other of the Saxon nation, the travels of Alured bishop of Worcester through Hungarie to Constantinople, and so by Asia the lesse into Phœnicia and Syria, and the like course of Ingulphus, not long afterward Abbot of Croiland, set downe particularly by himselfe, are things in mine opinion right worthy of memorie. After the comming in of the Normans, in the yeere 1096, in the reigne of William Rufus, and so downward for the space of above 300 yeeres, such was the ardent desire of our nation to visite the Holy land, and to expell the Saracens and Mahumetans, that not only great numbers of Erles, Bishops, Barons, and Knights, but even Kings, Princes, and Peeres of the blood Roiall, with incredible devotion, courage and alacritie intruded themselves into this glorious expedition. A sufficient proofe hereof are the voiages of prince Edgar the nephew of Edmund Ironside, of Robert Curtois brother of William Rufus, the great benevolence of king Henry the 2. and his vowe to have gone in person to the succour of Jerusalem, the personall going into Palæstina of his sonne king Richard the first, with the chivalrie, wealth, and shipping of this realme; the large contribution of king John, and the travels of Oliver Fitz-Roy his sonne, as is supposed, with Ranulph Glanvile Erle of Chester to the siege of Damiata in Ægypt: the prosperous voyage of Richard Erle of Cornwall, elected afterward king of the Romans, and brother to Henry the 3, the famous expedition of prince Edward, the first king of the Norman race of that name; the journey of Henry Erle of Derbie, duke of Hereford, and afterward king of this realme, by the name of Henry the 4. against the citie of Tunis in Africa, and his

THE
SECOND VOLVME

OF THE PRINCIPAL NA-
VIGATIONS, VOYAGES, TRAF-

fiques and Difcoueries of the *Englifh Nation*, made by
Sea or ouer-land, to the South and South-eaft parts of the
World, at any time within the compaffe of thefe 1600. yeres:
Diuided into two feuerall parts:

Whereof the firft containeth the perfonall trauels, &c.
of the *Englifh*, through and within the Streight of *Gibraltar*, to *Al-*
ger, *Tunis*, and *Tripolis* in *Barbary*, to *Alexandria* and *Cairo* in *AEgypt*, to the Ifles
of *Sicilia*, *Zante*, *Candia*, *Rhodus*, *Cyprus*, and *Chio*, to the Citie of *Conftantinople*, to diuers parts
of *Afia minor*, to *Syria* and *Armenia*, to *Ierufalem*, and other places in *Iudæa*; As alfo to *A-*
rabia, downe the Riuer of *Euphrates*, to *Babylon* and *Balfara*, and fo through the *Per-*
fian gulph to *Ormuz*, *Chaul*, *Goa*, and to many Iflands adioyning vpon the
South parts of *Afia*; And likewife from *Goa* to *Cambaia*, and to all the
dominions of *Zelabdim Echebar* the great *Mogor*, to the mighty
Riuer of *Ganges*, to *Bengala*, *Aracan*, *Bacola*, and *Chon-*
deri, to *Pegu*, to *Iamahai* in the kingdome of *Si-*
am, and almoft to the very fron-
tiers of *China*.

The fecond comprehendeth the Voyages, Trafficks, &c.
of the *Englifh Nation*, made without the Streight of *Gibral-*
tar, to the Iflands of the *Açores*, of *Porto Santo*, *Madera*, and the *Canaries*,
to the kingdomes of *Barbary*, to the Ifles of *Capo Verde*, to the Riuers of *Senega*, *Gam-*
bra, *Madrabumba*, and *Sierra Leona*, to the coaft of *Guinea* and *Benin*, to the Ifles
of *S.Thomé* and *Santa Helena*, to the parts about the Cape of *Buena Efpe-*
ranza, to *Quitangone* neere *Mozambique*, to the Ifles of *Comoro* and
Zanzibar, to the citie of *Goa*, beyond *Cape Comori*, to the Ifles
of *Nicubar*, *Gomes Polo*, and *Pulo Pinaom*, to the
maine land of *Malacca*, and to the kingdome of *Iunfalaon*.

¶ By RICHARD HACKLVYT Preacher, and fometime Student of Chrift-Church in Oxford.

❧ Imprinted at London by *George Bifhop*,
Ralph Newbery, and *Robert Barker*.
ANNO 1599.

TO SIR ROBERT CECIL

preparation of ships and gallies to go himselfe into the Holy land, if he had not on the sudden bene prevented by death; the travel of John of Holland brother by the mothers side to king Richard the 2 into those parts. All these, either Kings, Kings sonnes, or Kings brothers, exposed themselves with invincible courages to the manifest hazard of their persons, lives, and livings, leaving their ease, their countries, wives and children, induced with a Zelous devotion and ardent desire to protect and dilate the Christian faith. These memorable enterprises in part concealed, in part scattered, and for the most part unlooked after, I have brought together in the best Method and brevitie that I could devise. Where-unto I have annexed the losse of Rhodes, which although it were originally written in French, yet maketh it as honourable and often mention of the English nation, as of any other Christians that served in that most violent siege. After which ensueth the princely promise of the bountifull aide of king Henry the 8 to Ferdinando newly elected king of Hungarie, against Solyman the mortall enemie of Christendome. These and the like Heroicall intents and attempts of our Princes, our Nobilitie, our Clergie, & our Chivalry, I have in the first place exposed and set foorth to the view of this age, with the same intention that the old Romans set up in wax in their palaces the Statuas or images of their worthy ancestors; whereof Salust in his treatise of the warre of Jugurtha, writeth in this maner: Sæpe audivi ego Quintum maximum, Publium Scipionem, præterea civitatis nostræ præclaros viros solitos ita dicere, cum majorum imagines intuerentur, vehementissimè animum sibi ad virtutem accendi. Scilicet non ceram illam, neque figuram, tantam vim in sese habere, sed memoria rerum gestarum flammam eam egregiis viris in pectore crescere, neque prius sedari, quàm virtus eorum famam & gloriam adæquaverit. I have often heard (quoth he) how Quintus maximus, Publius Scipio, and many other worthy men of our citie were woont to say, when they beheld the images and

THE EPISTLE DEDICATORIE

portraitures of their ancestors, that they were most vehemently inflamed unto vertue. Not that the sayd wax or portraiture had any such force at all in it selfe, but that by the remembring of their woorthy actes, that flame was kindled in their noble breasts, and could never be quenched, untill such time as their owne valure had equalled the fame and glory of their progenitors. So, though not in wax, yet in record of writing have I presented to the noble courages of this English Monarchie, the like images of their famous predecessors, with hope of like effect in their posteritie. And here by the way if any man shall think, that an universall peace with our Christian neighbours will cut off the emploiment of the couragious increasing youth of this realme, he is much deceived. For there are other most convenient emploiments for all the superfluitie of every profession in this realme. For, not to meddle with the state of Ireland, nor that of Guiana, there is under our noses the great & ample countrey of Virginia; the In-land whereof is found of late to bee so sweete and holesome a climate, so rich and abundant in silver mines, so apt and capable of all commodities, which Italy, Spaine, and France can affoord, that the Spaniards themselves in their owne writings printed in Madrid 1586, and within few moneths afterward reprinted by me in Paris, and in a secret mappe of those partes made in Mexico the yeere before for the king of Spaine, (which originall with many others is in the custodie of the excellent Mathematician M. Thomas Hariot) as also in their intercepted letters come unto my hand, bearing date 1595. they acknowledge the In-land to be a better and richer countrey then Mexico and Nueva Spania it selfe. And on the other side their chiefest writers, as Peter Martyr ab Angleria, and Francis Lopez de Gomara, the most learned Venetian John Baptista Ramusius, and the French Geographers, as namely, Popiliniere and the rest, acknowledge with one consent, that all that mightie tract of land from 67. degrees Northward to the latitude almost of Florida was first discovered

out of England, by the commaundement of king Henry
the seventh, and the South part thereof before any other
Christian people of late hath bene planted with divers
English Colonies by the royal consent of her sacred
Majestie under the broad seale of England, whereof one
as yet remaineth, for ought we know, alive in the
countrey. Which action, if upon a good & godly peace
obtained, it shal please the Almighty to stirre up her
Majesties heart to continue with her favourable countenance (as upon the ceasing of the warres of Granada, hee
stirred up the spirite of Isabella Queene of Castile, to
advaunce the enterprise of Columbus) with transporting of
one or two thousand of her people, and such others as
upon mine owne knowledge will most willingly at their
owne charges become Adventurers in good numbers with
their bodies and goods ; she shall by Gods assistance, in
short space, worke many great and unlooked for effects,
increase her dominions, enrich her cofers, and reduce
many Pagans to the faith of Christ. The neglecting
hitherto of which last point our adversaries daily in many
of their bookes full bitterly lay unto the charge of the
professors of the Gospell. No sooner should we set
footing in that pleasant and good land, and erect one or
two convenient Fortes in the Continent, or in some Iland
neere the maine, but every step we tread would yeeld us
new occasion of action, which I wish the Gentrie of our
nation rather to regard, then to follow those soft unprofit-
able pleasures wherein they now too much consume their
time and patrimonie, and hereafter will doe much more,
when as our neighbour warres being appeased, they are
like to have lesse emploiment then nowe they have,
unlesse they bee occupied in this or some other the like
expedition. And to this ende and purpose give me leave
(I beseech you) to impart this occurrent to your honourable and provident consideration : that in the yere one
thousand five hundred eighty and seven, when I had
caused the foure voyages of Ribault, Laudonniere, and
Gourges to Florida, at mine owne charges to bee printed

in Paris, which by the malice of some too much affectioned to the Spanish faction, had bene above twentie yeeres suppressed, assoone as that booke came to the view of that reverend and prudent Counseller Monsieur Harlac the lord chiefe Justice of France, and certaine other of the wisest Judges, in great choler they asked, who had done such intollerable wrong to their whole kingdome, as to have concealed that woorthie worke so long? Protesting further, that if their Kings and the Estate had throughly followed that action, France had bene freed of their long civill warres, and the variable humours of all sortes of people might have had very ample and manifold occasions of good and honest emploiment abroad in that large and fruitfull Continent of the West Indies. The application of which sentence unto our selves I here omit, hastening unto the summarie recapitulation of other matters contained in this worke. It may please your Honour therefore to understand, that the second part of this first Treatise containeth our auncient trade and traffique with English shipping to the Ilands of Sicilie, Candie, and Sio, which by good warrant herein alleaged, I find to have bene begun in the yeere 1511. and to have continued untill the yeere 1552. and somewhat longer. But shortly after (as it seemeth) it was intermitted, or rather given over (as is noted in master Gaspar Campions discreet letters to master Michael Lock and master William Winter inserted in this booke) first by occasion of the Turkes expelling of the foure and twentie Mauneses or governours of the Genouois out of the Ile of Sio, and by taking of the sayd Iland wholie into his owne hand in Aprill, 1566. sending thither Piali Basha with fourescore gallies for that purpose; and afterward by his growing over mightie and troublesome in those Seas, by the cruell invasion of Nicosia and Famagusta, and the whole Ile of Cyprus by his lieutenant Generall Mustapha Basha. Which lamentable Tragedie I have here againe revived, that the posteritie may never forget what trust may bee given to the oath of a

Mahumetan, when hee hath advauntage and is in his choler.

Lastly, I have here put downe at large the happie renuing and much increasing of our interrupted trade in all the Levant, accomplished by the great charges and speciall industrie of the worshipfull and worthy Citizens, Sir Edward Osborne Knight, M. Richard Staper, and M. William Hareborne, together with the league for traffike onely betweene her Majestie and the Grand Signior, with the great privileges, immunities, and favours obteyned of his imperiall Highnesse in that behalfe, the admissions and residencies of our Ambassadours in his stately Porch, and the great good and Christian offices which her Sacred Majestie by her extraordinary favour in that Court hath done for the king and kingdome of Poland, and other Christian Princes : the traffike of our Nation in all the chiefe Havens of Africa and Egypt : the searching and haunting the very bottome of the Mediterran Sea to the ports of Tripoli and Alexandretta, of the Archipelagus, by the Turkes now called The white sea, even to the walles of Constantinople : the voyages over land and by river through Aleppo, Birrha, Babylon and Balsara, and downe the Persian gulfe to Ormuz, and thence by the Ocean sea to Goa, and againe over-land to Bisnagar, Cambaia, Orixa, Bengala, Aracan, Pegu, Malacca, Siam, the Iangomes, Quicheu, and even to the Frontiers of the Empire of China : the former performed diverse times by sundry of our nation, and the last great voyage by M. Ralph Fitch, who with M. John Newbery and two other consorts departed from London with her Majesties letters written effectually in their favour to the kings of Cambaia and China in the yere 1583, who in the yeere 1591. like another Paulus Venetus returned home to the place of his departure, with ample relation of his wonderfull travailes, which he presented in writing to my Lord your father of honourable memorie.

Now here if any man shall take exception against this our new trade with Turkes and misbeleevers, he shall shew himselfe a man of small experience in old and new Histories, or wilfully lead with partialitie, or some worse humour. *For who knoweth not, that king Salomon of old, entred into league upon necessitie with Hiram the king of Tyrus, a gentile? Or who is ignorant that the French, the Genouois, Florentines, Raguscans, Venetians, and Polonians are at this day in league with the Grand Signior, and have beene these many yeeres, and have used trade and traffike in his dominions? Who can deny that the Emperor of Christendome hath had league with the Turke, and payd him a long while a pension for a part of Hungarie? And who doth not acknowledge, that either hath travailed the remote parts of the world, or read the Histories of this later age, that the Spaniards and Portugales in Barbarie, in the Indies, and elsewhere, have ordinarie confederacie and traffike with the Moores, and many kindes of Gentiles and Pagans, and that which is more, doe pay them pensions, and use them in their service and warres? Why then should that be blamed in us, which is usuall and common to the most part of other Christian nations? Therefore let our neighbours, which have found most fault with this new league and traffike, thanke themselves and their owne foolish pride, whereby we were urged to seeke further to provide vent for our naturall commodities. And herein the old Greeke proverbe was most truely verified, That evill counsaile proveth worst to the author and deviser of the same.

Having thus farre intreated of the chiefe contents of the first part of this second Volume, it remayneth that I briefly acquaint your Honor with the chiefe contents of the second part. It may therefore please you to understand, that herein I have likewise preserved, disposed, and set in order such Voyages, Navigations, Traffikes, and Discoveries, as our Nation, and especially the worthy inhabitants of this citie of London, have painefully performed to the South and Southeast parts of the world, without the Streight of Gibraltar, upon the coasts of Africa, about the Cape of Buona Sperança, to and

*1. King. cap. 5. 2. Chron. cap. 2.

TO SIR ROBERT CECIL

beyonde the East India. To come more neere unto particulars, I have here set downe the very originals and infancie of our trades to the Canarian Ilands, to the kingdomes of Barbarie, to the mightie rivers of Senega and Gambra, to those of Madrabumba, and Sierra Leona, and the Isles of Cape Verde, with twelve sundry voyages to the sultry kingdomes of Guinea and Benin, to the Isle of San Thomé, with a late and true report of the weake estate of the Portugales in Angola, as also the whole course of the Portugale Caracks from Lisbon to the barre of Goa in India, with the disposition and qualitie of the climate neere and under the Equinoctiall line, the sundry infallible markes and tokens of approching unto, and doubling of The Cape of good Hope, the great variation of the compasse for three or foure pointes towards the East betweene the Meridian of S. Michael one of the Islands of the Azores, and the aforesaid Cape, with the returne of the needle againe due North at the Cape Das Agulias, and that place being passed outward bound, the swarving backe againe thereof towards the West, proportionally as it did before, the two wayes, the one within and the other without the Isle of S. Laurence, the dangers of privie rockes and quicksands, the running seas, and the perils thereof, with the certaine and undoubted signes of land. All these and other particularities are plainly and truely here delivered by one Thomas Stevens a learned Englishman, who in the yeere 1579 going as a passenger in the Portugale Fleete from Lisbon into India, wrote the same from Goa to his father in England : Whereunto I have added the memorable voyage of M. James Lancaster, who doth not onely recount and confirme most of the things above mentioned, but also doth acquaint us with the state of the voyage beyond Cape Comori, and the Isle of Ceilon, with the Isles of Nicubar and Gomes Polo lying within two leagues of the rich Island Samatra, and those of Pulo Pinaon, with the maine land of Junçalaon and the streight of Malacca. I have likewise added a late intercepted letter of a

THE EPISTLE DEDICATORIE

Portugall revealing the secret and most gainefull trade of Pegu, which is also confirmed by Cæsar Fredericke a Venetian, and M. Ralph Fitch now living here in London.

And because our chiefe desire is to find out ample vent of our wollen cloth, the naturall commoditie of this our Realme, the fittest places, which in al my readings and observations I find for that purpose, are the manifold Islands of Japan, & the Northern parts of China, & the regions of the Tartars next adjoyning (whereof I read, that the countrey in winter is Assi fria como Flandes, that is to say, as cold as Flanders, & that the rivers be strongly overfrozen) and therefore I have here inserted two speciall Treatises of the sayd Countries, the one beginning pag. 68, the other, pag. 88 : which last discourse I hold to be the most exact of those parts that is yet come to light, which was printed in Latine in Macao a citie of China, in China-paper, in the yeere a thousand five hundred and ninetie, and was intercepted in the great Carack called Madre de Dios two yeeres after, inclosed in a case of sweete Cedar wood, and lapped up almost an hundred fold in fine calicut-cloth, as though it had beene some incomparable jewell.

But leaving abruptly this discourse, I thinke it not impertinent, before I make an end, to deliver some of the reasons, that moved me to present this part of my travailes unto your Honour. The reverend antiquitie in the dedication of their workes made choyse of such patrons, as eyther with their reputation and credite were able to countenance the same, or by their wisedome and understanding were able to censure and approove them, or with their abilitie were likely to stand them or theirs in steade in the ordinarie necessities and accidents of their life. Touching the first, your descent from a father, that was accounted Pater patriæ, your owne place and credite in execution of her Majesties inward counsailes and publike services, added to your well discharging your forren imployment (when the greatest cause in Christendome was handled) have not onely drawen mens eyes upon you,

TO SIR ROBERT CECIL

but also forcibly have moved many, and my selfe among
the rest to have our labours protected by your authoritie.
For the second point, when it pleased your Honour in
sommer was two yeeres to have some conference with me,
and to demaund mine opinion touching the state of the
Country of Guiana, and whether it were fit to be planted
by the English: I then (to my no small joy) did admire
the exact knowledge which you had gotten of those
matters of Indian Navigations: and how carefull you
were, not to be overtaken with any partiall affection to the
Action, appeared also, by the sound arguments which you
made pro & contra, of the likelihood and reason of good
or ill successe of the same, before the State and common
wealth (wherein you have an extraordinarie voyce) should
be farther engaged. In consideration whereof I thinke
my selfe thrise happie to have these my travailes censured
by your Honours so well approved judgement. Touching the third and last motive I cannot but acknowledge
my selfe much indebted for your favourable letters heretofore written in my behalfe in mine honest causes.
Whereunto I may adde, that when this worke was to
passe unto the presse, your Honour did not onely
intreate a worthy knight, a person of speciall experience,
as in many others so in marine causes, to oversee and
peruse the same, but also upon his good report with your
most favourable letters did warrant, and with extraordinarie commendation did approve and allow my
labours, and desire to publish the same. Wherefore to
conclude, seeing they take their life and light from
the most cheerefull and benigne aspect of your favour, I
thinke it my bounden dutie in all humilitie and with
much bashfulnesse to recommend my selfe and them unto
your right Honorable and favourable protection, and
your Honour to the mercifull tuition of the most High.
From London this 24. of October. 1599.

Your Honors most humble
to be commanded,
Richard Hakluyt preacher.

THE EPISTLE DEDICATORIE IN THE THIRD VOLUME
OF THE SECOND EDITION, 1600.

To the Right Honourable Sir Robert Cecil Knight,
principall Secretary to her Majestie, master of
the Court of Wards and Liveries, and one of
her Majesties most honourable privie Councel.

Ight honourable, your favourable accep-
tance of my second volume of The English
voyages offred unto you the last yere,
your perusing of the same at your convenient leasure, your good testimony of
my selfe and of my travailes therein,
together with the infallible signes of your
earnest desire to doe mee good, which very lately, when
I thought least thereof, brake forth into most bountiful
and acceptable effects: these considerations have throughly
animated and encouraged me to present unto your prudent censure this my third and last volume also. The
subject and matter herein contained is the fourth part
of the world, which more commonly then properly is
called America: but by the chiefest authors The new
world. New, in regard of the new and late discovery
thereof made by Christopher Colon, aliàs Columbus, a
Genouois by nation, in the yere of grace 1492. And
world, in respect of the huge extension thereof, which
to this day is not throughly discovered, neither within
the Inland nor on the coast, especially toward the North
and Northwest, although on the hither side it be knowen
unto us for the space of five thousand leagues at the least,
compting and considering the trending of the land, and

THE

THIRD AND LAST
VOLVME OF THE VOY-
AGES, NAVIGATIONS, TRAF-

fiques, and Difcoueries of the *Englifh Nation*, and in
fome few places, where they haue not been, of ftrangers, performed within and before the time of thefe hundred yeeres, to all
parts of the *Newfound* world of *America*, or the *Weft Indies*, from 73.
degrees of Northerly to 57. of Southerly latitude:

As namely to *Engronland*, *Meta Incognita*, *Eftotiland*,
Tierra de Labrador, *Newfoundland*, vp *The grand bay*, the gulfe of *S. Lau-*
rence, and the Riuer of *Canada* to *Hochelaga* and *Saguenay*, along the coaft of *Aram-*
bec, to the fhores and maines of *Virginia* and *Florida*, and on the Weft or backfide of them
both, to the rich and pleafant countries of *Nueua Bifcaya*, *Cibola*, *Tiguex*, *Cicuic*,
Quiuira, to the 15. prouinces of the kingdome of *New Mexico*, to the
bottome of the gulfe of *California*, and vp the
Riuer of *Buena Guia*:

And likewife to all the yles both fmall and great lying before the
cape of *Florida*, *The bay* of *Mexico*, and *Tierra firma*, to the coafts and Inlands
of *Newe Spaine*, *Tierra firma*, and *Guiana*, vp the mighty Riuers of *Orenoque*,
Deffekebe, and *Marannon*, to euery part of the coaft of *Brafil*, to the Riuer of *Plate*,
through the Streights of *Magellan* forward and backward, and to the
South of the faid Streights as farre as 57. degrees:

And from thence on the backfide of *America*, along the coaftes, harbours,
and capes of *Chili*, *Peru*, *Nicaragua*, *Nueua Efpanna*, *Nueua Galicia*, *Culiacan*,
California, *Nova Albion*, and more Northerly as farre as 43. degrees:

Together with the two renowmed, and profperous voyages of Sir *Francis Drake*
and M. *Thomas Candifh* round about the circumference of the whole earth, and
diuers other voyages intended and fet forth for that courfe,

Collected by RICHARD HAKLVYT *Preacher, and fometimes*
ftudent of Chrift-Church in Oxford.

¶ Imprinted at London by *George Bifhop*, *Ralfe*
Newberie, and ROBERT BARKER.

ANNO DOM. 1600.

The material originally positioned here is too large for reproduction in this
reissue. A PDF can be downloaded from the web address given on page iv
of this book, by clicking on 'Resources Available'.

TO SIR ROBERT CECIL

for 3000. more on the backeside in the South Sea from the Streight of Magellan to Cape Mendoçino and Nova Albion. So that it seemeth very fitly to be called A newe worlde. Howbeit it cannot be denied but that Antiquitie had some kinde of dimme glimse, and unperfect notice thereof. Which may appeare by the relation of Plato in his two worthy dialogues of Timæus and Critias under the discourse of that mighty large yland called by him Atlantis, lying in the Ocean sea without the Streight of Hercules, now called the Streight of Gibraltar, being (as he there reporteth) bigger then Africa & Asia : And by that of Aristotle in his booke De admirandis auditionibus of the long navigation of certaine Carthaginians, who sayling forth of the aforesaid Streight of Gibraltar into the maine Ocean for the space of many dayes, in the ende found a mighty and fruitfull yland, which they would have inhabited, but were forbidden by their Senate and chiefe governours. Moreover, above 300. yeeres after these wee have the testimony of Diodorus Siculus lib. 5. cap. 7. of the like mighty yland discovered in the Westerne Ocean by the Tyrrheni, who were forbidden for certaine causes to inhabite the same by the foresaid Carthaginians. And Seneca in his tragedie intituled Medea foretold above 1500. yeeres past, that in the later ages the Ocean would discover new worlds, and that the yle of Thule would no more be the uttermost limite of the earth. For whereas Virgile had said to Augustus Cæsar, Tibi serviat ultima Thule, alluding thereunto he contradicteth the same, and saith, Nec sit terris ultima Thule. Yea Tertullian one of our most ancient and learned divines, in the beginning of his treatise de Pallio alludeth unto Plato his Westerne Atlantis, which there by another name he calleth Aeon, saying, Aeon in Atlantico nunc quæritur. And in his 40. chapter de Apologetico he reporteth the same to be bigger then all Africa and Asia. Of this New world and every speciall part thereof in this my third volume I have brought to light the best & most perfect relations of such as were

THE EPISTLE DEDICATORIE

chiefe actours in the particular discoveries and serches of the same, giving unto every man his right, and leaving every one to mainteine his owne credit. The order observed in this worke is farre more exact, then heretofore I could attaine unto: for whereas in my two former volumes I was enforced for lacke of sufficient store, in divers places to use the methode of time onely (which many worthy authors on the like occasion are enforced unto) being now more plentifully furnished with matter, I always follow the double order of time and place. Wherefore proposing unto my selfe the right situation of this New world, I begin at the extreme Northerne limite, and put downe successively in one ranke or classis, according to the order aforesaide, all such voyages as have bene made to the said part: which comming all together, and following orderly one upon another, doe much more lighten the readers understanding, and confirme his judgement, then if they had bene scattered in sundry corners of the worke. Which methode I observe from the highest North to the lowest South. Now where any country hath bene but seldome hanted, or any extraordinary and chiefe action occurreth, if I finde one voyage well written by two severall persons, sometimes I make no difficultie to set downe both those journals, as finding divers things of good moment observed in the one, which are quite omitted in the other. For commonly a souldier observeth one thing, and a mariner another, and as your honour knoweth, Plus vident oculi, quàm oculus. But this course I take very seldome and sparingly. And albeit my worke do carry the title of The English voyages, aswell in regard that the greatest part are theirs, and that my travaile was chiefly undertaken for preservation of their memorable actions, yet where our owne mens experience is defective, there I have bene carefull to supply the same with the best and chiefest relations of strangers. As in the discovery of the Grand Bay, of the mighty river of S. Laurence, of the countries of Canada, Hochelaga, and Saguenay, of Florida, and the Inland

lxxvi

TO SIR ROBERT CECIL

of Cibola, Tiguex, Cicuic, and Quivira, of The gulfe of California, & the Northwesterne sea-coast to Cabo Mendoçino and Sierra Nevada: as also of the late & rich discovery of 15. provinces on the backside of Florida and Virginia, the chiefest wherof is called the kingdome of New Mexico, for the wealth, civil government, and populousnesse of the same. Moreover, because since our warres with Spaine, by the taking of their ships, and sacking of their townes and cities, most of all their secrets of the West Indies, and every part thereof are fallen into our peoples hands (which in former time were for the most part unknowen unto us,) I have used the uttermost of my best endevour, to get, and having gotten, to translate out of Spanish, and here in this present volume to publish such secrets of theirs, as may any way availe us or annoy them, if they drive and urge us by their sullen insolencies, to continue our courses of hostilitie against them, and shall cease to seeke a good and Christian peace upon indifferent and equal conditions. What these things be, and of how great importance your honour in part may understand, if it please you to vouchsafe to reade the Catalogues conteyning the 14. principal heads of this worke. Whereby your honor may farther perceive that there is no chiefe river, no port, no towne, no citie, no province of any reckoning in the West Indies, that hath not here some good description thereof, aswell for the inland as the seast-coast. And for the knowledge of the true breadth of the Sea betweene Nova Albion on the Northwest part of America, and the yle of Japan lying over against the kingdomes of Coray and China, which until these foure yeeres was never reveiled unto us, being a point of exceeding great consequence, I have here inserted the voyage of one Francis Gualle a Spaniard made from Acapulco an haven on the South sea on the coast of New Spaine, first to the Philippinas, and then to the citie of Macao in China, and homeward from Macao by the yles of Japan, and thence to the back of the West Indies in the Northerly latitude of 37. degrees ½. In

which course betweene the said ylands and the maine he
found a wide and spacious open Ocean of 900. leagues
broad, which a little more to the Northward hath bene set
out as a Streight, and called in most mappes The Streight
of Anian. In which relation to the viceroy hee constantly
affirmeth three severall times, that there is a passage that
way unto the North parts of Asia. Moreover, because I
perceive by a letter directed by her Majestie to the Emperour of China (and sent in the last Fleet intended for
those parts by The South Sea under the charge of Ben-
jamin Wood, chiefly set out at the charges of sir Robert
Duddeley, a gentleman of excellent parts) that she useth
her princely mediation for obtaining of freedome of
traffique for her marchants in his dominions, for the better
instruction of our people in the state of those countries,
I have brought to light certaine new advertisements of the
late alteration of the mightie monarchie of the confronting
yle of Japan, and of the new conquest of the kingdome of
Coray, not long since tributarie to the king of China, by
Quabacondono the monarch of all the yles and prince-
domes of Japan; as also of the Tartars called Jezi, adjoyning on the East & Northeast parts of Coray, where I
thinke the best utterance of our natural and chiefe commoditie of cloth is like to be, if it please God hereafter
to reveile unto us the passage thither by the Northwest.
The most exact and true information of the North parts
of China I finde in an history of Tamerlan, which I have
in French, set out within these sixe yeres by the abbat of
Mortimer, dedicated to the French king that now reigneth,
who confesseth that it was long since written in the
Arabian tongue by one Alhacen a wise and valiant Captaine, employed by the said mighty prince in all his conquests of the foresaid kingdome. Which history I would
not have failed to have translated into English, if I had
not found it learnedly done unto my hand.

And for an appendix unto the ende of my worke, I
have thought it not impertinent, to exhibit to the grave
and discreet judgements of those which have the chiefe

TO SIR ROBERT CECIL

places in the Admiraltie and marine causes of England,
Certaine briefe extracts of the orders of the Contractation
house of Sivil in Spaine, touching their government in
sea-matters; together with The streight and severe
examination of Pilots and Masters before they be admitted to take charge of ships, aswell by the Pilot mayor,
and brotherhood of ancient Masters, as by the Kings
reader of The lecture of the art of Navigation, with the
time that they be enjoyned to bee his auditors, and some
part of the questions that they are to answere unto.
Which if they finde good and beneficial for our seamen,
I hope they wil gladly imbrace and imitate, or finding out
some fitter course of their owne, will seeke to bring such
as are of that calling unto better government and more
perfection in that most laudable and needfull vocation.
To leave this point, I was once minded to have added
to the end of these my labours a short treatise, which I
have lying by me in writing, touching The curing of
hot diseases incident to traveilers in long and Southerne
voyages, which treatise was written in English, no doubt
of a very honest mind, by one M. George Wateson, and
dedicated unto her sacred Majestie. But being carefull
to do nothing herein rashly, I shewed it to my worshipfull friend M. doctour Gilbert, a gentleman no lesse
excellent in the chiefest secrets of the Mathematicks (as
that rare jewel lately set foorth by him in Latine doeth
evidently declare) then in his owne profession of physicke:
who assured me, after hee had perused the said treatise,
that it was very defective and unperfect, and that if hee
might have leasure, which that argument would require,
he would either write something thereof more advisedly
himselfe, or would conferre with the whole Colledge of
the Physicions, and set downe some order by common
consent for the preservation of her Majesties subjects.
Now as the foresaid treatise touched the cure of diseases
growing in hot regions, so being requested thereunto by
some in authoritie they may adde their judgements for
the cure of diseases incident unto men employed in cold

THE EPISTLE DEDICATORIE

regions, which to good purpose may serve our peoples turnes, if they chance to prosecute the intermitted discovery by the Northwest, whereunto I finde divers worshipfull citizens at this present much inclined. Now because long since I did foresee, that my profession of divinitie, the care of my family, and other occasions might call and divert me from these kinde of endevours, I have for these 3. yeeres last past encouraged and furthered in these studies of Cosmographie and forren histories, my very honest, industrious, and learned friend M. JOHN PORY, one of speciall skill and extraordinary hope to performe great matters in the same, and beneficial for the common wealth.

Thus Sir I have portrayed out in rude lineaments my Westerne Atlantis or America : assuring you, that if I had bene able, I would have limned her and set her out with farre more lively and exquisite colours : yet, as she is, I humbly desire you to receive her with your wonted and accustomed favour at my handes, who alwayes wil remaine most ready and devoted to do your honour any poore service that I may ; and in the meane season will not faile unfainedly to beseech the Almighty to powre upon you the best of his temporall blessings in this world, and after this life ended with true and much honour, to make you partaker of his joyes eternall. From London the first of September, the yeere of our Lord God 1600.

Your Honours most humble to be commanded,

RICHARD HAKLUYT, Preacher.

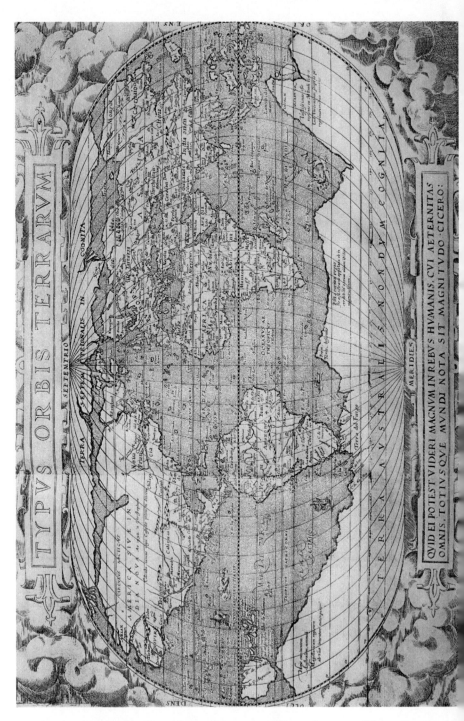

The material originally positioned here is too large for reproduction in this reissue. A PDF can be downloaded from the web address given on page iv of this book, by clicking on 'Resources Available'.

THE FIRST VOLUME

OF THE

Principall Navigations, Voyages, Traffiques and Discoveries of the English Nation

Made to the North and Northeast quarters of the
World, with the directions, letters, priviledges
discourses, and observations incident
to the same

Certeine testimonies concerning K. Arthur and
his conquests of the North regions, taken
out of the historie of the Kings of Britaine,
written by Galfridus Monumetensis, and newly
printed at Heidelberge, Anno 1587.

Lib. 9. cap. 10.

Nno Christi, 517. Arthurus, secundo regni sui anno, subjugatis totius Hyberniæ partibus, classem suam direxit in Islandiam, eámque debellato populo subjugavit. Exin divulgato per cæteras insulas rumore, quòd ei nulla Provincia resistere poterat, Doldavius rex Gotlandiæ, & Gunfacius rex Orcadum ultrò venerunt, promissóque vectigali subjectionem fecerunt. Emensa deinde hyeme, reversus est in Britanniam, statúmque regni in firmam pacem renovans, moram duodecim annis ibidem fecit.

The same in English.

IN the yere of Christ, 517. king Arthur in the second yeere of his reigne, having subdued all parts of Ireland, sailed with his fleet into Island, and brought it and the people thereof under his subjection. The rumour afterwards being spread thorowout all the other Islands, that no countrey was able to withstand him, Doldavius the king of Gotland, and Gunfacius the king of Orkney, came voluntarily unto him, and yeelded him their obedience, promising to pay him tribute. The

Winter being spent, he returned into Britaine, and establishing his kingdome in perfect peace, he continued there for the space of twelve yeres.

Lib. 9 cap. 12.

MIssis deinde in diversa regna Legatis, invitantur tam ex Galliis, quàm ex collateralibus Insulis Oceani, qui ad curiam venire deberent, &c. Et paulò post : Ex collateralibus autem Insulis, Guillaumurius rex Hyberniæ, Malvasius rex Islandiæ, Doldavius rex Gotlandiæ, Gunnasius rex Orchadum, Lot rex Noruegiæ, Aschilius rex Danorum.

The same in English.

AFter that king Arthur sending his messengers into divers kingdomes, he summoned such as were to come to his Court, aswell out of France, as out of the adjacent Islands of the sea, &c. and a little after : From those adjacent Islands came Guillaumurius king of Ireland, Malvasius king of Island, Doldavius king of Gotland, Gunnasius king of Orkney, Lot the king of Norway, and Aschilius the king of Denmarke.

Lib. 9 cap. 19.

AT reges cæterarum Insularum, quoniam non duxerant in morem equites habere, pedites quot quisque debebat, promittunt, ita ut ex sex Insulis, videlicet, Hyberniæ, Islandiæ, Gotlandiæ, Orcadum, Noruegiæ, atque Daciæ, sexies viginti millia essent annumerata.

[I. 2.]
The same in English.

BUt the kings of the other Islands, because it was not their custome to breed up horses, promised the king as many footmen, as every man was bound to send : so that out of the six Islands, namely, of Ireland, Island, Gotland, Orkney, Norway, and Denmarke, the king had sixe score thousand souldiers sent him.

KING ARTHUR

A testimonie of the right and appendances of
the crowne of the kingdome of Britaine,
taken out of M. Lambard his Ἀρκαιονομία, fol.
137. pag. 2.

ARthurus qui fuit quondam inclytissimus Rex Britonum, vir magnus fuit & animosus, & miles
illustris. Parum fuit ei regnum istud, non fuit animus
ejus contentus regno Britanniæ. Subjugavit igitur sibi
strenuè Scantiam totam, quæ modo Norweia vocatur, &
omnes insulas ultra Scantiam, scz. Islandiam, & Grenlan-
diam, quæ sunt de appendiciis Norweiæ, & Suechordam,
& Hyberniam, & Gutlandiam, & Daciam, Semelandiam,
Winlandiam, Curlandiam, Roe, Femelandiam, Wirelan-
diam, Flandriam, Cherelam, Lappam, & omnes alias terras
& insulas, Orientalis Oceani usque Russiam (in Lappa
scilicet posuit Orientalem metam regni Britanniæ) &
multas insulas ultra Scantiam, usque dum sub Septen-
trione, quæ sunt de appendicibus Scantiæ, quæ modo
Norweia vocatur. Fuerunt autem ibi Christiani occultè.
Arthurus autem Christianus optimus fuit, & fecit eos
baptizari, & unum Deum per totam Norweiam venerari,
& unam fidem Christi semper inviolatam custodire, &
suscipere. Ceperunt universi proceres Norweiæ uxores
suas de nobili gente Britonum tempore illo, unde Norwegienses dicunt se exiisse de gente & sanguine regni
hujus. Impetravit enim temporibus illis Arthurus rex
à domino Papa, & à Curia Romana, quod confirmata sit
Norweia, in perpetuum coronæ Britanniæ in augmentum
regni hujus, vocavítque illam dictus Arthurus Cameram
Britanniæ. Hac verò de causa dicunt Norwegienses, se
debere in regno isto cohabitare & dicunt se esse de
corpore regni hujus, scilicet de corona Britanniæ. Malu-
erunt enim manere in regno isto, quàm in terra eorum
propria. Terra enim eorum arida est, & montuosa, &
sterilis, & non sunt ibi segetes nisi per loca. Ista verò
opulenta est, & fertilis, & crescunt hic segetes, & cætera
universa. Qua ex causa sæpius per vices gesta sunt bella

5

atrocissima inter Anglos & Norwegienses, & interfecti
sunt innumerabiles. Occupaverunt verò Norwegienses
terras multas & insulas regni hujus, quas adhuc detinent
occupatas, nec potuerunt unquam postea penitus evelli.
Tandem modò confederati sunt nobis fide, & sacramento,
& per uxores suas, quas postea ceperunt de sanguine
nostro, & per affinitates, & conjugia. Ita demum con-
stituit, & eis concessit bonus rex Edouardus propinquus
noster (qui fuit optimus filius pacis) per commune consilium totius regni. Qua de causa possent, & debent
prædicti de cætero nobiscum cohabitare, & remanere in
regno, sicut conjurati fratres nostri.

The same in English.

ARthur which was sometimes the most renowmed
king of the Britains, was a mightie, and valiant
man, and a famous warriour. This kingdome was too
litle for him, & his minde was not contented with it.
He therefore valiantly subdued all Scantia, which is now
called Norway, and all the Islands beyond Norway, to wit,
Island and Greenland, which are apperteining unto Norway, Sweveland, Ireland, Gotland, Denmarke, Semeland,
Windland, Curland, Roe, Femeland, Wireland, Flanders,
Cherilland, Lapland, and all the other lands & Islands of
the East sea, even unto Russia (in which Lapland he
placed the Easterly bounds of his Brittish Empire) and
many other Islands beyond Norway, even under the
North pole, which are appendances of Scantia, now called
Norway. These people were wild and savage, and had
not in them the love of God nor of their neighbors,
because all evill commeth from the North, yet there were
among them certeine Christians living in secret. But
king Arthur was an exceeding good Christian, and caused
them to be baptized, and thorowout all Norway to worship
one God, and to receive and keepe inviolably for ever,
faith in Christ onely. At that time all the noble men of
Norway tooke wives of the noble nation of the Britaines,
whereupon the Norses say, that they are descended of the

race and blood of this kingdome. The aforesayd king
Arthur obteined also in those dayes of the Pope & court
of Rome, that Norway should be for ever annexed to the
crowne of Britaine for the inlargement of this kingdome,
and he called it the chamber of Britaine. For this cause
the Norses say, that they ought to dwell with us in this
kingdome, to wit, that they belong to the crowne of
Britaine : for they had rather dwell here then in their
owne native countrey, which is drie and full of mountaines, [I. 3.]
and barren, and no graine growing there, but in certeine
places. But this countrey of Britaine is fruitfull, wherein
corne and all other good things do grow and increase : for
which cause many cruell battels have bene oftentimes
fought betwixt the Englishmen and the people of Norway,
and infinite numbers of people have bene slaine, & the
Norses have possessed many lands and Islands of this
Empire, which unto this day they doe possesse, neither
could they ever afterwards be fully expelled. But now at
length they are incorporated with us by the receiving of
our religion and sacraments, and by taking wives of our
nation, and by affinitie, and mariages. For so the good
king Edward (who was a notable mainteiner of peace)
ordeined and granted unto them by the generall consent
of the whole kingdome, so that the people may, and
ought from henceefoorth dwell and remaine in this kingdome with us as our loving sworne brethren.

A testimonie out of the foresayd Galfridus Monu-
    metensis, concerning the conquests of Malgo,
    king of England. Lib. 11. cap. 7.

Ortiporio successit Malgo, omnium ferè Britanniæ
pulcherrimus, multorum tyrannorum depulsor,
robustus armis, largior cæteris, & ultra modum
probitate præclarus. Hic etiam totam Insulam obtinuit,
& sex conprovinciales Oceani Insulas : Hyberniam videlicet, atque Islandiam, Gotlandiam, Orcades, Noruegiam,
Daciam, adjecit dirissimis præliis potestati suæ.

7

The same in English.

MAlgo succeeded Vortiporius which was the goodliest man in person of all Britaine, a prince that expulsed many tyrants. He was strong and valiant in warre, taller then most men that then lived, and exceeding famous for his vertues. This king also obteined the government of the whole Island of Britaine, and by most sharpe battailes he recovered to his Empire the sixe Islands of the Ocean sea, which before had bene made tributaries by king Arthur, namely Ireland, Island, Gotland, Orkney, Norway, and Denmarke.

The conquest of the Isles of Anglesey and Man by Edwin the Saxon king of Northumberland written in the second Booke and fift Chapter of Beda his Ecclesiasticall historie of the English nation.

EDuinus Nordanhumbrorum gentis, id est, ejus quæ ad borealem Humbri fluminis plagam inhabitat, majore potentia cunctis qui Britanniam incolunt, Anglorum pariter & Britonum populis præfuit, præter Cantuarios tantùm, necnòn & Menavias Britonum insulas, quæ inter Hiberniam & Britanniam sitæ sunt, Anglorum subjecit potestati.

The same in English.

EDwin king of the people of Northumberland, that is to say, of them which inhabit to the North of the river Humber, being of greater authoritie then any other potentate in the whole Isle of Britaine, bare rule as well over the English as the British nation, except onely the people of Kent : who also brought in subjection under the English, the Isles of Man and Anglesey, and the other Northwesterne Isles of the Britons, which are situate betweene Britaine and Ireland.

8

Another testimonie alledged by Beda to the same
purpose. Lib. 2. cap. 9.

ANno ab incarnatione Domini sexcentesimo vicesimo
quarto, gens Nordanhumbrorum, hoc est, ea natio
Anglorum quæ ad aquilonarem Humbri fluminis plagam
habitat, cum rege suo Eduino, verbum fidei (prædicante
Paulino, cujus supra meminimus) suscepit : cui videlicèt
regi in auspicium suscipiendæ fidei, & regni cœlestis
potestas,. & terreni creverat imperii : ita ut (quod nemo
Anglorum ante eum fecit) omnes Britanniæ fines, qua vel
ipsorum vel Britonum Provinciæ habitabantur, sub ditione
acceperit.   Quìn & Menavias insulas (sicut & supra
docuimus) imperio subjugavit Anglorum.   Quarum prior
quæ ad austrum est, & situ amplior, & frugum proventu
atque ubertate fœlicior, nongentarum sexaginta familiarum
mensuram, juxta æstimationem Anglorum, secunda tre-
centarum & ultrà spatium tenet.

The same in English.

[I. 4.]

IN the yeere from the incarnation of our Lord, sixe
hundreth twentie and foure, the people of Northumberland, to wit, those English people which inhabit
on the North side of the river of Humber, together with
their king Edwin, at the Christian preaching and per-
swasion of Paulinus above mentioned, embraced the
Gospel.   Under which king, after he had once accepted
of the Christian faith, the power both of the heavenly
& of his earthly kingdome was inlarged ; insomuch, that
he (which no English king had done before him) brought
under his subjection all the provinces of Britaine, which
were inhabited either by the English men themselves, or
by the Britons.   Moreover, he subdued unto the crowne
of England (as we have above signified) the Hebrides,
commonly called the Westerne Islands.   The principall
wherof being more commodiously and pleasantly seated
towards the South, and more abounding with corne then
the rest, conteineth according to the estimation of the

9

English, roome enough for 960. families, and the second
for 300. and above.

The voyage of Bertus, generall of an armie sent into Ireland by Ecfridus king of Northumberland, in the yere of our Lord 684, out of the 4. Booke and 26. Chapter of Beda his Ecclesiasticall Hystorie.

Nno Dominicæ incarnationis sexcentesimo
octogesimo quarto, Ecfridus rex Nordan-
humbrorum, misso Hiberniam cum excer-
citu duce Berto, vastavit miserè gentem
innoxiam, & nationi Anglorum semper
amicissimam, ita ut nec ecclesiis quidem
aut monasteriis manus parceret hostilis.
At insulani & quantum valuere armis arma repellebant,
& invocantes divinæ auxilium pietatis cœlitus se vindicari
continuis diù imprecationibus postulabant.   Et quamvis
maledici regnum Dei possidere non possint, creditum
tamen est, quòd hi qui merito impietatis suæ maledice-
bantur, ocyùs Domino vindice, pœnas sui reatus luerent.

The same in English.

IN the yeere of our Lord 684, Ecfrid the king of
Northumberland sent captaine Bert into Ireland with
an armie, which Bert miserably wasted that innocent
nation being alwayes most friendly unto the people of
England, insomuch that the fury of the enemy spared
neither churches nor monasteries.   Howbeit the Islanders
to their power repelled armes with armes, and craving
Gods aid from heaven with continuall imprecations and
curses, they pleaded for revenge.   And albeit cursed
speakers can by no meanes inherit the kingdome of God,
it was thought notwithstanding, that they which were
accursed for their impiety did not long escape the ven-
geance of God imminent for their offences.

The voyage of Octher made to the Northeast parts
beyond Norway, reported by himselfe unto
Alfred the famous king of England, about the
yere 890.

Cther said, that the countrey wherein he
dwelt was called Helgoland. Octher tolde
his lord king Alfred that he dwelt furthest
North of any other Norman. He sayd
that he dwelt towards the North part of
the land toward the West coast : and
affirmed that the land, notwithstanding it
stretcheth marveilous farre towards the North, yet it is all
desert and not inhabited, unlesse it be very few places, here
and there, where certeine Finnes dwell upon the coast,
who live by hunting all the Winter, and by fishing in *Fynnes live by*
Summer. He said that upon a certeine time he fell into *hunting &*
a fantasie and desire to proove and know how farre that *fishing.*
land stretched Northward, and whether there were any
habitation of men North beyond the desert. Whereupon
he tooke his voyage directly North along the coast, having
upon his steereboord alwayes the desert land, and upon
the leereboord the maine Ocean : and continued his
course for the space of 3. dayes. In which space he was
come as far towards the North, as commonly the whale *The place*
hunters use to travell. Whence he proceeded in his *whither the*
course still towards the North so farre as he was able to *whale hunters*
saile in other 3. dayes. At the end whereof he perceived *traveile.*
that the coast turned towards the East, or els the sea
opened with a maine gulfe into the land, he knew not
how farre. Well he wist and remembred, that he was
faine to stay till he had a Westerne winde, and somewhat
Northerly : and thence he sailed plaine East along the
coast still so far as he was able in the space of 4. dayes.
At the end of which time he was compelled againe to stay [I. 5.]
till he had a full Northerly winde, forsomuch as the coast
bowed thence directly towards the South, or at least wise

11

the sea opened into the land he could not tell how farre : so that he sailed thence along the coast continually full South, so farre as he could travaile in 5. dayes ; and at the fifth dayes end he discovered a mightie river which opened very farre into the land. At the entrie of which river he stayed his course, and in conclusion turned backe againe, for he durst not enter thereinto for feare of the inhabitants of the land : perceiving that on the other side of the river the countrey was thorowly inhabited : which was the first peopled land that he had found since his departure from his owne dwelling : whereas continually thorowout all his voyage, he had evermore on his steereboord, a wildernesse and desert countrey, except that in some places, he saw a few fishers, fowlers, and hunters, which were all Fynnes : and all the way upon his leereboord was the maine ocean. The Biarmes had inhabited and tilled their countrey indifferent well, notwithstanding he was afrayed to go upon shore. But the countrey of the Terfynnes lay all waste, and not inhabited, except it were, as we have sayd, whereas dwelled certeine hunters, fowlers, and fishers. The Biarmes tolde him a number of stories both of their owne countrey, and of the countreyes adjoyning. Howbeit, he knew not, nor could affirme any thing for certeine trueth : forsomuch as he was not upon land, nor saw any himselfe. This onely he judged, that the Fynnes and Biarmes speake but one language. The principall purpose of his traveile this way, was to encrease the knowledge and discoverie of these coasts and countreyes, for the more commoditie of fishing of ‖ horsewhales, which have in their teeth bones of great price and excellencie : whereof he brought some at his returne unto the king. Their skinnes are also very good to make cables for shippes, and so used. This kinde of whale is much lesse in quantitie then other kindes, having not in length above seven elles. And as for the common kind of whales, the place of most and best hunting of them is in his owne countrey : whereof some be 48. elles of length, and some 50. of which sort he affirmed that he

A Desert
countrey.

Fynnes.

Biarmia.

Terfynnes.

The Fynnes
and Biarmes
speake one
language.
‖ Or, morsses,
their teeth
commended.
Use of ye
Morsses skinne
for cables.

himselfe was one of the sixe, which in the space of 3. dayes killed threescore. He was a man of exceeding wealth in such riches, wherein the wealth of that countrey doth consist. At the same time that he came to the king, he had of his owne breed 600. tame Deere, of that kinde which they call Rane Deere : of the which number 6. were stall Rane Deere, a beast of great value, and marveilously esteemed among the Fynnes, for that with them they catch the wilde Rane Deere. He was among the chiefe men of his countrey one : and yet he had but 20. kine, and 20. swine, and that little which he tilled, he tilled it all with horses. Their principall wealth consisteth in the tribute which the Fynnes pay them, which is all in skinnes of wilde beasts, feathers of birds, whale bones, and cables, and tacklings for shippes made of Whales or Seales skinnes. Every man payeth according to his abilitie. The richest pay ordinarily 15. cases of Marterns, 5. Rane Deere skinnes, and one Beare, ten bushels of feathers, a coat of a Beares skinne, two cables threescore elles long a piece, the one made of Whales skin, the other of Seales.

He sayd, that the countrey of Norway was very long and small. So much of it as either beareth any good pasture, or may be tilled, lieth upon the Sea coast, which notwithstanding in some places is very rockie and stonie : and all Eastward, all along against the inhabited land, lie wilde and huge hilles and mountaines, which are in some places inhabited by the Fynnes. The inhabited land is broadest toward the South, & the further it stretcheth towards the North, it groweth evermore smaller and smaller. Towards the South it is peradventure threescore miles in bredth or broader in some places : about the middest, 30. miles or above, and towards the North where it is smallest, he affirmeth that it proveth not three miles from the Sea to the mountaines. The mountaines be in breadth of such quantitie, as a man is able to traveile over in a fortnight, and in some places no more then may be traveiled in sixe dayes. Right over against this land, in the other side of the mountaines, somewhat towards the

Sixe hundreth tame Deere.

The Fynnes tribute.

Note.

Cables of Whales and Seales skins.

A description of Norway.

The bredth of the mountaines of Norway.

A.D.
c. 890.

Swethland.
Queeneland.

South, lieth Swethland, and against the same towards the North, lieth Queeneland. The Queenes sometimes passing the mountaines, invade and spoile the Normans : and on the contrary part, the Normans likewise sometimes spoile their countrey. Among the mountaines be many and great lakes in sundry places of fresh water, into the which the Queenes use to carie their boats upon their backs over land, and thereby invade and spoile the countrey of the Normans. These boats of theirs be very little and very light.

Boats caried
on mens backs.

The voyage of Octher out of his countrey of Halgoland into the sound of Denmarke unto a port called Hetha, which seemeth to be Wismer or Rostorke.

OCther sayd that the countrey wherein he dwelled, was called Halgoland : and affirmed that there was no man dwelling towards the North from him. From this countrey towards the South, there is a certeine || port called Scirings hall, whither, he sayth, that a man was not able to saile in a moneths space, if he lay still by night, although he had every day a full winde. And he shall saile all the way along the coast, having on his steereboord, first Jutland and the Islands which lie betwixt this countrey & Jutland, still along the coast of this countrey, till he came to Scirings hall, having it on his larboord. At Scirings hall there entreth into the land a maine gulfe of the Sea, which is so broad, that a man cannot see over it : and on the other side against the same, is Gotland, and then Silland. This sea stretcheth many hundreth miles up into the land. From Scirings hall he sayd that he sailed in 5. dayes to the port which is called Hetha, which lieth betwixt the countries of || Wendels, Saxons, and Angles, whereunto it is subject. And as he sailed thitherward from Scirings hall, he had upon his steereboord Denmarke, and on his leereboord the maine sea, for the space of 3. dayes : and 2. dayes before, he arrived in

[I. 6.]
|| *Or, streight.*
It seemeth to
be about
Elsenborg.

The descrip-
tion of the sound
of Denmarke.

Gotland.

|| *Vandals.*

14

Hetha, he had Gotland on leerboord, and Silland, with divers other Islands. In that countrey dwelt English men, before they came into this land. And these 2. dayes he had upon his leereboord the Islands that are subject to Denmarke.

*Hetha but two
dayes sayling
from Seland.
It seemeth to
be Wismer or
Rostocke.*

Wolstans navigation in the ‖ East sea, from Hetha to Trusco, which is about Dantzig.

*‖ Within the
sound of Den-
marke.*

Olstan sayd, that he departed from Hetha, and arrived at Trusco, in the space of 7. dayes, and 7. nights : during which time, his shippe kept her course continually under saile. All this voyage Wenedland was still upon his steerboord, and on his leerboord was Langland, Layland, Falster, and Sconie : all which countreyes are subject to Denmarke. Upon his leerboord also, was Bargenland, which hath a private king, unto whom it is subject. Having left Bargenland, he passed by Blekingie, Meere, Eland and Gotland, having them on his leerboord : all which countreys are subject to Sweden : and Wenedland was all the way upon his steerboord, until he came to Wixel mouth. Wixel is a very great river which runneth along betwixt Witland and Wenedland. Witland is apperteining to the Easterlings : and the river of Wixel runneth out of ‖ Wenedland into Eastmeere, which Eastmeere is at the least 15. miles in breadth. There runneth also another river called Ilsing from the East, and falleth into Eastmeere, out of another lake upon the banke, whereupon is situated Fruso. So that Ilsing comming out of ‖ Eastland, and Wixel out of Wenedland, fall both together into Eastmeere, and there Wixel depriveth Ilsing of his name, and runneth thence West & North into the sea ; whereof the place is called Wixelmouth.

*Bargenland,
or Bornholme.*

*Wixel is the
river that
falleth into the
sea by
Dantzig.*

‖ Or, Prussia.

Fruso.

*‖ Or,
Lituania.*

Eastland is a very large land, and there be many cities and townes within it, and in every one of them is a king : whereby there is continually among them great strife

*The descrip-
tion of
Eastland.*

and contention. There is great plentie of hony and fish.

The wealthiest men drinke commonly Mares milke, and the poore people and slaves meade. There is no ale brewed among the Easterlings, but of mead there is plentie.

The navigation of King Edgar, taken out of Florentius Wigorniensis, Hóveden, and M. Dee his discourse of the Brittish Monarchie, pag. 54, 55, &c.

 Have often times (sayd he) and many wayes looked into the state of earthly kingdomes, generally the whole world over (as farre as it may be yet knowen to Christian men commonly) being a studie of no great difficultie, but rather a purpose somewhat answerable to a perfect Cosmographer, to finde himselfe Cosmopolites, a citizen and member of the whole and onely one mysticall citie universall, and so consequently to meditate of the Cosmopoliticall government thereof, under the King almightie, passing on very swiftly toward the most dreadfull and most comfortable terme prefixed.

And I finde (sayd he) that if this Brittish Monarchie would heretofore have followed the advantages which they have had onward, they might very well, yer this, have surpassed by justice, and godly sort, any particular Monarchie els, that ever was on earth since mans creation : and that to all such purposes as to God are most acceptable, and to all perfect common wealths, most honorable, profitable, and comfortable.

But yet (sayd he) there is a little locke of Lady Occasion flickering in the aire, by our hands to catch hold on, whereby we may yet once more (before all be utterly past, and for ever) discreetly and valiantly recover and enjoy, if not all our ancient & due appurtenances to this

16

Imperiall Brittish monarchie, yet at the least some such
notable portion thereof, as (al circumstances duely and
justly apperteining to peace & amitie with forrein princes [I. 7.]
being offred & used) this may become the most peaceable, most rich, most puissant, & most florishing monarchie of al els (this day) in christendome. Peaceable, I
say, even with the most part of the selfe same respects
that good king Edgar had (being but a Saxon) and by
sundry such meanes, as he chiefly in this Empire did put
in proofe and ure triumphantly, whereupon his sirname
was Pacificus, most aptly and justly. This peaceable
king Edgar had in his minde about six hundred yeeres
past, the representation of a great part of the selfe same
Idæa, which from above onely, & by no mans devise
hath streamed downe into my imagination, being as it
becommeth a subject carefull for the godly prosperitie
of this British Empire under our most peaceable Queene
Elizabeth.

For, Ædgarus pacificus, Regni sui prospiciens utilitati, *Flores*
pariter & quieti, quatuor millia octingentas sibi robustas *Historiarum.*
congregavit naves è quibus mille ducentas, in plaga Angliæ
Orientali, mille ducentas in Occidentali, mille ducentas in
Australi, mille ducentas in Septentrionali pelago con-
stituit, ut ad defensionem regni sui, contra exteras nationes,
bellorum discrimina sustinerent.

O wisedome imperiall, most diligently to be imitated,
videlicet, prospicere, to foresee. O charitable kingly parent,
that was touched with ardent zeale, for procuring the
publike profite of his kingdome, yea and also the peaceable
enjoying therof. O, of an incredible masse of treasure,
a kingly portion, yet, in his coffers remayning : if then he
had, (or late before) any warres, seeing no notable taxe, or
contribution publike is historically mentioned to have bene
for the charges levied : if in peace he himselfe flourished
so wealthily : O marveilous politicall, & princely prudencie,
in time of peace to foresee, and prevent, (and that most
puissantly, and invincibly) all possible malice, fraude, force,
and mischiefe forrain. O most discreet liberalitie to such

excellent uses, powring out his treasure so abundantly. O
faithfull English people (then,) and worthy subjects, of
such an Imperiall and godly Governour. O your true,
and willing hearts, and blessed ready hands (then,) so to
impart such abundance of victuals for those huge Navies
maintenance : so (I say) as neither dearth of famine,
seemed (fondly) to be feared of you, for any intolerable
want likely to ensue thereby, nor prices of victuals complained of to be unreasonable enhaunsed by you, finding
for their great sales so good, and rare opportunitie.

This peaceable king Edgar, was one of the perfect Imperiall Monarches of this British Empire, and therefore
thus his fame remaineth (for ever) recorded.

Charta Regia,   Anglici orbis Basileus, flos, & Decus Ædgarus, non
Henrici   minùs memorabilis Anglis, quàm Cyrus Persis,
secundi.   Romulus Romanis, Alexander Macedonibus,
Arsaces Parthis, Carolus Francis, Anno vitæ 37.
Regni sui cum fratre, & post 21. Idibus Julii obiit,
& apud Glascon sepelitur.

O Glastonbury, Glastonbury, the treasurie of the carcases of so famous, and so many persons (Quæ olim mater
sanctorum dicta es, & ab aliis, tumulus sanctorum, quam
ab ipsis discipulis Domini, ædificatam fuisse venerabilis
habet Antiquorum authoritas) how lamentable is thy case
nowe! howe hath hypocrisie and pride wrought thy desolation! though I omit here the names of very many other,
both excellent holy men, and mighty princes, whose carcases
are committed to thy custody, yet that Apostolike Joseph,
that triumphant British Arthur, and nowe this peaceable
and provident Saxon king Edgar, doe force me with
a certaine sorowful reverence, here to celebrate thy
memorie.

This peaceable king Edgar (as by ancient Recordes
may appeare) his Sommer progresses, and yerely chiefe
pastimes were, the sailing round about this whole Isle
of Albion, garded with his grand navie of 4000. saile
at the least, parted into 4. equall parts of petie Navies,

18

eche one being of 1000. ships, for so it is anciently recorded.

Idem quoque Ædgarus, 4000. naves congregavit, ex quibus omni anno, post festum Paschale, 1000. naves ad quamlibet Angliæ partem statuit, sic, æstate Insulam circumnavigavit : hyeme verò, judicia in Provincia exercuit : & hæc omnia ad sui exercitium, & ad hostium fecit terrorem.

Ranulphus Cestrensis.

COuld, and would that peaceable & wise king Edgar, before need, as being in peace and quiet with all nations about him, and notwithstanding mistrusting his possible enemies, make his pastimes so roially, politically, and triumphantly, with so many thousand ships, and at the least with ten times so many men as ships, and that yerely? and shall we being not assured of such neighbors friendship, as may become to us as cruel and tyrannicall enemies as never king Edgar needed to dread the like, and they as many and mighty princes, as never king Edgar coped with the like, shall we (said he) not judge it some part of wisdome, to imitate carefully in some litle proportion (though not with so many thousands) the prosperous pastimes of peaceable king Edgar, that Saxonicall Alexander? yea, prosperous pastimes these may bee justly counted, by which he also made evident to the whole world, that as he wisely knew the ancient bounds and limits of this British Empire, so that he could and would royally, justly, and trium- [I. 8.] phantly enjoy the same, spite of the devil, and maugre the force of any forreine potentate. And al that, so highly and faithfully to the glory of God finally intended and brought to passe, as the wisest and godliest Prelates and counsellors of those dayes (so counted of and recorded) coulde best advise and direct him, or perchance, but sincerely commend and duetifully incourage him in, he being of himselfe so bent, as purposing first invincibly to fortifie the chiefe and uttermost walles of his Islandish Monarchie, against all forreine encombrance possible. And in that fortification furthering and assuring to trust best his owne

oversight and judgement, in yeerely viewing the same in
every quarter thereof, and that as it were for his pastime
Imperiall, also in Sommer time, to the ende that afterward
in all securitie, hee might in Winter time (vacare) be at
convenient leisure on land, chiefly to set foorth Gods due
honour, and secondly to understand, and diligently to
listen to the causes and complaints of his commons. For
as Matthæus Westmonasteriensis of him to his Imperiall
commendation hath left us a remembrance.

> Habebat autem præterea consuetudinem, per omnes
> Regni provincias transire, ut intelligeret quomodo
> legum jura, & suorum statuta decretorum, à
> principibus observarentur, & ne pauperes à
> potentibus præjudicium passi, opprimerentur,
> diligenter investigare solebat : in uno fortitudini,
> in altero Justitiæ studens, & Reipub. regníque
> utilitati consulens in utroque. Hinc hostibus
> circumquáque timor, & amor omnium erga eum
> excreverat subditorum.

Thus we see how in opportunitie, this peaceable Edgar
procured to this Empire such prosperous securitie, that
his true and faithfull subjects, all maner of wayes (that is
at home and also at sea, both outward and inward) might
peaceably, safely and securely employ their wits and travels
for the marveilous enriching of this kingdome, and
pleasuring very many other, carying forth the naturall commodities of this land, abounding here above our necessary
uses (and due store reserved) and likewise againe furnish-
ing the same with all necessary and not superfluous
forreine commodities, fet from farre or forrein countreys.
This was in deed (as before is recorded) a kingly provi-
dence, Reipub. Regníque utilitati consulens, &c. besides
with great utilitie and profite publique foreseene, and by
his meanes enjoyed, he himselfe used most gladly the
advantage of that securitie, in ministring of justice, or
causing the same to be executed all his kingdome over,
not squemishly, frowningly or skornefully shunning the

KING EDGAR

ragged and tattered sleeve of any suppliant, holding up to him a simple soiled bill of complaint or petition, and that homely contrived, or afrayde at, and timerously hasting from the sickly pale face or feeble limmed suter, extreemely constrained so to speake for himselfe, nor parcially smoothering his owne conscience, to favour or mainteine the foule fault and trespasse unlawfull of any his subjects, how mightie or necessary soever, they (els) were, but diligently made search, least Pauperes à potentibus præjudicium passi, opprimerentur.

Thus did publique securitie from forrein foe abroad, and true love of his owne subjects, garding him at home, and the heavenly spirit directing all his good purposes, cause justice and equitie in all quarters of this Albion to flourish. For which his peaceable and prosperous benefits at the eternall king his hand obteined, hee became not insolent or declined to tyrannicall regiment (as some princes in other countreis have made their lives Comicotragical) but with all his foresaide invincible Seaforce, aboundant wealth, triumphant peace, with securitie and Justice over all his Monarchie prevailing, his heart was continually, and most zealously bent to set foorth the glory, laude and honour of the Almightie Creator, the heavenly and everlasting king, by such principall and princely meanes, as (then) were deemed to God most acceptable, as many monuments yet to our dayes remaining, do of him undoubtedly testifie : As this, for one.

Altitonantis Dei largiflua clementia, qui est rex Regum, Ego Ædgarus Anglorum Basileus omniúmque Regum, Insularum, Oceaníque Britanniam circumjacentis, cunctarúmque nationum quæ infra eam includuntur, Imperator, & Dominus, gratias ago ipsi Deo omnipotenti, Regi meo, qui meum Imperium sic ampliavit, & exaltavit super regnum patrum meorum : qui licet Monarchiam totius Angliæ adepti sunt à tempore Athelstani (qui primus regnum Anglorum, & omnes Nationes, *Ex charta fundationis Ecclesiæ Cathedralis Wigorniæ.*

quæ Britanniam incolunt, sibi Armis subegit)
nullus tamen eorum ultra ejus fines imperium suum
dilatare aggressus est. Mihi autem concessit pro-
pitia Divinitas, cum Anglorum Imperio, omnia
regna Insularum Oceani, cum suis ferocissimis
Regibus, usque Noruegiam, maximámque partem
Hyberniæ, cum sua nobilissima Civitate Dublinia,
Anglorum regno subjugare : Quos etiam omnes,
meis Imperiis colla subdere (Dei favente gratia)
coegi. Quapropter & ego Christi gloriam, &
laudem exaltare, & ejus servitium amplificare
devotus disposui, & per meos fideles Fautores,
Dunstanum viz. Archiepiscopum, Athelwoldum, &
Oswaldum episcopos (quos mihi patres spirituales,
& Consiliatores elegi) magna ex parte, secundum
quod disposui, effeci, &c.

[I. 9.] And againe this in another Monument.

*Fundatio
Ecclesiæ
Cathedralis
Eliensis.* OMnipotentis Dei, &c. Ipsius nutu & gratia suffultus,
Ego Ædgarus Basileus dilectæ Insulæ Albionis, subditis nobis sceptris Scotorum, Cumbrorum, ac Brytonum,
& omnium circumcirca Regionum, quieta pace perfruens,
studiosus sollicitè de laudibus creatoris omnium occupor
addendis : Ne nunc inertia, nostrísque diebus (plus æquo)
servitus ejus tepescere videatur, &c. 18. mei terreni
Imperii anno, &c. Anno Incarnationis Dominicæ, 973.

Ego Ædgarus totius Albionis Basileus hoc privilegium
(tanta roboratum authoritate) crucis Thaumate con-
firmavi.

So that by all these rehearsed Records, it is most evident
that the peaceable king Edgar, was one of those Monarchs,
in whose handes (if life had suffised) the incredible value
and priviledge granted by God and nature unto this
British monarchie, might have bene peaceably purchased in
such sort, as the very blessing and favour of the divine
Trinitie hath laid meanes for our industrie to attaine to,
and enjoye the same by.

KING EDGAR

And though sundry other valiant princes and kings of this land I could recite, which in times past have either by intent gone about, or by wise and valiant exploit, have meetely well prospered towards this Islandish appropriate supremacie attaining, yet never any other reasonable meanes was used, or by humane wit, or industrie can be contrived, to al purposes sufficient, but only by our sea forces prevailing, and so by our invincible enjoying al within the sea limites of our British royaltie contained.

To which incredible political mysterie attaining, no easier, readier, or perfecter plat and introduction, is (as yet) come to my imagination, then is the present and continuall service of threescore good and tall warlike ships, with twentie smaller barkes, and those 80. ships (great and smal) with 6660. apt men furnished, and all singularly well appointed for service both on sea and land, faithfully and diligently to be done in such circumspect and discreet order, as partly I have in other places declared, and further (upon good occasion offered) may declare.

This grand navie of peaceable king Edgar, of so many thousand ships, and they furnished with an hundred thousand men at the least, with all the finall intents of those sea forces, so invincible, continually mainteined, the order of the execution of their service, the godly and Imperial successe thereof, are in a maner kingly lessons and prophetical incouragements to us left, even now to bee as provident for publique securitie as he was, to be as skilful of our sea right and royal limits, and wisely to finde our selves as able to recover and enjoy the same as he was, who could not chuse, but with the passing and yeerely sayling about this Brittish Albion, with all the lesser Isles next adjacent round about it, he could not chuse I say, but by such ful and peaceable possession, find himselfe (according to right, and his hearts desire) the true and soveraigne Monarch of all the British Ocean, environing any way his empire of Albion and Ireland, with the lesser Islands next adjacent : with memorial whereof, as with one very precious jewel Imperial, hee adorned the title and crowne

23

of his regalitie, as with the testimonie annexed of the states and nobles of his Empire, to commit to perpetuall memorie, the stile of his chiefe worldly dignitie, in this very tenor of words before also remembred.

Ego Ædgarus Anglorum Basileus, omniúmque Regum, Insularum, Oceaníque Britanniam circumjacentis, cunctarúmque nationum, quæ infra eam includuntur, Imperator, & Dominus.

The voyage of Edmund and Edward the sonnes of King Edmund Ironside into Hungarie, Anno D. 1017. Recorded by Florentius Wigorniensis pag. 391.

Edit consilium Edricus Canuto regi, ut clitunculos Eadwardum & Eadmundum regis Eadmundi filios necaret. Sed quia magnum dedecus sibi videbatur, ut in Anglia perimerentur, parvo elapso tempore, ad regem Suavorum occidendos misit. Qui, licèt fœdus esset inter eos, precibus illius nullatenùs voluit acquiescere, sed illos ad regem Hungarorum Salomonem nomine misit nutriendos vitæque reservandos. Quorum unus scilicet Eadmundus processu temporis ibidem vitam finivit. Eadwardus verò Agatham filiam Germani Imperatoris Henrici in matrimonium accepit, ex qua Margaretam Scotorum reginam, & Christinam Sanctimonialem, & Clitonem Eadgarum suscepit.

The same in English.

EDric counselled king Kanutus to murther the yong princes Edward and Edmund the sonnes of King Edmund. But because it seemed a thing very dishonourable unto him to have them put to death in England, hee sent them, after a short space, unto the king of Sweden to be slaine. Who, albeit there was a league betweene them, would in no case condescend unto Canutus his bloody request, but sent them unto Salomon the king of Hungarie to be nourished and preserved alive. The one whereof namely Edmund in processe of time there deceased. But Edward received to wife Agatha daughter unto the Germane Emperour Henry, of whom he begot Margaret the Queene of the Scots, and Christina a Nunne, and Clito Edgar.

A Chronicle of the Kings of Man, taken out of M. Camdens Chorographie.

IN the yeere of our Lord 1066. Edward King of England, of famous memory deceased, whom Harald sonne of Godwin succeeded in his kingdome; against which Harald the king of Norwaie called Harald Harfager fought a battel at Stainford bridge, where the English winning the fielde put all the Norwegians to flight: out of which flight one Godredus sirnamed Crovan (the sonne of Harald the blacke, who had before time fled out of Island) repaired unto Godred sonne of Syrric, who then reigned in Man, and was right friendly and honourably enterteined by him.

In the very same yeere William the Conquerour subdued England, and Godred the sonne of Syrric, king of Man, deceased, after whom succeeded his sonne Fingal. *Fingal.*

In the yeere 1066. Godredus Crovan gathered a fleete of ships, and sailed unto Man, and giving battell unto the people of the countrey, was vanquished and put to flight. The second time also having gathered his armie and ships together, hee came unto Man, fought with the inhabitants, lost the victorie, and was chaced away. Yea, the third time he assembled a great multitude, and comming by night unto the port which is called Ramsa, hid 300. of his men in a wood standing upon the side of the hill called Scacafel. The Sunne was no sooner up, but the Mannians arranged themselves and with great furie set upon Godred.

And in the midst of the skirmish, the foresaid 300. men rising out of their ambush, and comming upon the backes of the Mannians, molested them so sore, that they were enforced to flie. But when they saw y^t they were overcome and had no place of refuge to retire unto (for the tide of the sea had filled the chanel of the river of Ramsa) and seeing the enemie so fiercely pursuing them on the other side, they which remained, with lamentable outcries beseeched Godred to spare their lives. Then hee being mooved with compassion, and pitying their extreme calamitie, because hee had bene of late sustained and nourished among them, sounded a retreat and forbad his souldiers to make any longer pursuit. The day following Godred put his souldiers to their choice, whether they would divide Man among themselves and inhabite it, or whether they would take the wealth of the countrey, and so returne unto their owne home. Howbeit, it pleased them better to waste the whole Island and to enrich themselves with the commodities thereof, and so to returne from whence they came. Nowe Godred himselfe with a fewe Islanders which had remained with him, tooke possession of the South part of the Island, and unto the remnant of the Mannians he granted the North part thereof, upon condition, that none of them should at any time afterward dare once to chalenge any parcell of the said ground by title of inheritance. Whereupon it commeth to passe, that unto this day the whole Island is the kings owne Fee-simple, and that all the revenues thereof pertaine unto him. Also Godredus subdued Dublin unto himselfe & a great part of Lainestir. And he so tamed the Scots, that none of them durst build a ship or a boate, with above three yron nailes in it. Hee reigned 16. yeeres and died in the Island called Yle. He left behinde him three sonnes, Lagman, Harald, and Olavus. Lagman being the eldest chalenged the kingdome and reigned seven yeeres. Howbeit Harald his brother rebelled against him a long time, but being at length taken by Lagman, hee was gelt and had his eyes put out. After-

Boats having not past three yron nailes in them.

26

ward Lagman repenting him that he had put out the eyes
of his brother, did of his owne accord relinquish his
kingdome, and taking upon him the badge of the crosse,
he went on pilgrimage to Jerusalem, in which journey
also he died.

In the yeere 1075. all the principall men of the Islands
having intelligence of the death of Lagman, sent messengers unto Murecardus O-Brien King of Irland, requesting
him that hee would send some wel-disposed person of his
owne kinred and blood royall, untill Olavus sonne of
Godred were come to full age. The king most willingly [I. 11.]
condescended unto their request, and sent unto them one
Dopnald the sonne of Tade, charging and commaunding
him that with all meekenesse and modestie, hee should
governe that kingdome, which of right belonged not unto
him. Howbeit he, after he had once attained unto the
kingdome, neglecting the commaundement of his lord,
usurped the government with great tyrannie, committing
many heinous crimes, and so he reigned very disorderly
for the space of three yeeres. Then all the princes of
the Islands making a generall conspiracie, banded themselves against him, and expelled him out of their
dominions. And he flying into Irland returned no
more unto them.

In the yeere 1077. one Ingemundus was sent from the
king of Norway, to take possession of the kingdome of
the Islands. And being come unto the Island of Leodus, *Lewis.*
hee sent messengers unto all the princes of the Islands to
come unto him, commaunding them to assemble themselves,
and to appoint him to be their King. In the meane
season he and his companions spent their time in robbing
and rioting, ravished women and virgines, and addicted
themselves to filthy pleasures and to the lustes of the
flesh. And when these things were reported unto the
princes of the Islands, who had assembled themselves to
chuse him king, being mightely incensed thereat, they
made haste towards him, and comming upon him in the
night, they burnt the house wherein hee was, and slue

both him and the rest of his company, partly with sword,
and partly with fire.

In the yeere 1098. the abbey of S. Maries at Cistertium
was founded. In the same yeere also Antiochia was
taken by the Christians, and a Comet appeared.

Moreover, the same yeere there was a battel fought
betweene the inhabitants of Man, at Santwat, and they of
the North obtained the victory. In which battell were
slaine Earle Othor and Mac-Maras, chieftaines of both
parts.

The same yeere Magnus king of Norway, sonne of
Olavus, sonne of Harald Harfagre, being desirous to
view the corps of S. Olavus king and Martyr, gave commaundement that his monument should be opened. But
the Bishop and the Clergie withstanding this his attempt,
the king went very boldly and by his kingly authoritie,
caused the cophin to be opened. And when hee had
seene with his eyes, and handled with his hands the
incorrupt body of the foresaid King and Martyr, a sudden
feare came upon him, and he departed with great haste.
The night following Olavus king and Martyr appeared
unto him in a vision, saying: Chuse (I say) unto your
selfe one of these two, either within 30. dayes to lose
your life with your kingdome, or else to depart from
Norway and never to see it againe. The King so soone
as he was awaked out of sleepe, called his Princes and
Senatours, and expounded the foresaide vision unto them.
And they also being astonished thereat gave him this
counsell, that with all speed he should depart out of
Norway. Then he without any further delay caused a
Navie of 160. ships to be provided, and so sailed unto the
Islands of Orkney, which hee presently subdued, and
passing along through all the Islands and conquering
them, at length he came unto the Isle of Man, where
he was no sooner arrived, but hee went unto the Isle of
S. Patric to see the place of battell, where the inhabitants
of Man had of late fought, because many of the dead
bodies were as yet unburied. And seeing that it was a

most beautifull Island, it pleased him exceeding well, and therefore hee made choice to inhabite therein his owne selfe, and built forts there which are at this day called by his owne name. He had the people of Galway in such awe, that he constrained them to cut downe their owne timber, and to bring it unto his shore for the building of his fortes. Hee sailed on further unto the Isle of Anglesey neere unto Wales, and finding two Earles therein (either of them being called by the name of Hugo) he slue the one, and the other hee put to flight, and so subdued the Island. But the Welshmen presented many gifts unto him, and so bidding them farewell he returned unto Man. Unto Murecard king of Irland he sent his shooes, commaunding him that he should cary them on his shoulders, upon the birth-day of our Lord through the midst of his Palace, in the sight of his Embassadours, that thereby it might appeare unto them, that he was subject unto king Magnus. Which when the Irishmen heard, they tooke it grievously and disdeined much thereat. But the King being better advised, I had rather (said he) not only beare his shooes, but eate his shooes, then that king Magnus should destroy any one province in Irland. Wherefore he fulfilled his commaundement, and honourably enterteined his Embassadours. Many gifts also he sent unto king Magnus by them, and concluded a league. But the messengers returning unto their lord, tolde him of the situation of Irland, of the beautie thereof, of the fruitfulnesse of the soile, and of the holesomnesse of the aire. Magnus hearing these things was fully resolved to conquer all Irland unto himselfe. And for the same purpose he commaunded that a Fleet should be made ready. But he taking his voyage with sixteene ships, & being desirous to view the land, when he had undiscreetly departed from his Navie, he was suddenly invironed by the Irish, and was himselfe slaine, together with all that were with him almost. Hee was interred neere unto the Church of S. Patric in Armagh. Hee reigned six yeeres. After his death the Princes of the

Islands sent for Olavus the sonne of Godredus Crovan, who lived in the Court of Henry King of England son unto William the Conquerour.

In the yeere 1102. Olavus sonne of Godredus Crovan beganne his reigne and reigned fourtie yeeres : he was a peaceable man being in league with all the Kings of Scotland and Irland in his time. He tooke to wife Affrica the daughter of Fergusius of Galway, of whom he begat Godredus. Of his concubines he begat Regnaldus, Lagmannus, and Haraldus, and many daughters, whereof
‖ Argile.
one married unto Sumerledus king of ‖ Herergaidel, which afterward occasioned the overthrow of the whole kingdome of the Islands. He begat foure sonnes by her, namely Dulgallus, Raignaldus, Engus, and Olavus.

In the yeere 1134. Olavus gave unto Yvo the Abbat of Furnes a portion of his owne ground in Man to build an Abbey in the place which is called Russin. Also hee inriched with revenues and indued with priviledges al places of religion within his Islands.

In the yere 1142. Godredus ye son of Olavus sailed unto the K. of Norway called Hinge, and doing his homage unto him he remained with him, & was by him honorably enterteined. The same yere the 3. sonnes of Harald brother unto Olavus, who were brought up at the citie of Dublin, gathering together a great multitude of people, and all the fugitives and vagabonds of the kingdome resorted unto Man, and demaunded of the said king the one halfe of al the kingdome of the Islands. Which thing when the king heard, being desirous to pacifie them, he answered that he would consult about that matter. And a day and place being appointed, where the consultation should bee kept, in the meane time those miscreants conspired together, about the murthering of the King. And when the day appointed was come, both companies assembled themselves unto the haven towne called Ramsa, and they sate in order, the king with his nobilitie on the one side, and they with their confederates on the other side. Howbeit Regnaldus who had an

intention to slay the king, stoode a-side in the midst of the
house talking with one of the Princes of the lande.   And
being called to come unto the king he turned himselfe about
as if hee would have saluted him, and lifting up his glittering
axe, he chopt the kings head quite off at a blow.   Nowe 1143.
having committed this outragious vilanie, within a short
space they divided the Island betweene themselves, and
gathering an armie together sailed unto Galway, intending
to subdue that also; howbeit the people of Galway
assembled themselves, and with great furie encountred
with them.   Then they immediately turning their backs
with great confusion fled unto Man.   And as touching all
the Galwedians which inhabited in the said Island, some of
them they slue, and the residue they banished.

In the yeere 1143. Godredus sonne of Olavus returning
out of Norway was created king of Man; who in revenge
of his fathers death, put out the eyes of two of Haralds
sonnes and slue the thirde.

In the yeere 1144. Godredus began his reigne, and hee
reigned thirtie yeeres.   In the thirde yeere of his reigne
the citizens of Dublin sent for him and created him king
of Dublin, against whom Murecardus king of Irland made
warre, and encamping himselfe at the citie called Coridelis,
he sent his brother Osibel with 3000. horsemen unto
Dublin, who was slaine by Godred and the Dubliners, the
rest of his company being put to flight.   These things
being thus finished, Godredus returned unto Man, and
began to exercise tyrannie, disinheriting certaine of his
nobles, of whom one called Thorfinus the sonne of Oter,
being mightier then the rest, went unto Sumerledus, and
named Dubgal the sonne of Sumerledus, king of the
Islands, and subdued many of the said Islands on his
behalfe.   Whereof when Godred had intelligence by one
Paulus, providing a Navie, hee went to meete Sumerledus
comming against him with 80. ships: and in the yeere
1156. upon the night of the feast of Epiphanie, there was 1156.
a Sea-battell fought, and many being slaine on both parts,
the day folowing they were pacified, and divided the

31

kingdome of the Islands among themselves, and it continued two kingdomes from that day unto this present time. And this was the cause of the ruine of the monarchie of the Islands, from which time the sonnes of Sumerled injoyed the one halfe thereof.

In the yeere 1158. Sumerled came unto Man with 53. ships, putting Godred to flight and wasting the Island: and Godred sailed unto Norway to seeke for aide against Sumerled. In the yere 1164. Sumerled gathered a fleete of 160. ships together; and arrived at Rhinfrin, intending to subdue all Scotland unto himselfe: howbeit, by Gods just judgement being overcome by a few, together with his sonne, and an innumerable multitude of people, he was slaine. The very same yere there was a battel fought at Ramsa, betweene Reginald the brother of Godred, and the inhabitants of Man, but by the stratageme of a certaine Earle the Mannians were put to flight. Then began Reginald to usurpe the kingly authoritie. Howbeit his brother Godred within foure dayes after, comming out of Norway with a great power of armed men, apprehended his brother Reginald, gelt him, and put out his eyes. The same yeere deceased
[I. 13.] Malcolme the king of Scots, and his brother William succeeded in the kingdome.

In the yeere 1166. two Comets appeared in the moneth of August, before the rising of the Sunne, one to the South and another to the North.

In the yeere 1171. Richard earle of Penbroke sailed into Irland, and subdued Dublin with a great part of Irland.

In the yere 1176. John Curcy conquered Ulster unto himselfe. And at the same time also Vivianus legate from the sea of Rome came into Man, & caused king Godred to bee lawfully wedded unto his wife Phingola, daughter of Maclotlen son of Murkartac king of Irland, mother of Olavus, who was then 3. yeeres old. Silvanus the abbat married them, unto whom the very same day, king Godred gave a portion of ground in Mirescoge, where he

32

THE KINGS OF MAN

built a Monastery : howbeit, in processe of time, the said land with the monkes, was granted unto the abbey of Russin.

In the yere 1172. Reginaldus the son of Eacmarcat (a man descended of the blood royal) comming into Man with a great multitude of people, in the absence of the king, at the first conflict hee put to flight certaine watchmen which kept the shoare, & slue about 30. persons. Whereupon the very same day the Mannians arranging themselves put him, & almost al his folowers to the sword.

In the yere 1183. O-Fogolt was vicount of Man.

In the yere 1185. the Sunne was ecclipsed upon the feast of S. Philip and Jacob.

In the yere 1187. deceased Godred king of the Islands, upon the 4. of the Ides of November, and the next sommer his body was translated unto the island of Hy. He left 3. sonnes behinde him, Reginaldus, Olavus, and Yvarus. In his life time he ordeined his sonne Olavus to be his heire apparant, because he onely was borne legitimate. But the Mannians, when Olavus was scarce ten yeeres olde, sent unto the islands for Reginald and created him king.

In the yeere 1187. began Reginald the sonne of Godred to reigne over the islands : and Murchardus a man of great power throughout all the kingdome of the islands was put to death.

In the yere 1192. there was a battel fought betweene Reginald and Engus the two sonnes of Sumerled : but Engus obtained the victory. The same yere was the abbey of Russin remooved unto Dufglas, howbeit within foure yeeres after the monkes returned unto Russin.

In the yere 1203. Michael bishop of the islands deceased at Fontanas, and Nicholas succeeded in his roome.

In the yere 1204. Hugo de Lacy invaded Ulster with an armie and encountered with John de Curcy, tooke him prisoner & subdued Ulster unto himselfe. Afterward he permitted the said John to goe at libertie, who comming unto king Reginald was honourably enterteined by him, because he was his sonne in lawe, for John de Curcy had taken to wife Affrica the daughter of Godredus, which founded the abbey of S. Mary de jugo domini, and was there buried.

In the yeere 1205. John de Curcy & Reginald king of the islands invading Ulster with a hundreth ships at the port which is called Stranfeord did negligently besiege the castle of Rath : but Walter de Lacy comming upon them with his armie, put them to flight, & from that time Curcy never recovered his land. In the yere 1210. Engus the son of Sumerled & his 3. sonnes were slaine.

At the same time John king of England conducted a fleet of 500. ships into Irland, and subdued it unto himselfe : and sending a certaine earle named Fulco, unto the isle of Man, his souldiers almost utterly wasted it in the space of 15. dayes, and having taken pledges they returned home into their owne countrey. King Reginald and his nobles were at this time absent from Man.

In the yere 1217. deceased Nicolas bishop of the islands, and was buried in Ulster, in the house of Benchor, whom Reginald succeeded.

I thinke it not amisse to report somewhat more concerning the two foresaid brethren Reginaldus and Olavus.

REginald gave unto his brother Olavus, the island called Lodhus or Lewes, which is saide to be larger then the rest of the islands, but almost destitute of inhabitants, because it is so ful of mountaines & quarreis, being almost no where fit for tillage. Howbeit the inhabitants thereof do live for the most part upon hunting and fishing. Olavus therefore went to take possession of this Island, and dwelt therein leading a poore life : and when he saw that it would by no meanes suffice for the sustentation of himselfe & his folowers, hee went boldly unto his brother Reginald, who as then remained in the islands, & spake on this wise unto him. My brother (said he) and my lord and king, you know that the

kingdom of the islands pertained unto me by right of
inheritance, howbeit because the Lord had chosen you to
beare the scepter, I doe not envie that honour unto you,
neither doeth it any whit grieve mee that you are exalted
unto this royall dignitie. Nowe therefore I beseech you
to provide mee some portion of land in the islands,
whereby I may honestly live. For the Island of Lewis [I. 14.]
which you gave me is not sufficient for my maintenance.
Which his brother Reginald hearing said that he would
consult about the premisses. And on the morow, when
Olavus was sent for to parle, Reginald commanded him to
be attached, and to be caried unto William king of
Scotland, and with him to remaine prisoner : and Olavus
remained in prison almost for the space of 7. yeres. But
at the 7. yeres end William king of Scots deceased, and
Alexander his sonne reigned in his stead. The foresaid
William, before his death, commanded that all prisoners
should be set at libertie. Olavus therefore being at
libertie came unto Man, and immediatly with a great
company of nobles tooke his journey unto S. James : and
his brother Reginald caused the said Olavus to take unto
wife, the daughter of a certaine noble man of Kentyre,
cousine german unto his owne wife, & by name being
called Lavon, and he granted unto him the possession of
Lewis. After a few dayes Reginald the bishop of the
Islands having gathered a Synod, separated Olavus and
Godred his sonne, and Lavon his wife, namely because
shee was cousin german unto his former wife. Afterward
Olavus maried Scristina daughter unto Ferkarus earle of
Rosse.

Hereupon the wife of Reginald Queene of the Islands
being incensed, sent letters unto the Island of Sky in
K. Reginald his name to her sonne Godred willing him to
take Olavus. Which commandement Godred putting in
practise, & entring the isle of Lewis for ye same purpose,
Olavus fled in a litle skiffe unto his father in law the earle
of Rosse, & in the meane time Godred wasted the isle of
Lewis. At the very same time Pol the son of Boke

vicount of Sky, being a man of power in al the Islands, because he would not consent unto Godred, fled, & dwelt together with Olavus in the dominions of the earle of Rosse, & making a league with Olavus, they went both in a ship unto Sky. To be short, sending certaine spies, they were informed that Godred remained secure with a smal company in a certaine Isle called ye isle of S. Columba. And uniting unto themselves their friends and acquaintance, & others that would goe voluntarily with them, in the dead of the night, having lanched 5. ships from the next sea-shore, which was distant about the space of 2. furlongs from the foresaid Island, they environed the said Island on all sides. Now Godred and his company rising early in the morning, and seeing themselves beset with their enemies on all sides, they were utterly astonied. Howbeit arming themselves they began stoutly to make resistance, but altogether in vaine. For about 9. of the clocke in the morning, Olavus and the foresaid vicount Pol, with al their souldiers, entred the Island, and having slaine all whom they found without the precincts of the Church, they apprehended Godred, gelding him, and putting out his eyes. Unto which action Olavus gave not his consent, neither could he withstand it, by reason of the forenamed vicount the son of Boke. This was done in the yere of Christ 1223. The next sommer folowing Olavus having received pledges from all the chiefe men of the Islands, with a fleet of 32. ships sailed unto Man, and arrived at Rognolfwaht. At the same time Reginald and Olavus divided the kingdome of the Islands betweene themselves, Man being granted unto Reginald, & besides his portion the name of a king also. Olavus having received certaine victuals of the people of Man, returned, together with his company, unto his owne portion of Islands. The yeere folowing Reginald taking unto him Alanus lord of Galway, together with his subjects of Man, sailed unto the Islands, that hee might take away that portion of ground from his brother Olavus, which he had granted unto him, and subdue it unto himselfe. How-

The Isle of Man advaunced to a kingdome.

36

beit, by reason that the people of Man had no list to fight against Olavus or the Islanders, because they bare good will towards them, Reginald and Alanus lord of Galway being defeated of their purpose, returned home unto their owne. Within a short space after Reginald, under pretense of going unto the Court of his lord the king of England, received an 100. markes of the people of Man, and tooke his journey unto Alanus lord of Galway. Which the people of Man hearing tooke great indignation thereat, insomuch that they sent for Olavus, and appointed him to be their king.

In the yeere 1226. Olavus recovered his inheritance, that is to say the kingdome of Man and of the Islands, which Reginald his brother had governed for the space of 38. yeeres, and he reigned two yeeres in safetie.

In the yeere 1228. Olavus with all his nobles of Man, and the stronger part of his people, sailed unto the Islands. A short space after Alanus lord of Galway, Thomas earle of Athol, & king Reginald came unto Man with a mightie army, and wasted all the South part of Man, spoiled the Churches, and slue all the men whom they coulde take, insomuch, that the South part of the saide Island was brought almost into desolation. And then Alanus returned with his army into his owne land, leaving behind him bailiffes and substitutes in Man, which should gather up and render unto him the tribute of the countrey. Howbeit king Olavus came suddenly upon them, chaced them away and recovered his kingdome. And the Mannians which of late were dispersed and scattered abroad, began to unite themselves, and to inhabite without feare. The same yeere, in the time of Winter, upon the sudden, and in the very dead of the night came king Reginald out of Galway with five ships, and burnt all [I. 15.] the ships of his brother Olavus, and of the nobles of Man, at the Isle of S. Patric, & concluding a peace with his brother, remained at the port of Ragnolwath 40. dayes : in the meane while hee allured unto himselfe all the Islanders upon the South part of Man, who sware, that they would adventure their lives, untill hee had gotten the one halfe of his kingdome : contrarywise Olavus joyned unto himselfe them of the North part, & upon the 14. of February in the place called Tingvalla, a field was fought betweene the two brothers, wherein Olavus got the victory, and Reginald the king was by certaine souldiers slaine without the knowledge of his brother. Also certaine pirates comming to the south part of Man, wasted & spoiled it. The monkes of Russin conveyed the body of K. Reginald, unto the abbey of S. Mary of Fournes, & there he was interred in the place, which his owne selfe had chosen for the purpose. After these things Olavus traveiled unto the king of Norway, but before he was arrived there, Haco king of Norway appointed a certaine noble man named Husbac the son of Owmund, to be king of the Islands of the Hebrides & called his name Haco. Then came the said Haco with Olavus & Godred Don the son of Reginald, and a multitude of Norwegians, unto the islands : and while they were giving an assault unto a castle in the island of Both, Haco being hit with a stone died, and was buried in Iona.

In the yere 1230. came Olavus, with Godredus Don, & certeine Norwegians unto Man, and they parted the kingdome among themselves, Olavus stil reteining Man. Godred as he was going unto the islands, was slaine in the isle of Lewis, & Olavus injoyed the kingdome of the islands also.

In the yere 1237. upon the 12. of the Kalends of June, Olavus sonne of Godred king of Man deceased in the isle of S. Patric, and was interred in the abbey of Russin. He reigned 11. yeres, two while his brother was alive, and nine after his death.

Haraldus his sonne being of the age of 14. yeres, succeeded, and he reigned 12. yeeres. The first yere of his reigne taking his journey unto the islands, he appointed one Loglen his kinsman to be his deputie in Man. The Autumne folowing Haraldus sent the three sonnes of Nel, namely Dufgaldus, Torquellus, & Molmore, and his friend

Joseph unto Man, that they might enter into consultation together. Wherfore the 25. day they assembled themselves at Tingvalla : and malice growing betweene the sonnes of Nel, and Loglen, they fel to blowes and skirmished sore on both parts, Molmore, Dufgald, and the foresaid Joseph being all slaine in the fray. The Spring folowing, king Harald came into the isle of Man, and Loglen fleeing into Wales, was himselfe, together with Godred the sonne of Olavus his pupil, and 40. others, drowned by shipwracke.

In the yere 1238. Gospatricius and Gillescrist sonne of Mac-Kerthac came from the king of Norway unto Man, expelling Harald out of the said island, and taking tribute on the behalfe of the Norwegian king, because the said Harald refused to come unto his Court.

In the yere 1240. Gospatricius deceased and was buried in the abbey of Russin.

In the yere 1239. Haraldus went unto the king of Norway, who within two yeres confirmed unto him, his heires and successors, under seale, all the islands which his predecessors enjoyed.

In the yeere 1242. Haraldus returned out of Norway unto Man, and being honourably received by the inhabitants, he lived in peace with the kings of England and Scotland.

In the yeere 1247. Haraldus (like as his father also before him) was knighted by the king of England, and so being rewarded with many gifts, he returned home. The same yere he was sent for by the king of Norway, and he maried his daughter. And in the yere 1249. as he was returning home with his wife, with Laurence the elect of Man, and with many other nobles, neere unto the confines of Radland, he was drowned in a tempest.

In the yere 1249. Reginald the sonne of Olavus, and brother unto Harald began to reigne the day next before the Nones of May : and upon the 30. day of the same moneth he was slaine by Yvarus a souldier, and other of his complices, in the South part of a certaine medow,

39

neere unto the Church of the holy Trinitie, and he was buried at the Church of S. Marie at Russin.

The same yere Alexander king of Scots provided a great navie of ships, that he might conquere the islands unto himselfe : howbeit falling into an ague at the isle of Kerwary, he deceased.

Then Haraldus the sonne of Godred Don usurped the name of a king over the islands, hee banished also all the princes of Harald the sonne of Olavus, and ordeined his fugitives to bee princes and nobles in their stead.

In the yere 1250. Haraldus the son of Godred Don being summoned by letters went unto the king of Norway, who deteined him in prison because he had unjustly possessed the kingdome. The same yeere Magnus the sonne of Olavus, and John the sonne of Dugalt arrived at Roghalwaht, which John named himselfe king, but the Mannians taking it grievously, that Magnus was not nominated, drave them from their shoare, and many of the company perished by shipwracke.

In the yeere 1252. came Magnus the sonne of Olavus unto Man, and was ordeined king. The yere folowing he tooke his journey unto the king of Norway, & there he remained one whole yere.

[I. 16.] In the yeere 1254. Haco king of Norway ordeined Magnus the sonne of Olavus king of the Islands, confirming them to him and to his heires, and by name unto Harald his brother.

In the yere 1256. Magnus tooke his journey into England, and was by the king of England created knight.

In ye yere 1257. the Church of S. Maries of Russin was dedicated by Richard bishop of Soder.

In the yeere 1260. Haco king of Norway came into the parts of Scotland, and without atchieving ought, turning his course towards the Orcades he there deceased at Kirwas, and was buried at Bergen.

In the yeere 1265. Magnus the sonne of Olavus king of Man and of the Islands died at the castle of Russin, and was buried at the Church of S. Mary at Russin.

THE KINGS OF MAN

In the yere 1266. the kingdome of the Islands was translated unto Alexander king of Scots.

That which followeth was written in a new character or letter, and of a divers kinde from the former.

IN the yeere 1270. upon the seventh day of October the Fleete of Alexander king of Scots arrived at Roghalwath, and the next day before the Sunne rising there was a battell fought betweene the Mannians and the Scots, in the which conflict there were slaine 535. Mannians : whereupon a certaine versifier writeth to this effect :

> Five hundreth fourtie men are slaine :
>   against ill haps,
> Yee Mannians arme your selves, for feare
> of afterclaps.

In the yeere 1313. Robert king of Scots besieged the castle of Russin, which Dingaway Dowil held against him, howbeit at the last the king tooke the castle.

In the yeere 1316. upon the feast of Ascension, Richard le Mandevile and his brethren, with divers great personages of Irland arrived at Ramaldwath, demaunding to have victuals and money ministred unto them, because they had bene spoyled by their enemies, which made continuall warre upon them. But when the whole company of the Mannians answered that they would give nothing, they proceeded against them in warlike maner with two bands, till they were come under the side of the hill called Warthfel, in the fielde where John Mandevile remained, and there having fought a battell, the Irish overcame the people of Man, and spoiled the Island and the Abbey of Russin also : and when they had reveled a whole moneth in the Island, lading their ships they returned home.

The mariage of the daughter of Harald, slaine by
William the Conquerour, unto Jeruslaus duke of
Russia, taken out of the 9. Booke of the Danish
historie written by Saxo Grammaticus. An. D.
1067.

1067.

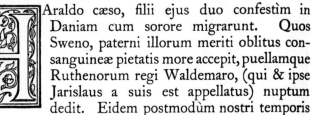Araldo cæso, filii ejus duo confestìm in
Daniam cum sorore migrarunt. Quos
Sweno, paterni illorum meriti oblitus con-
sanguineæ pietatis more accepit, puellamque
Ruthenorum regi Waldemaro, (qui & ipse
Jarislaus a suis est appellatus) nuptum
dedit. Eidem postmodùm nostri temporis
dux, ut sanguinis, ita & nominis hæres, ex filia nepos
obvenit. Itaque hinc Britannicus, indè Eous sanguis
in salutarem nostri principis ortum confluens communem
stirpem duarum gentium ornamentum effecit.

The same in English.

HArald being slaine his two sonnes with their sister
sped themselves immediatly into Denmarke. Whom
Sweno forgetting their fathers deserts received in most
kinde and friendly maner, and bestowed the yong damosell
in mariage upon Waldemarus king of Russia who was
also called by his subjects Jarislaus. Afterward the said
Waldemarus had by his daughter a nephew being duke
at this present, who succeeded his predecessour both in
lineal descent and in name also. Wherefore the English
blood on the one side and the Russian on the other
side concurring to the joyfull birth of our prince, caused
that mutual kinred to be an ornament unto both nations.

[I. 17.] The state of the shipping of the Cinque ports from
Edward the Confessour and William the Conquerour, and so downe to Edward the first,
faithfully gathered by the learned Gentleman

M. Willaim Lambert in his Perambulation of Kent, out of the most ancient Records of England.

Finde in the booke of the generall survey of the Realme, which William the Con-querour caused to bee made in the fourth yeere of his reigne, and to be called Domesday, because (as Matthew Parise saith) it spared no man but judged all men indifferently, as the Lord in that great day wil do, that Dover, Sandwich, and Rumney, were in the time of K. Edward the Confessour, discharged almost of all maner of imposicions and burdens (which other townes did beare) in consideration of such service to bee done by them upon the Sea, as in their special titles shall hereafter appeare.

Whereupon, although I might ground reasonable con-jecture, that the immunitie of the haven Townes (which we nowe call by a certaine number, the Cinque Ports) might take their beginning from the same Edward : yet for as much as I read in the Chartre of K. Edward the first after the conquest (which is reported in our booke of Entries) A recitall of the graunts of sundry kings to the Five Ports, the same reaching no higher then to William the Conquerour, I will leave my conjecture, and leane to his Chartre : contenting my selfe to yeelde to the Conquerour, the thankes of other mens benefits, seeing those which were benefited, were wisely contented (as the case then stood) to like better of his confirmation (or second gift) then of K. Edwards first graunt, and endowment.

And to the ende that I may proceed in some maner of array, I will first shewe, which Townes were at the begin-ning taken for the Five Ports, and what others be now reputed in the same number : secondly, what service they ought, and did in times passed : and lastly, what privi-ledges they have therefore, and by what persons they have bene governed.

*Which be the
Five Ports.*

If I should judge by the common, and rude verse,
<dd>*Dover, Sandwicus, Ry, Rum, Frigmare ventus,*</dd>
I must say, that Dover, Sandwich, Rie, Rumney, and
Winchelsey, (for that is, Frigmare ventus) be the Five
Ports : Againe, if I should be ruled by the Rolle which
reciteth the Ports that send Barons to the Parliament, I
must then adde to these, Hastings and Hyde, for they also
have their Barons as well as the other : and so should I
not onely, not shew which were the first Five, but also
(by addition of two others) increase both the number, and
doubtfulnesse.   Leaving the verse therefore, for ignorance
of the authour and suspition of his authoritie, and for-
saking the Rolle (as not assured of the antiquitie) I will

1250.

flee to Henry Bracton, a man both ancient, learned, and
credible, which lived under K. Henry the thirde, and
wrote (above three hundreth yeeres since) learnedly of the
lawes of this Realme.

He (I say) in the third booke of his worke, and treatise
of the Crowne, taking in hand to shewe the articles inquir-
able before the Justice in Eire, (or Itinerent, as we called
them, because they used to ride from place to place
throughout the Realme, for administration of justice)
setteth forth a special fourme of writs, to be directed
severally to the Bailifes of Hastings, Hithe, Rumney,
Dover, and Sandwich, commanding them, that they should

*Citizens were
called Barons
in old time.*

cause twentie & foure of their Barons (for so their
Burgesses, or townesmen, and the citizens of London
likewise, were wont to be termed) to appeare before the
Kings Justices at Shipwey in Kent (as they accustomed to
do) there to enquire of such points, as should be given in
charge.   Which done, hee addeth moreover, that forso-

*Contention
betweene Yar-
mouth, and the
Five Ports.*
1250.
*Antiquitie of
Yarmouth
fishing.*

much as there was oftentimes contention betweene them of
the Five Ports, & the inhabitants of Yarmouth in
Norfolke and Donwich in Suffolke, there should be severall
writs directed to them also, returnable before the same
Justices at the same day and place, reciting, that where the
King had by his former writs sommoned the Pleas of the
Five Ports to bee holden at Shipwey, if any of the same

44

townes had cause to complaine of any (being within the liberties of the said Ports) he should be at Shipwey to propound against him, and there to receive according to law and Justice.

Thus much I recite out of Bracton, partly to shew that Shipwey was before K. Edward the firsts time, the place of assembly for the Plees of the Five Ports : partly to notifie the difference, and controversie that long time since was betweene these Ports, and those other townes : But purposely, and chiefly, to prove, that Hastings, and Hithe, Dover, Rumney, and Sandwich, were in Bractons time accompted the Five principall havens or Ports, which were endowed with priviledge, and had the same ratified by the great Chartre of England.

Neither yet will I deny, but that soone after, Winchelsey and Rie might be added to the number. For I find in an old recorde, that king Henry the third tooke into his owne hands (for the better defence of the Realme) the townes of Winchelsey, and Rie, which belonged before to the Monasterie of Fescampe in Normandie, and gave therefore in exchange, the Manor of Chiltham in Gloucestershire, & divers other lands in Lincolneshire. This he did, partly to conceale from the Priors Aliens the intelligence of the secret affaires of his Realme, and partly because of a great disobedience & excesse, that was committed by the inhabitants of Wincelsey, against Prince Edward his eldest sonne. And therefore, although I can easily be led to thinke, that he submitted them for their correction to the order, and governance of the Five ports, yet I stand doubtfull whether hee made them partners of their priviledges, or no, for that had bene a preferment, and no punishment unto them : but I suspect rather, that his sonne king Edward the first, (by whose encouragement and aide, olde Winchelsey was afterward abandoned, and the newe towne builded) was the first that apparelled them with that preeminence.

By this therefore let it appeare, that Hastings, Dover, Hithe, Rumney, and Sandwich, were the first Ports of

1268.
[I. 18.]

*Winchelsey
first builded.*
1277.

priviledge : which (because they were 5. in number) both
at the first gave, and yet continue, to all the residue, the
name of Cinque Ports, although not onely Winchelsey and
Rie, be (since that time) incorporated with them as
principals, but divers other places also (for the ease of
their charge) be crept in, as partes, lims, and members of
the same.

Now therefore, somewhat shalbe said, as touching the
services that these Ports of duetie owe, and in deed have
done, to the Princes : whereof the one (I meane with what
number of vessels, in what maner of furniture, and for
how long season, they ought to wait on the king at the
Sea, upon their owne charges) shall partly appeare by that
which we shall presently say, and partly by that which shall
followe in Sandwich, and Rumney : The other shall bee
made manifest by examples, drawne out of good histories :
and they both shall be testified by the words of king
Edward the first in his owne Chartre.

The booke of Domesday before remembred, chargeth
Dover with twentie vessels at the sea, whereof eche to be
furnished with one and twentie men for fifteene dayes
together : and saith further, that Rumney and Sandwich
answered the like service. But now whether this (like)
ought to be understoode of the like altogether, both in
respect of the number and service, or of the (like) in
respect of service, according to the proportion of their
abilitie onely, I may not hereby take upon me to determine. For on the one side, if Rumney, Sandwich, and
the residue, should likewise finde twentie vessels a piece,
then (as you shall anone see) the five Ports were subject
to a greater charge at that time, then King Edward the
first layd upon them : And on the other side, if they were
onely chargeable after their proportion, then know I not
how farre to burthen them, seeing the Record of Domesday
it selfe, bindeth them to no certeintie. And therefore
leaving this as I find it, I must elsewhere make inquisition
for more lightsome proofe. And first I will have recourse
to king Edward the first his Chartre in which I read, that

At ech time that the King passeth over the sea, the Ports ought to rigge up fiftie and seven ships, (whereof every one to have twentie armed souldiers) and to mainteine them at their owne costes, by the space of fifteene dayes together.

And thus it stoode with the Ports for their generall charge, in the sixt yeere of his reigne, for then was this Chartre sealed.   But as touching the particular burthen of ech one, I have seene two divers testimonies, of which the first is a note in French (bearing the countenance of a Record) and is intituled, to have bene renued in the two and twentie yeere of the Reigne of the same king, by Stephan Penchester, then Constable of Dover Castle, in which the particular charge is set downe in this maner.

The Port of Hastings ought to finde three ships.

The lowie of Pevensey, one.

Bulverhithe and Petit Jahn, one.

Bekesborne in Kent, seven.

Grenche at Gillingham in Kent, two men and armour, with the ships of Hastings.

The towne of Rie, five.

To it was Tenterdene annexed, in the time of King Henrie the sixt.

The towne of Winchelsey, tenne.

The Port of Rumney, foure.

Lydde, seven.

The Port of Hythe, five.

The Port of Dover, nineteene.

The towne of Folkestone, seven.

The towne of Feversham, seven.

The Port of Sandwich, with Stonor, Fordwich, Dale, &c. five.

These ships they ought to finde upon fortie dayes [I. 19.] summons, armed and arrayed at their owne charge, and in ech of them twentie men, besides the Master of the Mariners: all which they shall likewise mainteine five dayes together at their owne costs, giving to the Maister sixe pence by the day, to the Constable sixe pence, and to

ech other Mariner three pence. And after those five
dayes ended, the King shall defray the charges.

The other is a Latine Custumall of the towne of Hyde,
the which although it pretend not so great antiquity as
the first, yet seemeth it to me to import as much or more
likelihood and credit: It standeth thus.

These be the Five Ports of our soveraigne Lord the King
having liberties, which other Ports have not: Hasting,
Romenal, Heth, Dover, Sandwich, the chiefe Townes.
The services due by the same.

Hasting shall finde 21. ships, in every ship 21. men,
and a Garcion, or Boy, which is called a Gromet. To it
perteine (as the members of one towne) the Seashore in
Seford, Pevenshey, Hodeney, Winchelsey, Rie, Ihame,
Bekesbourne, Grenge, Northie, Bulwerheth.

Romenal 5. ships, in every ship 21. men, and a
Garcion: To it perteine, as members thereof, Promhell,
Lede, Eastwestone, Dengemareys, olde Rumney.

Hethe 5. ships, as Romenal before. To it perteineth
the Westhethe.

Dover 21. ships, as Hasting before. To it perteine,
Folkstane, Feversham, and S. Margarets, not concerning
the land, but for the goods and cattels.

Sandwich 5. ships, as Romenal, and Hethe. To it
perteine Fordwich, Reculver, Serre, and Dele, not for the
soile, but for the goods.

Summe of ships 57.
Summe of the men 1187. and 57. Garcions.

This service, the Barons of the Five Ports doe acknowledge to owe to the King, upon summons yerely (if it
happen) by the space of 15. dayes together, at their owne
costs and charges, accounting that for the first day of the
15. in which they shall spread their sailes to goe towards
those parts that the King intendeth: and to serve so long
after 15. dayes, as the King will, at his owne pay and
wages.

Thus much out of these ancient notes, whereby your

selfe may easily discerne the difference: but whether the
one or the other, or (by reason of some latter dispensa-
tion) neither of these, have place at this day, I must
referre it to them that be privie, and of counsell with the
Ports: and so leaving this also undecided, holde on the
way, wherein I am entred.

This duetie of attendance therefore (being devised for
the honourable transportation, and safe conduct of the
Kings owne person or his armie over the narrow Seas)
the Ports have not onely most diligently ever since that
time performed, but furthermore also valiantly behaved
themselves against the enemie from time to time, in
sundrie exploits by water, as occasion hath bene profered,
or the necessitie of the Realme required.

And amongst other feats not unwoorthy perpetuall re- *The good ser-*
membrance, after such time as Lewes (the eldest sonne of *vice of the five*
the French King) had entred the Realme to aide Stephan *Ports.*
Langton the Archbishop, and the Nobilitie, in the life of
King John, and had sent into France for new supply of
souldiers after his death, Hubert of Borough (then   1217.
captaine of Dover) following the opinion of Themistocles
in the exposition of the oracle of the woodden walles,
by the aide of the Port townes, armed fortie tall ships,
and meeting with eightie saile of French men upon
the high seas, gave them a most couragious encounter,
in which he tooke some, sunke others, and discomfited
the rest.

King Henrie the third also, after that he came to riper
age, had great benefit by the service of the Cinque Ports:
And king Edward the first in his Chartre, maketh their
continuall faithfull service (and especially their good
endevour, then lately shewed against the Welshmen) the   1278.
principall cause, and motive of that his liberall grant.

Furthermore, about the midst of the reigne of the same
king, an hundreth saile of the Navie of the Ports fought
at the Sea with a fleet of 200. French men, all which   1293.
(notwithstanding the great oddes of the number) they
tooke, and slew, and sunke so many of the Mariners, that

France was thereby (for a long season after) in maner destitute, both of Seamen, and shipping.

Finally, and to conclude this part, in the dayes of king Henrie the fourth, the navie of the Five Ports, under the conduct of one Henrie Paye, surprised one hundreth and twentie French ships, all laden with Salt, Iron, Oile, and no woorse merchandize.

The priviledges of these Ports, being first granted by Edward the Confessour, and William the Conquerour, and then confirmed and increased by William Rufus, Henrie the second, Richard the first, Henrie the third, and king Edward the first, be very great, considering either the honour and ease, or the freedome and exemption, that the inhabitants have by reason of the same.

Part of an Epistle written by one Yvo of Narbona unto the Archbishop of Burdeaux, conteining the confession of an Englishman as touching the barbarous demeanour of the Tartars, which had lived long among them, and was drawen along perforce with them in their expedition against Hungarie: Recorded by Mathew Paris in the yere of our Lord 1243.

THe Lord therefore being provoked to indignation, by reason of this and other sinnes committed among us Christians, is become, as it were, a destroying enemie, and a dreadfull avenger. This I may justly affirme to be true, because an huge nation, and a barbarous and inhumane people, whose law is lawlesse, whose wrath is furious, even the rod of Gods anger, overrunneth, and utterly wasteth infinite countreyes, cruelly abolishing all things where they come, with fire and sword. And this present Summer, the foresayd nation, being called Tartars, departing out of Hungarie, which they had surprised by treason, layd siege unto the

very same ‖ towne, wherein I my selfe abode, with many thousands of souldiers: neither were there in the sayd

towne on our part above 50. men of warre, whom, together
with 20. crosbowes, the captaine had left in garrison. All
these, out of certeine high places, beholding the enemies
vaste armie, and abhorring the beastly crueltie of Anti-
christ his complices, signified foorthwith unto their
governour, the hideous lamentations of his Christian
subjects, who suddenly being surprised in all the province
adjoyning, without any difference or respect of condition,
fortune, sexe, or age, were by manifolde cruelties, all of
them destroyed : with whose carkeises, the Tartarian
chieftains, and their brutish and savage followers, glutting
themselves, as with delicious cates, left nothing for vultures but the bare bones. And a strange thing it is to
consider, that the greedie and ravenous vultures disdeined
to praye upon any of the reliques, which remained. Olde,
and deformed women they gave, as it were, for dayly
sustenance, unto their Canibals : the beautifull devoured
they not, but smothered them lamenting and scritching,
with forced and unnaturall ravishments. Like barbarous
miscreants, they quelled virgins unto death, and cutting
off their tender paps to present for deinties unto their
magistrates, they engorged themselves with their bodies.

Howbeit, their spials in the meane time discrying from
the top of an high mountaine the Duke of Austria, the
King of Bohemia, the Patriarch of Aquileia, the Duke of
Carinthia, and (as some report) the Earle of Baden, with
a mightie power, and in battell aray, approching towards
them, that accursed crew immediatly vanished, and all
those Tartarian vagabonds retired themselves into the
distressed and vanquished land of Hungarie; who as they
came suddenly, so they departed also on the sudden :
which their celeritie caused all men to stand in horrour
and astonishment of them. But of the sayd fugitives, the
prince of Dalmatia tooke eight : one of which number the
Duke of Austria knew to be an English man, who was
perpetually banished out of the Realme of England, in
regard of certaine notorious crimes by him committed.
This fellow, on the behalfe of the most tyrannicall king of

the Tartars, had bene twise, as a messenger and interpreter, with the king of Hungarie, menacing and plainely
foretelling those mischiefes which afterward happened,
unlesse he would submit himselfe and his kingdome unto
the Tartars yoke. Well, being allured by our Princes to
confesse the trueth, he made such oathes and protestations, as (I thinke) the devill himselfe would have beene
trusted for. First therefore he reported of himselfe, that
presently after the time of his banishment, namely about
the 30. yere of his age, having lost all that he had in the
citie of Acon at dice, even in the midst of Winter, being
compelled by ignominious hunger, wearing nothing about
him but a shirt of sacke, a paire of shooes, and a haire
cappe onely, being shaven like a foole, and uttering an
uncoth noise as if he had bene dumbe, he tooke his
journey, and so traveiling many countreyes, and finding in
divers places friendly enterteinment, he prolonged his life
in this maner for a season, albeit every day by rashnesse of
speech, and inconstancie of heart, he endangered himselfe
to the devill. At length, by reason of extreame travaile,
and continuall change of aire and of meats in Caldea, he
fell into a grievous sickenesse, insomuch that he was wearie
of his life. Not being able therefore to go forward or
backeward, and staying there a while to refresh himselfe,
he began (being somewhat learned) to commend to writing
those wordes which hee heard spoken, and within a short
space, so aptly to pronounce, and to utter them himselfe,
that he was reputed for a native member of that countrey:
and by the same dexteritie he attained to manie languages.
This man the Tartars having intelligence of by their spies,
drew him perforce into their societie : and being admonished by an oracle or vision, to challenge dominion over
[I. 21.] the whole earth, they allured him by many rewards to
their faithfull service, by reason that they wanted Interpreters. But concerning their maners and superstitions,
of the disposition and stature of their bodies, of their
countrey and maner of fighting &c, he protested the
particulars following to be true : namely, that they were

above all men, covetous, hasty, deceitfull, and mercilesse :
notwithstanding, by reason of the rigour and extremitie of
punishments to be inflicted upon them by their superiours,
they are restreined from brawlings, and from mutuall
strife and contention. The ancient founders and fathers
of their tribes, they call by the name of gods, and at
certaine set times they doe celebrate solemne feasts unto
them, many of them being particular, & but foure onely
generall. They thinke that all things are created for
themselves alone. They esteeme it none offence to exercise cruelty against rebels. They be hardie and strong in
the breast, leane and pale-faced, rough and huf-shouldred,
having flatte and short noses, long and sharpe chinnes,
their upper jawes are low and declining, their teeth long
and thinne, their eye-browes extending from their foreheads downe to their noses, their eies inconstant and
blacke, their countenances writhen and terrible, their
extreame joynts strong with bones and sinewes, having
thicke and great thighes, and short legs, and yet being
equall unto us in stature : for that length which is wanting
in their legs, is supplied in the upper parts of their bodies.
Their countrey in olde time was a land utterly desert and
waste, situated far beyond Chaldea, from whence they
have expelled Lions, Beares, & such like untamed beasts,
with their bowes, and other engines. Of the hides of
beasts being tanned, they use to shape for themselves light,
but yet impenetrable armour. They ride fast bound unto
their horses, which are not very great in stature, but
exceedingly strong, and mainteined with little provender.
They use to fight constantly and valiantly with javelins,
maces, battle-axes, and swords. But specially they are
excellent archers, and cunning warriers with their bowes.
Their backs are slightly armed, that they may not flee.
They withdraw not themselves from the combate, till they
see the chiefe Standerd of their Generall give backe.
Vanquished, they aske no favour, and vanquishing, they
shew no compassion. They all persist in their purpose of
subduing the whole world under their owne subjection, as

if they were but one man, and yet they are moe then millions in number. They have 60000. Courriers, who being sent before upon light horses to prepare a place for the armie to incampe in, will in the space of one night gallop three dayes journey. And suddenly diffusing themselves over an whole province, and surprising all the people thereof unarmed, unprovided, dispersed, they make such horrible slaughters, that the king or prince of the land invaded, cannot finde people sufficient to wage battell against them, and to withstand them. They delude all people and princes of regions in time of peace, pretending that for a cause, which indeed is no cause. Sometimes they say, that they will make a voyage to Colen, to fetch home the three wise kings into their owne countrey; sometimes to punish the avarice and pride of the Romans, who oppressed them in times past; sometimes to conquere barbarous and Northren nations; sometimes to moderate the furie of the Germans with their owne meeke mildnesse; sometimes to learne warlike feats and stratagems of the French; sometimes for the finding out of fertile ground to suffice their huge multitudes; sometimes againe in derision they say, that they intend to goe on pilgrimage to S. James of Galicia. In regard of which sleights and collusions certaine undiscreet governors concluding a league with them, have granted them free passage thorow their territories, which leagues notwithstanding being violated, were an occasion of ruine and destruction unto the foresayd governours &c.

Libellus historicus Joannis de Plano Carpini, qui
missus est Legatus ad Tartaros anno Domini
1246. ab Innocentio quarto Pontifice maximo.
Incipit Prologus in librum Tartarorum.

Mnibus Christi fidelibus ad quos præsens
scriptum pervenerit, frater Joannes de
Plano Carpini ordinis fratrum minorum,
Apostolicæ sedis Legatus, nuncius ad Tartaros & nationes alias Orientis, Dei gratiam
in præsenti, & gloriam in futuro, & de
inimicis suis gloriam triumphalem. Cum
ex mandato sedis Apostolicæ iremus ad Tartaros & nationes
alias Orientis, & sciremus Domini Papæ & venerabilium
Cardinalium voluntatem, elegimus priùs ad Tartaros proficisci. Timebamus enim ne per eos in proximo ecclesiæ
Dei periculum immineret. Et quamvis a Tartaris & aliis
nationibus timeremus occidi, vel perpetuo captivari, vel
fame, siti, algore, æstu, contumelia, & laboribus nimiis, [I. 22.]
& quasi ultra vires affligi (quæ omnia multo plusquam
prius credidimus, excepta morte vel captivitate perpetua
nobis multipliciter evenerunt) non tamen pepercimus nobis
ipsis, ut voluntatem Dei secundum Domini papæ mandatum adimplere possemus, & ut proficeremus in aliquo
Christianis, ut saltem scita veraciter voluntate & intentione
ipsorum, possemus illam patefacere Christianis, ne forte
subito irruentes invenirent eos imparatos, sicut peccatis
hominum exigentibus alia vice contigit : & fecerunt
magnam stragem in populo Christiano. Unde quæcunque
pro vestra utilitate vobis scribimus ad cautelam, tanto
securius credere debetis, quanto nos cuncta vel ipsi
vidimus oculis nostris, qui per annum & quatuor menses *Annus & 4.*
& amplius ambulavimus per ipsos & cum ipsis, ac *menses &*
fuimus inter eos, vel audivimus a Christianis qui *amplius.*
sunt inter eos captivi, & ut credimus fide dignis.
Mandatum etiam a supremo pontifice habebamus, ut
cuncta perscrutaremur & videremus omnia diligenter.

*Frater Bene-
dictus Polonus
comes Joannis
de Plano Car-
pini.*

Quod tam nos quàm frater Benedictus ejusdem ordinis
qui nostræ tribulationis fuit socius & interpres fecimus
studiose.

De terra Tartarorum, situ, qualitate & dispositione aeris in eadem. Cap. 1.

Olentes igitur facta scribere Tartarorum, ut
lectores facilius valeant invenire, hoc modo per
capitula describemus. Primo quidem dicemus
de terra. Secundo de hominibus. Tertio de ritu.
Quarto de moribus. Quinto de ipsorum imperio. Sexto
de bellis. Septimo de terris quas eorum dominio
subjugaverunt. Octavo quomodo Bello occurratur
eisdem. De terra possumus hoc modo tractare. In
principio quidem dicemus de situ ipsius : secundo de
qualitate : tertio de dispositione aeris in eadem. Terra
vero prædicta est in ea posita parte Orientis in qua oriens
sicut credimus conjungitur Aquiloni. Ab Oriente autem
est terra posita Kytaiorum & etiam ‖ Solangorum : a
meridie sunt terræ Saracenorum : inter Occidentem &
Meridiem Huyrorum. Ab Occidente provincia Naymanorum ; ab Aquilone mari oceano circundatur. Hæc
vero in parte aliqua est nimium montuosa, & in aliqua est
campestris, sed fere tota admixta glarea, raro argillosa,
plurimum est arenosa. In aliqua parte terræ sunt aliquæ
modicæ sylvæ : alia vero est sine lignis omnino. Cibaria
autem sua decoquunt & sedent tam imperator quàm
principes & alii ad ignem factum de boum stercoribus &
equorum. Terra autem prædicta non est in parte
centesima fructuosa : nec etiam potest fructum portare
nisi aquis fluvialibus irrigetur. Sed aqua & rivi ibidem
sunt pauci : flumina vero rarissima unde ibidem villæ
sunt paucæ ; nec aliquæ civitates excepta una, quæ esse
dicitur satis bona ; nos autem non vidimus illam, sed
fuimus prope ad dimidium diem, cum apud Syram ordam
essemus, quæ curia est major imperatoris eorum. Et licet
aliàs infructuosa sit, quamvis non multum, tamen competenter est alendis pecoribus apta. Aer in ipsa est

*‖ Al. Sclango-
rum.*

*Oceanus ab
Aquilone.*

*Syra orda,
curia major
imperatoris.*

mirabiliter inordinatus. In media etiam æstate quando in
aliis partibus solet calor maximus abundare ; ibi sunt
tonitrua magna & fulgura, ex quibus homines quàm
plurimi occiduntur. Cadunt etiam ibi eodem tempore
maximæ nives. Ibi sunt etiam frigidissimorum ventorum
tam maximæ tempestates, quod cum labore vix possunt
homines aliquando equitare. Unde cum essemus apud
ordam (sic enim stationes imperatoris apud eos & principum
appellantur) jacebamus in terra præ magnitudine venti
prostrati, & propter pulveris multitudinem videre minime
poteramus. In ea etiam in hyeme nusquam pluit, sed in
æstate : & tam modicum, quod vix potest aliquando
pulverem & radices graminum madidare. Grando etiam
ibi sæpe maxima cadit. Unde eo tempore quando fuit
electus, & in sede regni poni debuit imperator, nobis in
curia existentibus, tanta cecidit grando, quod ex subita
resolutione, sicut plenius intelleximus, plusquam centum &
quadraginta homines in eadem curia fuerunt submersi.
Res autem & habitacula plura deducta fuerunt. Ibi est
etiam in æstate subito magnus calor, & repente maximum
frigus. In hyeme vero in aliqua parte cadunt maximæ
nives, in alia autem parvæ. Et ut breviter de terra con-
cludam, magna est, sed aliter, sicut vidimus oculis
nostris, (quia per ipsam circuendam quinque mensibus
& dimidium ambulavimus) multo vilior est, quàm
dicere valeamus.

*Maximæ
nives in æstate
in Tartaria.*

*Grando
maxima.*

*Maxima inun-
datio ex subita
grandinis
resolutione.*

*Iter quinque
mensium &
dimidii.*

De formis Tartarorum, de conjugio, vestibus & habitaculis eorum. Cap. 2.

DIcto de terra, de hominibus est dicendum. Primò
quidem formas describemus personarum. Secundò
de ipsorum conjugio supponemus. Tertio de vestibus. Quarto de habitaculis. Quinto de rebus
eorum. Forma personarum ab hominibus aliis est
remota. Inter oculos enim & genas plusquam alii
homines sunt lati. Genæ etiam satis prominent a
maxillis. Graciles sunt generaliter in cingulo exceptis
quibusdam paucis. Pene omnes sunt mediocris staturæ.

[I. 23.]

Barba fere omnibus minime crescit. Aliqui tamen in
inferiori labio & in barba modicos habent crines, quos
minime tondent. Super verticem capitis in modum
clericorum habent coronas, & ab aure una usque ad
aliam, ad latitudinem trium digitorum similiter omnes
radunt. Quæ rasuræ coronæ prædictæ junguntur. Super
frontem etiam ad latitudinem duorum digitorum similiter
omnes radunt. Illos autem capillos qui sunt inter
coronam & prætaxatam rasuram crescere usque ad supercilia sinunt. Et ex utraque parte frontis tondendo
plusquam in medio crines faciunt longos : reliquos vero
crines permittunt crescere ut mulieres. De quibus faciunt
duas cordas, & ligant unamquamque post aurem. Pedes
etiam modicos habent. Uxores vero habet unusquisque
quot potest tenere. Aliquis centum, aliquis quinquaginta,
aliquis decem, aliquis plures vel pauciores : & omnibus
parentibus generaliter junguntur, excepta matre, filia, vel
sorore ex eadem matre, sororibus etiam ex patre : tamen
& uxores patris post mortem ducere possunt. Uxorem
etiam fratris alter frater junior post mortem vel alius de
parentela junior ducere tenetur. Reliquas mulieres omnes
sine ulla differentia ducunt in uxores, & emunt eas valde
pretiosè a parentibus suis. Post mortem maritorum de
facili ad secunda conjugia non migrant, nisi quis velit

Vestes. suam novercam ducere in uxorem. Vestes autem tam
virorum quàm mulierum sunt uno modo formatæ.
Palliis, cappis vel capputiis vel pellibus non utuntur.
Tunicas vero portant de Bukeramo, purpura, vel Baldaquino
in hunc modum formatas. A supremo usque deorsum
sunt scissæ, quia ante pectus duplicantur. A latere vero
sinistro una, & in dextris tribus ligaturis nectuntur, & in
latere & in sinistro usque ad brachiale sunt scissæ. Pellicia
cujuscunque sunt generis in eundem modum formantur :
superius tamen pellicium exterius habet pilum, sed a
posterioribus est apertum. Habet autem caudulam unam
usque ad genua retro. Mulieres vero quæ sunt maritatæ
habent tunicam valde amplam & usque ad terram ante
scissam. Super caput vero habent unum quid rotundum

de viminibus vel de cortice factum, quod in longum protenditur ad unam ulnam, & in summitate desinit in
quadrum : & ab imo usque ad summum in amplitudine
semper crescit, & in summitate habet virgulam unam
longam & gracilem de auro vel de argento seu de ligno,
vel etiam pennam : & est assutum super unum pileolum,
quod protenditur usque ad humeros. Instrumentum
prædictum est tectum de buccaramo, sive purpura vel
baldaquino : sine quo instrumento coram hominibus
nunquam vadunt, & per hoc ab aliis mulieribus cognos-
cuntur. Virgines autem & juvenes mulieres cum magna
difficultate a viris suis possunt discerni : quum per omnia
vestiuntur ut viri. Pileola habent alia quàm aliæ nationes,
quorum formam intelligibiliter describere non valemus.
Stationes rotundas habent in modum tentorii præparatas, *Tabernacula.*
de virgis & baculis subtiliter factas. Supra vero in medio
rotundam habent fenestram unde lumen ingreditur, & ut
possit fumus exire : quia semper in medio ignem faciunt.
Parietes autem & tecta filtro sunt cooperta. Ostia etiam
de filtro sunt facta. Quædam stationes sunt magnæ,
quædam parvæ, secundum dignitatem & hominum
parvitatem. Quædam solvuntur subito & reparantur, &
super somarios deferuntur. Quædam dissolvi non possunt,
sed in curribus deferuntur. Minoribus autem in curru
ad deferendum unos bos ; majoribus tres vel quatuor, vel
etiam plures, vel quod est magis, sufficiunt ad portandum.
Quocunque vadunt sive ad bellum, sive aliàs, semper illas
deferunt secum. In animalibus sunt divites valde : in *Opes in pecore.*
camelis, bobus, ovibus, capris, & equis. Jumentorum
tantam habent multitudinem, quantam non credimus habere
totum mundum. Porcos & alias bestias minime habent.

De cultu & de hiis quæ credunt esse peccata, & de
    divinationibus & ritu funeris eorum, & de
    purgationibus suorum peccatorum. Cap. 3.

DIcto de hominibus, dicendum est de ritu : de
   quo tractabimus in hunc modum. Primo de cultu :
secundo de hiis quæ credunt esse peccata : tertio de

divinationibus, & purgationibus peccatorum : quarto de ritu funeris. Unum Deum credunt, quem credunt esse factorem omnium visibilium & invisibilium. Et credunt eum tam bonorum in hoc mundo quàm pœnarum esse factorem : non tamen orationibus vel laudibus, aut ritu aliquo ipsum colunt. Nihilominus habent idola quædam de filtro ad imaginem hominis facta ; & illa ponunt ex utraque parte ostii stationis, & subtus illa ponunt quiddam de filtro in modum uberis factum, & illa credunt esse pecorum custodes, & eis beneficium lactis & pullorum præstare. Alia vero faciunt de pannis sericis, & illa multum honorant. Quidam ponunt illa in pulchro curru tecto ante ostium stationis : & quicunque aliquid de illo curru furatur, sine ulla miseratione occiditur. Duces, millenarii, & centenarii unum semper habent in medio stationis. Prædictis idolis offerunt primum lac omnis pecoris & jumenti. Et cum primo comedere & bibere incipiunt, primo offerunt eis de cibariis & potu. Et cum bestiam aliquam occidunt, offerunt cor Idolo quod est in curru in aliquo cypho, & dimittunt usque mane, & tunc auferunt de præsenti ejus, & decoquunt & manducant. Primo etiam imperatori faciunt idolum, quod ponunt in curru, ante quam stationem honorifice, sicut vidimus ante ordam imperatoris istius, offerunt munera multa. Equos etiam offerunt ei, quos nullus audet ascendere usque ad mortem. Alia etiam animalia eidem offerunt. Quæ vero occidunt ad manducandum, nullum os ex eis confringunt, sed igni comburunt. Et etiam ad meridiem tanquam Deo inclinant, & inclinare faciunt alios nobiles, qui se reddunt eisdem. Unde nuper contigit quod Michael, qui fuit unus de magnis ducibus Russiæ, cum ivisset ad se reddendum Bati, fecerunt eum prius inter duos ignes transire : Post hoc dixerunt, quod ad meridiem Cyngis can inclinaret. Qui respondit, quod Bati & servis suis inclinaret libenter, sed imagini hominis mortui non inclinaret, quia non licet hoc facere Christianis. Et cum sæpe diceretur, quod inclinaret, & nollet, mandavit ei prædictus per filium

[I. 24.]

Jeroslai, quod occideretur si non inclinaret. Qui respondit, quod potius vellet mori, quàm hoc faceret, quia non liceret. At ille satellitem unum misit, qui tam diu contra cor eum in ventre calce percussit, quousque deficeret. Tunc quidam de suis militibus qui astabat confortans eum dixit : Esto robustus quia hæc pœna non diu tibi durabit, & statim sequetur gaudium sempiternum : post hoc fuit caput ejus cultello præcisum. Militi vero prædicto fuit caput etiam cultello amputatum. Solem igitur lumina & ignem venerantur & adorant, & aquam & terram, eis ciborum & potus primitias offerentes, & mane potissime antequam comedant & bibant : quia de cultu Dei nullam legem observant. Neminem cogunt suam fidem vel legem negare. Accidit tamen dum adhuc nuper essemus in terra quod Andreas dux de ‖ Sarvogle quæ est in Russia fuit apud Bati accusatus, quod educeret equos Tartarorum de terra & venderet aliàs, & cum tamen non esset probatum fuit occisus : quod audiens junior frater ejus, venit cum uxore occisi ad ducem prædictum Bati, volens supplicare, ne terra tolleretur eisdem. Qui dixit par esse, quod uxorem fratris carnalis prædicti duceret in uxorem : & mulieri præcepit ducere illum in virum secundum consuetudinem Tartarorum. Qui respondit, quod prius vellet occidi, quàm faceret contra legem. At ille nihilominus tradidit eam illi, quamvis renuerat quantum posset : & duxerunt ambo in lecto, & posuerunt pucrum super illam plorantem & clamantem, & cogerunt eos commisceri coactione non conditionali, sed absoluta. Quamvis de justitia facienda, vel peccato cavendo nullam habeant legem, nihilominus tamen habent aliquas traditiones, quas dicunt esse peccata : quas confinxerunt ipsi & patres eorum. Unum est, cultellum figere in igne, vel etiam quocunque modo tangere cum cultello : vel cum cultello extrahere carnes de caldario : juxta ignem etiam incidere cum securi. Credunt etiam quod sic auferri caput debeat igni. Item appodiare se ad flagellum, cum quo percutitur equus : Ipsi enim calcaribus non utuntur. Item tangere flagellis sagittas. Item juvenes aves occidere, vel accipere :

cum frœno equum percutere. Item os cum osse alio
frangere. Item lac vel aliquem potum vel cibum super
terram effundere. In statione mingere, sed si voluntarie
facit occiditur : si autem aliter, oportet quod pecunia
solvatur incantatori, qui purificet eos : faciat etiam
stationem & ea quæ in ipsa sunt inter duos ignes transire.
Sed antequam sic purificetur nullus audet intrare vel
aliquid de ipsa portare. Item si alicui morsus imponitur,
& deglutire non potest, & de ore suo ejicit eum, fit foramen sub statione, & extrahunt per illud foramen, & sine
ulla misericordia occiditur. Item si aliquis calcat limen
stationis alicujus ducis interficitur eodem modo.   Et

ἀθεότης.   multa habent similia, de quibus longum est narrare. Sed
homines occidere, aliorum terras invadere, res aliorum
accipere, quocunque injusto modo fornicari, aliis hominibus injuriari, facere contra Dei prohibitiones & Dei
præcepta, nullum est peccatum apud eos. De vita æterna
& damnatione perpetua, nihil sciunt. Credunt tamen quod
post mortem in alio seculo vivant, greges multiplicent,
comedant, bibant, & alia faciant, quæ in hoc seculo a
viventibus hominibus fiunt. Divinationibus, auguriis,
aruspiciis, veneficiis, incantationibus multum intendunt. Et
cum a dæmonibus ipsis respondetur, credunt quod Deus
ipsis loquatur, quem Deum vocant Itoga : sed Comani
Cham, id est, imperatorem ipsum appellant, quem mirabiliter timent & reverentur : ac oblationes offerunt multas,
& primitias cibi & potus. Secundum autem responsa

Cultus lunæ.   ipsius faciunt universa. In principio etiam lunationis vel
plenilunio incipiunt quicquid novi agere volunt. Unde
illam magnum imperatorem appellant, eique genua flectunt
& deprecantur. Solem dicunt esse matrem lunæ, eo quod
lumen a sole recipiat. Et ut breviter dicam per ignem
credunt omnia purificari. Unde cum nuncii veniunt ad
eos, vel principes, vel qualescunque personæ, oportet ipsos
& munera quæ portant per duos ignes transire, ut purificentur. Item si cadit ignis de cœlo super pecora, vel

[I. 25.]   super homines, quod ibidem sæpe contingit, sive aliquid
talium evenerit eis, per quod immundos seu infortunatos

se reputant, oportet similiter per incantatores mundari. Et
quasi omnem spem suam in talibus posuerunt. Quando *Ritus funebris.*
aliquis eorum infirmatur, ponitur in statione ejus una
hasta, & contra illam filtrum circumvolvitur nigrum : &
ex tunc nullus audet alienus postes stationum intrare. Et
quando incipit agonizare, omnes recedunt ab eo ; quoniam
nullus de iis qui morti ejus assistunt, potest ordam alicujus
ducis vel imperatoris usque ad novam lunationem intrare.
Cum autem mortuus est, si est de majoribus, sepelitur
occulte in campo ubi placuerit : sepelitur autem cum
statione sedendo in medio ejus, & ponunt mensam ante
eum, & alveum carnibus plenum, & cyphum lactis
jumentini : Sepelitur autem cum eo unum jumentum cum
pullo, & equus cum fræno & sella : & alium equum comedunt & stramine corium implent, & super duo vel quatuor
ligna altius ponunt, ut habeat in alio mundo stationem ubi
moretur, & jumentum de quo lac habeat, & possit sibi
equos multiplicare, & equos etiam in quibus valeat
equitare. Aurum & argentum sepeliunt eodem modo cum
ipso. Currus in quo ducitur frangitur, & statio sua
destruitur, nec nomen proprium ejus usque ad tertiam
generationem audet aliquis nominare. Alius etiam est
modus sepeliendi quosdam majores. Vaditur in campo
occultè, & ibi gramina removent cum radicibus, & faciunt
foveam magnam, & in latere illius foveæ faciunt unam sub
terra, & illum servum quem habet dilectum ponunt sub
eo, qui jacet tam diu sub eo donec incipit agonizare,
deinde extrahunt eum ut valeat respirare, & sic faciunt
ter. Et si evadet, postea est liber, & facit quicquid ei
placuerit, & est magnus in statione, ac inter parentes illius.
Mortuum autem ponunt in foveam, quæ est in latere facta *Idem mos*
cum his quæ superius dicta sunt. Deinde replent foveam *sepeliendi fere*
quæ est ante foveam suam, & desuper gramina ponunt, ut *in Florida.*
fuerant prius, ad hoc, ne locus ulterius valeat inveniri.
Alia faciunt ut dictum est. In terra eorum sunt cœmeteria
duo. Unum in quo sepeliuntur imperatores, duces &
nobiles omnes : & ubicunque moriuntur, si congruè fieri
potest, illuc deferuntur. Sepelitur autem cum eis aurum

& argentum multum. Aliud est in quo sepeliuntur illi qui in Hungaria interfecti fuerunt : multi enim ibidem occisi fuerunt. Ad illa cœmeteria nullus audet accedere præter custodes, qui ad custodiendum positi sunt ibidem. Et si aliquis accesserit, capitur, spoliatur & verberatur, & valde malè tractatur. Unde nos ipsi ncscientes intravimus terminos cœmeterii eorum qui in Hungaria occisi fuerunt, & venerunt super nos sagittæ volantes : sed quia eramus nuncii consuetudinem terræ nescientes, nos liberos dimi-

Lustrationis ritus. serunt abire. Parentes autem & omnes alii qui morantur in stationibus suis oportet purificari per ignem : quæ purificatio fit hoc modo. Faciunt duos ignes, & duas hastas ponunt juxta ignes, & unam cordam in summitate hastarum : & ligant super cordam illam quasdam scissuras de buccharamo : sub qua corda & ligaturis inter illos duos ignes transeunt homines, bestiæ & stationes : Et sunt duæ mulieres, una hinc, & alia inde aquam projicientes, & quædam carmina recitantes. Et si aliqui currus ibi franguntur, vel etiam res ibi cadunt aliquæ, incantatores accipiunt. Et si aliquis occiditur à tonitruo, omnes illos homines qui morantur in stationibus illis, oportet prædicto modo ignes transire. Statio, lectus, filtra, currus, vestes, & quicquid talium habuerint, a nullo tanguntur, sed tanquam immunda ab omnibus respuuntur.

De consuetudinibus bonis & malis & cibis eorum.
Cap. 4.

DIcto de ritu, dicendum est de moribus : de quibus tractabimus hoc modo. Primo dicemus de bonis, secundo de malis : tertio de consuetudinibus : quarto de cibis. Prædicti homines, scilicet Tartari sunt magis

Obedientia. obedientes Dominis suis, quàm aliqui homines in hoc mundo, sive religiosi, sive seculares : & magis reverentur eosdem : neque de facili mentiuntur eis. Verbis ad invicem rarò aut nunquam contendunt, factis verò nunquam. Bella, rixæ, vulnera, homicidia inter eos non

Abstinentia. contingunt. Prædones & fures magnarum rerum non inveniuntur inter eos. Unde stationes & currus eorum,

ubi habent thesaurum suum setis aut vectibus non
firmantur. Si aliquæ bestiæ perduntur, quicunque invenerit eas vel dimittit sic esse, vel ducit eas ad homines
illos, qui positi sunt ad hoc. Homines autem quorum
sunt bestiæ apud eosdem illas requirunt, & absque ulla
difficultate recipiunt illas. Unus alium satis honorat : & *Comitas.*
ad invicem sunt satis familiares : Et cibaria quamvis inter
illos sint pauca, tamen inter se satis competenter com-
municant illa ; & satis sunt sufferentes. Unde quum *Temperantia.*
jejunant uno die vel duobus diebus nihil comedentes
omninò de facili non videntur impatientes, sed cantant &
ludunt quasi comederunt bene. In equitando multum
sustinent frigus, & calorem nimium patiuntur. Non sunt
homines delicati. Invidi ad invicem non videntur. Inter
eos quasi nulla placita sunt : nullus alium spernit, sed
juvat & promovet quantum congruè potest. Mulieres *Castitas*
eorum sunt castæ : nec de impudicitia earum inter eas *mulierum.*
aliquid auditur. Verba tamen quædam ex eis in joco satis [I. 26.]
habent turpia & impudica. Seditiones verò inter eas rarò
vel nunquam audiuntur. Et quamvis multum inebrientur,
in ebrietate sua tamen verbis vel facto nunquam contendunt. Nunc de malis moribus eorum est suppon-
endum. Superbissimi aliis hominibus sunt, & despiciunt *Insolentia ad-*
omnes : ideò quasi pro nihilo reputant, sive nobiles sint, *versus exteros.*
sive ignobiles. Vidimus enim in curia Imperatoris nobi-
lem virum Jeroslaum, magnum Ducem Russiæ, filium
etiam Regis & Reginæ Georgiæ, & Soldanos multos,
duces etiam Soldanorum nullum honorem debitum recipere inter eos. Sed Tartari qui erant eis assignati,
quantumcunque erant viles, antecedebant eos, & semper
primum locum & summum tenebant : immò sæpè opor-
tebat eos post eorum posteriora sedere. Iracundi multum *Iracundia.*
& indignantis naturæ sunt : & etiam aliis hominibus plus
sunt mendaces, & ferè nulla veritas invenitur in eis. In *Mendacitas.*
principio quidem sunt blandi, sed in fine pungunt ut
scorpio. Subdoli sunt & fraudulenti, & si possunt astutia *Fraudulentia.*
circumveniunt omnes. Homines sunt immundi, sumendo *Sordes.*
cibum & potum, & aliis factis suis. Qui cum volunt

aliquid mali facere aliis hominibus, miro modo occultant, ut prævidere non possint, vel contra eorum astutias re- *Temulentia.* medium invenire. Ebrietas honorabilis est apud eos: & quum multum quis bibit, ibidem rejicit, nec propter hoc *Extortio.* dimittit quin iterum bibat. Valdè sunt cupidi & avari, exactores maximi ad petendum: tenacissimi retentores, & *Crudelitas.* parcissimi donatores. Aliorum hominum occisio pro nihilo est apud illos. Et, ut breviter dicam, omnes mali mores eorum propter prolixitatem in scripto redigi non *Cibi.* possunt. Cibi eorum sunt omnia quæ mandi possunt. Comedunt canes, lupos, vulpes, & equos; & in necessitate carnes humanas. Unde quando pugnaverunt contra quandam civitatem Kytaorum, ubi morabatur imperator ipsorum; eam obsederunt tam diu, quod defecerunt ipsis Tartaris omninò expensæ. Et quia non habebant quòd manducarent omninò, tunc accipiebatur de decem hominibus unus ad manducandum. Abluviones etiam quæ egrediuntur de jumentis cum pullis manducant. Imò vidimus etiam eos pediculos manducare: vidimus etiam eos comedere mures. Mensalibus & manutergiis non utuntur: panem non habent, nec olera, nec legumina, nec aliquid aliud nisi carnes: & tam paucas habent, quòd aliæ nationes vix inde vivere possent. Cum pinguedine carnium multum polluunt manus: quando verò comederunt, tunc manus ad ocreas suas, vel ad gramina, vel ad aliquid talium tergunt. Solent etiam honestiores habere aliquos panniculos parvos, cum quibus ultimo tergunt manus, quando carnes manducarunt. Cibum unus eorum incidit, & alius accipit cum puncto cultelli morsellos, & unicuique præbet, quibusdam plus, quibusdam minus, secundum quod plus vel minus volunt eos honorare. Scutellas non lavant, & si aliquando cum brodio lavant carnium, iterum cum carnibus in olla reponunt. Ollas etiam vel caldaria, vel alia vasa ad hoc deputata si abluunt, simili modo lavant. Apud eos est magnum peccatum, si de cibo vel potu perire permittatur aliquid. Unde ossa, nisi priùs extrahatur medulla, dari canibus non permittunt. Vestes etiam non lavant, nec lavari permittunt, & maximè quo tonitrua ab illa hora incipiunt donec desinant. Lac jumentinum bibunt in maxima quantitate si habent: bibunt etiam ovinum, caprinum, vaccinum, & camelorum. Vinum, cervisiam, & medonem non habent, nisi ab aliis nationibus mittatur, vel donetur eisdem. In hyeme, nisi divites sint, lac jumentinum non habent. Millium, cum aqua decoquunt, quod tam tenue faciunt, quòd non comedere sed bibere possunt. Et unus quisque ex eis bibit cyphum unum vel duos in mane, & nil plus in die manducant. In sero unicuique parum de carnibus datur, & brodium de carnibus bibunt. In æstate autem, quia tunc habent satis de lacte jumentino carnes rarò manducant, nisi fortè donentur eis, aut venatione aliquam bestiam ceperint, sive avem. Legem etiam sive *Pœna* consuetudinem habent occidendi virum & mulierem quos *adulterii.* in adulterio invenerint manifestè. Similiter & virginem si fornicata fuerit, mulierem occidunt & virum. Si aliquis invenitur in præda vel in furto manifesto in terra potes- *Furti.* tatis eorum sine ulla miseratione occiditur. Item si aliquis *Arcani* eorum deundat consilium, maximè quando volunt ire ad *evulgati.* bellum, centum plagæ dantur super posteriora, quanto majores dare cum baculo magno unus rusticus potest. Item quando aliqui de minoribus offendunt in aliquo à suis majoribus non parcitur eis, sed verberibus graviter affliguntur. Item inter filium concubinæ & uxoris nulla est differentia, sed dat pater unicuique eorum quod vult, et si est de genere ducum, ita est dux filius concubinæ, sicut filius legitimus. Et cum unus Tartarus habet Πολυγαμία. multas uxores, unaquæque per se suam stationem, & familiam habet: & cum una comedit, & bibit, & dormit una die, & altera die cum alia. Una tamen ex ipsis major est inter alias, & frequentius cum illa quam cum aliis commoratur. Et cum tam multæ sint inter se tamen de facili non contendunt. Viri nihil operantur omninò ex- ceptis sagittis: & etiam de gregibus aliquantulam habent curam, sed venantur, & exercent se ad sagittandum: Omnes enim à parvo usque ad magnum sagittarii sunt & boni. Et statim pueri eorum, cum sunt duorum anno- rum vel trium, incipiunt equitare. Equos eorum regunt

& currunt in eis: & dantur eis arcus secundùm suam
ætatem, & instruunt ad sagittandum. Agiles enim sunt &
audaces valdè. Virgines & mulieres equitant, & agiliter
in equis currunt ut viri. Vidimus enim eas arcus &
pharetras portare. Et tam viri quàm mulieres diu in
equitando possunt durare. Brevissimas habent strepas:
equos valdè custodiunt: imo rerum omnium sunt magni
conservatores. Mulieres eorum omnia operantur. Pel-

*Fœminæ
Metæ incog-
nitæ eodem
modo vestiun-
tur.*

licia, vestes, calceos, ocreas, & omnia opera quæ de corio
fiunt. Currus etiam ducunt & reparant, camelos onerant,
& velocissimæ sunt & strenuæ in omnibus operibus suis:
fœmoralibus omnes utuntur: aliquæ, sicut viri, sagittant.

De ipsorum Imperio. Cap. 5.

DIcto de eorum consuetudinibus, dicendum est de
eorum imperio. Et primò de ipsius principio.
Secundò de principibus ejus. Tertio de dominio Impera-
toris & principum. Terra quædam est in partibus
Orientis, de qua dictum est suprà, quæ Mongol nominatur.
Hæc terra quondam quatuor populos habuit. Et unus
Yek a Mongol, id est, magni Mongali vocabatur. Se-

*Tartariæ
populi.
Tartar
fluvius.*

cundus Sumongol, id est Aquatici Mongali. Ipsi autem
se ipsos Tartaros appellabant, à quodam fluvio, qui currit
per terram eorum, qui Tartar nominatur. Alius appellatur
Merkat, quartus Metrit. Hii populi omnes unam
formam personarum, & unam linguam habebant: quamvis
inter se per principes & provincias essent divisi. In terra

*Cyngis ortus
& res gestæ.*

Yeka-Mongol fuit qui vocabatur Cyngis. Iste incepit
esse robustus venator coram Domino. Didicit enim
homines furari, rapere, prædari. Ibat autem ad alias
terras, & quoscunque potuit capere, & sibi associare non
demittebat: homines verò suæ gentis ad se inclinabat,
qui tanquam ducem ipsum sequebantur ad omnia male-
facta. Hic autem incepit pugnare cum Sumongal, sive
Tartaris, postquam homines aggregaverat sibi, & interfecit ducem eorum, & multo bello omnes Tartaros sibi
subjugavit & in suam servitutem redegit. Post hæc cum
omnibus his pugnavit, cum Merkat, qui erant positi juxta

JOHN DE PLANO CARPINI

A.D.
1246.

terram Tartarorum, quos etiam bello sibi subjecit: Inde
procedens pugnavit contra Metritas, & etiam illos devicit.
Audentes itaque Naymani, quod Cyngis erat taliter *Naymani.*
elevatus, indignati fuerunt. Ipsi enim habuerunt Imperatorem, qui fuerat strenuus valdè, cui dabant tributum
omnes nationes prædictæ. Qui debitum universæ carnis
exsolvens, filii ejus successerunt loco ejus; sed juvenes
erant & stulti, & populum nesciebant tenere: sed invicem *Fratres*
divisi erant & scissi: unde medio tempore Cyngis erat *discordantes*
taliter exaltatus, nihilominus insultum faciebant in terras *oppressi.*
superius annotatas, viros & mulieres, & pueros occidebant,
& capiebant prædam eorum. Cyngis hoc audiens, omnes
sibi subjectos homines aggregavit. Naymani & Kara *Kara Kitai.*
Kitai, id est, nigri Kitai, ex adverso in quandam vallem
strictam inter montes duos, per quam nos euntes ad imperatorem eorum transivimus, similiter conveniunt: &
commissum est prælium, in quo Naymani & Kara Kitai a
Mongallis sunt devicti, & major pars eorum occisa: &
alii qui evadere non potuerunt in servitutem redacti sunt.
In terra autem prædictorum Kara Kytaorum Occaday can *Occoday can.*
filius Cyngis can, postquam positus fuit imperator, quandam civitatem ædificavit, quam ‖Omyl appellavit. Propè ‖ *Vel Chanyl.*
quam ad meridiem est quoddam desertum magnum, in
quo sylvestres homines pro certo habitare dicuntur, qui *Homines*
nullo modo loquuntur, nec in cruribus habent juncturas: *sylvestres.*
& si quando cadunt, per se surgere sine adjutorio aliorum
minimè possunt, aliquantam tamen habent discretionem.
Mongali autem in terram eorum revertentes se contra
Kytaos in prælium præparaverunt, qui castra moventes
terram eorum intraverunt. Imperator autem Kytaorum *De mutua*
hoc audiens venit contra eos cum exercitu suo; & com- *victoria*
missum est prælium durum; in quo prælio Mongali *Mongalorum*
fuerunt devicti: & omnes nobiles Mongallorum qui *Tartarorum*
erant in prædicto exercitu fuerunt occisi usque ad septem. *Kytaina*
Cyngis verò & alii qui remanserunt in terram suam *clades.*
fugerunt. Et quum aliquantulum quievisset Cyngis,
præparavit se rursus ad prælium & contra terram
Huyrorum processit ad bellum. Isti homines Christiani

69

de secta Nestorianorum erant, quos etiam bello devicit, &
eorum literas acceperunt. Nam prius scripturam aliquam

Novæ victoriæ
literæ.

non habebant. Nunc autem eandem literam Mongallorum
appellant. Inde processit contra terram Saruiuorum, &

Vel Saruiur.
Vel Karanita-
rum.
Vel Hudirat.

contra terram Karavitarum, & contra terram Voyrat, &
contra terram Comana, quas terras omncs devicit. Inde
est in terram suam reversus. Et cum aliquantulum
quievisset, convocatis omnibus gentibus supradictis, contra
Kytaos ad bellum processit, & cum diu contra eos pug-
nasset magnam partem terræ Kytaorum vicerunt : Imperatorem autem eorum concluserunt in sua civitate majori :
quam cum tam diu obsiderunt, quod exercitui defecerunt
expensæ, & cum non haberent quod manducarent, præcepit illis Cyngis can, quod de decem hominibus unum
darent ad manducandum. Illi autem de civitate pugna-

Argentum loco
lapidum in
hostem pro-
jectum.

bant viriliter contra illos sagittis & machinis : Et cum
deficerent lapides, pro lapidibus projecerunt argentum, &
maximè liquefactum. Civitas enim hæc multis divitiis
erat plena. Et cum diu pugnassent, & eam bello vincere
minimè possent, fecerunt unam magnam viam sub terra ab
exercitu usque ad mediam civitatem, & aperientes subitò

[I. 28.]
Kytai victi.

terram, eis nescientibus prosilierunt in medio civitatis, &
pugnabant cum hominibus civitatis, & illi qui erant extra
simili modo pugnabant, & concidentes portas intraverunt
civitatem : & occidentes Imperatorem & homines plures,
civitatem possidebant : & aurum & argentum, & omnes
divitias abstulerunt. Et cum terræ prædictæ Kytaorum
suos homines præfecissent, in terram propriam sunt reversi.

Cyngis
salutatur
Imperator.
Kythaiæ pars
in mari posita.
Kytaorum
litera, &
religio.

Et tunc Imperatore Kytaorum devicto factus est Imperator.
Quandam autem partem terræ Kytaorum, quæ posita est
in mari, usque in hodiernum diem nullatenus devicerunt.
Kytai autem, de quibus superiùs diximus, homines sunt
Pagani, qui habent literam specialem : & habent novum &
vetus Testamentum ; & habent vitas patrum, & Eremitas
& domos quasi Ecclesias factas, in quibus orant temporibus
suis : Et dicunt se quosdam sanctos habere. Unum
Deum colunt : Dominum nostrum Jesum Christum
honorant, & credunt vitam æternam, sed minimè bap-

tizantur. Scripturam nostram honorant & reverentur :
Christianos diligunt, & Ecclesias faciunt plures. Homines
benigni & humani satis videntur : barbam non habent, &
in dispositione faciei satis concordant cum Mongalis, non
tamen sunt in facie ita lati. Linguam propriam habent : *Opificiorum*
meliores artifices non inveniuntur in toto mundo in *laus.*
omnibus operibus, in quibus solent homines exercitari.
Terra eorum est opulenta valdè in frumento, vino, auro,
argento, & serico, & omnibus rebus in quibus solet sus-
tentari humana natura. Et cum aliquantulum quievissent,
suos exercitus diviserunt. Unum de filiis Tossuch *Thossuch can*
nomine, quem etiam Can appellabant, id est Imperatorem, *Cyngis filius*
misit cum exercitu contra Comanos, quos multo bello *Comanos de-*
devicit : & postquam vicerat eos in terram suam reverte- *vicit.*
batur. Alium etiam filium misit cum exercitu contra
Indos ; qui minorem Indiam devicerunt. Hii autem *India minor*
nigri sunt Saraceni, qui Æthiopes nuncupantur. Hic *debellata.*
autem exercitus contra Christianos, qui sint in India
majori in pugnam processit. Quod audiens rex terræ
illius, qui vulgò Præsbyter Johannes appellatur, venit con- *Presbyter*
tra eos exercitu congregato. Et faciens imagines cupreas *Joannes :*
hominum in sella posuit super equos, ponens ignem *ejusdem*
interius, & posuit hominem cum folle post imaginem *stratagema.*
cupream super equum : & cum multis imaginibus, &
equis taliter præparatis venerunt contra prædictos ad
pugnandum. Et cum ad locum prælii pervenissent, istos
equos unum juxta unum præmiserunt. Viri autem, qui
erant retro, posuerunt nescio quid super ignem qui erat in
prædicta imagine, & cum follibus fortiter sufflaverunt.
Unde factum est, quod de fumo illo aer est denigratus.
Et tunc super Tartaros jecerunt sagittas, ex quibus multi *Victoria de*
interfecti & vulnerati fuerunt. Et sic cum confusione eos *Tartaris.*
de finibus suis ejecerunt : Et nunquam audivimus, quod
ultra ad eos redierunt. Cum autem per deserta redirent,
in quandam terram venerunt in qua quædam monstra *De monstrosis*
fœmineas imagines habentia repererunt. Et cum inter- *mulieribus &*
rogassent eas per multos interpretes ubi essent viri terræ *canibus mon-*
illius, responderunt quod in illa terra quæcunque fœminæ *strosa narratio.*

nascebantur, habebant formam humanam : Masculi verò
formam caninam. Et dum moram protraherent in terra
prædicta, Canes in alia parte convenerunt in unum : Et
dum esset hyems asperrima, se omnes projecerunt in
aquam : & post hæc incontinenti in pulverem movebantur,
& ita pulvis admixtus aquæ super eos congelavit : & dum

Glacies. sæpè hoc fecissent, glacies densa facta est super eos : Unde
cum magno impetu cum Tartaris convenerunt ad pugnam.
At illi quum sagittas super eos jactabant, ac si super
lapides sagitassent, retro sagittæ redibant : Alia etiam
arma eorum in nullo eos lædere potuerunt. Canes verò
insultum facientes in eos morsibus vulneraverunt, multos
etiam occiderunt, & ita ejecerunt eos de finibus suis. Et

Burutabeth dum reverteretur exercitus ille, venit ad terram Buruta-
regio. beth, quos bello vicerunt : qui sunt Pagani. Qui consuetudinem mirabilem imo potius miserabilem habent.
Quia cum aliquis patrum suorum humanæ naturæ debitum
exsolvit, omnem congregant parentelam, & comedunt

Incolarum eum. Isti pilos in barba non habent : immo quoddam
mores. ferrum in manibus portant, cum quo barbam semper
depilant, si fortè aliquis crinis crescit in ipsa : & multum
etiam deformes sunt. Inde exercitus ille revertebatur in
terram suam. Cyngis can etiam eo tempore quo divisit
exercitus illos, misit in expeditione contra Orientem per

Terra Kergis terram Kergis, quos bello non vicit : & usque ad Caspios
Orientalis. montes pervenit, montes autem illi sunt de lapide adamantino. Unde eorum sagittas & arma ferrea ad se traxerunt.
Homines inter Caspios montes conclusos viderunt, qui
jam montem fregerunt : sed nubes quædam erat posita
ante ipsos, ad quam accedere non poterant ullo modo, quia
statim moriebantur, cum perveniebant ad illam. Sed
antequam pervenirent ad prædictum montem plusquam

Nota iter per mensem vastam solitudinem transierunt. Inde pro-
duorum men- cedentes adhuc contra Orientem plusquam per mensem
sium versus per magnum desertum iverunt. Et pervenerunt ad quan-
Orientem. dam terram, ubi viderunt vias tritas, sed nullum hominem
poterant invenire. Sed tantum quæsiverunt per terram,
quod invenerunt hominem cum uxore sua ; quos ante

Cyngis can adduxerunt. Et cum interrogasset, ubi essent homines terræ illius, responderunt quod in terra sub montibus habitarent. At Cyngis can retenta uxore misit *Troglodytæ.* virum illum cum nunciis suis mandans hominibus illis ut [I. 29.] venirent ad mandatum ipsius. Illi verò euntes ad eos, narraverunt omnia quæ Cyngis can mandaverat. Qui responderunt quod tali die venirent ad mandatum suum faciendum. Medio vero tempore congregaverunt se per vias occultas sub terra, & venerunt contra istos ad pugnandum : & irruentes subitò super eos plurimos occiderunt. At illi, Cyngis can videlicet & sui fugam ineuntes, terram exierunt prædictam. Illos tamen homines, virum scilicet & mulierem secum duxerunt, qui usque ad mortem in terra Tartarorum fuerunt. Interrogati verò quare sub *Videtur hic* terra habitarent, dixerunt quod uno tempore anni quum *sonitus fieri,* sol oritur, tantus sonitus est, quod homines nulla ratione *glaciei, &* possunt sustinere. Immo etiam tunc percutiebant in *nivium de* organis & tympanis, & aliis instrumentis, ut illum sonitum *montibus.* non audirent. Et dum Cyngis de terra illa reverteretur, defecerunt ei victualia, & habebant maximam famem. Et tunc recentia interiora unius bestiæ eos contigit invenire : quæ accipientes, depositis tamen stercoribus decoxerunt ; & coram Cyngis can portantes cum suis illa comedit. Et *Cyngis lex.* ex hoc statutum fuit ab eo, ut nec sanguis, nec interiora, nec aliquid de bestia quod manducari potest, exceptis stercoribus, projiciatur. Et deinde in terram propriam est reversus : & ibidem leges & statuta multiplicia fecit, quæ Tartari non violabiliter observant. Ex quibus tantum duo dicemus. Unum est, quod quicunque in superbia erectus, propria authoritate sine electione principum esse voluerit imperator, sine ulla miseratione debet occidi. Unde ante electionem ipsius Cuynch propter hoc unus de principibus, nepos ipsius Cyngis can fuit occisus. Volebat enim sine electione regnare. Aliud statutum est, quod sibi debent subjugare omnem terram : nec cum aliqua gente debent pacem habere, nisi prius eis subdatur, quo usque veniat tempus occisionis eorum. Debent enim occidi, ut prophetatum est eis : Et illi qui evadere poterunt, ut dicunt, debent illam legem tenere quam tenent alii, qui eos bello devincunt. Statuit etiam quod per millenarios, & centenarios & Decanos debeat eorum exercitus ordinari.

Interitus. Post hoc ab ictu tonitrui est occisus, peractis suis ordinationibus & statutis. Hic autem habuit quatuor filios:

Liberi. Unus vocabatur Occoday, secundus Tossuch can, tertius Thaaday : & nomen quarti ignoramus. Isti quatuor filii cum aliis majoribus qui tunc erant, primum filium videlicet Occoday elegerunt imperatorem, filii autem istius

Nepotes. Occoday Cuyne, qui nunc est imperator, Cocthen & Cyrenen. Et si plures habuerit filios ignoramus. Filii autem Tossuch can Bati : iste est ditior & potentior post imperatorem : Ordu, iste est senior omnium ducum : Syban, Bora, Bercuthanth : aliorum filiorum Tossuch can nomina ignoramus. Filii Thaaday sunt Burin & Chadan, nomina aliorum filiorum nescimus. Alterius autem filii Cyngis can, cujus nomen nescimus, filiorum nomina sunt hæc. Unus vocatur Mengu, cujus mater est Seroctan. Ista domina inter omnes Tartaros, excepta matre imperatoris, est magis nominata : & potentior est omnibus excepto Bati. Alius vocatur Becas. Alios filios habuit

Duces. plures, sed eorum nomina ignoramus. Hæc sunt ducum nomina. Ordu : iste fuit in Polonia & in Hungaria : Bati, Cathan, Syban, Bureth. Omnes isti fuerunt in Hungaria, Cyrpodan, iste est adhuc ultra mare contra Soldanum Damasci. Isti remanserunt in terra : Mangu, Cuthen, Syrennen, Hybilay, Seremum, Synocur, Thuatamur, Cyragay, Sybedey, senex quidam miles inter eos, Bora, Berca, Mauci, Choranca : sed iste inter alios est minimus. Alii verò duces sunt plures, sed eorum nomina ignoramus.

Imperatoris Tartarorum servile in omnes imperium. Imperator autem Tartarorum habet mirabile dominium super omnes. Nullus audet in aliqua parte morari, nisi ipse assignet ei. Ipse autem assignat ubi maneant duces : millenarii centenariis, Centenarii decanis. Insuper quicquid præcipitur in quocunque tempore, quocunque loco, sive ad bellum, sive ad mortem, sive ad vitam, sine ulla contradictione obediunt. Etiam si petit filiam virginem

vel sororem, sine contradictione dant ei. Aut singulis
annis, aut intermissis aliquibus annis virgines colligit ex
omnibus finibus Tartarorum. Si ipse vult sibi retinere
aliquas retinet: alias dat suis hominibus, sicut videtur ei
expedire. Nuncios quoscunque, quotcunque & ubicunque
transmittit, oportet quod dent ei sine mora equos subdititios & expensas. Undecunque venerint ei tributa vel
nuncii, oportet quod equi, currus, & expensæ similiter
dentur eis. Nuncii qui veniunt aliunde in magna miseria
sunt in victu pariter & vestitu : quia expensæ viles sunt
& paucæ : & maximè cum veniunt ad principes, & ibi   *Inhumanitas*
debent moram contrahere. Tunc ita parum datur decem   *erga Legatos.*
hominibus, quod inde vix possint vivere duo. Nec etiam
in curiis principum, nec in via datur eis comedere, nisi
semel in die, & satis parum. Insuper si aliquæ injuriæ
sibi fiunt, conqueri de facili minimè possunt. Unde eos
oportet illa patienter portare. Insuper multa tam à principibus, quam ab aliis nationibus et minoribus ab eis ex-
iguntur : & si non daretur, vili pendunt eos, immò quasi
pro nihilo habent eos. Et si à magnis viris mittuntur,
nolunt ab eis modicum munus habere : sed dicunt: A
magno homine venistis, & cur modicum datis? & accipere
dedignantur. Et si nuncii benè volunt facere facta sua,
oportet eos dare majora. Idcirco magnam partem rerum,
quæ nobis à fidelibus erant datæ, oportuit nos de necessitate muneribus dare. Et sciendum, quod ita omnia sunt [I. 30.]
in manu Imperatoris prædicti, quod nemo audet dicere,
hoc est meum vel illius ; sed omnia sunt Imperatoris, res,
jumenta, & homines. Et super hoc etiam nuper emanavit
Imperatoris statutum. Idem dominium per omnia habent
duces super homines suos. Divisi enim sunt homines
Tartari, videlicet etiam alii inter duces. Nuncii etiam
ducum, quocunque eos transmittunt, & homines tam
Imperatoris quàm alii omnes equos subdititios & expensas,
& qui equos custodiant, & etiam nunciis serviant sine
contradictione dare tenentur. Imperatori autem jumenta
ut habeat ex eis lac ad annum vel ad duos, vel ad tres,
sicut placuerit ei, tam duces quàm alii pro redditu dare

tenentur. Et homines ducum idem facere tenentur dominis suis. Inter eos enim nullus est liber. Et ut breviter dicam, Quicquid Imperator & Duces volunt, & quantum volunt de rebus suis accipiunt. De personis etiam eorum disponunt per omnia, sicut volunt. Mortuo Imperatore, sicut superius dictum est, convenerunt Duces *Occoday secun-* & elegerunt Occoday filium Cyngis can prædicti Impera-
dus Imperator torem. Qui habito consilio principum divisit exercitus.
Tartarorum. Bati, qui in secundo gradu attinebat ei, misit contra Altisoldanum, & contra terram Biserminorum. Hii erant Saraceni, & Comanicum loquebantur. Et cum intrasset terram illorum pugnavit contra eos, & bello eos sibi
‖ *Barthra* subjecit. Quædam autem civitas quæ ‖ Barthra dicitur,
civitas vel diu restitit ei, fecerant enim foveas multas in circuitu
Barchin. civitatis & operuerant illas; & quando illi veniebant cadebant in foveas. Unde non potuerunt capere civitatem, donec illas foveas replessent. Homines autem de quadam
‖ *Vel Sarguit.* civitate quæ vocatur ‖ Iakint hæc audientes exierunt obviam eis, se sponte in manus eorum tradentes: unde civitas eorum non erat destructa, sed plures eorum occiderunt, & alios transtulerunt. Et accepto spolio civitatis, ipsam aliis hominibus repleverunt. Et venerunt contra
Orna super civitatem quæ vocatur Orna. Ista civitas erat nimium
Don fluvium. populosa: Christiani ibi erant plures; Gazari videlicet, Rutheni, & Alani, & alii: nec non & Saraceni. Saracenorum enim erat dominium civitatis. Hæc autem civitas erat divitiis multum plena. Est enim posita super fluvium qui vocatur Don, qui intrat in mare. Unde est quasi portus: & forum maximum habebant de illa civitate alii Saraceni. Et cum non possent aliter devincere, præciderunt fluvium, qui currebat per civitatem, & illam cum rebus omnibus submerserunt. Quo facto: postea intraverunt terram Tortorum, qui similiter sunt Pagani: quam devincentes, iverunt contra Russiam, & fecerunt magnam stragem in terra Russiæ, civitates & castra destruxerunt,
Kiovia civitas. & homines occiderunt: etiam Kioviam quæ erat Metropolis Russiæ obsederunt: & cum diu obsedissent, illam ceperunt, & occiderunt homines civitatis. Inde procedentes

pugnando destruxerunt totam Russiam. De Russia autem & Comania processerunt duces prædicti, & pugnaverunt contra Hungaros & Polonos. Ex quibus Tartaris in Polonia & in Hungaria plures interfecti fuerunt. Et si non fugissent, sed viriliter restitissent Hungari exivissent Tartari de finibus suis : quia tunc habuerunt timorem, quod omnes fugere attentabant. Sed Bati vaginato gladio in faciem eis restitit, dicens : Nolite fugere : quia si fugitis nullus evadet : Et si debemus mori, moriamur omnes : quia futurum est, ut Cyngis can prædixit, quod interfici debeamus : Et si nunc est tempus, sustineamus. Et sic animati sunt & remanserunt, & Hungariam destruxerunt. Inde revertentes iverunt in terram Morduanorum, qui sunt Pagani, & bello devicerunt. Inde procedentes contra Bileros, id est, Bulgariam magnam, & ipsam destruxerunt omnino. Inde procedentes ad Aquilonem adhuc contra Bascart, id est, Hungariam magnam, & eos etiam devicerunt. Inde egredientes iverunt ad Aquilonem, & venerunt ad Parossitas qui habent parvos stomachos & os parvulum, nec manducant, sed decoquunt carnes : quibus decoctis ponunt se inter fumum & ollam, & recipiunt fumum, & de hoc solo reficiuntur : Sed etiamsi aliquid manducant, hoc valdè modicum est. Inde procedentes venerunt ad Samogedos. Hii autem homines tantùm de venationibus vivunt : tabernacula & vestes habent tantummodo de bestiarum pellibus. Inde ultra procedentes venerunt ad quandam terram super Oceanum, ubi invenerunt quædam monstra quæ per omnia formam humanam habebant, sed pedes desinebant in pedes bovinos, & faciem per omnia habebant ut canis : duo verba loquebantur more humano & tertio latrabant ut canis : & sic per intervalla temporum latratum interponebant : tum ad naturam suam redibant : & sic intelligi poterat quod dicebant : Inde redierunt in Comaniam, & usque nunc quidam ex eis morantur ibidem. Cyrpodan vero eodem tempore misit Occoday can cum exercitu ad meridiem contra Kergis, quos etiam bello devicit. Hii autem homines sunt pagani, qui pilos in barba non habent. Quorum consuetudo est talis. Cum

Morduanorum terra.

Bulgaria magna.

Hungaria magna.

Parossitæ.

Samogedi.

Oceanus Septentrionalis. Similes Frobisheri hominibus.

Expeditio Cyrpodanis.

pater moritur alicujus, præ dolore quasi unam corrigiam in signum lamenti ab aure usque ad aurem de facie sua levant. Quibus devictis, ad meridiem ivit contra Armenos. Sed cum per deserta transiret, etiam quædam monstra effigiem humanam habentia invenerunt: sed non nisi unum brachium cum manu in medio pectoris, & unum pedem habebant: & duo sagittarunt cum uno arcu, & isti ita fortiter currebant, quod equi eos investigare non poterant. Currebant enim saltando super illum unum pedem, & cum essent fessi taliter eundo, ibant super manum & pedem, removendo se quasi rota; & sic cum essent fessi iterum currebant secundum modum priorem: aliquos tamen occidebant ex eis. Inde procedentes venerunt in Armeniam, quam bello vicerunt, & partem Georgiæ: & alia pars venit ad mandatum eorum; & quadraginta millia yperperorum singulis annis dederunt, & adhuc faciunt idem. Inde procedentes ad terram Soldani Deurum, qui erat satis magnus & potens, cum eo pugnaverunt & devicerunt. Inde procedentes ultra debellando & vincendo usque ad terram Soldani Halapiæ & nunc terram illam impugnant: nec postea usque in hodiernum diem in terram suam fuerunt reversi. Alius exercitus ivit contra terram Calif de Baldach, quam sibi etiam subdiderunt: Et quadraginta bisantia exceptis Baldachinis & aliis muneribus omni die dant pro tributo: Et omni anno pro Calif, ut ad eos veniat, nuncios mittunt: qui cum tributo munera magna mittit, rogans ut eum supportent. Ipse vero imperator munera accipit, & nihilominus ut veniat mittit pro eo.

Qualiter Tartari se habent in præliis. Cap. 6.

DIcto de imperio, dicendum est hoc modo de bello. Primo de ordinatione acierum. Secundo de armis. Tertio de astutiis in congressione, quarto de crudelitate quam faciunt in captivos. Quinto de oppugnatione castrorum & civitatum. Sexto de perfidia quam exercent cum hiis qui se reddunt eisdem. De ordinatione acierum dicemus hoc modo. Cyngis can ordinavit, ut decem

hominibus præponeretur unus : & ille secundum nos
appellatur Decanus. Decem autem Decanis præponeretur
unus, qui centenarius nuncupatur : Decem vero Centenariis
præponeretur unus qui millenarius nuncupatur : decem
millenariis præponeretur unus, & ille numerus vocatur
tenebre apud eos. Cuncto vero expercitui præponuntur
duo duces vel tres, ita tamen quod habeant respectum ad
unum. Cum autem omnes sunt in bello si de decem
hominibus fugit unus vel duo, vel tres, vel etiam plures,
omnes occiduntur. Et ut breviter dicam, nisi communiter
cedant, omnes qui fugiunt occiduntur. Item si unus vel
duo aut plures audacter ad pugnam accedunt, & decem alii
non sequuntur, etiam occiduntur. Item si unus de decem
vel plures capiuntur, & alii socii sui non liberant eos, etiam
occiduntur. Duo arcus vel tres, vel unum bonum ad minus,
& tres pharetras magnas plenas de sagittis & unam
securim, & funes ad machinas trahendas habere debet
unusquisque. Divites autem habent gladios acutos in fine,
ex una tantum parte incidentes, & aliquantulum curvos :
& habent equum armatum, crura etiam tecta. Galeas &
loricas quidam habent de corio in hunc modum formatas.
Habent quasdam corrigias de bove ad latitudinem unius
manus, & bituminant tres vel quatuor simul, & ligant
illas corrigiolis vel cordis. In corrigia superiori ponunt
cordulas in fine ; in inferiori ponunt in medio, & sic
faciunt usque ad finem. Unde quum se inclinant in
inferiores, corrigiæ superiores ascendunt & sic duplicantur
super corpus, vel triplicantur. De coopertura equi faciunt
quinque partes : ex una parte faciunt unam, ex alia parte
faciunt aliam, quam partem ducunt à cauda usque ad caput :
quæ ligantur ad sellam, & post sellam in dorso & etiam in
collo, super renes etiam partem aliam ponunt, ubi duæ
partium ligaturæ junguntur : in qua pecia faciunt unum
foramen, per quod caudas exponunt : & ante pectus ponunt
etiam unam : quæ omnes protenduntur usque ad crurium
juncturas. Et ante frontem laminam ferream ponunt, quæ
ex utraque parte colli partibus prædictis ligatur. Lorica
vero etiam quatuor partes habet, una pars protenditur à

fœmore usque ad collum ; sed est facta secundum dispo-
sitionem humani corporis : quia ante pectus est stricta : in
rotundum obvolvitur circa corpus à brachiis inferius :
Super humeros autem retro ad renes habent aliam peciam,
quæ protenditur a collo usque ad aliam peciam, quæ
revolvitur circa corpus : Super humeros autem istæ duæ
peciæ anterior videlicet & posterior, ad duas laminas
ferreas quæ sunt in utroque humero fibulis connectuntur.
Et in utroque brachio unam habent peciam, quæ ab
humero protenduntur usque ad manus, quæ etiam inferius
sunt aptæ. Et in utroque crure unam habent peciam :
quæ peciæ omnes fibulis conjunguntur. Galea autem
superius est ferrea. Sed illud quod protegit in circuitu
collum & gulam de corio fit. Et omnes istæ peciæ de
corio sunt formatæ secundum modum superius annotatum.
Quidam autem omnia quæ superius diximus habent de
ferro in hunc modum formata. Unam laminam tenuem ad
latitudinem unius digiti faciunt, & ad longitudinem palmæ
unius. Et in hunc modum faciunt laminas multas : & in
unaquaque lamina octo foramina parvula faciunt, & interius
tres corrigias strictas & fortes ponunt, & laminas unam
super aliam ponunt, quasi ascendendo per gradus : &
ligant laminas prædictas ad corrigias tenuibus corrigiolis,
[I. 32.] quas mittunt per foramina superius annotata : Et in
superiori parte consuunt corrigiolam unam, ut laminæ
prædictæ bene & firmiter cohæreant sibi. Et faciunt ex
laminis quasi corrigiam unam, & postea ligant per pecias
per omnia, sicut superius dictum est. Et ista faciunt tam
ad equorum quam ad hominum armaturas. Et faciunt illa
ita lucere, quod potest homo in eis faciem suam videre.
Aliqui eorum lanceas habent : & in fine ferri lanceæ unum
habent uncum, cum quo trahunt hominem de sella si
possunt. Longitudo sagittarum est duorum pedum &
unius palmæ, & duorum digitorum. Et quia diversi sunt
pedes, mensuram pedum geometricam ponimus. Duodecim
grana hordei pollicis transversio est. Sexdecim pollices
transversi faciunt unum geometricum pedem. Ferramenta
sagittarum sunt acutissima, & ex utraque parte incidentia

quasi gladius biceps, & semper portant limas juxta pharetram ad acuendum sagittas. Ferramenta prædicta caudam
habent acutam ad longitudinem unius digiti, quam imponunt in lignum. Scutum habent de viminibus vel de
virgulis factum. Sagittas habent alias ad sagittandum aves
bestias & homines inermes ad trium digitorum latitudinem.
Sagittas alias habent diversimodas ad aves & bestias sagit-
tandas. Quum ad bellum procedere volunt præcursores
præmittunt, qui nihil secum portant præter filtra sua,
equos & arma. Isti nihil rapiunt, domos non comburunt,
bestias non occidunt : Sed tamen homines vulnerant
& mortificant, & si non possunt aliud, mittunt in fugam ;
multo libentius tamen occidunt, quam fugant, post istos
sequitur exercitus, qui cuncta quæ invenit accipit, &
homines etiam, si inveniri possunt, accipiunt & occidunt.
Quum autem ad flumina perveniunt, hoc modo transeunt *Mos tranandi*
illa etiamsi sunt magna. Majores unum rotundum & *flumina.*
leve corium habent, in quo in summitate per circuitum
crebras faciunt ansas, in quibus funem imponunt, &
stringunt ita quod in circuitu faciunt quendam ventrem,
quem replent vestibus, & aliis rebus, & fortissime comprimunt ad invicem : post hoc in medio ponunt sellas
& alias res duriores : homines autem in medio sedent : &
ligant ad caudam equi navem hanc taliter præparatam, &
unum hominum qui equum regat faciunt pariter cum equo
ante natare : vel habent aliquando duos remos, & cum illis
remigant ultra aquam, & sic transeunt fluvium. Equos
vero pellunt in aqua, & unus homo juxta unum equum,
quem regit, natat : & alii equi illum sequuntur. Et sic
transeunt aquas & flumina magna. Alii vero pauperiores
unam bursam de corio bene consutam unusquisque tenetur
habere : in qua bursa vel in quo sacco vestes & omnes res
suas imponunt; & in summitate saccum fortissime ligant,
& suspendunt ad caudam equi, & transeunt, ut supradictum est. Sciendum est, quod cum vident hostes tunc
vadunt ad eos, & unusquisque jacit tres sagittas vel quatuor
contra adversarios : Et si vident quod eos superare non
possunt, retro gradiuntur ad suos : Et hoc faciunt in

fraudem, ut adversarii eos sequantur ad loca ubi insidias paraverunt : Et si inimici eorum sequuntur ad prædictas insidias, circundant eos & sic vulnerant & occidunt. Item si vident quod magnus exercitus est contra eos, aliquando divertunt ab eo per unam dietam vel duas, & aliam partem terræ invadunt & spoliant : & interficiunt homines, & terram destruunt & devastant. Et si vident quod hoc etiam facere non possunt, cedunt retro ad decem vel duodecim dietas : aliquando etiam morantur in loco tuto, quousque adversariorum exercitus separetur, & tunc furtim veniunt, & depopulantur totam terram. In bellis etiam astutissimi sunt : quia jam per quadraginta annos & amplius cum aliis gentibus dimicarunt. Cum autem volunt ad pugnam accedere, omnes acies ordinant sicut deberent pugnare. Duces sive principes exercitus bellum non intrant, sed stant à longe contra inimicorum exercitum, & juxta se habent pueros in equis & mulieres & equos. Et faciunt aliquando imagines hominum, & ponunt super equos. Hoc ideo faciunt, ut multitudo magna bellantium esse credantur. Contra faciem equorum unam aciem captivorum & aliarum gentium quæ sunt inter eos transmittunt : & forsitan aliqui Tartari vadunt cum eis. Alias acies fortiorum hominum longe mittunt à dextris & à sinistris, ut non videantur ab adversariis suis : & sic circundant adversarios & colligunt in medium, & pugnare incipiunt ex omni parte. Et cum sunt aliquando pauci, putantur ab adversariis qui circundati sunt, esse multi. Et maxime cum videant illos, qui sunt cum duce vel principe exercitus pueros & mulieres & equos, & homines fictos, ut dictum est supra : quos credunt esse pugnatores : & per hoc terrentur & confunduntur. Et si forte adversarii bene pugnant, faciunt eis viam ut fugiant : & statim cum fugere incipiunt, ab invicem separati insequuntur eos, & plures tunc occidunt fuga, quàm mortificare possent in bello. Sciendum tamen est, quod si aliud possunt, non libenter congrediuntur, sed homines & equos sagittis vulnerant & occidunt. Munitiones in hunc modum expugnant. Si est talis munitio ipsam circundant, immo aliquando ita

82

sepiunt, ut nullus ingredi vel exire possit. Expugnant
fortissime machinis & sagittis : & nec die nec nocte
cessant a prælio, ut illi qui sunt in munitionibus non
quiescant. Ipsi Tartari quiescunt : quia acies dividunt &
una succedit alteri in pugnam ut non nimium fatigentur.
Et si eam taliter habere non possunt græcum projiciunt
ignem. Imo solent aliquando accipere arvinam hominum
quos occidunt, & liquefactum projiciunt super domos :
Et ubicunque venit ignis super pinguedinem illam, quasi [I. 33.]
inextinguibiliter ardet. Et si ita non prævalent, & si
civitas illa vel castrum habeat flumen, obstruunt illud, vel
faciunt alium alveum & submergunt illam munitionem si
possunt. Si autem non possunt suffodiunt illam, & sub
terra armati in ipsam ingrediuntur. Et cum jam intraverunt, una pars ignem imponit ut comburatur : & alia
pars cum illius munitionis hominibus pugnat. Si autem
nec sic illam vincere possunt, castrum vel munitionem
suam faciunt contra illam, ut ab inimicorum jaculis non
graventur, & contra illam multo tempore jacent : nisi forte
exterius adjutorium exercitus qui pugnat cum eis adhibeat,
& vi removeant ipsos. Sed cum jacent ante munitionem *Punica fides.*
blande eis loquuntur, & multa promittunt, ad hoc ut se in
eorum manus tradant : Et si illi se eis tradiderint, dicunt :
Exite, ut secundum morem nostrum vos muneremus. Et
cum illi ad eos exeunt, quærunt qui sunt artifices inter
eos, & illos reservant : alios autem, exceptis illis quos
volunt habere pro servis cum securi occidunt. Et si
aliquibus aliis parcunt, ut dictum est, nobilibus & honestis
nunquam parcunt. Et si fortè aliquo casu contingente
reservant aliquos nobiles ; nec prece nec precio ultra de
captivitate possunt exire. In bellis autem quoscunque
capiunt occidunt, nisi forte velint aliquos reservare ut
habeant eos pro servis. Occidendos autem dividunt per
centenarios, ut cum bipenni interficiantur ab eis. Ipsi vero
post hoc dividunt captivos, & unicuique servo ad inter-
ficiendum dant decem aut plures vel pauciores, secundum
quod majoribus placet.

De terris quas eorum dominio subjugarunt.
Cap. 7.

SCripto quomodo pugnant, dicendum est de terris, quas eorum dominio subjugarunt. De quo isto modo scribemus. Primo dicemus quomodo faciunt cum hominibus pacem. Secundo de terrarum nominibus quas sibi subdiderunt. Tertio de tyrannide quam exercent in eis. Quarto de terris quæ viriliter restiterunt. Sciendum est quod cum nullis hominibus faciunt pacem, nisi subdentur eis : quia, ut dictum est supra, Cyngis can habent mandatum, ut cunctas si possunt sibi subjiciant nationes. Et hæc sunt illa quæ petunt ab eis, ut vadant cum eis in exercitu contra omnem hominem quando placet, & ut dent decimam de omnibus tam de hominibus, quàm de rebus. Computant enim decem, & unum accipiunt. De puellis faciunt illud idem, quos in terram eorum deducunt & tenent eos pro servis : reliquos numerant & ordinant secundum morem. Sed quando plene habent dominium super eos, si aliquid promiserunt eis nihil observant : sed quascunque possunt congrue occasiones inveniunt contra eos. Nam cum essemus in Russia, missus fuit Saracenorum ex parte Cuynthcan ut dicebatur & Bati : & præfectus ille a quolibet homine qui habebat tres pueros unum accipiebat : & quicunque viri non habebant uxores, illos deducebant, & faciebant de mulieribus etiam illud idem quæ viros legitimos non habebant. Pauperes etiam qui mendicando suum victum quærebant similiter deportabunt. Reliquos autem secundum eorum consuetudinem numeravit, præcipiens ut unusquisque tam parvus quam magnus, & infans unius diei, sive pauper sive dives esset, tale *Ursi albi.* tributum præberet : ut scilicet daret unum pellem albi ursi, & unum nigrum castorem, & unum Zabulum, & unam nigram pellem cujusdam animalis quod in terra latibulum habet, cujus nomen nescio in latinum transferre, ‖ *Vel illic.* sed Teutonice dicitur ‖ illit : Poloni autem & Rutheni *Dochon.* appellant illam Dochon : & unam nigram pellem vulpinam. Et quicunque ista non dat, inter Tartaros debet duci, & in

84

eorum redigi servitutem. Mitunt etiam pro principibus
terrarum, ut ad eos veniant sine mora : & cum venerint,
debitum honorem nullum recipiunt, sed habentur ut aliæ
viles personæ : & oportet ut eis munera magna præsentent,
tam ducibus quàm uxoribus eorum, & officialibus, millenariis & centenariis. Imo omnes generaliter, & ipsi
etiam servi ab eis cum magna importunitate munera
quærunt : Et non solum ab ipsis, sed etiam à nunciis
eorum cum mittuntur. Aliquibus etiam inveniunt occasiones ut eos occidant. Sicut de Michaele & aliis actum
est. Aliquos vero alliciunt, quos permittunt redire.
Aliquos etiam potionibus perimunt vel veneno. Eorum
enim intentio est, ut ipsi soli dominentur in terra. Idcirco
quærunt occasiones contra nobiles, ut eos occidant. Ab
illis vero quos redire permittunt petunt eorum filios aut
fratres, quos ulterius nunquam dimittunt. Sicut factum
est de filio Jeroslai, & de quodam duce Alanorum, & aliis
plurimis. Et si moritur pater vel frater sive hæres, filium
vel fratrem nunquam dimittunt : immo illius principatum
totaliter accipiunt sibi. Sicut de quodam Solangorum *Solangi.*
vidimus esse factum. Baschathos suos ponunt in terris *Bascha, vox*
eorum quos redire permittunt, quibus oportet ut ad nutum *Tartarica, qua*
tam duces quàm alii debeant obedire. Et si homines *utuntur Turci.*
alicujus civitatis vel terræ non faciunt quod volunt, isti
Baschathi imponunt eis, quod sunt Tartaris infideles : &
sic civitatem illam vel terram destruunt, & homines qui
sunt in ea occidunt, per manum validam Tartarorum, qui
ex mandato principis illius cui obedit terra illa veniunt eis
nescientibus, & subito irruunt super eos : sicut nuper
contigit cum in terra Tartarorum essemus de quadam [I. 34.]
civitate. Quod ipsummet de Ruthenis fecerunt in terra
Comanorum. Et non solum princeps Tartarorum qui
terram usurpavit, sed præfectus ipsius, & quicunque
Tartarus per civitatem illam sive terram transit quasi
dominatur eidem, & maxime qui major est apud eos. In
super aurum & argentum, & alia quæ volunt & quando
libet ad imperatorem vadant Tartarorum ad placitandum.
Sicut nuper contigit de duobus filiis regis Georgiæ. Unus

enim erat legitimus, & alter de adulterio natus, qui vocabatur David : legitimus autem Melic vocabatur. Filio adulteræ terræ partem relinquebat pater. Alius vero, qui junior erat, veniebat cum matre ad Tartarorum imperatorem, pro eo quod David prædictus ad ipsum iter arripuerat veniendi. Mater alterius scilicet Melic regina Georgiæ, per quam maritus tenebat regnum, quia per fœminas illud regnum tenebatur, mortua fuit in via. Illi autem cum venerunt dederunt maxima munera : & maxime legitimus filius, qui repetebat terram quam reliquerat pater filio suo David, cum non deberet habere, quia adulteræ filius erat. Ille vero respondit : Licet sim filius concubinæ, peto tamen ut fiat mihi justitia secundum legem Tartarorum, qui nullam differentiam faciunt inter filios legitimæ & ancillæ : unde fuit data sententia contra filium legitimum, ut ille Davidi qui major erat subesset, & terram haberet quiete & pacifice, quam dederat ei pater : & sic donaria quæ dederat, & causam quam contra fratrem suum David habuerat, amisit. Ab illis etiam nationibus quæ longe sunt ab eis, & conjunctæ sunt aliis nationibus quas aliquo modo timent, quæ non sunt eis subjectæ, tributum accipiunt & quasi misericorditer agunt cum eis, ut non adducant exercitum super eos, vel etiam ut alii non terreantur, se tradere eis. Sicut factum est de Obesis sive Georgianis, a quibus quinquaginta vel quadraginta millia, ut dictum est, yperperorum sive Bysantiorum accipiunt pro tributo : aliâs ad hoc in pace esse permittunt. Tamen, secundum quod intelleximus ab eis, rebellare proponunt.

Terrarum nomina quas vicerunt sunt hæc. Kytai, Naymani, Solangi, Kara Kytai, sive nigri Kytai, Comania, Tumat, Voyrat, Caraniti, Huyur, Soboal, Merkiti, Meniti, Baryhryur, Gosmit, Saraceni, Bisermini, Turcomani, Byleri, magna Bulgaria, Baschare, magna Hungaria, Kergis, Colona, Thorati, Buritabeth, Parossiti, Sassi, Jacobiti, Alani, sive Assi, Obesi sive Georgiani, Nestoriani, Armeni, Cangiti, Comani Brutachi, qui sunt Judæi, Mordui, Torci, *Samogedi* Gazari, Samogedi, Perses, Thoas, India minor sive *aquilonares.* Æthiopia, Yrchasi, Rutheni, Baldach, Sarthi : Aliæ terræ

sunt plures, sed earum nomina ignoramus. Vidimus etiam
viros & mulieres fere de omnibus terris supra nominatis.
Hæc autem sunt nomina Terrarum quæ eis viriliter restiterunt, nec sunt adhuc subditæ eis, India magna, Mangia ; *Mangia.*
Quædam pars Alanorum, Quædam pars Kytaorum, Sayi.
Quandam enim civitatem Sayorum prædictorum obsede-
derunt & debellare tentaverunt. At ipsi fecerunt machinas
contra machinas eorum, & Tartarorum machinas omnes
fregerunt, nec civitati appropinquare poterant ad pugnam
contra machinas & balistas. Tandem unam viam sub terra
fecerunt, & prosiluerunt in civitatem, & alii tentabant
incendere civitatem, alii pugnabant. Homines autem
civitatis unam partem populi ad extinguendum ignem
posuerunt, & alia pars fortiter pugnabat cum hiis qui intraverunt civitatem, & multos occiderunt ex eis, & alios
vulneraverunt, compellentes eos ad suos redire. At ipsi
videntes quod nihil possent facere, & multi homines
morerentur, recesserunt ab eis. In terra Saracenorum &
aliorum ubi sunt quasi inter eos domini, accipiunt omnes
artifices meliores, & in omnibus operibus suis ponunt.
Alii autem artifices dant eis de opere suo tributum.
Segetes omnes condunt in horreis dominorum : & unicuique unum pondus satis modicum dant in die : nihil
aliud nisi ter in septimana modicum quid de carnibus eis
prebent. Et illi hoc tantum artificibus faciunt qui in civitatibus commorantur. Item quando dominis placet juvenes
omnes accipiunt, & post se cum omnibus famulis suis ire
cogunt : qui de cætero certo sunt numero Tartarorum ;
immo potius de numero captivorum; quia etsi inter ipsos
sunt numerati, non tamen habentur in reverentia sicut
Tartari ; sed habentur pro servis, & ad omnia pericula ut
alii captivi mittuntur. Ipsi enim in bello sunt primi :
Etiam si debet palus vel aqua periculosa transiri, eos
oportet primo vadum tentare. Ipsos est etiam necesse
operari omnia quæ sunt facienda. Ipsi etiam si in aliquo
offendunt, vel si non obediunt ad nutum, ut asini verberantur. Et ut breviter dicam, modicum quid manducant,
& etiam modicum bibunt, & pessime induuntur; nisi forte

aliquid possunt lucrari, nisi sunt aurifabri & alii artifices
boni. Sed aliqui tam malos dominos habent, quod nihil
eis dimittunt, nec habent tempus præ multitudine operum
dominorum, ut sibi aliquid operentur, nisi furentur sibi
tempus, quando forsitan debent quiescere vel dormire. Et
hoc si uxores vel propriam stationem permittuntur habere.
Alii autem qui tenentur in domo pro servis omni miseria
sunt repleti. Vidi enim eos ire in bracis sæpissime, &
toto corpore nudos in maximo solis ardore. Et in hyeme
patiuntur maximum frigus. Vidimus etiam aliquos pedi-
cas & digitos manuum de magno frigore perdidisse. Audivimus etiam alios esse mortuos, vel etiam de magno
algore quasi in omnibus membris inutiles esse factos.

[I. 35.]   Quomodo bello occurratur Tartaris. Cap. 8.

DIcto de terris, quæ obediunt eis, supponendum est
quomodo bello occurratur eisdem. Quod videtur
nobis hoc modo dicendum. Primo scribendum est quid
intendunt. Secundo de armis & ordinatione acierum.
Tertio quomodo occurratur astutiis eorum in congressione.
Quarto de munitione castrorum & civitatum. Quinto
quid faciendum sit de captivis eorum. Intentio Tartarorum
est subjicere sibi totum mundum si possunt. Et de hoc
Cyngischan habent mandatum, sicut superius dictum est.
Idcirco eorum imperator sic in literis suis scribit. Dei
fortitudo, Omnium Imperator. Et in superscriptione
sigilli sui hoc habet.
   Dominus in cœlo, & Cuynch Chan super terram. Dei
fortitudo, omnium hominum imperatoris sigillum. Et
ideo cum nullis hominibus faciunt pacem, ut dictum est,
nisi forte se in eorum manibus tradunt. Et quia excepta
Christianitate nulla est terra in orbe quam timent, idcirco
se ad pugnam præpararunt contra nos. Unde noverint
universi quod nobis existentibus in terra eorum in solenni
curia, quæ jam ex pluribus annis indicta erat, fuimus, ubi
elegerent Cuynch imperatorem in presentia nostra, qui in
lingua eorum dicitur Chan. Qui Cuynch Chan prædictus
erexit cum omnibus principibus vexillum contra ecclesiam

dei & Romanum imperium, & contra omnia regna Christianorum & populos occidentis, nisi forsan facerent ea, quæ mandat Domino Papæ, & potentibus ac omnibus Christianorum populis Occidentis: quod nulla ratione faciendum est: tum propter nimiam servitutem & intolerabilem, quæ est hactenus inaudita, quam vidimus oculis nostris, in quam redigunt omnes gentes sibi subjectas: tum propterea quod nulla in eis est fides: nec potest aliqua gens confidere in verbis eorum: quia quicquid promittunt non observant, quando vident sibi tempora favere: & subdoli sunt in omnibus factis & promissis eorum. Intendunt etiam delere omnes principes, omnes nobiles, omnes milites de terra, ut superius dictum est : sed hoc faciunt subdole & artificiose in subditos suos: Tum etiam quia indignum est quod Christiani subdantur eisdem, propter abominationes eorum, & quia in nihilum redigitur cultus dei, & animæ pereunt, & corpora ultra quam credi possit multitudine affliguntur. In primo quidem sunt blandi, sed postea ut scorpio cruciant & affligunt. Tum quia pauciores sunt numero, & corpore debiliores quam populi Christiani. In prædicta autem curia sunt bellatores & principes & exercitus assignati. De decem hominibus mittuntur tres cum familiis eorum, de omni terra potestatis eorum. Unus exercitus debet intrare per Hungariam: secundus per Poloniam. Veniunt autem pugnaturi continue octodecem annis. Tempus est etiam eis assignatum, In Martio An. Dom. 1247. si de terra sua movebunt. Venient autem in tribus vel in quatuor ‖ annis usque ad Comaniam. De Comania autem insultum facient in terras superius annotatas. Hæc omnia firma sunt & vera, nisi Dominus aliquod impedimentum pro sua gratia faciat eis. Sicut fecit quando venerunt in Hungariam & Poloniam. Debebant enim procedere tunc pro certo triginta annis. Sed interfectus fuit tunc imperator eorum veneno: & propter hoc quieverunt à præliis usque nunc. Sed modo, quia positus est imperator de novo, iterum se de novo ad pugnam incipiunt præparare. Adhoc sciendum est, quod imperator dixit ore suo, quod vellet mittere exercitum in Livoniam & Prussiam. Et

‖ Forte mensibus.

Tartari proponunt invadere Livoniam & Prussiam.

quoniam omnem terram volunt delere vel in servitutem redigere, quæ servitus est intolerabilis nostræ genti, ut superius dictum est: Occurrendum est igitur eis in bello. Sed si una provincia non vult alteri opem ferre, terra illa delebitur contra quam pugnant, & cum illis hominibus quos capiunt pugnabunt contra aliam terram; & in acie erunt primi. Si male pugnant occidentur ab eis: Si autem bene, ipsos cum promissis adulationibus tenent: & etiam ut ab ipsis non fugiant promittunt eis quod facient eos dominos magnos : & post hoc quando securi esse possunt de ipsis, ut non redeant, faciunt eos infœlicissimos servos. Ac de mulieribus quas volunt in concubinas tenere pro servitiis faciunt illud idem. Et ita cum hominibus devictæ provinciæ destruunt aliam terram. Nec est aliqua provincia quæ per se possit resistere eis: quia de omni terra potestatis eorum, ut dictum est, homines congregant ad bellum. Unde si Christiani seipsos & suam terram, & Christianitatem volunt servare, oportet quod in unum conveniant reges, principes & barones, & terrarum rectores, & mittant de communi consilio homines contra eos ad pugnam, antequam ipsi incipiant in terras diffundi. Quoniam postquam incipiunt spargi per terras, undique homines quærunt, & nullus congrue auxilium alteri potest præbere: quoniam ipsi catervatim undique quærunt homines & occidunt. Et si claudunt se in castris, ponunt tria millia vel quatuor millia hominum contra castrum vel civitatem, qui obsideant eam ; & ipsi nihilominus diffunduntur per terras homines occidentes. Quicunque autem volunt pugnare cum eis, hæc arma debent habere. Arcus bonos & fortes, & balistas, quas multum timent, & sagittas sufficientes: & bonum dolabrum de bono ferro, & scutum cum longo *Temperamen-* manubrio. Ferramenta sagittarum de arcu vel de balista *tum ferri.* debent, ut Tartari, quando sunt calida, temperari in aqua *[I. 36.]* cum sale mixta, ut fortia sint ad penetrandum arma eorum. Gladios & etiam lanceas cum unco, qui valeant ad trahendum eos de sellis: quia de eis facillime cadunt; ac cultellos ac loricas duplicatas; quia illos eorum sagittæ non penetrant: & galeam & arma alia ad protegendum corpus &

JOHN DE PLANO CARPINI

equum ab armis & sagittis eorum. Et si aliqui non sunt
ita bene armati, ut dixi; debent ire post alios ut faciunt
Tartari: & trahere contra eos de armis & sagittis. Nec
debent parcere pecuniæ, quoniam comparent arma, ut possint animas & corpora, libertatem & res alias conservare.
Acies debent ordinari, ut ipsi, per millenarios, centenarios,
& decanos & duces exercitus: qui duces nequaquam debent
prælium intrare, sicut nec duces eorum, sed debent exercitus videre & ordinare: legemquè debent ponere ut simul
incedant ad bellum, sive aliâs, sicut sunt ordinati. Et quicunque relinquit alium sive ad bellum procedentem, sive
pugnantem, vel quicunque fugerit, nisi omnes communiter
cedant, gravissime puniatur: quia tunc pars bellantium sequitur fugientes, & sagittis eorum occidunt, & pars cum
hiis qui remanent pugnant, & sic confunduntur & occiduntur remanentes & fugientes. Similiter quicunque conversus fuerit ad prædam tollendam, antequam omnino sit
exercitus contrariorum devictus, maxima pœna mulctetur.
Talis enim apud Tartaros sine ulla miseratione occiditur.
Locus ad præliandum est eligendus, si fieri potest ut campus sit planus, & possint undique videre: & si possunt
habeant sylvam magnam a tergo vel a latere: ita tamen
quod non possunt intrare inter ipsos & sylvam: nec debent
simul omnes convenire in unum, sed facere acies multas,
& diversas ab invicem, nec tamen multum distantes. Et
contra illos qui post veniunt debent unam aciem mittere
qui eis occurrat. Et si Tartari simulant fugam, non multum vadant post eos, nisi forte quantum possunt videre,
ne forte ipsos ad paratas insidias trahant, sicut facere
solent : Et alia sit parata ad juvandum aciem illam, si
fuerit opportunum. Insuper habeant speculatores ex *Speculatores.*
omni parte, ut videant quando veniant aliæ acies
Tartarorum retro, à dextris & à sinistris: & semper
debent mittere aciem contra aciem quæ eis occurrat. Ipsi
enim semper nituntur concludere adversarios eorum in
medio, unde magnam cautelam debent habere ne hoc
facere possint, quia sic exercitus facillime debellatur.
Omnes acies hoc debent cavere, ne diu currant post eos,

propter insidias quas solent præparare: plus enim fraudulentia quàm fortitudine pugnant. Duces exercitus semper debent esse parati ad mittendum adjutorium, si necesse est, illis qui sunt in pugna, & propter hoc etiam debent vitare nimium cursum post eos: ne forte fatigentur equi eorum ; quoniam nostri multitudinem equorum non habent. Sed Tartari illum quem equitant una die, illum non ascendunt in tribus vel in quatuor diebus post hoc. Unde non curant si fatigentur equi eorum propter multitudinem quam habent. Et si Tartari cedunt, non tamen nostri debent recedere, vel ab invicem separari: quia simulando hoc faciunt, ut exercitus dividatur, & post hoc terram libere ingrediantur, & eam destruant. Debent etiam cavere ut non faciant nimias expensas, ut solent ; ne propter penuriam redire compellantur, & dent Tartaris viam, ut ipsos & alios occidant, & destruant omnem terram ; & propter eorum superfluitatem nomen Domini blasphemetur. Et hoc debent facere diligenter : ut si contingat aliquos pugnatores recedere, quod alii loco eorum succedant. Duces etiam nostri debent die noctéque facere exercitum custodiri, ne repente & subito irruant super ipsos : quia Tartari ut dæmones, multas excogitant iniquitates & artes nocendi : Immo tam de die quam de nocte semper debent esse parati : sed nec spoliati debent jacere nec deliciose ad mensam sedere, ne imparati inveniantur, quia Tartari semper vigilant, ut possint nocere. Homines vero terræ qui Tartaros expectant, vel super se timent venire, occultas foveas debent habere, in quibus sagittas, & alia debent reponere, propter duo : ut videlicet Tartari non possint ea habere ; & si propitius fuerit eis Deus, valeant ea postea invenire ; Eis fugientibus de terra, debent fœnum & stramina comburere, ut equi Tartarorum ad comedendum minus inveniant. Civitates autem & castra si volunt munire, videant prius qualia sint in situ. Situs enim talis debet esse in castris, quod machinis & sagittis expugnari non possit ; & aquam habeant sufficientem & lignum, & si fieri potest, quod introitus & exitus eis tolli non possit : & quod habeant homines sufficientes qui possint vicissim pugnare. Et debent vigilare diligenter ne aliqua astutia possint castrum furari. Expensas ad multos annos debent habere sufficientes : custodiant tamen diligenter illas, & in mensura manducent, quia nesciunt quanto tempore eos in castris oportet esse inclusos. Quum enim incipiunt, tunc multis annis obsident unum castrum. Sic fit hodierna die in terra Alanorum de quodam monte, quem, ut credo, jam obsederunt per duodecem annos ; qui viriliter restiterunt, & multos Tartaros & nobiles occiderunt. Alia autem castra & civitates, quæ talem situm non habent debent fortiter vallari foveis profundis munitis, & muris bene præparatis ; & arcus & sagittas sufficientes : & lapides ac fundas debent habere. Et debent diligenter cavere, quod non permittant Tartaros ponere machinas suas ; & suis machinis debent eos repellere. Et si forte aliquo ingenio vel arte erigunt Tartari machinas suas, debent eas destruere machinis suis si possunt. Balistis etiam, fundis & machinis debent resistere ne civitati appropinquent. Aliàs etiam debent esse parati, ut superius dictum est. De castris & civitatibus, quæ sunt in fluminibus positæ, diligenter debent videre ne possint submergi. Sed ad hoc sciendum est, quod Tartari plus diligunt, quod homines claudant se in civitatibus, quàm quod pugnent cum eis in campo. Dicunt enim eos esse suos porcellos in hara conclusos. Unde ponunt eis custodes, ut supradictum est. Si autem aliqui Tartari de equis suis in bello projiciuntur, statim sunt capiendi : quia cum sunt in terra fortiter sagittant, & equos & homines vulnerant & occidunt. Et si servantur tales, potest esse, quod habeatur pro eis pax perpetua, aut pecunia magna redimantur : quoniam se adinvicem satis diligunt. Sed quomodo Tartari cognoscantur, superius dictum est ubi forma eorum fuit expressa. Tamen quando capiuntur, si debent servari, ne fugiant diligens est custodia adhibenda. Sunt etiam aliæ multæ gentes cum eis, quæ per formam superius annotatam possunt ab ipsis cognosci. Est etiam hoc sciendum, quod multi in exercitu eorum sunt, qui si

Obsidio 12.
annorum.

[I. 37.]

93

viderent tempus, & haberent fiduciam, quod nostri non occiderent eos, ex omni parte exercitus, sicut ipsimet nobis dixerunt, pugnarent cum eis, & plura mala facerent ipsis, quàm alii, qui sunt eorum adversarii manifesti.

THe long and wonderful voyage of Frier John de Plano Carpini, sent ambassadour by Pope Innocentius the iiii. An. Do. 1246 to the great CAN of Tartaria ; wherin he passed through Bohemia, Polonia, Russia, and so to the citie of Kiow upon Boristhenes, and from thence rode continually post for the space of sixe moneths through Comania, over the mighty and famous rivers of Tanais, Volga, and Iaic, & through the countries of the people called Kangittæ, Bisermini, Kara-Kitay, Naimani, & so to the native countrie of the Mongals or Tartars, situate in the extreme Northeasterne partes of all Asia: and thence backe againe the same way to Russia, and Polonia, and so to Rome ; spending in the whole voyage among the sayd Tartars one whole yeere & above foure moneths : Taken out of the 32. booke of Vincentius Beluacensis his Speculum historiale.

LIBRI XXXII.

De prima missione Fratrum Prædicatorum & Minorum ad Tartaros.   Cap. 2.

Ascelinus.
¶ *Vide*
Mechovium
lib. 1. *cap.* 5.

Oc etiam tempore misit Innocentius IIII. Papa Fr. Ascelinum de ordine Prædicatorum cum tribus aliis Fratribus, auctoritate, qua fungebantur, de diversis ordinis sui conventibus sibi associatis, cum literis Apostolicis ad exercitum Tartarorum, in quibus hortabatur eos, ut ab hominum strage desisterent, & fidei veritatem reciperent.   Et ego quidem ab uno Fratrum Prædicatorum,

Simon San-
quintinianus.

videlicet à Fr. Simone de S. Quintino, jam ab illo itinere regresso, gesta Tartarorum accepi, illa duntaxat, quæ

94

JOHN DE PLANO CARPINI

superius per diversa loca juxta congruentiam temporum huic operi inserui. Siquidem & eo tempore quidam Frater ordinis Minorum, videlicet Fr. Johannes de Plano carpini, cum quibusdam aliis missus fuit ad Tartaros, qui etiam, ut ipse testatur, per annum & quatuor menses & amplius cum eis mansit, & inter eos ambulavit. A summo namque Pontifice mandatum, ut omnia, quæ apud eos erant, diligenter scrutaretur, acceperat, tam ipse, quàm Fr. Benedictus Polonus ejusdem ordinis, qui suæ tribulationis particeps & socius erat. Et hic ergo Fr. Joannes de his, quæ apud Tartaros vel oculis propriis vidit, vel à Christianis fide dignis, qui inter illos captivi erant, audivit, libellum historialem, conscripsit, qui & ipse ad manus nostras pervenit. De quo etiam hîc quasi per epilogum inserere libet aliqua, videlicet ad supplementum eorum, quæ desunt in prædicta Fr. Simonis historia.

De situ & qualitate terræ Tartarorum. Cap. 3.
Johannes de Plano Carpini.

ESt in partibus Orientis terra, quæ Mongal sive Tartaria dicitur, in ea scilicet parte sita, in qua Oriens Aquiloni conjungi creditur. Ab Oriente quidem habet terram Kythaorum & etiam Solangorum, à meridie verò terram Sarracenorum. Inter ‖ Orientem & meridiem terram Huynorum, & ab Occidente provinciam Naymanorum, ab Aquilone verò circundatur Oceano. In parte aliqua nimium est montuosa, & in aliqua campestris, sed tota ferè admixta glarea plurimum arenosa, nec est in centesima parte fructuosa. Nec enim potest fructum portare, nisi aquis fluvialibus irrigetur, quæ ibi sunt rarissimæ. Unde nec villæ nec aliquæ civitates ibidem reperiuntur, excepta una, quæ Cracurim appellatur, & satis bona esse dicitur. Nos quidem illam non vidimus, sed ad dimidiam dietam prope fuimus, cùm apud Syram ordam, quæ curia major Imperatoris eorum est, essemus. Licet autem aliâs infructifera sit illa terra, tamen alendis pecoribus est apta. In aliqua ejus parte sunt aliquæ sylvæ modicæ, alia verò sine lignis est omninò. Itaque

A.D. 1246.

Joannes de Plano Carpini.

Benedictus Polonus.

Libellus historialis Joannis de Plano Carpini.

Tartariæ descriptio.

‖Vel Occidentem.

[I. 38.]

Syra orda.

95

tam Imperator quàm Principes, & omnes alii sedent, & cibaria sua decoquunt ad focum, de boum & equorum stercoribus factum. Ipse quoque aër inordinatus est ibidem mirabiliter. In media siquidem æstate ibi tonitrua magna & fulgura fiunt, ex quibus plurimi occiduntur homines, & eodem quoque tempore cadunt ibidem maximæ nives. Sunt & ibi ventorum frigidissimorum tam maximæ tempestates, quòd aliquando vix possunt equitare homines.

Unde cùm ante ordam essemus (sic enim apud eos stationes Imperatoris & Principum appellantur) præ venti magnitudine in terra prostrati jacebamus, & videre propter pulveris magnitudinem minimè poteramus. Nunquam ibi pluit in hyeme, sed frequenter in æstate, & tam modicum, ut vix posset aliquando pulverem & radicem graminum madefacere. Ibi quoque maxima grando cadit sæpè. Unde cùm Imperator electus in sede regni debuit poni, nobis in curia tunc existentibus, tanta cecidit grando, quod ex subita resolutione plusquam CLX. homines in eadem curia fuerunt submersi. Res etiam & habitacula plura fuerunt deducta. Ibi etiam est in æstate subitò calor magnus, & repentè maximum frigus.

De forma & habitu & victu eorum. Cap. 4.

MOngalorum autem sive Tartarorum forma ab omnibus aliis hominibus est remota. Inter oculos enim, & inter genas, lati sunt plus cæteris, genæ quoque satis prominent à maxillis. Nasum habent planum & modicum, oculos etiam parvos, & palpebras usque ad supercilia elevatas, ac super verticem in modum Clericorum coronas.

Ex utraque parte frontis tondendo, plusquam in medio crines longos faciunt, reliquos autem sicut mulieres crescere permittunt. De quibus duas cordas faciunt, & unamquamque post aurem ligant. Pedes quoque modicos habent.

Vestes tam virorum quàm mulierum uno modo formatæ sunt. Palliis vel cappis vel caputiis non utuntur. Tunicas verò miro modo formatas portant de buccaramo, vel purpurato, vel baldaquino. Pellicium habet pilos exterius,

sed apertum est à posterioribus. Habet tamen caudulam

unam usque ad genua retrò. Vestes suas non lavant, nec
lavari permittunt, & maximè à tempore, quo tonitrua
incipiunt, usquequo desinat illud tempus. Stationes *Tabernacula*
habent rotundas in modum tentorii de virgulis & baculis
subtilibus præparatas. Supra verò in medio rotundam
habent fenestram, unde ingrediatur lumen, & fumus exire
possit : quia semper in medio faciunt ignem : parietes
autem & tecta filtro sunt operta. Ostia quoque de filtro
sunt facta. Harum quædam subitò solvuntur, & reparantur, & super summarios deferuntur : quædam verò dissolvi
non possunt sed in curribus portantur. Et quocunque
sive ad bellum sive aliâs vadunt, semper illas secum
deferunt. In animalibus valde divites sunt, ut in Camelis *Opes in pecore.*
& bobus, capris & ovibus. Jumenta & equos habent in
tanta multitudine, quantam non credimus totum mundi
residuum habere. Porcos autem & alias bestias non
habent. Imperator ac Duces atque alii magnates in auro &
argento ac serico & gemmis abundant. Cibi eorum sunt *Victus.*
omnia, quæ mandi possunt. Vidimus eos etiam manducare
pediculos. Lac bibunt animalium, & in maxima quantitate, si habent, jumentinum. Porro in hyeme, quia nisi
divites sint, lac jumentinum non habent, millium cum
aqua decoquunt, quod tam tenue faciunt, ut illud bibere
valeant. Unde quilibet eorum scyphum bibit unum vel
duos in mane, & quandoque nihil amplius manducant in
die. In sero autem unicuique datur de carnibus modicum,
& bibunt ex eis brodium. Porrò in æstate quando satis
habent de lacte jumentino, carnes comedunt rarò, nisi fortè
donentur eisdem, aut venatione bestiam aliquam ceperint
vel avem.

De moribus eorum bonis & malis. Cap. 5.

HAbent autem mores quosdam quidem commendabiles, Πειθαρχία.
& quosdam detestabiles. Magis quippe sunt obedientes Dominis suis, quàm aliqui qui in mundo sint
homines, sive religiosi sive seculares. Nam eos maximè
reverentur, nec illis de facili mentiuntur verbis factisve :
rarò vel nunquam ad invicem contendunt, belláque vel

Abstinentia.

Comitas.

Temperantia.

[I. 39.]

Castitas.

Insolentia adversus exteros.

Iracundia.

Fraudulentia.

Sordes.

Temulentia.

rixæ, vulnera vel homicidia nunquam inter eos contingunt. Prædones etiam ac fures rerum magnarum ibi nequaquam inveniuntur, ideoque stationes & currus eorum, ubi thesauros habent, seris aut vectibus non firmantur. Si aliqua bestia perdita fuerit, quicunque invenit eam vel dimittit, vel ad illos, qui ad hoc positi sunt, cam ducit. Apud quos ille, cujus est bestia, illam requirit, & absque ulla difficultate recipit. Unus alium satis honorat, & familiaritatem ac cibaria, quamvis apud eos sint pauca, liberaliter satis communicat. Satis etiam sunt sufferentes, nec cùm jejunaverint uno die, vel duobus, omninò sine cibo, videntur impatientes, sed cantant & ludunt, ac si bene comedissent. In equitando multum sustinent frigus, calorem quoque nimium patiuntur. Inter eos quasi nulla placita sunt, & quamvis multum inebrientur, tamen in ebrietate sua nunquam contendunt. Nullus alium spernit, sed juvat & promovet, quantum congruè potest. Castæ sunt eorum mulieres, nec aliquid inter eos auditur de ipsarum impudicitia. Quædam tamen ex iis verba turpia satis habent & impudica. Porrò erga cæteros homines iidem Tartari superbissimi sunt, omnesque nobiles & ignobiles quasi pro nihilo reputantes despiciunt. Unde vidimus in curia Imperatoris magnum Russiæ ducem, & filium regis Georgianorum, ac Soldanos multos & magnos nullum honorem debitum recipere apud eos. Quinetiam Tartari eisdem assignati, quantumcunque viles essent illos antecedebant, sempérque primum locum & summum tenebant, imò etiam sæpè oportebat illos post eorum posteriora sedere. Præterea iracundi sunt, & indignantis naturæ. multum erga cæteros homines, & ultra modum erga eosdem mendaces. In principio quidem blandi sunt, sed postmodum ut Scorpiones pungunt. Subdoli enim & fraudulenti sunt, & omnes homines si possunt astutia circumveniunt. Quicquid mali volunt eis facere, miro modo occultant, ut sibi non possint providere, vel contra eorum astutias remedium invenire. Immundi quoque sunt in cibo & potu sumendis, & in cæteris factis suis. Ebrietas apud illos est honorabilis : cumque multum aliquis

98

biberit, ibidemque rejicit, non ideo cessat, quin iterum
bibat. Ad petendum maximi sunt exactores, tenacissimi
retentores, parcissimi donatores. Aliorum hominum *Δωροδοκία.*
occisio apud illos est pro nihilo.

De legibus & consuetudinibus eorum. Cap. 6.

HOc autem habent in lege sive consuetudine, ut *Poena*
occidant viros & mulieres, si quando inveniantur in *adulterii.*
adulterio manifestè. Similiter etiam virginem, si fornicata
fuerit cum aliquo, occidunt eam cum eo. Præterea si
aliquis in præda vel furto manifesto invenitur, sine ulla *Furti.*
miseratione occiditur. Item si quis denudavit consilia,
maximè quando volunt ad bellum procedere, dantur ei
super posteriora centum plagæ, quanto majores unus *Arcani*
rusticus cum magno baculo potest dare. Similiter cùm *evulgati.*
aliqui de minoribus offendunt in aliquo, non eis à majoribus suis parcitur, sed verberibus graviter affliguntur.
Matrimonio autem generaliter conjunguntur omnibus, *Leges matri-*
etiam propinquis carne, excepta matre & filia & sorore ex *moniorum.*
eadem matre. Nam sororem tantùm ex patre, & uxorem
quoque patris, post ejus mortem solent ducere. Uxorem
etiam fratris alius frater junior, post ejus mortem, vel
alius de parentela, tenetur ducere. Unde dum adhuc *Andreas Dux*
essemus in terra, Dux quidam Russiæ, Andreas nomine, *Russiæ.*
apud Baty, quòd equos Tartarorum de terra educeret, & ¶ *Vide Her-*
aliis venderet, accusatus est : quod licet non esset pro- *bersteinium de*
batum, occisus est. Hoc audiens junior frater, & uxor *chovi pag. 8. b.*
occisi, pariter venerunt ad præfatum Ducem, supplicare
volentes, ne terra auferretur eisdem. At ille parvo præcepit, ut fratris defuncti duceret uxorem, mulieri quoque
ut illum in virum duceret, secundum Tartarorum consuetudinem. Quæ respondit, se potius occidi velle, quàm
sic contra legem facere. At ille nihilominus eam illi
tradidit quamvis ambo renuerent, quantum possent. Itaque
ducentes eos in lectum, clamantem puerum & plorantem
super illam posuerunt, ipsosque commisceri pariter coëg-
erunt. Denique post mortem maritorum, uxores Tartarorum non de facili solent ad secunda conjugia transire, nisi

fortè quis velit sororiam aut novercam suam ducere. Nulla
verò differentia est apud eos inter filium uxoris & concubinæ, sed dat pater quod vult unicuique. Itaque si sunt
etiam ex Ducum genere, ita fit Dux filius concubinæ, sicut
Melich &
David fratres
Georgiani.
filius uxoris legitimæ. Unde cùm rex Georgiæ duos filios
nuper, unum scilicet nomine Melich legitimum, alterum
verò David ex adulterio natum haberet, moriensque terræ
partem adulteræ filio reliquisset, Melich, cui etiam ex parte
matris regnum obvenerat, quia per fœminas tenebatur,
perrexit ad Imperatorem Tartarorum, eo quòd & David
iter arripuerat ad illum. Ambobus igitur ad curiam venientibus, datisque maximis muneribus, petebat adulteræ filius,
ut fieret ei justitia secundum morem Tartarorum. Dataque
est sententia contra Melich, ut David, qui major erat
natu, subesset, ac terram à patre sibi concessam quietè
πολυγαμία.
ac pacificè possideret. Cumque Tartarorum unus habet
uxorum multitudinem, unaquæque per se suam habet
familiam & stationem. Et una die Tartarus comedit
& bibit & dormit cum una, altera die cum alia. Una
tamen inter cæteras major habetur, cum qua frequentius quam cum aliis commoratur. Et licet, ut dictum
est, sint multæ, nunquam tamen de facili contendunt
inter se.

De superstitiosis traditionibus ipsorum. Cap 7.

ἐθελοθρησκεία.
QUibusdam verò traditionibus indifferentia quædam
esse peccata dicunt, quas vel ipsi vel antecessores
eorum confinxerunt. Unum est, cultellum in ignem
figere, vel quocunque modo ignem cultello tangere, vel
etiam de caldaria cum cultello carnes extrahere, vel cum
[I. 40.]
securi juxta ignem incidere. Credunt enim, quòd sic
auferri debeat caput igni. Aliud est appodiare se ad
flagellum, quo percutitur equus : ipsi enim non utuntur
calcaribus. Item flagello sagittas tangere, juvenes aves
capere vel occidere, cum fræno equum percutere, os cum
osse alio frangere. Itemque lac, vel aliquem potum aut
cibum super terram effundere, in statione mingere. Quod
si voluntariè facit, occiditur, si autem aliter, oportet quòd

pecuniam multam incantatori solvat, à quo purificetur.
Qui etiam faciat, ut statio cum omnibus, quæ in ipsa sunt,
inter duos ignes transeat. Antequam sic purificetur,
nullus audet intrare, nec aliquid de illa exportare. Præterea
si alicui morsellus imponitur, quem deglutire non possit,
& illum de ore suo ejicit, foramen sub statione fit, per
quod extrahitur, ac sine ulla miseratione occiditur. Iterum ἀθεότης.
si quis calcat super limen stationis Ducis alicujus, interficitur. Multa etiam habent his similia, quæ reputant
peccata. At homines occidere, aliorum terras invadere, ac
res illorum diripere, & contra Dei præcepta vel prohibitiones facere, nullum apud eos est peccatum. De vita
æterna & damnatione perpetua nihil sciunt. Credunt
tamen, quòd post mortem in alio seculo vivant, gregésque
multiplicent, comedant & bibant, & cætera faciant, quæ
hîc à viventibus fiunt. In principio lunationis vel in *Cultus lunæ.*
plenilunio incipiunt, quic quid novi agere volunt, ipsamque
Lunam Imperatorem magnum appellant, eamque depre-
cantes genua flectunt. Omnes, qui morantur in stationibus suis, oportet per ignem purificari. Quæ scilicet purificatio fit hoc modo. Duos quidem ignes faciunt, & duas *Lustrationis*
hastas juxta eos, unamque cordam in summitate hastarum *ritus.*
ponunt. Ligantque super cordam illam quasdam de
Bucaramo scissiones, sub qua scilicet corda & ligaturis inter
illos ignes transeunt homines, ac bestiæ ac stationes.
Sunt etiam duæ mulieres, una hinc, & alia inde aquam
projicientes, ac quædam carmina recitantes. Cæterum si
aliquis à fulgure occiditur, oportet prædicto modo per
ignes transire omnes illos, qui in illis stationibus morantur.
Statio siquidem ac lectus & currus, filtra & vestes, &
quicquid talium habent, à nullo tanguntur, sed ab hominibus tanquam immunda respuuntur. Et ut breviter dicam,
omnia purificari credunt per ignem. Unde quando *Ignis*
veniunt ad eos nuncii, vel Principes, aut qualescunque *superstitiosa*
personæ, oportet ipsos & munera sua per duos ignes, *efficacitas.*
ut purificentur, transire, ne fortè veneficia fecerint, aut
venenum seu aliquid mali attulerint.

De initio imperii sive Principatus eorum.
Cap. 8.

*Tartariæ
populi.*

TErra quidem illa Orientalis, de qua dictum est suprà, quæ Mongal nominatur, quatuor quondam habuisse populos memoratur. Unus eorum Yeka Mongal, id est, magni Mongali vocabantur. Secundus Sumongal, id est, aquatici Mongali, qui seipsos appellabant Tartaros, à quodam fluvio per eorum terram currente, qui Tartar nominatur. Tertius appellabatur Merkat. Quartus verò Metrit. Omnes unam personarum formam & unam linguam habebant hi populi, quamvis inter se per Principes ac provincias essent divisi. In terra Yeka Mongal quidam

*Chingis ortus
& res gestæ.*

fuit, qui vocabatur Chingis. Iste cœpit robustus venator esse : didicit enim homines furari, & prædam capere. Ad alias terras ibat, & quoscunque poterat, captivabat, sibique associabat. Homines quoque suæ gentis inclinavit ad se, qui tanquam Ducem sequebantur ipsum ad malè agendum. Cœpit autem pugnare cum Sumongal, sive cum Tartaris, & Ducem eorum interfecit, multoque bello sibi Tartaros omnes subjecit, & in servitutem redegit. Post hæc cum istis omnibus contra Merkatas, juxta terram positos Tartarorum pugnavit, quos etiam bello sibi subjecit. Inde procedens contra Metritas pugnam exercuit, & illos etiam

Naymani.
¶ *Infra cap.*
25.

obtinuit. Audientes Naymani, quòd Chingis taliter elevatus esset, indignati sunt. Ipsi enim habuerant Imperatorem strenuum valdè, cui dabant tributum cunctæ nationes prædictæ. Qui cùm esset mortuus, filii ejus

*Fratres
discordantes
oppressi.*

successerunt loco ipsius. Sed quia juvenes ac stulti erant, populum tenere nesciebant, sed ad invicem divisi ac scissi erant. Unde Chingi prædicto modo jam exaltato, nihilominus in terras prædictas faciebant insultum, & habitatores occidebant, ac diripiebant prædam eorum. Quod audiens Chingis, omnes sibi subjectos congregavit. Naymani & Karakytay ex adverso similiter in quandam vallem strictam convenerunt, & commissum est prælium, in quo Naymani & Karakytay à Mongalis devicti sunt. Qui etiam pro

A.D.
1246.

majori parte occisi fuerunt, & alii, qui evadere non potuerunt, in servitutem redacti sunt.   In terra prædictorum
Karakytaorum Occoday Cham, filius Chingischam, post- *Occoday*
quam imperator fuit positus, quandam civitatem ædificavit, *Cham.*
quam Chanyl appellavit.   Prope quam ad Meridiem est
quoddam desertum magnum, in quo pro certo sylvestres *Homines syl-*
homines habitare dicuntur, qui nullatenus loquuntur, *vestres.*
nec juncturas in cruribus habent, & si quando cadunt,
per se surgere non valent.   Sed tamen discretionem
tantam habent, quòd filtra de lana Camelorum, quibus
vestiuntur, faciunt & contra ventum ponunt.   Et si
quando Tartari pergentes ad eos vulnerant eos sagittis,
gramina in vulneribus ponunt, & fortiter ante ipsos
fugiunt.

De mutua victoria ipsorum & Kythaorum.   [L. 41.]
Cap. 9.

MOngali autem in terram suam revertentes, se contra* **Haythono &*
Kythaos ad prælium paraverunt, & castra moventes, *Paulo Veneto*
eorum terram intraverunt.   Quod audiens eorum Impera- *sunt Cathay.*
tor, venit cum exercitu suo contra illos, & commissum est *Tartarorum*
prælium durum, in quo Mongali sunt devicti, omnesque *Cathayna*
nobiles eorum, qui erant in exercitu, præter septem occisi *clades.*
sunt.   Unde cùm illis volentibus aliquam impugnare
regionem, minatur aliquis stragem, adhuc respondent :
Olim etiam occisi non nisi septem remansimus, & tamen
modò crevimus in multitudinem magnam, ideoque non
terremur de talibus.   Chingis autem & alii, qui remanserunt, in terram suam fugerunt.   Cumque quievisset
aliquantulum, præparavit se rursus ad prælium, & processit contra terram Huyrorum.   Isti sunt homines
Christiani de secta Nestorianorum.   Et hos etiam Mon- *Novæ*
gali devicerunt, eorumque literam acceperunt ; prius enim *victoriæ.*
scripturam non habebant, nunc autem eandem Mongal- *Literæ.*
orum literam appellant.   Inde contra terram Saruyur, &
contra terram Karanitarum, & contra terram Hudirat processit, quos omnes bello devicit.   Inde in terram suam
rediit, & aliquantulum quievit.   Deinde convocatis omni-

bus hominibus suis, contra Kythaos pariter processerunt, diuque contra illos pugnantes, magnam partem terræ illorum vicerunt, eorumque Imperatorem in civitatem suam majorem concluserunt. Quam & tam longo tempore obsederunt, quod exercitus expensæ omninò defecerunt. Cumque jam quod manducarent, penitus non haberent, præcipit Chingischam suis, ut de decem hominibus unum ad manducandum darent. Illi verò de civitate machinis & sagittis viriliter contra istos pugnabant, & cùm deficerent

lapides, argentum & maximè liquefactum projiciebant. Civitas siquidem illa multis erat divitiis plena. Cumque diu Mongali pugnassent, & eam bello vincere non possent, unam magnam sub terra viam ab exercitu usque ad medium civitatis fecerunt, & prosilientes in medium ejus, contra cives pugnaverunt. Illi quoque, qui extra remanserant, eodem modo contra illos pugnabant. Denique concidentes portas civitatis intraverunt, & imperatorem cum pluribus occidentes urbem possederunt, aurumque & argentum, & omnes ejus divitias abstulerunt. Et cùm illi terræ suos homines præfecissent, in terram propriam reversi sunt.

Tunc primum Imperatore Kythaorum devicto, factus est Chingischam imperator. Quandam tamen partem illius terræ, quia posita erat in mari, nullatenus devicerunt usque hodie. Sunt autem Kytai homines pagani, habentes literam specialem, & etiam, ut dicitur, veteris & novi Testamenti scripturam. Habent etiam vitas patrum & eremitas & domos, in quibus orant temporibus suis, ad modum Ecclesiarum factas. Quosdam etiam sanctos habere se dicunt, & unum Deum colunt. Christum JESUM Dominum venerantur, & credunt vitam æternam, sed non baptizantur. Scripturam nostram honorant ac reverentur. Christianos diligunt, & eleemosynas plures faciunt, homines benigni satis & humani videntur. Barbam non habent, & in dispositione faciei cum Mongalis in parte concordant.

Meliores artifices in mundo non inveniuntur in omnibus operibus, in quibus homines exercentur. Terra eorum est opulenta nimis in frumento & vino, auro & serico ac rebus cæteris.

De pugna ipsorum contra Indiam minorem & majorem. Cap. 10.

CUm autem Mongali cum Imperatore suo Chingischam post præfatam victoriam aliquantulum quievissent, exercitus suos diviserunt. Imperator siquidem unum de filiis suis nomine Thosut, quem etiam Can, id est, Imperatorem appellabant, cum exercitu contra Comanos misit, quos ille multo bello devicit, & postmodum in terram suam rediit. Alium verò filium cum exercitu contra Indos misit, qui & minorem Indiam subjecit. Hi sunt nigri Sarraceni, qui Æthipes sunt vocati. Hic autem exercitus ad pugnam contra Christianos, qui sunt in India majori, processit. Quod audiens Rex illius terræ, qui vulgò* Presbyter Johannes appellatur, contra illos venit exercitu congregato. Et faciens imagines cupreas hominum, unamquanque posuit in sella super equum. Posuit & interius ignem, & hominem cum folle super equum post imaginem. Itaque cum multis equis & imaginibus, taliter præparatis, ad pugnam contra Mongalos seu Tartaros processerunt. Et cùm ad locum prælii pervenissent, equos istos unum juxta alium præmiserunt. Viri autem, qui erant retrò, nescio quid super ignem, qui erat intra imagines, posuerunt, & cum follibus fortiter sufflaverunt. Unde factum est, ut ex Græco igne homines & equi comburerentur, & etiam aër ex fumo denigraretur. Túmque super Tartaros sagittas jecerunt Indi, ex quibus multi vulnerati fuerunt & interfecti. Sícque ejecerunt illos cum magna confusione de suis finibus, nec unquam, quod ad ipsos ultra redierint audivimus.

Thossut Can, Chingis F.

India minor debellata.

Regis majoris Indiæ stratagema.
Vide scolion in lib. 1. cap. 51. M. Pauli Veneti.

Victoria.

Qualiter ab hominibus caninis repulsi, Burithabethinos vicerunt. Cap. 11.

[I. 42.]

CUm autem per deserta redirent, in quandam terram venerunt, in qua, sicut nobis apud Imperatoris curiam per clericos Ruthenos, & alios, qui diu fuerant inter ipsos, firmiter asserendo referebatur, monstra quædam, imaginem

A.D.
1246.

*De monstrosis
mulieribus &
canibus mon-
strosa narratio.*

¶ *Forsan
autem videri
allegorica
allusio possit
ad Canibales
de quibus
Petrus Mar-
tyr Mediolan.
de rebus
Oceanicis.*

fœmineam habentia, repererunt. Quas cùm per multos interpretes interrogassent, ubi viri terræ illius essent, responderunt, quòd in illa terra quæcunque fœminæ nascebantur, habebant formam humanam, masculi vero speciem caninam. Dumque moram in terra illa protraherent, Canes in alia fluvii parte convenerunt. Et cùm esset hyems asperrima omnes se in aquam projecerunt. Post hæc incontinenti sponte in pulverem volvebantur, sicque pulvis admixtus aquæ super eos congelabatur, & ut ita pluries fecerunt, glacie super eos depressata, cum impetu magno contra Tartaros ad pugnam convenerunt. At verò cum illi sagittas super eos jaciebant, ac si super lapides sagittassent, retrò sagittæ redibant. Alia quoque arma eorum in nullo eos lædere poterant. Ipsi verò Canes insultum in Tartaros facientes, morsibus vulneraverunt multos, & occiderunt, sicque illos de suis finibus ejecerunt. Unde adhuc inter illos est proverbium de hoc facto, quod dicunt ad invicem ridendo : Pater meus vel frater meus à Canibus fuit occisus. Mulieres autem illorum, quas ceperant, ad terram suam duxerunt, & usque ad diem mortis eorum ibidem fuerunt. Cùm autem exercitus ille

*Burithabeth
regio.*

*Incolarum
mores.*

Mongalorum rediret, venit ad terram Burithabeth, cujus habitatores pagani sunt, & hos Tartari bello vicerunt. Hi consuetudinem habent mirabilem, imò potius miserabilem. Cùm enim alicujus pater humanæ naturæ solvit debitum, congregant omnem parentelam, & comedunt eum. Hi pilos in barba non habent, imò ferrum quoddam in manibus, sicut vidimus, portant, cum quo semper barbam, si forte crinis aliquis in ea crescit, depilant. Multum etiam deformes sunt. Inde verò ille Tartarorum exercitus in terram suam est reversus.

Qualiter à montibus Caspiis, & ab hominibus subterraneis repulsi sunt. Cap. 12.

*Alia Chingis
expeditio.*

CHingischam etiam illo tempore, quo dimisit alios exercitus contra Orientem, per terram Kergis cum expeditione perrexit, quos tamen tunc bello non vicit, & ut nobis dicebatur, ibidem usque ad montes Caspios

pervenit. At illi montes in ea parte, ad quam applica-
verunt, de lapide Adamantino sunt: ideóque sagittas &
arma ferrea illorum ad se traxerunt. Homines autem
inter Caspios montes conclusi clamorem exercitus, ut
creditur, audientes, montem frangere cœperunt, & cùm
alio tempore post decem annos redirent Tartari, montem
confractum invenerunt. Cumque ad illos accedere
attentassent, minimè potuerunt: quia nubes quædam erat
posita ante ipsos, ultra quam ire nullatenus poterant.
Omninò quippe visum amittebant, statim ut ad illam
perveniebant. Illi autem ex adverso credentes, quòd *¶ Vide an*
Tartari ad illos accedere formidarent, insultum contra eos *Hamsem*
fecerunt, sed statim ut pervenerunt ad nubem propter *regionem*
causam prædictam, procedere non potuerunt. Ac verò *Haythonus*
antequam ad montes prædictos pervenirent Tartari, plus- *cap.* 10.
quam per mensem per vastam solitudinem transierunt, &
inde procedentes adhuc contra Orientem, plusquàm per
mensem per magnum desertum perrexerunt. Itaque
pervenerunt ad quandam terram, in qua vias quidem tritas
videbant, sed neminem invenire poterant. Tandem
quærentes, unum hominem cum uxore sua repererunt,
quos in præsentiam Chingischam adduxerunt. Qui cùm
interrogasset illos, ubi homines illius terræ essent, responderunt, quòd in terra sub montibus habitarent. Tunc *Troglodytæ.*
Chingischam retenta uxore, misit ad eos virum illum,
mandans illis, ut venirent ad ipsius mandatum. Qui
pergens ad illos, omnia narravit, quæ Chingischam eis
mandavit. Illi verò respondentes dixerunt, quod die tali
venirent ad ipsum, ut facerent ejus mandatum. Ac ipsi
medio tempore per vias occultas sub terra se congregantes,
ad pugnam contra illos venerunt, & subitò super eos
irruentes, plurimos occiderunt. Solis quoque sonitus in *Fabulosus*
ortu suo sustinere non poterant, imò tempore, quo *Solis orientis*
oriebatur, oportebat eos unam aurem ad terram ponere, & *sonitus.*
superiorem fortiter obturare, ne sonum illum terribilem
audirent. Nec sic tamen cavere poterant, quin hac de
causa plurimi ex eis interirent. Videns ergo Chingischam
& sui, quòd nihil proficerent, sed potius homines suos

perderent, fugerunt, ac terra illa exierunt. Illum tamen virum cum uxore sua secum deduxerunt, qui etiam usque ad mortem in terra eorum fuerunt. Interrogati verò, cur in regione sua sub terra soleant habitare, dixerunt, quòd ibi quodam tempore anni, cúm oritur Sol, tantus fit sonitus, ut homines nulla ratione valeant sustinere. Quin etiam tunc in organis & tympanis cæterisque musicis instrumentis percutere solent, ut sonitum illum non audiant.

[I. 43.] De statutis Chingischam, et morte ipsius, et filiis ac Ducibus. Cap. 13.

CUm autem de terra illa reverteretur Chingischam, defecerunt eis victualia, famemque patiebantur maximam. Tunc interiora unius bestiæ recentia casu invenerunt: quæ accipientes, depositis tantum stercoribus, decoxerunt, & coram Chingischam deportata pariter

Chingis lex. comederunt. Ideoque statuit Chingischam, ut nec sanguis, nec interiora, nec aliquid de bestia, quæ manducari potest, projiciatur, exceptis stercoribus. Inde ergò in terram propriam reversus est, ibique leges & statuta edidit, quæ Tartari inviolabiliter observant, de quibus

Interitus. scilicet jam aliâs superiùs dictum est. Post hoc ab ictu
Liberi. tonitrui occisus est. Habuit autem quatuor filios: Occoday vocabatur primus, Thossut Can secundus, Thiaday tertius, quarti nomen ignoramus. Ab his iiii. descen-

Nepotes. derunt omnes Duces Mongalorum. Primus filiorum Occoday est Cuyne, qui nunc est Imperator. Hujus fratres Cocten & Chyrenen. Ex filiis autem Thossut Can sunt Bathy, Ordu, Siba, Bora. Bathy post Imperatorem omnibus ditior est ac potentior. Ordu verò omnium Ducum senior. Filii Thiaday, sunt Hurin & Cadan. Filii autem alterius filii Chingischam, cujus ignoramus nomen, sunt, Mengu & Bithat & alii plures. Hujus Mengu mater Seroctan est, Domina magna inter Tartaros, excepta Imperatoris matre plus nominata, omnibusque potentior, excepto Bathy. Hæc autem sunt nomina

Duces. Ducum: Ordu, qui fuit in Polonia, & Hungaria, Bathy

quoque & Huryn & Cadan & Syban & Ouygat, qui
omnes fuerunt in Hungaria. Sed & Cyrpodan, qui adhuc
est ultra mare contra quosdam Soldanos Sarracenorum, &
alios habitatores terræ transmarinæ. Alii verò remanserunt in terra, scilicet Mengu, Chyrenen, Hubilai, Sinocur,
Cara, Gay, Sybedey, Bora, Berca, Corrensa. Alii quoque
Duces eorum plures sunt, quorum nomina nobis ignota
sunt.

De potestate Imperatoris & Ducum ejus.
Cap. 14.

POrrò Imperator eorum, scilicet Tartarorum, super
omnes habet mirabile dominium. Nullus enim audet
in aliqua morari parte, nisi ubi assignaverit ipse. Et ipse
quidem assignat Ducibus ubi maneant. Duces autem loca
Millenariis assignant, Millenarii verò Centenariis, &
Centenarii Decanis. Quicquid autem eis præcipitur, quocunque tempore, quocunque loco, sive ad bellum, sive
ad mortem, vel ubicunque, sine ulla obediunt contradictione. Nam etsi petit alicujus filiam virginem, vel
sororem, mox ei sine contradictione exponunt eam, imò
frequenter colligit virgines ex omnibus Tartarorum finibus,
& si vult aliquas retinere, sibi retinet, alias verò dat suis
hominibus. Nuncios etiam quoscunque & ubicunque
transmittat, oportet quòd dent ei sine mora equos &
expensas. Similiter undecunque veniant ei tributa vel
nuncii, oportet equos & currus & expensas tribui. Ac
verò nuncii, qui aliunde veniunt, in magna miseria, &
victus & vestitus penuria sunt. Maximeque quando
veniunt ad Principes, & ibi debent moram contrahere.
Tunc adeò parum datur decem hominibus, quòd vix inde
possent duo vivere. Insuper & si aliquæ illis injuriæ
fiunt, minimè conqueri facile possunt. Multa quoque
munera tam à principibus quàm à cæteris ab illis petuntur:
quæ si non dederint, vilipenduntur, & quasi pro nihilo
reputantur. Hinc & nos magnam partem rerum, quæ
nobis pro expensis à fidelibus erant datæ, de necessitate
oportuit in muneribus dare. Denique sic omnia sunt in

*Imperatoris
Tartarorum
servile in om-
nes imperium.*

*Inhumanitas
erga Legatos.*

manu Imperatoris, quod nemo audet dicere, Hoc meum est vel illius, sed omnia, scilicet res & jumenta ac homines, sunt ipsius. Super hoc etiam nuper emanavit statutum ejusdem. Idem quoque per omnia dominium habent Duces super sibi subditos homines.

De electione Imperatoris Occoday, & legatione Ducis Bathy. Cap. 15.

Occoday sur-
rogatur patri.

MOrtuo, ut suprà dictum est, Cyngischam, convenerunt Duces, & elegerunt Occoday, filium ejus Imperatorem. Qui habito consilio Principum, divisit exercitus.

Bathy ejùsque
expeditio.

Misitque Bathy, qui in secundo gradu attingebat eum, contra terram Altissodan & contra terram Bisminorum, qui Sarraceni erant, sed loquebantur Comanicum. Qui terram illorum ingressus, cum eis pugnavit, eosque sibi bello sub-

Barchin
civitas.

jecit. Quædam autem civitas, nomine Barchin, diu restitit eis. Cives enim in circuitu civitatis foveas multas fecerant, propter quas non poterant à Tartaris capi, donec illas re-

Sarguit
civitas.

plevissent. Cives autem urbis Sarguit hoc audientes, exierunt obviam eis, spontè in manus eorum se tradentes. Unde civitas eorum destructa non fuit, sed plures eorum occiderunt, & alios transtulerunt, acceptisque spoliis, urbem aliis hominibus repleverunt, & contra civitatem

Orna civitas.
[I. 44.]

Orna perrexerunt. Hæc erat nimium populosa & divitiis copiosa. Erant enim ibi plures Christiani, videlicet Gasari & Rutheni, & Alani, & alii nec non & Sarraceni. Eratque Sarracenorum civitatis dominium. Est etiam posita super quendam magnum fluvium, & est quasi portus, habens forum maximum. Cumque Tartari non possent eos aliter vincere, fluvium, qui per urbem currebat, præciderunt, & illam cum rebus & hominibus submerserunt. Quo facto, contra Russiam perrexerunt, & magnam stragem in ea fecerunt, civitates & castra destruxerunt, & homines occiderunt. Kioviam, Russiæ metropolin, diu obsederunt,

¶ *Vide Mecho-*
vium, lib. 1.
ca. 3.

& tandem ceperunt, ac cives interfecerunt. Unde quando per illam terram ibamus, innumerabilia capita & ossa hominum mortuorum, jacentia super campum, inveniebamus. Fuerat enim urbs valdè magna & populosa, nunc quasi ad

nihilum est redacta : vix enim domus ibi remanserunt ducentæ, quarum etiam habitatores tenentur in maxima servitute. Porrò de Russia & de Comania Tartari contra
Hungaros & Polonos processerunt, ibique plures ex ipsis
interfecti fuerunt, & ut jam superius dictum est, si Hungari viriliter restitissent, Tartari ab eis confusi recessissent.
Inde revertentes in terram Morduanorum, qui sunt Pagani, *Morduani.*
venerunt, eosque bello vicerunt. Inde contra Byleros, id
est, contra Bulgariam magnam profecti sunt, & ipsam om- *Bulgaria*
ninò destruxerunt. Hinc ad Aquilonem adhuc contra *magna.*
Bastarcos, id est Hungariam magnam processerunt, & illos *Hungaria*
etiam devicerunt. Hinc ampliùs ad Aquilonem pergentes, *magna.*
ad Parossitas venerunt, qui parvos habentes stomachos & *Parossitæ.*
os parvum, non manducant, sed carnes decoquunt, quibus
decoctis, se super ollam ponunt, & fumum recipiunt, & de
hoc solo reficiuntur, vel si aliquid manducant, hoc valdè
modicum est. Hinc & ad Samogetas venerunt, qui tan- *Samogetæ.*
tùm de venationibus vivunt, & tabernacula vestesque tantum
habent de pellibus bestiarum. Inde ad quandam terram
super Oceanum pervenerunt, ubi monstra quædam invene- *Monstra*
runt, quæ per omnia formam humanam habebant, sed *aquilonaria.*
pedes bovinos, & caput quidem humanum, sed faciem ut
canis. Duo verba loquebantur ut homines, tertiò latrabant
ut canes. Hinc redierunt in Comaniam, & usque nunc ibi
morantur ex eis quidam.

† *De his regionibus Herbersteinius pag. 8.b. & 91.b.*
Paret enim hodie utraque Moschorum Principi. Item de
Bulgaria Guaguinus pag. 106.b.

De legatione Cyrpodan Ducis. Cap. 16.

EO tempore misit Occoday Can Cyrpodan Ducem cum *Expeditio*
exercitu ad meridiem contra Kergis, qui & illos bello *Cyrpodanis.*
superavit. Hi homines sunt Pagani, qui pilos in barba
non habent. Quorum consuetudo talis est, ut cùm alicujus pater moritur, præ dolore quasi unam corrigiam in
signum lamenti ab aure usque aurem de facie sua levet.
His autem devictis, Dux Cyrpodan contra Armenios ivit
ad meridiem cum suis. Qui cùm transirent per deserta

quædam, monstra invenerunt, effigiem humanam habentia, quæ non nisi unum brachium cum manu in medio pectoris, & unum pedem habebant, & duo cum uno arcu sagittabant, adeoque fortiter currebant, quòd equi eos investigare non poterant. Currebant autem super unum pedem illum saltando, & cùm essent fatigati, taliter eundo ibant super manum & pedem, se tanquam in circulo revolvendo. Cumque sic etiam fesse essent, iterum secundùm priorem modum currebant. Hos Isidorus Cyclopedes appellat. Et ex eis Tartari nonnullos occiderunt. Et sicut nobis à Ruthenis Clericis in curia dicebatur, qui morantur cum Imperatore prædicto, plures ex eis nuncii venerunt in legatione ad curiam Imperatoris, superiùs annotati, ut possent habere pacem cum illo. Inde procedentes venerunt in Armeniam, quam bello devicerunt, & etiam Georgiæ partem. Alia verò pars venit ad mandatum eorum, & singulis annis dederunt, & adhuc dant ei pro tributo xx. millia Yperperarum. Hinc ad terram Soldani Deurum, potentis & magni, processerunt, cum quo etiam pugnantes, ipsum devicerunt. Denique processerunt ulterius debellando ac vincendo usque ad terram Soldani Halapiæ, & nunc etiam terram obtinent, alias quoque terras ultra illas proponentes impugnare: nec postea reversi sunt in terram suam usque hodiè. Idemque exercitus contra terram Caliphi Baldach perrexit, quam etiam sibi subdidit, & ut CCCC. Byzantios, exceptis Baldekinis cæterisque muneribus, ei quotidiè pro tributo daret, obtinuit. Sed & quolibet anno mittunt nuncios ad Caliphum, ut ad eos veniat. Qui cum tributo munera magna trasmittens, ut eum supportent, rogat. Ipse autem Imperator Tartarorum munera quidem accipit, & nihilominus ut veniat, pro eo mittit.

Cyclopedes.

Armenia & Georgia subacta.

Soldanus Halapiæ.

✝
Calipha Baldacensis.

Qualiter Tartari se habent in præliis. Cap. 17.

Tartarorum militaris disciplina.

ORdinavit Chingischam Tartaros per Decanos & centenarios & millenarios. Decem quoque millenariis præponunt unum, cunctoque nihilominus exercitui duos aut tres Duces, ita tamen ut ad unum habeant respectum. Cumque in bello contra aliquos congrediuntur, nisi communiter cedant, omnes qui fugiunt, occiduntur. Et si unus aut duo, vel plures ex decem audacter accedunt ad pugnam, alii verò ex illo Denario non sequuntur, similiter occiduntur. Sed etiam si unus ex decem vel plures capiuntur, socii eorum si non eos liberant, ipsi etiam occiduntur. Porrò arma debent habere talia. Duos arcus vel *Armatura.* unum bonum ad minus. Tresque pharetras sagittis plenas, & unam securim & funes ad machinas trahendas. Divites autem habent gladios in fine acutos, ex una parte tantùm incidentes, & aliquantulum curvos. Habent & equos armatos, crura etiam tecta, galeas & loricas. Verùm loricas & equorum cooperturas quidam habent de corio, super corpus artificiosè duplicato vel etiam triplicato. Galea verò superius est de chalybe, vel de ferro: sed illud, quod in circuitu protegit collum & gulam, est de corio. Quidam autem de ferro habent omnia supradicta, in hunc modum formata. Laminas multas tenues ad unius digiti latitudinem & palmæ longitudinem faciunt, & in qualibet octo foramina parvula facientes, interius tres corrigias strictas & fortes ponunt. Sicque laminas, unam alii quasi per gradus ascendendo, supponunt. Itaque laminas ad corrigias, tenuibus corrigiolis per foramina prædicta immissis, ligant, & in superiori parte corrigiolam unam ex utraque parte duplicatam cum alia corrigiola consuunt, ut laminæ simul benè firmiterque cohæreant. Hæc faciunt tam ad cooperturas equorum, quàm ad armaturas hominum. Adeoque faciunt illa lucere, quod in eis potest homo faciem suam videre. Aliqui verò in collo ferri lanceæ uncum habent, cum quo de sella, si possunt, hominem detrahant. Sagittarum eorum ferramenta sunt acutissima, ex utraque parte quasi gladius biceps incidentia, semperque juxta pharetram portant limas ad acuendum sagittas. Habent verò scuta de viminibus, aut de virgulis facta. Sed non credimus, quòd ea soleant portare, nisi ad castra & ad custodiam Imperatoris ac principum, & hoc tantùm de nocte. In bellis astutissimi sunt: *Usus bellorum.* quia per annos xlii. cum cæteris gentibus dimicârunt. Cùm autem ad flumina pervenerunt, majores habent *Mos tranandi* rotundum ac leve corium, in cujus summitate per circui- *flumina.*

tum ansas crebras facientes, funem imponunt ac stringunt, ita quod in circuitu quasi ventrem efficiunt, quem vestibus ac rebus cæteris replent, fortissimeque ad invicem comprimunt. In medio autem ponunt sellas & alias res duriores: ibi quoque sedent homines. Hujusmodi navim ad equi caudam ligant, & hominem, qui equum regat, pariter natare faciunt, vel habent aliquando duos remos, cum quibus remigant. Equo igitur in aquam impulso, omnes alii equi sequuntur illum, & sic transeunt fluvium. Pauperior autem quilibet unam bursam vel saccum de corio benè consutum habet, in quo res suas omnes imponit, & in summitate fortiter ligatum, ad equi caudam suspendit, sicque modo prædicto transit.

Qualiter resistendum sit eis. Cap. 18.

NUllam æstimo provinciam esse, quæ per se possit eis resistere : quia de omni terra potestatis suæ solent homines ad bellum congregare. Et siquidem vicina provincia non vult eis opem ferre, quam impugnant, delentes illam, cum hominibus, quos ex illa capiunt, contra aliam pugnant. Et illos quidem in acie primos ponunt, & si malè pugnant, ipsos occidunt. Itaque si Christiani eis resistere volunt, oportet quòd Principes ac rectores terrarum in unum conveniant, ac de communi consilio eis resistant. Habeantque pugnatores arcus fortes & balistas, quas multùm timent, sagittasque sufficientes, dolabrum quoque de bono ferro, vel securim cum manubrio longo. Ferramenta verò sagittarum more Tartarorum, quando sunt calida, temperare debent in aqua, cum sale mixta, ut fortia sint ad penetrandum illorum arma. Gladios etiam & lanceas cum uncis habeant, qui volunt, ad detrahendum illos de sella, de qua facillimè cadunt. Habeant & galeas & arma cætera, ad protegendum corpus & equum ab armis & sagittis eorum, & si qui non ita sunt armati, debent more illorum post alios ire, & contra ipsos arcubus vel balistis trajicere. Et sicut dictum est suprà de Tartaris, debent acies suas ordinare, ac legem pugnantibus imponere. Quicunque conversus fuerit ad prædam ante victoriam,

Παραίνεσις
de bello contra
Tartaros
gerendo.

Ferri tempera-
mentum.

maximam debet pœnam subire : talis enim apud illos occiditur absque miseratione. Locus ad prælium, si fieri potest, eligendus est planus, ut undique possint videre, nec omnes debent in unum convenire, sed acies multas & divisas, nec tamen nimis distantes ab invicem, facere. Contra illos, qui primò veniunt, debent unam aciem mittere, & alia parata sit ad juvandum illam opportuno tempore. Habeant & speculatores ex omni parte, qui videant, quando veniunt acies cæteræ. Nam ideò semper debent aciem contra aciem, ut ei occurrant, mittere, quoniam illi semper nituntur adversarios in medio concludere. Hoc autem acies caveant, ne si etiam illi fugere videantur, diu post illos currant, ne fortè, sicut facere solent, ipsos ad paratas insidias trahant : quia plus fraudulentia quàm fortitudine pugnant. Et iterum ne fatigentur equi eorum : quia nostri multitudinem non habent equorum. Tartari verò quos equitant die una, non ascendunt tribus diebus, vel quatuor postea. Præterea si cedunt Tartari, non ideò debent nostri recedere, vel ab invicem separari : quoniam hoc simulando faciunt, ut exercitus [I. 46.] dividatur, & sic ad terræ destructionem liberè ingrediantur. Cæterùm Duces nostri die noctúque facere debent exercitum custodiri : nec jacere spoliati, sed semper ad pugnam parati : quia Tartari quasi Dæmones semper vigilant, excogitantes artem nocendi. Porrò si aliqui Tartarorum in bello de suis equis projiciuntur, statim capiendi sunt, quia quando sunt in terra fortiter sagittant, & equos hominesque vulnerant.

De itinere Fratris Johannis de Plano carpini usque ad primam custodiam Tartarorum. Cap. 19.

NOs igitur ex mandato sedis Apostolicæ cùm iremus ad Orientis nationes, elegimus prius ad Tartaros proficisci : quia timebamus, ne per illos in proximo Ecclesiæ Dei periculum immineret. Itaque pergentes, ad regem *Itinerarium* Boëmorum pervenimus : qui cùm esset nobis familiaris, *Joann. &* consuluit, ut per Poloniam & Russiam iter ageremus. *sociorum legatorum.* Habebat enim consanguineos in Polonia, quorum auxilio

Boleslaus Dux
Silesiæ.

* Mazoviæ.

* Grimislaua,
ut Mechovius
lib. 1. cap. 9.

Literæ Papæ
ad Russos.

Daniel, frater
Basilii.

Lituani.

Russiam intrare possemus. Datisque literis & bono conductu, fecit & expensas nobis dari per curias & civitates
ejus, quo usque ad Ducem Slesiæ Bolezlaum, nepotem
ejus, veniremus, qui etiam erat nobis familiaris & notus.
Hinc & ipse nobis similiter fecit, donec veniremus ad
Conradum, Ducem * Lautisciæ, ad quem tunc, Dei gratia
nobis favente, venerat Dominus Wasilico, Dux Russiæ, à
quo etiam plenius de facto audivimus Tartarorum : quia
nuncios illuc miserat, qui jam redierant ad ipsum. Audito
autem, quòd oporteret nos illis munera dare, quasdam
pelles castorum & aliorum animalium fecimus emi, de hoc,
quod datum nobis fuerat in eleemosynam ad subsidium
viæ. Quod agnoscentes Dux Conradus & * Ducissa
Cracoviæ, & Episcopus & quidam milites, plures etiam
nobis dederunt hujusmodi pelles. Denique Dux Wasilico
à Duce Cracoviæ, & Episcopo atque Baronibus pro nobis
attentè rogatus, secum nos in terram suam duxit, & ut
aliquantulum quiesceremus, aliquot diebus nos in expensis
suis detinuit. Et cùm rogatus à nobis, fecisset Episcopos
suos venire, legimus eis literas Domini Papæ, monentis
eos, ad sanctæ matris Ecclesiæ unitatem redire. Ad idem
quoque nos ipsi monuimus eos, & induximus, quantum
potuimus, tam Ducem quàm Episcopos & alios. Sed quia
Dux Daniel, frater Wasiliconis prædicti, præsens non erat,
quoniam ad Baty profectus erat, non potuerunt eo tempore
finaliter respondere. Post hæc Dux Wasilico transmisit
nos usque in Kioviam metropolin Russiæ, cum serviente
uno. Ibamus tamen in periculo capitis semper propter
Lituanos, qui sæpè faciebant insultum super terram Russiæ,
& in illis maximè locis, per quos debebamus transire. At
per prædictum servientem eramus securi à Ruthenis,
quorum etiam maxima pars occisa vel captivata erat à
Tartaris. Porrò in Danilone usque ad mortem tunc
infirmati fuimus. Nihilominus tamen in vehiculo per
nivem & frigus magnum trahi nos fecimus. Cùm ergò
Kioviam pervenimus, habuimus de via nostra consilium
cum millenario ac cæteris ibidem nobilibus. Qui responderunt nobis, quòd si duceremus equos illos, quos tunc

habebamus, ad Tartaros, cùm essent magnæ nives, morerentur omnes : quia nescirent herbam fodere sub nive, sicut equi faciunt Tartarorum, nec inveniri posset aliquod pro eis ad manducandum, cùm Tartari nec stramina nec fœnum habeant, nec pabulum. Itaque decrevimus eos illic dimittere cum duobus pueris, deputatis eorum custodiæ. Ideoque nos oportuit millenario dare munera, ut ipsum haberemus propitium, ad dandum nobis equos subductitios & conductum. Secundo igitur die post festum Purificationis cepto itinere, venimus ad villam Canovæ, quæ sub Tartaris erat immediatè. Cujus præfectus nobis dedit equos & conductum usque ad aliam, in qua reperimus præfectum Micheam, omni malitia plenum. Qui tamen acceptis à nobis muneribus secundum velle suum, duxit nos usque ad primam custodiam Tartarorum.

*Pabulum equo-
rum Tartaric.*

*Micheas
πάγκακος.*

Qualiter primô cum sociis suis receptus est à Tartaris. Cap. 20.

CUm ergo in prima sexta feria post diem cinerum, Sole ad occasum tendente, hospitaremur. Tartari super nos armati horribiliter irruerunt, quærentes cujusmodi homines essemus : cumque respondissemus, quòd Domini Papæ nuncii essemus, quibusdam cibariis à nobis acceptis, continuó discesserunt. Porrò mane facto, cùm surgentes aliquantulum processissemus, majores illorum, qui erant in custodia, nobis occurrerunt, interrogantes, cur ad eos veniremus ? & quid negotii haberemus ? Quibus respondimus, Domini Papæ nuncii sumus, qui Christianorum pater est ac Dominus. Hic nos idcircò tam ad Regem quàm ad Principes, omnesque Tartaros, mittit, quia placet ei, quòd omnes Christiani Tartarorum sint amici, & pacem habeant cum ipsis. Desiderat insuper, ut apud Deum in cœlo sint magni, & idcircò monet eos tam per nos quàm per literas suas, ut efficiantur Christiani, fidemque recipiant Domini nostri Jesu Christi, quia non possunt aliter salvari. Mandat præterea, quòd miratur de tanta occisione hominum, & maximè Christianorum, ac potissimè Hungarorum, Montanorum, & Polonorum, qui sunt ei subjecti, facta per

*Papa Christi-
anorum pater
& Dominus.*

*Legationis
mandata.
[I. 47.]*

Tartaros, cùm in nullo læsissent, aut lædere attentassent eos. Et quia Dominus Deus graviter est super hoc offensus, monet eos, ut à talibus de cætero caveant, & de commissis pœnitentiam agant. Super his etiam rogat, ut ei rescribant, quid facere velint de cætero, & quæ sit eorum intentio. Quibus auditis, & intellectis, dixerunt Tartari, se velle equos nobis subductitios usque ad Corrensam & ducatum præbere. Statimque munera petierunt, & à nobis acceperunt. Equis igitur acceptis, de quibus descenderant ipsi, cum eorum ducatu ad Corrensam arripuimus iter eundi. Ipsi tamen velociter equitantes, nuncium unum præmiserunt ad præfatum Ducem cum his verbis, quæ dixeramus eisdem. Est autem Dux iste Dominus omnium, qui positi sunt in custodia contra omnes Occidentis populos, ne fortè subitò & improvisò irruant aliqui super illos. Et iste dicitur habere sexaginta millia hominum armatorum sub se.

Corrensa.

Dux limitis occidentalis.

Qualiter recepti sunt apud Corrensam.
Cap. 21.

Mos salutandi Tartaricos proceres.

CUm ergò pervenissemus ad ejus curiam, fecit nobis longè à se poni stationem, & misit ad nos procuratores suos, ut quærerent à nobis, cum quo ei vellemus inclinare, id est, quæ ei munera inclinando vellemus offerre. Quibus respondimus, quòd Dominus Papa non mittebat aliqua munera ; quia non erat certus, quòd ad illos pervenire possemus, & insuper veneramus per loca valdè periculosa. Veruntamen in quantum de his, quæ habebamus ex gratia Dei & Domini Papæ ad victum nostrum, sicut poterimus, honorabimus ipsum. Acceptisque muneribus duxerunt nos ad ordam sive tentorium ipsius, & instructi fuimus, ut ante ostium stationis ter cum sinistro genu inclinaremus, & caveremus attentè, ne pedem super limen ostii poneremus. Et postquam intravimus, oportuit nos coram Duce omnibusque majoribus, qui ad hoc erant vocati, dicere flexis genibus ea, quæ dixeramus superiùs. Literas etiam Dom. Papæ obtulimus : sed interpres, quem de Kyovia, dato pretio, duxeramus, non erat sufficiens ad interpretandum, nec aliquis alius habebatur idoneus. Hinc equi nobis dati sunt, & tres Tartari, qui nos ducerent festinanter ad ducem Bathy. Ipse est apud eos potentior excepto Imperatore, cui tenentur præ cunctis principibus obedire. Itaque iter arripuimus secunda feria post primam dominicam ‖ xl. & equitando, quantum equi trotare poterant, quoniam habebamus equos recentes ferè ter aut quater omni die, properabamus de mane usque ad noctem, imò etiam de nocte sæpissimè, nec tamen ante quartam feriam majoris hebdomadæ potuimus ad ipsum pervenire. Ibamus autem per terram Comanorum, quæ tota est plana, & flumina quatuor habet magna. Primum appellatur * Neper, juxta quod ex parte Russiæ ambulabat Correnza & Montii, qui major est illo ex altera parte per campestria. Secundum appellatur * Don, super quod ambulat quidam Princeps, habens in conjugio sororem Baty, qui vocatur Tirbon. Tertium dicitur * Volga, quod est magnum valdè, super quod incedit Bathy. Quartum nominatur * Iaec, super quod duo millenarii vadunt, unus ex parte fluminis una, & alter ex altera. Hi omnes in hyeme ad mare descendunt, & in æstate super ripam eorundem fluminum ad montes ascendunt. Hoc est mare magnum, de quo brachium sancti Georgii exit, quod in Constantinopolin vadit. Hæc autem flumina sunt piscibus valdè plena, maximè Volga, intrantque mare Græciæ, quod dicitur Magnum mare. Super Nepre autem multis diebus ivimus per glaciem. Super littora quoque maris Græciæ satis periculosè per glaciem ivimus in pluribus locis multis diebus. Congelantur enim circa littora undæ ad tres leucas inferiùs. Prius autem quàm ad Bathy perveniremus, duo ex nostris Tartaris præcesserunt, ad indicandum ei omnia verba, quæ apud Corrensam dixeramus.

Bathy ejúsque potentia.

‖ *Quadragesimæ.*

Comania.

* *Veteribus Borysthenes.*

* *Tanais.*

* *Rha.*

* *Rhymnus.*

Pontus Euxinus.

Volga non intrat.

Qualiter recepti sunt apud Bathy magnum Principem. Cap. 22.

POrrò cùm in finibus terræ Comanorum ad Bathy perveniremus, benè positi fuimus per unam leucam à stationibus ejus. Cumque duci debuimus ad curiam

Ceremonia per duos ignes transeundi.

ipsius, dictum fuit nobis, quòd inter quos ignes transire deberemus. Nos autem hoc nulla ratione facere volebamus. At illi dixerunt nobis : Ite securè, quia pro nulla causa volumus hoc facere, nisi tantùm, ut si vos aliquid malum cogitatis Domino nostro, vel portatis venenum, ignis auferat omne malum. Quibus respondimus : quod propter hoc, ne de tali re suspectos redderemus nos, transiremus. Cùm igitur ad Ordam pervenissemus,

Eldegay.

interrogati à procuratore ipsius Eldegay, cum quo inclinare vellemus ? idem quod prius apud Corrensam respondimus,

[I. 48.]

datisque muneribus & acceptis, auditis etiam itineris causis, introduxerunt nos in stationem Principis, prius facta inclinatione, & audita de limine non calcando, sicut

Bathy audit legatos.

prius, admonitione. Ingressi autem flexis genibus, verba nostra proposuimus, deinde literas obtulimus, & ut nobis darentur interpretes ad transferendum eas, rogavimus. Qui etiam in die Parasceve dati fuerunt nobis, & eas in litera Ruthenica, Sarracenica & in Tartarica diligenter cum ipsis transtulimus. Hæc interpretatio Bathy præsentata fuit : quam & legit, & attentè notavit. Tandem ad nostram stationem reducti fuimus, sed nulla cibaria nobis dederunt, nisi semel aliquantulum millii in una scutella, scilicet in prima nocte quando venimus.

Gerit se regi-ficè.

Iste Bathy magnificè se gerit, habens ostiarios & omnes officiales ad modum Imperatoris, & sedet in eminenti loco velut in throno cum una de uxoribus suis. Alii verò tam fratres sui & filii, quàm alii majores inferiùs sedent in medio super bancum, & homines cæteri post eos in terra deorsum, sed viri à dextris, & fœminæ à sinistris. Tentoria quoque de panno lineo habet pulchra & magna satis, quæ fuerunt Hungariæ regis. Nec aliquis ad ejus tentorium audet accedere præter familiam, nisi vocatus, quantumcunque sit potens & magnus, nisi forte sciatur, quòd sit voluntas ipsius. Nos etiam dicta causa sedimus à sinistris : Sic etenim & omnes nuncii faciunt in eundo : sed in redeundo ab Imperatore, semper ponebamur à dextris. In medio ponitur mensa ejus prope ostium stationis, super quam apponitur potus in aureis &

argenteis vasis. Nec unquam bibit Bathy, vel aliquis *Ejusdem* Tartarorum Princeps, maximè quando in publico sunt, *bibendi ad* nisi cantetur ei vel cytharizetur. Et cùm equitat, semper *Symphonia·* portatur solinum, vel tentoriolum super caput ejus in hasta. *cantum mos.* Sícque faciunt cuncti majores Principes Tartarorum, & etiam uxores eorum. Idem verò Bathy satis est hominibus *Authoritas.* suis benignus, valdè tamen ab eis timetur, & in pugna est crudelissimus, sagax est multum & astutissimus in bello : quia jam pugnavit tempore longo.

Qualiter recedentes à Bathy per terram Comanorum & Kangittarum transierunt. Cap. 23.

IN die porrò Sabbathi sancti ad stationem fuimus vocati, *Legati* & exivit ad nos procurator Bathy prædictus, dicens *jubentur ad* ex parte ipsius, quòd ad Imperatorem Cuyne in terram *Cuyne Impe-* ipsorum iremus, retentis quibusdam ex nostris sub hac *rat. pergere.* specie, quòd vellent eos remittere ad Dominum Papam, quibus & literas dedimus de omnibus factis nostris, quas deferrent eidem. Sed cùm rediissent usque ad Montii Ducem supradictum, ibi retenti fuerunt usque ad reditum nostrum. Nos autem in die Paschæ officio dicto, & facta comestione qualicunque cum duobus Tartaris, qui nobis apud Corrensam fuerant assignati, cum multis lacrymis recessimus, nescientes utrum ad mortem vel vitam pergeremus. Eramus tamen ita infirmi corpore, quòd vix poteramus equitare. In tota siquidem illa quadragesima fuerat cibus noster millium cum aqua & sale tantùm, & in aliis similiter diebus jejuniorum. Nec habebamus aliquid ad bibendum præter nivem in caldario liquefactam. Ibamus autem per Comaniam equitando fortissimè, quoniam habebamus equos recentes quinquies aut pluries in die, nisi quando per deserta ibamus, & tunc equos meliores atque fortiores, qui possent continuum sustinere laborem, accipiebamus. Et hoc ab ineunte quadragesima usque ad octo dies post Pascha. Hæc terra Comania ab Aquilone *Comaniæ de-* immediatè post Russiam habet Morduynos Byleros, id *scriptio.* est, magnam Bulgariam, Bastarcos, id est, magnam Hungariam, post Bastarcos, Parositas & Samogetas. Post

Samogetas, illos, qui dicuntur habere faciem caninam in
Oceani littoribus desertis. A meridie habet Alanos,
Circassos, Gazaros, Græciam & Constantinopolin, ac
terram Iberorum, Cathos, Brutachios, qui dicuntur esse
Judæi, caput radentes per totùm, terram quoque Cithorum
atque Georgianorum & Armeniorum & Turcorum. Ab
occidente autem Hungariam habet atque Russiam. Et
est Comania terra maxima & longa. Cujus populos,
scilicet Comanos, Tartari occiderunt, quidam tamen à facie
eorum fugerunt, & quidam in eorum servitutem redacti
sunt. Plurimi autem ex eis, qui fugerunt, ad ipsos

redierunt. Post hæc intravimus terram Kangittarum, quæ
magnam habet in plurimis locis penuriam aquarum, in
qua etiam homines pauci morantur propter aquæ de-

fectum. Unde homines Jeroslai, Ducis Russiæ, cùm ad
ipsum in terram Tartarorum perrexerunt, plures eorum in
illo deserto præ siti mortui sunt. In hac etiam terra &
in Comania multa invenimus capita & ossa mortuorum
hominum, super terram jacentia tanquam sterquilinium.
Per hanc itaque terram ivimus ab octo diebus post Pascha
ferè usque ad Ascensionem Dominicam. Hujusque
habitatores Pagani erant, & tam ipsi quàm Comani non
laborabant, sed tantùm de animalibus vivebant, nec domos
ædificabant, sed in tabernaculis habitabant. Istos etiam
Tartari deleverunt, & habitabant in terris eorum, illique
qui remanserunt, redacti sunt in servitutem ipsorum.

Qualiter ad primam Imperatoris futuri curiam
devenerunt. Cap. 24.

POrrò de terra Kangittarum intravimus terram Biserminorum, qui loquuntur lingua Comanica, sed
legem tenent Sarracenorum. In hac etiam terra invenimus urbes innumeras cum castris dirutas, villasque

multas desertas. Hujus Dominus dicebatur Altisoldanus,
qui cum tota sua progenie à Tartaris est destructus.

Habet autem hæc terra montes maximos. Et à meridie
quidem habet Hierusalem & Baldach, totamque
Sarracenorum terram. Atque in finibus illis propinquis

JOHN DE PLANO CARPINI

morantur duo fratres carnales, Tartarorum Duces, scilicet
Burin & Cadan, filii Thiaday, qui fuit filius Chingischam. *Burin.*
Ab Aquilone verò terram habet nigrorum Kythaorum & *Cadan.*
Oceanum. In illa verò moratur Syban, frater Bathy. *Oceanus ab Aquilone.*
Per hanc ivimus à festo Ascensionis dominicæ ferè usque *Syban, frater*
ad viii. dies ante festum sanct. Johan. Baptistæ. Deinde *Bathy.*
ingressi sumus terram nigrorum Kythaorum, in qua *Nigri*
Imperator ædificavit domum, ubi etiam vocati fuimus ad *Cathayni.*
bibendum. Et ille, qui erat ibidem ex parte imperatoris,
fecit majores civitatis, & etiam duos filios ejus, plaudere
coram nobis. Hinc exeuntes, quoddam mare parvum *Mare parvum.*
invenimus, in cujus littore quidam existit mons parvus.
In quo scilicet monte quoddam foramen esse dicitur, unde
in hyeme tam maximæ tempestates ventorum exeunt,
quòd homines inde vix & cum magno periculo transire
possunt. In æstate verò semper quidem ibi ventorum
sonitus auditur, sed de foramine tenuiter egreditur. Per
hujus maris littora plurimis diebus perreximus, quod *Plurimis*
quidem licet non multum sit magnum, plures insulas *diebus.*
habet, & illud in sinistris dimisimus. In terra verò illa *Plures insulæ.*
habitat Ordu, quem omnium Ducum Tartarorum anti- *Ordu.cap.13.*
quiorem diximus, & est orda, sive curia patris ipsius,
quam inhabitat, & regis una de uxoribus ejus. Consuetudo enim est apud Tartaros, quòd principum &
majorum curiæ non delentur, sed semper ordinantur
aliquæ mulieres, quæ illas regant, eísque donariorum
partes, sicut Dominis earum dari solebant, dantur. Sic
tandem ad primam Imperatoris curiam venimus, in qua *Prima curia*
erat una de uxoribus ipsius. *Imperatoris.*

Qualiter ad ipsum Cuyne, Imperatorem futurum pervenerunt. Cap. 25.

AT verò quia nondum Imperatorem videramus, noluerunt vocare nos, nec intromittere ad Ordam ipsius,
sed nobis in tentorio nostro secundum morem Tartarorum
valdè benè serviri fecerunt, & ut quiesceremus, nos
ibidem per unam diem tenuerunt. Inde procedentes in *Terra*
vigilia sanctorum Petri & Pauli, terram Naymanorum *Naymanorum.*

intravimus, qui sunt Pagani. In ipsa verò die Apostolorum ibidem cecidit magna nix, & habuimus magnum frigus. Hæc quidem terra montuosa & frigida est supra modum, ibique de planicie reperitur modicum. Istæ quoque duæ nationes prædictæ non laborabant, sed sicut & Tartari in tentoriis habitabant, quas & ipsi deleverant, per hanc etiam multis diebus perreximus. Deinde terram

Tartaria.

Mongalorum intravimus, quos Tartaros appellamus. Per has itaque terras, ut credimus, tribus septimanis equitando

Julii 22.
Acceleratum
legatorum iter.

fortiter ivimus, & in die Beatæ Mariæ Magdalenæ ad Cuyne Imperatorem electum pervenimus. Ideò autem per omnem viam istam valdè festinavimus, quia præceptum erat Tartaris nostris, ut citò nos deducerent ad curiam solennem, jam ex annis pluribus indictam, propter ipsius Imperatoris electionem. Idcircò de mane surgentes, ibamus usque ad noctem sine comestione, & sæpius tam tardè veniebamus, quòd non comedebamus in sero, sed quod manducare debebamus in vespere, dabatur nobis in mane. Mutatisque frequentius equis, nullatenus parcebatur eis, sed equitabamus velociter ac sine intermissione, quantum poterant equi trotare.

Qualiter Cuyne Fratres Minores suscepit.
Cap. 26.

Cuyne in lega-
tos benignitas.

CUm autem pervenimus ad Cuyne, fecit nobis dari tentorium & expensas, quales Tartaris dare solent, nobis tamen melius quàm aliis nunciis faciebant. Ad ipsum autem vocati non fuimus, eo quòd nondum electus erat, nec adhuc de imperio se intromittebat. Interpretatio tamen literarum Domini Papæ, ac verba etiam à nobis dicta, à prædicto Baty erant ei mandata. Cùm ergo stetissemus ibi per quinque vel sex dies, ad matrem suam nos transmisit, ubi adunabatur curia solennis. Et cùm

Tentorium
regium.

venissemus illuc, tam extensum erat tentorium magnum, de alba purpura præparatum, eratque tam grande nostro judicio, quòd plusquam duo millia hominum poterant esse sub illo. Et in circuitu factum erat ligneum tabulatum variis imaginibus depictum. Illuc ergò perreximus cum

Tartaris, nobis ad custodiam assignatis, ibique convenerant omnes duces, & unusquisque cum hominibus suis *Comitia.*
equitabat in circuitu per planiciem & colles. In prima [I. 50.]
die vestiti sunt omnes purpuris albis, in secunda verò
rubeis. Et tunc venit Cuyne ad tentorium illud. Porrò
tertia die fuerunt omnes in blaueis purpuris, & quarta in
optimis Baldakinis. In illo autem tabulato juxta tentorium
erant duæ majores portæ, per quarum unam solus Imperator debebat intrare, & ad illam nulla erat custodia,
quamvis esset aperta, quia per illam nullus audebat ingredi
vel exire: per aliam omnes, qui admittebantur, intrabant,
& ad illam custodes cum gladiis & arcubus & sagittis
erant. Itaque si quis tentorio propinquabat ultra terminos,
qui positi erant, si capiebatur, verberabatur, si fugiebat,
sagitta sive ferro sagittabatur. Multique ibi erant, qui in
fræniis, pectoralibus, sellis & hujusmodi, judicio nostro,
auri circiter viginti marcas habebant. Sic Duces infra
tentorium colloquebantur, & de Imperatoris electione
tractabant, ut à nobis creditur. Alius autem universus
populus longè extra tabulatum collocabatur, & ita ferè
usque ad meridiem morabantur. Tunc incipiebant lac
jumentinum bibere, & usque ad vesperas tantum bibebant,
quod erat visu mirabile. Nos autem vocaverunt interius, *Symposium*
& dederunt nobis cerevisiam: quia jumentinum lac non *procerum.*
bibebamus. Et hoc quidem nobis pro magno fecerunt
honore: sed tamen nos compellebant ad bibendum, quod
nullatenus poteramus propter consuetudinem sustinere.
Unde ostendimus eis, hoc esse nobis grave, ideoque nos
cessaverunt compellere. Foris autem erat Dux Jeroslaus *Jeroslaus Dux*
de Susdal Russiæ, pluresque Duces Kythaorum & Solan- *Russiæ.*
gorum. Duo quoque filii regis Georgiæ, nuncius etiam *Legati*
Caliphi de Baldach, qui erat Soldanus, & plus quam decem *diversarum*
alii Soldani Sarracenorum, ut credimus. Et sicut nobis à *nationum.*
procuratoribus dicebatur, erant ibi nunciorum plus quàm
quatuor millia, inter illos, qui tributa portabant, & illos,
qui deferebant munera, & Soldanos ac Duces alios, qui ad
tradendum seipsos veniebant, & illos, pro quibus ipsi
miserant, illosque, qui terrarum præfecti erant. Hi omnes

simul extra tabulatum ponebantur, eisque simul bibere
præbebatur. Nobis autem & Duci Jerozlao ferè semper
ab eis dabatur superior locus, quando cum eis eramus
exterius.

Qualiter in imperium sublimatus fuit. Cap. 27.

ET quidem, si benè meminimus, ibidem per septimanas
circiter quatuor fuimus. Credimusque, quòd ibi fuit
electio celebrata, non tamen ibidem fuit publicata. Propter hoc autem id maximè credebatur, quia semper,
quando Cuyne tentorio exibat, eidem cantabatur, & cum
virgis speciosis, in summitate lanam coccineam habentibus,
inclinabatur, quod alteri Ducum nulli fiebat, quousque
exterius morabatur. Hæc autem statio sive Curia nomi-

natur ab eis Syra orda. Hinc exeuntes, unanimiter omnes
equitavimus per tres aut quatuor leucas ad alium locum,
ubi erat in quadam pulchra planicie juxta rivum inter

montes aliud tentorium, quod apud ipsos appellatur Orda
aurea, præparatum. Ibi enim Cuyne debebat poni in sede
in die Assumptionis Dominæ nostræ. Sed propter
grandinem nimiam, quæ tunc, ut suprà dictum est, cecidit,

res dilata fuit. Eratque tentorium in columnis positum,
quæ laminis aureis erant tectæ, & clavis aureis cum aliis
lignis fixæ. Porrò de Baldakino erat tectum superius, sed
alii erant panni exterius. Fuimus autem ibi usque ad
festum Beati Bartholomæi, in quo maxima multitudo

convenit, & contra meridiem versis vultibus stetit. Et
quidam ad jactum lapidis longè à cæteris erant, semperque
orationes faciendo, ac genua flectendo, contra meridiem
longius, & longius procedebant. Nos autem utrum in-
cantationes facerent, aut genua Deo vel alteri flecterent,
nescientes, nolebamus facere genu flexiones. Cumque
diu ita fecissent, ad tentorium reversi sunt, & Cuyne in
sede imperiali posuerunt, Ducesque coram eo genua
flexerunt. Post hoc idem fecit universus populus,
exceptis nobis, qui eis subditi non eramus.

De ætate ac moribus ac sigillo ipsius. Cap. 28.

Hic autem Imperator quando sublimatus est in regnum, *Cuynæ ætas*
videbatur esse circiter xl. vel xlv. annorum. Medio- *& mores.*
cris erat staturæ, prudens valde, nimis astutus multumque
seriosus, & gravis in moribus. Nec unquam videbat
eum homo de facili ridere, vel aliquam levitatem facere,
sicut dicebant Christiani, qui cum ipso morabantur continuè. Dicebant etiam nobis asserendo firmiter Christiani,
qui erant de familia ejus, quòd deberet fieri Christianus.
Cujus signum erat, quod ipse Clericos Christianos tenebat, *Studium*
& expensas eis dabat. Habebat etiam semper capellam *Christianismi.*
Christianorum ante majus tentorium suum, ubi cantant
Clerici publicè & apertè, ac pulsant ad horas, ut cæteri
Christiani secundùm mores Græcorum, quantacunque sit
ibi multitudo Tartarorum, vel etiam aliorum hominum.
Hoc tamen non faciunt alii Duces ipsorum. Est autem *Majestas.*
mos Imperatoris ipsius, ut nunquam ore proprio loquatur
cum extraneo, quantumcunque magnus sit, sed audit & [I. 51.]
respondet per interpositam personam, & quandocunque
negotium proponunt, vel Imperatoris responsionem audi-
unt illi, qui sub eo sunt, quantumcunque sint magni,
flexis genibus usque ad finem verborum persistunt. Nec
alicui de consuetudine super aliquo negotio loqui licitum
est, postquam ab Imperatore definitum est. Habet autem
Imperator prædictus procuratorem & protonotarios, atque
scriptores, omnesque officiales in negotiis tam publicis
quàm privatis, exceptis Advocatis. Nam sine litium vel *Potestas*
judiciorum strepitu secundum arbitrium Imperatoris omnia *exlex* †.
fiunt. Alii quoque Principes Tartarorum de his, quæ ad
illos pertinent, idem faciunt. Hoc autem noverint universi, quia nobis tunc existentibus in solenni curia, jam ex
pluribus annis indicta, idem Cuyne Imperator, de novo
electus, cum omnibus suis Principibus erexit vexillum *Bellum in*
contra Ecclesiam Dei, ac Romanum Imperium, & contra *Christianos*
omnia regna Christianorum & populos Occidentis, nisi *cogitatum.*
fortasse, quod absit, facerent ea, quæ mandabat Domino
Papæ, atque potentibus, & omnibus Christianorum popu-

lis, videlicet ut ipsi subdantur eis. Nam excepta Christianitate, nulla est terra in orbe, quam timeant, & idcirco
contra nos ad pugnam se præparant. Hujus siquidem
Imperatoris pater, scilicet Occoday, necatus fuerat veneno,
& ob hoc à bellis quieverant tempore pauco. Intentio
autem eorum, ut dictum est suprà, est, sibi totum subjicere
mundum, sicut à Chingischam habent mandatum. Unde
& ipse Imperator in literis suis ita scribit: Dei fortitudo,
omnium hominum Imperator. In superscriptione quoque
sigilli ejus est hoc: Deus in cœlo, & Cuyne Cham super
terram, Dei fortitudo: omnium hominum Imperatoris
sigillum.

† *Contrà Xenophon:* δίκαιον ἐστι νόμιμον. *Et præclarè
Aristoteles Politic. lib.* 3. *cap.* 12. *in hanc sententiam:
Qui legem præesse vult, is velle videtur Deum ac leges
imperare: qui autem vult hominem, is etiam belluam ad-
jungit, cùm præsertim tale quid sit cupiditas & iracundia:
& magistratus & optimus quisque à recta via detorque-
antur &c. Adde quæ è Chrysippo adducuntur ff. li. i.
tit.* 3. *l.* 2.

De admissione Fratrum & nunciorum ad
Imperatorem. Cap. 29.

*Cuyne audit
legatos.*

IN loco illo, ubi positus est Imperator in throno, vocati
fuimus coram ipso. Cumque Chingay protonotarius
ejus nomina nostra scripsisset, illorumque à quibus missi
eramus, & Ducis Solangorum & aliorum, clamavit alta
voce, recitans illa coram Imperatore ac Ducum universitate.
Quo facto, flexit unusquisque nostrum quater genu sinistrum, & monuerunt, ne tangeremus limen deorsum.
Cumque pro cultellis nos diligentissimè scrutati fuissent, &
nullatenus invenissent, intravimus ostium ab Orientali
parte: quia nullus ab Occidente, nisi solus imperator, audet
intrare. Similiter & Dux ab illa parte ingreditur solus, si
est tentorium ejus. Minores autem non multum curant
de talibus. Tunc ergò primum in ejus præsentia suam intravimus stationem, videlicet postquam factus est Imperator ibidem. Omnes quoque nuncii tunc ab eo recepti sunt,

JOHN DE PLANO CARPINI

sed paucissimi tentorium ejus intraverunt. Ibi verò tanta *Munera*
donaria ab ipsis nunciis fuerunt ei præsentata, quòd quasi *eidem oblata.*
videbantur infinita, videlicet in samitis ac purpureis & baldakinis ac cingulis sericis cum auro præparatis, pellibus
etiam nobilibus, cæterisque muneribus. Quoddam etiam
Solinum, sive tentoriolum, quod super caput Imperatoris
portatur, fuit eidem præsentatum, quod totum erat cum
gemmis præparatum. Quidam verò præfectus unius provinciæ adduxit ei Camelos multos cum Baldakinis tectos.
Similiter sellæ positæ cum instrumentis quibusdam erant,
in quibus homines interius sedere valebant. Equos etiam
multos & mulos adducebant eidem phaleratos & armatos,
quosdam quidem de corio, & quosdam de ferro. Nos
etiam requisiti fuimus, an ei munera dare vellemus: sed
jam facultas non erat, quoniam omnia ferè nostra consump-
seramus. Ibidem longè à stationibus super montem erant *Currus*
positi currus plusquam quingenti, qui omnes auro & Θησαυρόφοροι.
argento ac sericis vestibus erant pleni. Cunctique inter
imperatorem & Duces divisi fuerunt, singulique Duces
inter homines suos partes suas, ut eis placuit, diviserunt.

De loco divisionis Imperatoris & matris suæ, & morte Jeroslai, Ducis Russiæ.

INde recedentes, venimus ad alium locum, ubi tentorium *Tentorium*
mirabile, totum de purpura rufa, quod Kitay dederant, *purpureum.*
erat positum. Illic interius introducti fuimus, & semper
cùm intrabamus nobis dabatur ad bibendum cerevisia vel
vinum, & etiam carnes coctæ, si volebamus, ad edendum.
Erátque solariolum unum, de tabulis altè præparatum, ubi *Solium ebur-*
thronus Imperatoris erat positus, ex ebore mirabiliter *num.*
sculptus, in quo etiam erat aurum, & lapides preciosi, si
benè meminimus, & illuc ascendebatur per gradus. Erátque rotundum superius. Banci verò erant positi in cir- [I. 52.]
cuitu sedis, ubi dominæ sedebant à parte sinistra in scamnis,
à dextris autem nemo sedebat superius, sed Duces sedebant
in Bancis inferius, & hoc in medio. Alii verò sedebant
post eos, & quolibet die veniebat dominarum maxima
multitudo. Ista verò tria tentoria, de quibus suprà dixi-

mus, erant valdè magna, aliaque habebant uxores ejus de filtro albo satis magna & pulchra. Ibidem Imperator divisus est à matre sua, quæ ivit in unam terræ partem, & Imperator in aliam ad judicia facienda. Capta siquidem erat amicà Imperatoris istius, quæ veneno interfecerat patrem ejus, eo tempore, quo exercitus eorum in Hungaria fuit. Propter quod etiam exercitus eorum, qui erat in partibus illis, recessit. De qua cum aliis pluribus factum fuit judicium, & occisi fuerunt. Eodem tempore mortuus fuit Jerozlaus. Dux magnus Soldal, quæ est quædam Russiæ pars. Vocatus enim ad matrem Imperatoris quasi pro honore, ut manducaret ac biberet de manu ipsius, in continenti ad hospitium est reversus, infirmatusque mortuus est post septem dies, totúmque corpus ejus miro modo glaucum effectum est, dicebaturque ab omnibus, quod ibidem, ut terram ejus liberè ac plenariè possiderent, fuisset impotionatus.

Nex Occoday vindicata Jeroslaus Dux Russiæ.

Qualiter tandem Fratres ad Imperatorem accedentes, literas dederunt & acceperunt. Cap. 31.

DEnique Tartari nostri nos ad Imperatorem duxerunt: qui cùm audisset per illos, nos ad eum venisse, jussit nos ad matrem redire. Volebat enim secundo die, sicut superiùs dictum est, contra totam Occidentis terram vexillum erigere, quod nos volebat ignorare. Itaque reversi stetimus paucis diebus, & iterum ad ipsum reversi sumus. Cum quo benè per mensem fuimus in tanta fame ac siti, quòd vix vivere poteramus. Nam expensæ, quæ nobis pro diebus quatuor dabantur, vix uni sufficiebant. Nec invenire poteramus aliquid ad emendum, quia forum erat nimis remotum. Sed Dominus nobis quendam Ruthenum, nomine Cosmam, aurifabrum præparavit, qui satis dilectus Imperatori, nos in aliquo sustentavit. Et hic nobis ostendit thronum Imperatoris, quem ipse fecerat, antequam poneretur in sede, & sigillum ejusdem, quod etiam fabricaverat ipse. Post hoc Imperator pro nobis misit, nobisque per Chingay protonotarium suum dici fecit, ut verba nostra

Cuyne cum legatis dissimulanter agit.

Cosmas Russus.

Chingay internuncius.

& negotia scriberemus, eique porrigeremus. Quod & fecimus. Post plures dies nos iterum vocari fecit, & utrum essent apud Dominum Papam, qui Ruthenorum vel Sarracenorum, aut etiam Tartarorum literam intelligerent, interrogavit. Cui respondimus, quòd nullam istarum literarum habebamus. Sarraceni tamen erant in terra, sed remoti erant à Domino Papa. Diximus tamen, quia nobis *Prudens de* expedire videbatur, quòd in Tartarico scriberent, & nobis *literis con-silium.* interpretarentur, nos autem in litera nostra diligenter scriberemus, & tam literam quàm interpretationem ad Dominum Papam deferremus. Tunc à nobis recesserunt, & ad Imperatorem iverunt. Porrò à die Beati Martini fuimus vocati. Tunc Kadac, totius imperii procurator, & Chingay & Bala, pluresque scriptores ad nos venerunt, nobisque literam de verbo ad verbum interpretati fuerunt. Et cùm in Latina litera scripsissemus, faciebant sibi per singulas orationes interpretari, volentes scire, si nos in aliquo verbo erraremus. Cùm igitur ambæ literæ fuissent scriptæ, fecerunt nos semel ac secundo legere, ne fortè minus aliquid haberemus. Dixerunt enim nobis, videte, quòd omnia benè intelligatis, quia non expediret, quòd non omnia benè intelligeretis. Literas etiam in Sarracenico scripserunt, ut aliquis in partibus nostris inveniri posset, qui eas, si opus esset, legeret.

Qualiter licentiati fuerunt. Cap. 32.

UT autem nobis Tartari nostri dixerunt, proposuit Imperator nuncios suos nobiscum mittere. Volebat tamen, ut credimus, quod nos id ab eo peteremus. Sed cùm unus de Tartaris nostris, qui senior erat, nos ad hoc petendum hortaretur, nobis quidem, ut venirent, ne quaquam bonum videbatur. Ideoque respondimus ei, quòd *Legati* non erat nostrum petere, sed si sponte ipse Imperator mit- *abhorrent à* teret eos, libenter eos securè conduceremus, Domino ad- *Tartarorum* juvante. Nobis autem ob plures causas ut venirent, non *legatione.* videbatur expedire. Prima quidem fuit, quia timuimus, ne visis dissentionibus aut guerris, quæ fiunt inter nos, magis animarentur ad veniendum contra nos. Secunda

fuit, timebamus eos exploratores terræ fieri. Tertia verò,
quia timebamus eos interfici. Gentes enim nostræ arro-
gantes sunt & superbæ. Unde quando servientes, qui
stant nobiscum, ex rogatu Cardinalis, legati scilicet Alemanniæ, in habitu Tartarico ibant ad ipsum, in via ferè
lapidati sunt à Teutonicis, & coacti sunt deponere habitum
illum. Consuetudo autem est Tartarorum, ut cum illis,
qui nuncios eorum occiderint, nunquam faciant pacem, nisi
sumant de ipsis ultionem. Quarta etiam causa fuit, quia

timebamus ne nobis auferrentur vi. Quinta verò causa
erat, quia de adventu eorum nulla foret utilitas, cùm
nullum haberent aliud mandatum vel potestatem, nisi quód
literas Imperatoris ad Dominum Papam & ad Principes
deferrent, quas videlicet literas ipsi nos habebamus, &
malum ex eorum adventu posse contingere credebamus.

Novemb. 13. Itaque tertia die post hoc, scilicet in festo beati Briccii
nobis dederunt licentiam & literam, Imperatoris sigillo

Honorantur munitam, mittentes nos ad ipsius Imperatoris matrem,
commeatu & quæ unicuique nostrum dedit pelliceum unum de pellibus
lautiis. vulpinis, quod habebat pilos de foris, & purpuram unam.
De quibus Tartari nostri furati sunt ex unaquaque unum
passum. De illa quoque, quæ dabatur servienti, meliorem
medietatem sunt furati. Quod nos quidem non ignoravi-
mus, sed inde verba movere noluimus.

Qualiter ab illo itinere redierunt. Cap. 33.

TUnc iter ad revertendum arripuimus, ac per totam
hyemem venimus, jacentes in desertis sæpiùs in nive,
nisi quantum poteramus nobis cum pede locum facere.

Difficilis Ibi quippe non erant arbores, sed planus campus. Et
legatorum sæpe manè nos inveniebamus totos nive, quam ventus
reditus. pellebat, coopertos. Sic venientes usque ad Ascensionem
Bathy. Domini pervenimus ad Bathy. A quo cùm inquireremus,
quid responderet Domino Papæ, dixit se nolle aliud, nisi
quod Imperator diligenter scripserat, demandare. Datisque nobis de conductu literis, ab eo recessimus, & sabbatho
infra octavas Pentecostes usque ad Montii pervenimus,
ubi erant socii nostri, ac servientes, qui fuerant retenti,

quos ad nos fecimus reduci. Hinc usque Corrensam *Corrensa.*
pervenimus, cui iterum à nobis donaria petenti non
dedimus, quia non habebamus. Deditque nobis duos
Comanos, qui erant ex Tartarorum plebe, usque ad
Kioviam Russiæ. Tartarus tamen noster non dimisit nos,
donec exiremus ultimam Tartarorum custodiam. Isti
verò alii, qui nobis à Corrensa dati sunt, in sex diebus ab
ultima custodia usque ad Kioviam nos duxerunt. Venimus autem illuc ante festum Beati Johannis Baptistæ xv.
diebus. Porrò Kiovienses adventum nostrum percipientes, *Junii 8.*
occurrerunt nobis omnes lætanter. Congratulabantur *Gratulationes*
enim nobis, tanquam à morte suscitatis. Sic fecerunt *reducibus*
nobis per totam Russiam, Poloniam & Bohemiam. Daniel *factæ.*
& Wasilico frater ejus festum nobis magnum fecerunt, & *Basilius &*
nos contra voluntatem nostram bene per octo dies *Daniel*
tenuerunt. Medioque tempore inter se & cum Episcopis, *Principes.*
cæterisque probis viris, super his, quæ locuti fueramus
eisdem, in processu nostro ad Tartaros consilium habentes,
responderunt nobis communiter, dicentes : quòd Dominum *Russi*
Papam habere vellent in specialem Dominum, & in patrem, *agnoscunt pri-*
sanctam quoque Romanam Ecclesiam in dominam & *matum Papæ*
magistram, confirmantes etiam omnia, quæ priùs de hac
materia per Abbatem suum transmiserant. Et super hoc
etiam nobiscum ad Dominum Papam nuncios suos &
literas transmiserunt.

[The voyage

The voyage of Johannes de Plano Carpini unto the Northeast parts of the world, in the yeere of our Lord, 1246.

Of the first sending of certaine Friers Prædicants and Minorites unto the Tartars, taken out of the 32. Booke of Vincentius Beluacensis his Speculum Historiale : beginning at the second Chapter.

Ascellinus.

Bout this time also, Pope Innocentius the fourth sent Frier Ascelline being one of the order of the Prædicants, together with three other Friers (of the same authoritie whereunto they were called) consorted with him out of divers Covens of their order, with letters Apostolicall unto the Tartars campe : wherein hee exhorted them to give over their bloudie slaughter of mankinde, and to receive the Christian faith. And I, in verie deede, received the relations concerning the deedes of the Tartars onelie, (which, according to the congruence of times, I have above inserted into this my woorke) from a Frier Minorite, called Simon de Sanct.

Simon Quintinianus. John de plano Carpini.

Quintin, who lately returned from the same voyage. And at that verie time also, there was a certaine other Frier Minorite, namely Frier John de Plano Carpini, sent with certaine associates unto the Tartars, who likewise (as himselfe witnesseth) abode and conversed with them a yeere and three moneths at the least. For both he & one

Benedictus Polonus.

Frier Benedict a Polonian being of the same order, and a partaker of all his miserie and tribulation, received straight commaundement from the Pope, that both of them shoulde diligently searche out all things that concerned the state of the Tartars. And therefore this Frier John hath written a litle Historie (which is come to our hands) of such

[I. 54.]

things, as with his owne eyes hee sawe among the Tartars, or which he heard from divers Christians worthy of credit, remaining there in captivitie. Out of which historie I thought good by way of conclusion, to insert somewhat for the supply of those things which are wanting in the said Frier Simon.

Of the situation and qualitie of the Tartars land, By Johannes de Plano Carpini. Chap. 3.

THere is towards the East a land which is called Mon- *A description* gal or Tartaria, lying in that part of the worlde which *of Tartaria.* is thought to be most North Easterly. On the East part it hath the countrey of Kythay and of the people called Solangi : on the South part the countrey of the Saracens : on the South east the land of the Huini : and on the West the province of Naimani : but on the North side it is *The North* invironed with the Ocean Sea. In some part thereof it is *Ocean.* full of mountaines, and in other places plaine and smoothe grounde, but everie where sandie and barren, neither is the hundreth part thereof fruitefull. For it cannot beare fruite unlesse it be moistened with river waters, which bee verie rare in that countrey. Whereupon they have neither villages, nor cities among them, except one which is called Cracurim, and is said to be a proper towne. We our selves sawe not this towne, but were almost within halfe a dayes journey thereof, when we remained at Syra Orda, *Syra Orda.* which is the great court of their Emperour. And albeit the foresaid lande is otherwise unfruitfull, yet is it very commodious for the bringing up of cattell. In certaine places thereof are some small store of trees growing, but otherwise it is altogether destitute of woods. Therefore the Emperour, and his noble men and all other warme themselves, and dresse their meate with fires made of the doung of oxen, and horses. The ayre also in that *The* countrey is verie intemperate. For in the midst of *intemperature* Sommer there be great thunders and lightnings, by the *of the aire.* which many men are slaine, and at the same time there falleth great abundance of snowe. There bee also such mightie tempestes of colde windes, that sometimes men are not able to sitte on horsebacke. Whereupon, being *What Orda* neere unto the Orda (for by this name they call the *signifieth.*

habitations of their Emperours and noble men) in regarde of the great winde we were constrained to lye groveling on the earth, and could not see by reason of the dust. There is never any raine in Winter, but onely in Sommer, albeit in so little quantitie, that sometimes it scarcely sufficeth to allay the dust, or to moysten the rootes of the grasse. There is often times great store of haile also. Insomuch that when the Emperour elect was to be placed in his Emperiall throne (my selfe being then present) there fell such abundance of haile, that, upon the sudden melting thereof, more then 160. persons were drowned in the same place : there were manie tentes and other thinges also caried away. Likewise, in the Sommer season there is on the sudden extreame heate, and suddenly againe intollerable colde.

Of their forme, habite, and maner of living. Chap. 4.

The shape of the Tartars.
THe Mongals or Tartars, in outward shape, are unlike to all other people. For they are broader betweene the eyes, and the balles of their cheekes, then men of other nations bee. They have flat and small noses, litle eyes, and eye liddes standing streight upright, they are shaven on the crownes like priests. They weare their haire somewhat longer about their eares, then upon their foreheads : but behinde they let it growe long like
Their habite.
womans haire, whereof they braide two lockes binding eche of them behind either eare. They have short feet also. The garments, as well of their men, as of their women are all of one fashion. They use neither cloakes, hattes, nor cappes. But they weare Jackets framed after a strange manner, of buckeram, skarlet, or Baldakines.
Like unto Frobishers men.
Their shoubes or gownes are hayrie on the outside, and open behinde, with tailes hanging downe to their hammes. They use not to washe their garments, neither will in any wise suffer them to bee washed, especially in
Their tabernacles.
the time of thunder. Their habitations bee rounde and cunningly made with wickers and staves in manner of

a tent. But in the middest of the toppes thereof, they have a window open to convey the light in and the smoake out. For their fire is alwayes in the middest. Their walles bee covered with felt. Their doores are made of felte also. Some of these Tabernacles may quickely be taken asunder, and set together againe, and are caried upon beastes backes. Other some cannot be taken insunder, but are stowed upon carts. And whithersoever they goe, be it either to warre, or to any other place, they transport their tabernacles with them. They are very rich in cattel, as in camels, oxen, sheep, and *Their cattell.* goats. And I thinke they have more horses and mares then all the world besides. But they have no kine nor other beasts. Their Emperors, Dukes, & other of their nobles doe abound with silk, gold, silver, and precious stones. Their victuals are al things that may be eaten : *Their* for we saw some of them eat lice. They drinke milke in *victuals.* great quantitie, but especially mares milke, if they have [I. 55.] it : They seeth Mill also in water, making it so thinne, that they may drinke thereof. Every one of them drinkes off a cup full or two in a morning, and sometime they eate nought else all the day long. But in the evening each man hath a little flesh given him to eate, and they drinke the broath thereof. Howbeit in summer time, when they have mares milke enough, they seldome eate flesh, unles perhaps it be given them, or they take some beast or bird in hunting.

Of their manners both good and bad. Chap. 5.

THeir manners are partly prayse-worthie, and partly *Their* detestable : For they are more obedient unto their *obedience.* lords and masters, then any other either clergie or laie-people in the whole world. For they doe highly reverence them, and will deceive them, neither in wordes nor deedes. They seldome or never fall out among themselves, and, as for fightings or brawlings, wounds or manslaughters, they never happen among them. There *Their* are neither theeves nor robbers of great riches to be *abstinence.*

found, and therefore the tabernacles and cartes of them that have any treasures are not strengthened with lockes or barres. If any beast goe astray, the finder thereof either lets it goe, or driveth it to them that are put in office for the same purpose, at whose handes the owner of the said beast demaundeth it, and without any

Their courtesie.

difficultie receiveth it againe. One of them honoureth another exceedingly, and bestoweth banquets very familiarly and liberally, notwithstanding that good victuals are daintie and scarce among them. They are also very hardie, and when they have fasted a day or two without any maner of sustenance, they sing and are merry as if they had eaten their bellies full. In riding, they endure much cold and extreme heat. There be, in a maner, no contentions among them, and although they use commonly to be drunken, yet doe they not quarell in their drunkennes. Noe one of them despiseth another but helpeth and furthereth him, as much as conveniently

Their chastity.

he can. Their women are chaste, neither is there so much as a word uttered concerning their dishonestie. Some of them will notwithstanding speake filthy and immodest

Their insolencie against strangers.

words. But towards other people, the said Tartars be most insolent, and they scorne and set nought by all other noble and ignoble persons whatsoever. For we saw in the Emperours court the great duke of Russia, the kings sonne of Georgia, and many great Soldanes receiving no due honour and estimation among them. So that even the very Tartars assigned to give attendance unto them, were they never so base, would alwaies goe before them, and take the upper hand of them, yea, and sometimes would constraine them to sit behinde their backes. More-over they are angrie and of a disdainefull nature unto other people, and beyond all measure deceitfull, and treacherous towards them. They speake fayre in the beginning, but in conclusion, they sting like scorpions. For craftie they are, and full of falshood, circumventing all men whom they are able, by their sleights. Whatso-ever mischiefe they entend to practise against a man, they

keepe it wonderfully secrete, so that he may by no meanes
provide for himselfe, nor find a remedie against their
conspiracies. They are unmanerly also and uncleanly in
taking their meat and their drinke, and in other actions.
Drunkennes is honourable among them, and when any of
them hath taken more drinke then his stomacke can well
beare, hee casteth it up and falles to drinking againe.
They are most intollerable exacters, most covetous
possessours, and most nigardly givers. The slaughter
of other people is accompted a matter of nothing with
them.

Of their lawes and customes.   Chap. 6.

MOreover, they have this law or custome, that *Punishments*
whatsoever man or woman be manifestly taken *of adultery.*
in adultery, they are punished with death. A virgine
likewise that hath committed fornication, they slay
together with her mate. Whosoever be taken in *Of theft.*
robberie or theft, is put to death without all pitie. Also, *Of secretes*
if any man disclose their secrets, especially in time of *disclosed.*
warre, he receiveth an hundreth blowes on the backe with
a bastinado, layd on by a tall fellow.   In like sort when any
inferiours offend in ought, they finde no favour at their
superiours handes, but are punished with grievous stripes.
They are joyned in matrimony to all in generall, yea, *Lawes of*
even to their neare kinsfolkes except their mother, *matrimonie.*
daughter and sister by the mothers side. For they use
to marrie their sister by the fathers side onely, and also
the wife of their father after his decease. The yonger
brother also, or some other of his kindred, is bound to
marry the wife of his elder brother deceased. For, at the
time of our aboad in the countrey, a certaine duke of *Andreas duke*
Russia named Andreas, was accused before duke Baty for *of Russia.*
conveying the Tartars horses out of the land, and for
selling them to others : and although it could not be
prooved, yet was he put to death. His yonger brother
and the wife of the party deceased hearing this, came
& made their supplication unto the forenamed duke, that

the dukedome of Russia might not be taken from them. But he commanded the youth to marrie his deceased brothers wife, and the woman also to take him unto her husband, according to the custome of the Tartars. She answered, that she had rather die, then so haynously transgresse the law. Howbeit, hee delivered her unto him, although they both refused as much as they could. Wherefore carying them to bed, they constrained the youth, lamenting and weeping, to lie downe and commit incest with his brothers wife. To be short, after the death of their husbands, the Tartars wives use very seldome to marrie the second time, unlesse perhaps some man takes his brothers wife or his stepmother in mariage. They make no difference betweene the sonne of their wife and of their concubine, but the father gives what he pleaseth unto each one : For of late the king of Georgia having two sonnes, one lawfully begotten called Melich ; but the other David, borne in adulterie, at his death left part of his lande unto his base sonne. Hereupon Melich (unto whome the kingdome fell by right of his mother, because it was governed before time by women) went unto the Emperour of the Tartars, David also having taken his journey unto him. Nowe both of them comming to the court and proffering large giftes, the sonne of the harlot made suite, that he might have justice, according to the custome of the Tartars. Well, sentence passed against Melich, that David being his elder brother, should have superioritie over him, and should quietly and peaceably possesse the portion of land granted unto him by his father. Whensoever a Tartar hath many wives, each one of them hath her family and dwelling place by her selfe. And sometime the Tartar eateth, drinketh and lieth with one, and sometime with another. One is accompted chiefe among the rest, with whom hee is oftener conversant, then with the other. And notwithstanding (as it hath bin said) they are many, yet do they seldome fal out among themselves.

*Melich &
David two
brothers.*

Of their superstitious traditions.   Chap. 7.

BUt by reason of certain traditions, which either they or their predecessors have devised, they accompt some things indifferent to be faults.   One is to thrust a knife into the fire, or any way to touch the fire with a knife, or with their knife to take flesh out of the cauldron, or to hewe with an hatchet neare unto the fire.   For they think by that means to take away the head or force from the fire.   Another is to leane upon the whip, wherewith they beate their horses : for they ride not with spurs. Also, to touch arrowes with a whip, to take or kill yong birds, to strike an horse with ye raine of their bridle, and to breake one bone against another.   Also, to powre out milke, meate, or any kinde of drinke upon the ground or to make water within their tabernacle : which whoso-ever doth willingly, he is slaine, but otherwise he must pay a great summe of money to the inchanter to be purified.   Who likewise must cause the tabernacle with all things therein, to passe betweene two fiers.   Before it be on this wise purified, no man dare once enter into it, nor conveigh any thing thereout.   Besides, if any man hath a morsell given him, which he is not able to swallow, and for that cause casteth it out of his mouth, there is an hole made under his tabernacle, by which hee is drawen forth and slaine without all compassion.   Likewise, who-soever treads upon the threshold of any of their dukes tabernacles, he is put to death.   Many other things there be, like unto these, which they take for heinous offences. But to slay men, to invade the dominions of other people, and to rifle their goods, to transgresse the commaundements and prohibitions of God, are with them no offences at all. They know nothing concerning eternall life, and ever-lasting damnation, and yet they thinke, that after death they shall live in another world, that they shall multiply their cattell, that they shal eate and drinke and doe other things which living men performe here upon earth.   At a new moone, or a full moone, they begin all enterprises that they take in hand, and they call the moone the Great Emperour, and worship it upon their knees. All men that abide in their tabernacles must be purified with *Their custome* fire : Which purification is on this wise, They kindle two *of purifying.* fires, and pitch two Javelines into the ground neere unto the said fires, binding a corde to the tops of the Javelines. And about the corde they tye certaine jagges of buckram, under which corde, and betweene which fires, men, beastes, and tabernacles do passe. There stand two women also, one on the right side, and another on the left casting water, and repeating certaine charmes. If any man be slaine by lightning, all that dwell in the same tabernacle with him must passe by fire in maner aforesaid. For their tabernacles, beds, and cartes, their feltes and garments, and whatsoever such things they have, are touched by no man, yea, and are abandoned by all men as things uncleane. And to bee short, they thinke that all things are to be purged by fire. Therefore, when any ambassadours, princes, or other personages whatsoever come unto them, they and their giftes must passe betweene two fires to be purified, lest peradventure they have practised some witchcraft, or have brought some poyson or other mischiefe with them.

[I. 57.] ## Of the beginning of their empire or government. Chap. 8.

The people of THe East countrie, whereof wee have entreated, which
Tartaria. is called Mongal, is reported to have had of olde time foure sortes of people. One of their companions was called Yeka Mongal, that is the great Mongals. The second company was called Sumongal, that is, the Water-Mongals, who called themselves Tartars of a certaine river running through their countrey named Tartar. The third was called Merkat, and the fourth Metrit. All these people had one and the same person, *The original* attire of body and language, albeit they were divided by
& the ex- princes and provinces. In the province of Yeka Mongal,
ploits of there was a certaine man called Chingis. This man
Chingis.

142

became a mighty hunter. For he learned to steale men,
& to take them for a pray. He ranged into other
countries taking as many captives as he could, and joining
them unto himselfe. Also hee allured the men of his
owne countrey unto him, who followed him as their
captaine and ringleader to doe mischiefe. Then began he
to make warre upon the Sumongals or Tartars, and slewe
their captaine, and after many conflicts, subdued them
unto himselfe, and brought them all into bondage.
Afterward he used their helpe to fight against the
Merkats, dwelling by the Tartars, whom also hee vanquished in battell. Proceeding from thence, he fought
against the Metrites, and conquered them also. The *The Naimani.*
Naimani hearing that Chingis was thus exalted, greatly
disdeined thereat. For they had a mighty & puissant
Emperour, unto whom all the foresaid nations payed
tribute. Whose sonnes, when he was dead, succeeded
him in his Empire. Howbeit, being young and foolish,
they knew not howe to governe the people, but were *The discord of*
divided, and fell at variance among themselves. Now *brethren.*
Chingis being exalted, as is aforesaid, they neverthelesse
invaded the forenamed countries, put the inhabitants to
the sword, and carried away their goods for a pray.
Which Chingis having intelligence of, gathered all his
subjects together. The Naimani also, and the people
called Karakitay assembled and banded themselves at a
certaine straight valley, where, after a battell foughten
they were vanquished by the Mongals. And being thus
vanquished, they were, the greater part of them, slaine ;
and others, which could not escape, were carried into
captivitie. In the land of the foresayd Karakytayans,
Occoday Cham, the sonne of Chingis Cham, after he was *Occoday*
created Emperour, built a certaine citie, which he called *Cham.*
Chanyl. Neare unto which citie, on the South side,
there is an huge desert, wherein wilde men are certainely
reported to inhabite, which cannot speake at all, and are
destitute of joynts in their legges, so that if they fall, they
cannot rise alone by themselves. Howbeit, they are of

discretion to make feltes of Camels haire, wherewith they
clothe themselves, and which they holde against the
winde. And if at any time, the Tartars pursuing them,
chance to wound them with their arrowes, they put herbes
into their wounds, and flye strongly before them.

Of the mutuall victories betweene them, and the
people of Kythay.   Chap. 9.

BUt the Mongals returning home into their owne
countrey, prepared themselves to battell against the
*Kythayans : Which their Emperour hearing, set forward
against them with his armie, and they fought a cruell
battell, wherein the Mongals were overcome, and all their
nobles in the armie, except seven, were slaine.   And for
this cause, when they, purposing to invade anie region,
are threatned by the inhabitants thereof to be slaine, they
doe, to this day, answere : in old time also our whole
number besides being slaine, we remayned but seven of us
alive, and yet notwithstanding we are now growen unto
a great multitude, thinke not therefore to daunt us with
such brags.   But Chingis and the residue that remained
alive, fled home into their countrey : And having breathed

him a little, he prepared himselfe to warre, and went forth
against the people called Huyri : These men were Christians of the sect of Nestorius.   And these also the
Mongals overcame, and received letters or learning from
them : for before that time they had not the arte of
writing, and nowe they call it the hand or letters of the
Mongals.   Immediately after, hee marched against the
countrey of Saruyur, and of the Karanites, and against
the land of Hudirat ; all which he vanquished.   Then
returned he home into his owne countrey, and breathed
himselfe.   Afterward, assembling his warlike troupes, they
marched with one accord against the Kythayans, and
waging warre with them a long time, they conquered a
great part of their land, and shut up their Emperour into
his greatest citie : which citie they had so long time besieged, that they began to want necessary provision for their

armie. And when they had no victuals to feede upon, Chingis Cham commaunded his souldiers, that they should eate every tenth man of the companie. But they of the [I. 58.] citie fought manfully against them, with engines, dartes, and arrowes, and when stones wanted they threw silver, *Silver cast at* and especially melted silver : for the same citie abounded *the enemie in stead of stones.* with great riches. Also, when the Mongals had fought a long time and could not prevayle by warre, they made a great trench underneath the ground from the armie unto the middest of the citie, and there issuing foorth they fought against the citizens, and the remnant also without the walles fought in like manner. At last, breaking open the gates of the citie, they entred, and putting the Emperour, with many other to the sworde, they tooke possession thereof and conveighed away the golde, silver, and all the riches therein. And having appointed certaine deputies over the countrey, they returned home into their owne lande. This is the first time, when the Emperour of the Kythayans being vanquished, Chingis Cham ob- *Chingis Cham* tayned the Empire. But some parte of the countrey, *proclaimed* *Emperour.* because it lyeth within the sea, they could by no meanes *Part of* conquere unto this day. The men of Kytay are Pagans, *Cathay in* having a speciall kinde of writing by themselves, and (as it *the sea.* is reported) the Scriptures of the olde and newe Testa- *The letters,* ment. They have also recorded in hystories the lives of *& the* their forefathers : and they have Eremites, and certaine *religion of the* houses made after the manner of our Churches, which *Cathayans.* in those dayes they greatly resorted unto. They say that they have divers Saints also, and they worship one God. They adore and reverence CHRIST JESUS our Lorde, and beleeve the article of eternall life, but are not baptized. They doe also honourably esteeme and reverence our Scriptures. They love Christians, and bestowe much almes, and are a very courteous and gentle people. They have no beardes, and they agree partly with the Mongals in the disposition of their *Their* countenance. In all occupations which men practise, *excellent* there are not better artificers in the whole worlde. *workmanship.*

Their countrey is exceeding rich, in corne, wine, golde, silke, and other commodities.

Of their warre against India major and minor. Chap. 10.

ANd when the Mongals with their emperour Chingis Cham had a while rested themselves after the foresayd victorie, they divided their armies. For the Emperour sent one of his sonnes named Thossut (whom also *Thossut Can* they called Can, that is to say, Emperour) with an armie *son of Chingis.* against the people of Comania, whom he vanquished with much warre, and afterward returned into his owne country. But he sent his other sonne with an armie *India minor* against the Indians, who also subdued India minor. *subdued.* These Indians are the blacke Saracens, which are also called Æthiopians. But here the armie marched forward to fight against Christians dwelling in India major. Which the King of that countrey hearing (who is commonly called Presbiter John) gathered his souldiers together, and came *The stratagem* foorth against them. And making mens images of copper, *of the king of* he set each of them upon a saddle on horsebacke, and put *India.* fire within them, and placed a man with a paire of bellowes on the horse backe behinde every image. And so with many horses and images in such sorte furnished, they marched on to fight against the Mongals or Tartars. And comming neare unto the place of the battell, they first of all sent those horses in order one after another. But the men that sate behind laide I wote not what upon the fire within the images, and blew strongly with their bellowes. Whereupon it came to passe, that the men and the horses were burnt with wilde fire, and the ayre was darkened with smoake. Then the Indians cast dartes upon the Tartars, of whom many were wounded and slain. And so they expelled them out of their dominions with great confusion, neither did we heare, that ever they returned thither againe.

How being repelled by monstrous men shapen
like dogs, they overcame the people of Burithabeth. Chap. 11.

BUt returning through the deserts, they came into a
certaine countrey, wherin (as it was reported unto us
in the Emperours court, by certaine clergie men of Russia,
and others, who were long time among them, and that by
strong and stedfast affirmation) they found certaine
monsters resembling women : who being asked by many
interpreters, where the men of that land were, they
answered, that whatsoever women were borne there, were
indued with the shape of mankinde, but the males were
like unto dogges. And delaying the time, in that countrey
they met with the said dogges on the other side of the river.
And in the midst of sharpe winter, they cast themselves
into the water : Afterward they wallowed in the dust upon
the maine land, and so the dust being mingled with water,
was frozen to their backes, and having often times so
done, the ice being strongly frozen upon them, with great
fury they came to fight against the Tartars. And when
the Tartars threwe their dartes, or shot their arrowes
among them, they rebounded backe againe, as if they had
lighted upon stones. And the rest of their weapons coulde
by no meanes hurt them. Howbeit, the Dogges made an
assault upon the Tartars, and wounding some of them
with their teeth, and slaying others, at length they drave
them out of their countries. And thereupon they have a
Proverbe of the same matter, as yet rife among them,
which they speake in jesting sorte one to another ; My
father or my brother was slaine of Dogges. The women
which they tooke, they brought into their owne countrey,
who remayned there till their dying day. And in traveiling homewardes, the sayd armie of the Mongals came unto
the lande of Burithabeth (the inhabitants whereof are
Pagans) and conquered the people in battell. These
people have a strange or rather a miserable kinde of

*A strange
report of cer-
tain monstrous
women and
dogs.*

[I. 59.]

*The region of
Burithabeth.*

147

custome. For when anie mans father deceaseth, he assembleth all his kindred, and they eate him. These men have no beards at all, for we saw them carie a certaine iron instrument in their hands, wherewith, if any haires growe upon their chinne, they presently plucke them out. They are also very deformed. From thence the Tartars armie returned to their owne home.

How they had the repulse at the Caspian mountaynes, and were driven backe by men dwelling in caves. Chap. 12.

MOreover Chingis Cham, at the same time when he sent other armies against the East, hee himselfe marched with a power into the lande of Kergis, which notwithstanding, he conquered not in that expedition, and as it was reported unto us, he went on forward even to the Caspian mountaines. But the mountaines on that part where they encamped themselves, were of adamant, and therefore they drew unto them their arrowes, and weapons of iron. And certaine men contained within those Caspian mountaynes, hearing, as it was thought, the noyse of the armie, made a breach through, so that when the Tartars returned unto the same place tenne yeeres after, they found the mountaine broken. And attempting to goe unto them, they could not : for there stood a cloud before them, beyond which they were not able to passe, being deprived of their sight so soone as they approched thereunto. But they on the contrary side thinking that the Tartars durst not come nigh them, gave the assault, & when they came at the cloud, they could not proceed for the cause aforesaid. Also the Tartars, before they came unto the said mountaines, passed for the space of a moneth and more, through a vast wildernes, & departing thence towards the East, they were above a moneth traveiling through another huge desert. At length, they came unto a land wherin they saw beaten waies, but could not find any people. Howbeit, at the last, diligently seeking, they found a man & his wife, whom they presented before

Chingis Cham : and demanding of them where the people of that countrey were, they answered, that the people inhabited under the ground in mountains. Then Chingis Cham keeping still the woman, sent her husband unto them, giving them charge to come at his command. And going unto them, he declared all things that Chingis Cham had commanded them. But they answered, that they would upon such a day visite him, to satisfie his desire. And in the meane season, by blinde & hidden passages under the earth, assembling themselves, they came against the Tartars in warlike manner, and suddenly issuing forth, they slewe a great number of them. This people were not able to endure the terrible noise, which in that place the Sunne made at his uprising : for at the time of the *A fabulous* Sunne rising, they were inforced to lay one eare upon the *narration of* ground, and to stoppe the other close, least they should *the sun rising.* heare that dreadfull sound. Neither could they so escape, for by this meanes many of them were destroyed. Chingis Cham therefore and his company, seeing that they prevailed not, but continually lost some of their number, fled and departed out of that land. But the man and his wife aforesaid they caried along with them, who all their life time continued in the Tartars countrey. Being demaunded why the men of their countrey doe inhabite under the ground, they sayd, that at a certeine time of the yeare, when the sunne riseth, there is such an huge noyse, that the people cannot endure it. Moreover, they use to play upon cymbals, drums, and other musicall instruments, to the ende they may not heare that sounde.

Of the statutes of Chingis Cham, of his death, of his sonnes, and of his dukes. Chap. 13.

BUt as Chingis Cham returned out of that countrey, his people wanted victuals, & suffered extreme famin. Then by chance they found ye fresh intrails of a beast : which they tooke, & casting away the dung therof, caused it to be sodden, brought it before Chingis Cham, & did *The lawe of* eat therof. And hereupon Chingis Cham enacted ; that *Chingis.*

[I. 60.]

neither the blood, nor the intrails, nor any other part of a beast which might be eaten, should be cast away, save onely the dunge. Wherefore he returned thence into his owne land, and there he ordayned lawes and statutes, which the Tartars doe most strictly and inviolably observe, *The death of* of the which we have before spoken. He was afterward *Chingis.* slaine by a thunderclap. He had foure sonnes : the first *His sonnes.* was called Occoday, the second Thossut Can, the third Thiaday : the name of the fourth is unknowen. From these foure descended all the dukes of the Mongals. The *His graund-* first sonne of Occoday is Cuyne, who is now Emperour : *children.* his brothers be Cocten and Chyrinen. The sonnes of Thossut Can are Bathy, Ordu, Siba, and Bora. Bathy, next unto the Emperour, is richer and mightier then all the rest. But Ordu is the seignior of all the dukes. The sonnes of Thiaday be Hurin and Cadan. The sonnes of Chingis Cham his other sonne, whose name is unknowen, are Mengu, Bithat, and certaine others. The mother of Mengu was named Seroctan, and of all others most honoured among the Tartars, except the Emperors mother, and mightier then any subject except Bathy. *The Tar-* These be the names of the dukes : Ordu, who was in *tarian dukes.* Poland and in Hungarie : Bathy also & Hurin & Cadan, and Siban, and Ouygat, all which were in Hungarie. In like maner Cyrpodan, who is as yet beyond the sea, making war against certaine Soldans of the Saracens, and other inhabitants of farre countries. Others remained in the land, as namely Mengu, Chyrinen, Hubilai, Sinocur, Cara, Gay, Sybedey, Bora, Berca, Corrensa. There be many other of their dukes, whose names are unknowen unto us.

Of the authoritie of the Emperour, and of his dukes. Chap. 14.

The absolute
and lordly
dominion of the
Tartarian
Emperour over
his subjects.

MOreover, the Emperour of the Tartars hath a wonderfull dominion over all his subjects. For no man dare abide in any place, unles he hath assigned him to be there. Also he himselfe appointeth to his dukes where they should inhabite. Likewise the dukes assigne places unto every Millenarie, or conducter of a thousand souldiers, the Millenaries unto each captaine of an 100. the captaines unto every corporall of ten. Whatsoever is given them in charge, whensoever, or wheresoever, be it to fight or to lose their lives, or howsoever it be, they obey without any gainsaying. For if he demandeth any mans daughter, or sister being a virgine, they presently deliver her unto him without all contradiction : yea, often times he makes a collection of virgines throughout all the Tartars dominions, and those whom he meanes to keepe, he retaineth unto himselfe, others he bestoweth upon his men. Also, whatsoever messenger he sendeth, or whithersoever, his subjects must without delay finde them horses and other necessaries. In like sorte, from what countrey soever tribute payers, or ambassadours come unto him, they must have horses, carriages, and expenses allowed them. Notwithstanding ambassadours comming from other places do suffer great misery, and are in much wante both of victuals, and of apparel : especially when they come to any of the dukes, and there they are constrayned to make some lingering abode. Then ten men *Their* are allowed so little sustenance, that scarcely two could *barbarous* live thereof. Likewise, if any injuries be offered them, *inhumanitie* they cannot without danger make complaint. Many gifts *ambassadours.* also are demaunded of them, both by dukes and others, which if they doe not bestow, they are basely esteemed, and set at nought. And hereupon, wee were of necessitie enforced to bestowe in giftes a great part of those things which were given us by well disposed people, to defray our charges. To be short, all things are so in the power and possession of the Emperour, that no man dare say, This is mine, or, this is my neighbours ; but all, both goods, cattell and men are his owne. Concerning this matter also he published a statute of late. The very same authority and jurisdiction, doe the dukes in like sorte exercise upon their subjects.

Of the election of Emperour Occoday, and of
the expedition of duke Bathy.   Chap. 15.

AFter the death of Chingis Cham aforesayd, the dukes
assembled themselves and chose Occoday his sonne
to be their Emperour.   And he, entering into consultation with his nobles, divided his armies, and sent duke

Bathy his nephew against the countrie of Altisoldan, and
against the people called Bisermini, who were Saracens,
but spake the language of Comania.   The Tartars invading their countrey, fought with them and subdued

them in battel.   But a certeine citie called Barchin resisted
them a long time.   For the citizens had cast up many
ditches and trenches about their citie, in regard whereof
the Tartars could not take it, till they had filled the said
ditches.   But the citizens of Sarguit hearing this, came
foorth to meete them, yeelding themselves unto them of
their owne accord.   Whereupon their citie was not
destroyed, but they slue manie of them and others they
carried away captive, and taking spoyles, they filled the

citie with other inhabitants, and so marched foorth against
the citie of Orna.   This towne was very populous and
exceeding rich.   For there were many Christians therein,
as namely Gasarians, Russians, and Alanians, with others,
and Saracens also.   The government of the citie was in
the Saracens hande.   It standeth upon a mighty river,
and is a kinde of porte towne, having a great marte
exercised therein.   And when the Tartars could not
otherwise overcome it, they turned the said river, running
through the citie, out of his chanell, and so drowned the
citie with the inhabitantes and their goods.   Which being
done, they set forward against Russia, and made foule
havocke there, destroying cities and castles and murthering the people.   They layd siege a long while unto Kiow
the chiefe citie of Russia, and at length they tooke it and
slue the citizens.   Whereupon, traveiling through that
countrey, wee found an innumerable multitude of dead
mens skulles and bones lying upon the earth.   For it was

a very large and a populous citie, but it is nowe in a
maner brought to nothing : for there doe scarce remaine
200. houses, the inhabitants whereof are kept in extreame
bondage. Moreover, out of Russia and Comania, they
proceeded forward against the Hungarians, and the
Polonians, and there manie of them were slaine, as is
aforesaid : and had the Hungarians manfully withstood
them, the Tartars had beene confounded and driven
backe. Returning from thence, they invaded the
countrey of the Morduans being pagans, and conquered *The*
them in battell. Then they marched against the people *Morduans.*
called Byleri, or Bulgaria magna, & utterly wasted the *Bulgaria*
countrey. From hence they proceeded towards the *magna.*
North against the people called Bastarci or Hungaria *Hungaria*
magna, and conquered them also. And so going on *magna.*
further North, they came unto the Parossitæ, who having *Parossitæ.*
little stomacks and small mouthes, eate not any thing at
all, but seething flesh they stand or sitte over the potte,
and receiving the steame or smoke thereof, are therewith
onely nourished, and if they eate anie thing it is very
little. From hence they came to the Samogetæ, who live *Samogetæ.*
onely upon hunting, and use to dwell in tabernacles onely,
and to weare garments made of beastes skinnes. From
thence they proceeded unto a countrey lying upon the
Ocean sea, where they found certaine monsters, who in *The North*
all things resembled the shape of men, saving that their *ocean.*
feete were like the feete of an oxe, and they had in deede
mens heads but dogges faces. They spake, as it were, *Northerne*
two words like men, but at the third they barked like *monsters.*
dogges. From hence they retired into Comania, and
there some of them remaine unto this day.

Of the expedition of duke Cyrpodan.   Chap. 16.

AT the same time Occoday Can sent duke Cyrpodan *Kergis.*
with an armie against Kergis, who also subdued
them in battell. These men are Pagans, having no
beardes at all. They have a custome when any of their
fathers die, for griefe and in token of lamentation to

drawe as it were, a leather thong overthwart their faces, from one eare to the other. This nation being conquered, duke Cyrpodan marched with his forces Southward against the Armenians. And travailing through certain desert places, they found monsters in the shape of men, which had each of them but one arme & one hand growing out of the midst of their breast, and but one foote. Two of them used to shoote in one bowe, and they ran so swiftly, that horses could not overtake them. They ran also upon that one foote by hopping and leaping, and being weary of such walking, they went upon their hand and their foote, turning themselves round, as it were in a circle. And being wearie of so doing, they ran againe according to their wonted manner. Isidore

calleth them Cyclopedes. And as it was told us in court, by the clergie men of Russia, who remaine with the foresayd Emperour, many ambassadours were sent from them unto the Emperours court, to obtaine peace. From thence they proceeded forth into Armenia, which they

conquered in battell, and part also of Georgia. And the other part is under their jurisdiction, paying as yet every yeare unto them for tribute, 20000. pieces of coyne called Yperpera. From thence they marched into the dominions of the puissant and mighty Soldan called Deurum, whom also they vanquished in fight. And to be short, they went on farther sacking and conquering, even unto the

Soldan of Aleppo his dominions, and now they have subdued that land also, determining to invade other countries beyond it : neither returned they afterward into their owne land unto this day. Likewise the same armie

marched forward against the Caliph of Baldach his countrey, which they subdued also, & exacted at his handes the daylie tribute of 400. Byzantines, besides Baldakines and other giftes. Also every yeare they send messengers unto the Caliph moving him to come unto them. Who sending back great gifts together with his tribute beseecheth them to be favourable unto him. Howbeit the Tartarian Emperour receiveth al his gifts,

& yet still nevertheles sends for him, to have him
come.

How the Tartars behave themselves in warre.   [I. 62.]
Chap. 17.

CHingis Cham divided his Tartars by captaines of *The military*
ten, captaines of an 100. and captaines of a 1000. *discipline of*
And over ten Millenaries or captains of a 1000, he *the Tartars.*
placed, as it were, one Colonel, and yet notwithstanding
over one whole armie he authorised two or three
dukes, but yet so that all should have especiall regard
unto one of the said dukes. And when they joine
battel against any other nation, unles they do all with
one consent give backe, every man that flies is put to
death. And if one or two, or more of ten proceed
manfully to the battel, but the residue of those ten
draw backe & follow not the company, they are in
like maner slaine. Also, if one among ten or more
bee taken, their fellowes, if they rescue them not, are
punished with death. Moreover they are enjoined to
have these weapons following. Two long bowes or one *Their*
good one at the least, three quivers full of arrowes, & one *weapons.*
axe, and ropes to draw engines withal. But the richer
sort have single edged swords, with sharpe points, and
somewhat crooked. They have also armed horses with
their shoulders and breasts defenced, they have helmets
and brigandines. Some of them have jackes, and caparisons
for their horses made of leather artificially doubled or
trebled upon their bodies. The upper part of their
helmet is of iron or steele, but that part which com-
passeth about the necke and the throate is of leather.
Howbeit some of them have all their foresaide furniture
of iron framed in maner following. They beate out
many thinne plates a finger broad, and a handful long,
and making in every one of them eight little holes,
they put thereunto three strong and streight leather
thongs. So they joine the plates one to another, as it
were, ascending by degrees. Then they tie the plates

unto the said thongs, with other small and slender
thongs, drawen through the holes aforesayd, and in the
upper part, on each side therof, they fasten one small
doubled thong unto another, that the plates may
firmely be knit together. These they make, as well for
their horses caparisons, as for the armour of their men :
And they skowre them so bright that a man may
behold his face in them. Some of them upon the
necke of their launce have an hooke, wherewithall they
attempt to pull men out of their saddles. The heads of
their arrowes are exceedingly sharpe cutting both wayes
like a two edged sworde, and they alwaies carie a file
in their quivers to whet their arrowheads. They have
targets made of wickers, or of small roddes. Howbeit
they doe not (as we suppose) accustome to carrie them,
but onely about the tents, or in the Emperours or
dukes guardes, & that only in the night season. They
are most politique in warres, having bene exercised
therein with other nations for the space of these 42.
yeres. When they come at any rivers, the chiefe men
of the company have a round and light piece of
leather, about the borders whereof making many loopes,
they put a rope into them to drawe it together like a
purse, and so bring it into the rounde forme of a ball,
which leather they fill with their garments and other
necessaries, trussing it up most strongly. But upon the
midst of the upper parte thereof, they lay their saddles
and other hard things, there also doe the men themselves sit. This their boate they tye unto an horse
tayle, causing a man to swimme before, & to guide
over the horse, or sometime they have two oares to row
themselves over. The first horse therefore being driven
into the water, all the other horses of the company
followe him, and so they passe through the river. But the
poorer sort of common souldiers have every man his leather
bag or sachell well sowen together, wherin he packs up all
his trinkets, and strongly trussing it up hangs it at his
horses tayle, and so passeth over, in maner aforesaid.

JOHN DE PLANO CARPINI

A.D.
1246.

Howe they may be resisted.   Chap. 18.

I Deeme not any one kingdome or province able to
resist them : because they use to take up souldiers
out of every countrey of their dominions. And if so
be the neighbour province which they invade, wil not
aide them, utterly wasting it, with the inhabitants
therof, whom they take from thence with them, they
proceed on to fight against another countrey. And
placing their captives in the forefront of the battell, if
they fight not couragiously, they put them to the
swerde. Wherefore, if Christians would withstande
them, it is expedient, that the provinces and governours
of countreies should agree in one, and so by common
counsell, should give them resistance. Their souldiers
also must be furnished with strong hand-bowes & cros-
bowes, which they greatly dread, & with sufficient
arrowes, with maces also of good iron, or an axe with
a long handle or staffe. When they make their arrow
heads, they must (according to ye Tartars custome) dip
them red-hot into water mingled with salte, that they
may be strong to pierce the enemies armour. They
that wil may have swords also & lances with hooks at the
ends, to pull them from their saddles, out of which they
are easilie removed. They must have helmets likewise
& other armour to defend themselves & their horses from
the Tartars weapons & arrowes, & they that are unarmed, must (according to ye Tartars custome) march
behinde their fellowes, and discharge at the enemie with
long bowes and cros-bowes. And (as it is above said
of the Tartars) they must orderly dispose their bandes
and troupes, and ordeine lawes for their souldiers.
Whosoever runneth to the pray or spoyle, before the
victorie be atchieved, must undergoe a most severe
punishment. For such a fellow is put to death among
the Tartars without all pitie or mercie. The place of
battel must be chosen, if it be possible, in a plaine
fielde, where they may see round about, neither must

*Counsel how
to wage warre
against the
Tartars.*

*A notable
temper of iron
or steele.*

[I. 63.]

all be in one company, but in manie and severall bandes, not very farre distant one from another. They which give the first encounter must sende one band before, and must have another in a readynesse to relieve and second the former in time convenient. They must have spies also on every side to give them notice when the rest of the enemies bandes approch. For therefore ought they alwayes to send forth band against band & troupe against troupe, because the Tartar ever practiseth to gette his enemie in the midst and so to environ him. Let our bands take this caveat also, if the enemie retire, not to make any long pursuit after him, lest peradventure (according to his custome) he might draw them into some secret ambush : for the Tartar fights more by policie then by maine force. And againe, lest our horses bee tired : for we are not so well stored with horses as they. Those horses which the Tartars use one day, they ride not upon three or foure dayes after. Moreover, if the Tartars draw homeward, our men must not therefore depart and casseir their bandes, or separate themselves asunder : because they doe this upon policie, namely to have our armie divided, that they may more securely invade and waste the countrey. And in very deede, our captaines ought both day and night to keepe their armie in a readines : and not to lie out of their armour, but at all assayes, to bee provided for battell. For the Tartars like divels are alwaies watching and devising howe to practise mischiefe. Furthermore, if in battell any of the Tartars be cast off their horse backes, they must presently bee layd holde on and taken, for being on foote they shoote strongly, wounding and killing both horses and men.

*Johannes de
plano Carpini

Of the journey of frier *John unto the first guard of the Tartars. Chap. 19.

WE therefore by the commaundement of the sea apostolique setting foorth towards the nations of the East, chose first to travel unto the Tartars, because

we feared that there might be great danger imminent
upon the Church of God next unto them, by their
invasions. Proceeding on therefore, we came to the
king of Bohemia, who being of our familiar acquaintance, advised us to take our journey through Polonia
and Russia. For we had kinsfolkes in Polonia, by
whose assistance, we might enter into Russia. Having
given us his letters, hee caused our charges also to be
defrayed, in all his chiefe houses and cities, till we
came unto his nephew Boleslaus duke of Slesia, who
also was familiar and well knowen unto us. The like
favour he shewed us also, till wee came unto Conradus
duke of * Lautiscia, unto whome then (by Gods especiall
favour towards us) lord Wasilico duke of Russia was
come, from whose mouth we heard more at large
concerning the deedes of the Tartars : for he had sent
ambassadours thither, who were returned backe unto him.
Wherefore, it being given us to understand, that we must
bestow giftes upon them, we caused certaine skinnes
of bevers and other beastes to be bought with part of
that money, which was given upon almes to succour us by
the way. Which thing duke Conradus and the * duches
of Cracow, and a bishop, and certaine souldiers being advertised of, gave us likewise more of the same skins. And
to be short, duke Wasilico being earnestly requested by the
duke of Cracow, and by the bishop and barons, on our
behalfe, conducted us with him, unto his owne land, and
there for certaine daies, enterteined us at his owne charges,
to the ende that we might refresh our selves a while. And
when, being requested by us, he had caused his bishops to
resort unto him, we reade before them the Popes letters,
admonishing them to returne unto the unitie of the Church.
To the same purpose also, we our selves admonished them,
and to our abilitie, induced as well the duke as the bishops
and others thereunto. Howbeit because duke Daniel the
brother of Wasilico aforesaid (having as then taken his
journey unto Baty) was absent, they could not at that time,
make a finall answere. After these things duke Wasilico

*The journey of
frier John &
his fellow
Legates.*

*Boleslaus duke
of Silesia.*

* Mazovia.

Grimslaua.

*Daniel
brother unto
Wasilico.*

sent us forward with one of his servants as farre as Kiow the chiefe citie of Russia. Howbeit we went alwayes in danger of our lives by reason of the Lituanians, who did often invade ye borders of Russia, even in those verie places by which we were to passe. But in regard of the foresayd servant, wee were out of the Russians daunger, the greatest part of whome were either slaine, or caried into captivitie by the Tartars. Moreover, at Danilon wee were feeble even unto the death. (Notwithstanding wee caused our selves to bee carried in a waggon through the snowe and extreme colde.) And being come unto Kiow, wee consulted with the Millenary, & other noble men there concerning our journey. They told us, that if wee carried

[I. 64.] those horses, which wee then had, unto the Tartars, great store of snowe lying upon the ground, they would all dye : be cause they knew not howe to digge up the grasse under

the snow, as the Tartarian horses doe, neither could there bee ought found for them to eate, the Tartars having neither hay nor strawe, nor any other fodder. We determined therefore to leave them behind at Kiow with two servants appointed to keepe them. And wee were constrayned to bestow gifts upon the Millenary, that we might obtaine his favour to allowe us poste horses and a guide. Wherefore beginning our journey the second daye after the feast of the Purification, wee arrived at the towne of Canow, which was immediatly under the dominion of the Tartars. The governour whereof allowed us horses and a guide unto

another towne, wherein wee found one Michæas to be governour, a man full of all malice and despight. Who notwithstanding, having received giftes at our handes, according to his maner conducted us to the first guarde of the Tartars.

How he and his company were at the first received of the Tartars. Chap. 20.

WHerefore, the first saturday next after Ash wednesday, having about the Sunnes going downe, taken up our place of rest, the armed Tartars came rushing upon us in uncivil and horrible maner, being very inquisitive of us what maner of persons, or of what condition we were : & when we had answered them that we were the Popes Legates, receiving some victuals at our handes, they immediatly departed. Moreover in the morning rising and proceeding on our journey, the chiefe of them which were in the guard met with us, demaunding why, or for what intent and purpose we came thither ? and what busines we had with them ? Unto whom we answered, We are the legates of our lord the Pope, who is the father & lord of the Christians. He hath sent us as well unto your Emperour, as to your princes, and all other Tartars for this purpose, because it is his pleasure, that all Christians should be in league with the Tartars, and should have peace with them. It is his desire also that they should become great or in favour with God in heaven, therfore he admonisheth them aswel by us, as by his own letters, to become Christians, and to embrace the faith of our Lord Jesu Christ, because they could not otherwise be saved. Moreover, he gives them to understand, that he much marveileth at their monstrous slaughters & massacres of mankind, & especially of Christians, but most of al of Hungarians, Mountaineirs, & Polonians, being al his subjects, having not injuried them in ought, nor attempted to doe them injurie. And because the Lord God is grievously offended thereat, he adviseth them from henceforth to beware of such dealing, & to repent them of that which they had done. He requesteth also, that they would write an answere unto him, what they purpose to doe hereafter, and what their intention is. All which things being heard and understood, the Tartars sayd that they would appoint us poste horses and a guide unto Corrensa. And immediately demanding gifts at our hands, they obtained them. Then receiving the same horses, from which they dismounted, together with a guide wee tooke our journey unto Corrensa. But they riding a swift pace, sent a messenger before unto the sayd duke Corrensa, to signifie the message, which we had delivered unto them. This

The contents of the legacie.

Corrensa.

The duke of the Westerne marches.

duke is governour of all them, which lie in guard against the nations of the West, least some enemy might on the sudden and at unawares breake in upon them. And hee is said to have 60000. men under him.

How they were received at the court of Corrensa. Chap. 21.

BEing come therefore unto his court, hee caused our tent to bee placed farre from him, and sent his agents to demaund of us with what we would incline unto him, that is to say, what giftes we would offer, in doing our obeisance unto him. Unto whome wee answered, that our lord the Pope had not sent any giftes at all, because he was not certaine that wee should ever bee able to come at them: for we passed through most dangerous places. Notwithstanding, to our abilitie, we will honour him with some part of those things, which have bene, by the goodnes of God, & the favour of the Pope, bestowed upon us for our sustenance. Having received our gifts, they conducted us unto the Orda or tent of the duke, & we were instructed to bow thrise with our left knee before the doore of the tente, and in any case to beware, lest wee set our foote upon the threshold of the sayd doore. And that after we were entred, wee should rehearse before the duke and all his nobles, the same wordes, which wee had before sayde, kneeling upon our knees. Then presented wee the letters of our lord the Pope : but our interpreter whome we had hired and brought with us from Kiow was not sufficiently able to interpret them, neither was there any other esteemed to bee meete for the same purpose. Here certaine poste

horses and three Tartars were appoynted for us to conduct us from hence with al speede unto duke Bathy. This

Bathy is the mightiest prince among them except the Emperour, & they are bound to obey him before all other princes. We began our journey towards his court the first tuesday in Lent, and riding as fast as our horses could trot (for we had fresh horses almost thrise or foure times a day) we posted from morning till night, yea very often in the night season also, and yet could we not come at him before Maundie thursday. All this journey we went through the land of Comania, which is al plaine ground, and hath foure mighty rivers running through it : The first is called ‡ Neper, on the side whereof towards Russia, *‡ Boristhenes.* duke Corrensa & Montii marched up and downe, which Montii on the other side upon the plaines is greater then he. The second is called ‡ Don, upon the banke whereof *‡ Tanais.* marcheth a certain prince having in mariage the sister of Baty, his name is Tirbon. The third is called ‡ Volga, *‡ Rha.* which is an exceeding great river, upon the bankes whereof duke Bathy marcheth. The fourth is called ‡ Iaec, upon *‡ Rhymnus.* which two Millenaries doe march, on each side of the river one. All these, in the winter time, descend down to the sea, & in summer ascend backe by the bankes of the said rivers up to the mountaines. The sea last named is the ‖ Great sea, out of which the arme of S. George proceedeth, *‖ Pontus* which runneth by Constantinople. These rivers do abound *Euxinus.* with plenty of fishes, but especially Volga, & they exon- *He is deceived,* erate themselves into the Grecian sea, which is called Mare *for albeit* major. Over Neper we went many daies upon the ice. *Neper & Don run into Mare* Along the shore also of the Grecian sea we went very dan- *major : yet* gerously upon the ice in sundry places, & that for many *Volga & Iaec* daies together. For about the shore the waters are frozen *flowe into the* three leagues into the sea. But before we came unto *Caspian sea.* Bathy, two of our Tartars rode afore, to give him intelligence of all the sayings which we had uttered in the presence of Corrensa.

How we were received at the court of the great prince Bathy. Chap. 22.

MOreover, when we came unto Bathy in the land of Comania, we were seated a good league distant from his tabernacles. And when we should be conducted unto *A ceremony* his court, it was tolde us that we must passe between two *of passing be-* fires. But we would by no means be induced thereunto. *tweene two* Howbeit, they said unto us : you may passe through *fiers.* without al danger : for we would have you to doe it for none other cause, but only that if you intend any mischiefe against our lord, or bring any poyson with you, fire may take away all evill.   Unto whom we answered, that to the end we might cleare ourselves from all suspition of any such matter, we were contented to passe through.   When therefore we were come unto the Orda, being demanded

by his agent Eldegay with what present or gift we would do our obeisance ?   Wee gave the same answere which we did at the court of Corrensa.   The gifts being given and received, the causes of our journey also being heard, they brought us into the tabernacle of the prince, first bowing our selves at the doore, & being admonished, as before,

not to tread upon the threshold.   And being entred, we spake unto him kneeling upon our knees, & delivered him our letters, and requested him to have interpreters to translate them.   Who accordingly on good friday were sent unto us, and we together with them, diligently translated our sayd letters into the Russian, Tartarian, and Saracen languages.   This interpretation was presented unto Bathy, which he read, & attentively noted.   At length wee were conducted home againe unto our owne lodging, howbeit no victuals were given unto us, except it were once a litle Millet in a dich, the first night of our

comming.   This Bathy caries himselfe very stately & magnificently, having porters and all officers after the maner of the Emperour, and sittes in a lofty seate or throne together with one of his wives.   The rest, namely, as well his brethren and sonnes, as other great personages sit underneath him in the midst upon a bench, and others sit downe upon the ground, behinde him, but the men on the right hand and the women on the left.   He hath very faire and large tentes of linnen cloth also, which were once the kings of Hungaria.   Neither dare any man come into his tent (besides them of his owne family) unles he be called, be he never so mighty and great, except perhaps it be knowen that it is his pleasure.   Wee also, for the same cause, sate on the left hand ; for so doe all ambassadors in going : but in returning from the Emperour, we were

JOHN DE PLANO CARPINI

A.D.
1246.

alwaies placed on the right hand.   In the middest stands
his table, neare unto the doore of the tent, upon the which
there is drinke filled in golden and silver vessels.   Neither *Their custome*
doth Bathy at any time drinke, nor any other of the *of drinking at*
Tartarian princes, especially being in a publique place, but *the sound of*
they have singing and minstrilsie before them.   And *musicke.*
alwaies, when hee rides, there is a canopie or small tent
caried over his head upon the point of a javeline.   And so
doe all the great princes of the Tartars, & their wives also.
The sayd Bathy is courteous enough unto his owne men,
and yet is hee had in great awe by them : he is most cruel
in fight: he is exceedingly prudent and politique in warre,
because he hath now continued a long time in martiall
affaires.

How departing from Bathy, they passed through [I. 66.]
    the land of Comania, and of the Kangittæ.
    Chap. 23.

MOreover, upon Easter even we were called unto the
tent, and there came forth to meete us the foresaid
agent of Bathy, saying on his masters behalfe, that we
should go into their land, unto the Emperor Cuyne,
deteining certaine of our company with this pretence, that
they would send them backe unto the Pope, to whom we
gave letters of al our affaires to deliver unto him.   But
being come as farre as duke Montii aforesaid, there they *They traveiled*
were kept untill our returne.   Upon Easter day, having *post from*
said our praiers, and taken a slender breakfast, in the *Easter day to*
company of two Tartars, which were assigned unto us by *the 22. of July*
Corensa we departed with many teares, not knowing *Eastward of*
whether we went to death or to life.   And we were so *Volga.*
feeble in bodie, that we were scarce able to ride.   For all
that Lent through, our meat was Millet onely with a little
water and salte.   And so likewise upon other fasting
dayes.   Neither had we ought to drinke, but snowe
melted in a skillet.   And passing through Comania we
rode most earnestly, having change of horses five times or
oftener in a day, except when we went through deserts, for

then we were allowed better and stronger horses, which could undergoe the whole labour. And thus farre had we travailed from the beginning of Lent untill eight dayes after Easter. The land of Comania on the North side immediately after Russia, hath the people called Morduyni Byleri, that is, Bulgaria magna, the Bastarci, that is, Hungaria magna, next unto the Bastarci, the Parositæ and the Samogetæ. Next unto the Samogetæ are those people which are sayd to have dogges faces, inhabiting upon the desert shores of the Ocean. On the South side it hath the Alani, the Circassi, the Gazari, Greece and Constantinople; also the land of Iberia, the Cathes, the Brutaches who are said to be Jewes shaving their heads all over, the landes also of Scythia, of Georgia, of Armenia, of Turkie. On the West side it hath Hungaria, and Russia. Also Comania is a most large and long countrey. The inhabitantes whereof called Comani the Tartars slewe, some notwithstanding fled from them, and the rest were subdued under their bondage. But most of them that fled are returned againe. Afterward wee entred the lande of the Kangittæ, which in many places hath great scarcetie of waters, wherin there are but fewe inhabitants by reason of the foresayd defect of water. For this cause divers of the servants of Jeroslaus duke of Russia, as they were travailing towards him into the land of Tartaria, died for thirst, in that desert. As before in Comania, so likewise in this countrey, wee found many skulles and bones of dead men lying upon the earth like a dunghill. Through this countrey we were travailing from the eight day after Easter untill Ascension day. The inhabitants therof were Pagans, and neither they nor the Comanians used to till the ground, but lived onely upon cattell, neither built they any houses but dwelled in tents. These men also have the Tartars rooted out, and doe possesse and inhabite their countrey, howbeit, those that remained are reduced into their bondage.

A description of Comania.

The North Ocean.

The land of the Kangittæ.

Jeroslaus duke of Russia.

How they came unto the first court of the new Emperour. Chap. 24.

MOreover, out of the land of the Kangittæ, we entered into the countrey of ye Bisermini, who speake the language of Comania, but observe the law of the Saracens. In this countrey we found innumerable cities with castles ruined, & many towns left desolate. The lord of this country was called Soldan Alti, who with al his progenie, was destroyed by the Tartars. This country hath most huge mountains. On the South side it hath Jerusalem and Baldach, and all the whole countrey of the Saracens. In the next territories adjoyning doe inhabite two carnall brothers dukes of the Tartars, namely, Burin and Cadan, the sonnes of Thyaday, who was the sonne of Chingis Can. On the North side thereof it hath the land of the blacke Kythayans, and the Ocean. In the same countrie Syban the brother of Bathy remaineth. Through this countrie we were traveiling from the feast of Ascension, until eight daies before the feast of S. John Baptist. And then we entred into the land of the blacke Kythayans, in which the Emperour built an house, where we were called in to drinke. Also the Emperours deputy in that place caused the chiefe men of the citie and his two sonnes to daunce before us. Departing from hence, wee founde a certaine small sea, upon the shore whereof stands a little mountaine. In which mountaine is reported to be a hole, from whence, in winter time such vehement tempests of winds doe issue, that traveilers can scarcely, and with great danger passe by the same way. In summer time, the noise in deede of the winde is heard there, but it proceedeth gently out of the hole. Along the shores of the foresaid sea we travailed for the space of many dayes, which although it bee not very great, yet hath it many islandes, and wee passed by leaving it on our left hande. In this lande dwelleth Ordu, whome wee sayde to bee auncient unto all the Tartarian dukes. And it is the Orda or court of his father which hee inhabiteth, and one of his

The land of the Bisermini.

Alti Soldanus.

Huge mountaines.

Burin and Cadan.

The North ocean.
Syban brother unto Bathy.

The blacke Kythayans.

A small sea.

Many dayes.

Ordu cap. 13.

The first court of the Emperour.

wives beareth rule there.   For it is a custome among the Tartars, that the Courts of Princes or of noble men are not dissolved, but alwayes some women are appointed to keepe and governe them, upon whom certaine gifts are bestowed, in like sort as they are given unto their Lords. And so at length we arrived at the first court of the Emperour, wherein one of his wives dwelt.

Howe they came unto Cuyne himselfe, who was forthwith to be chosen Emperour.   Chap. 25.

The land of Naymani.

BUt because we had not as yet seene the Emperour, they would not invite us nor admit us into his Orda, but caused good attendance and entertainement, after the Tartars fashion, to be given unto us in our owne tent, and they caused us to stay there, and to refresh our selves with them one day.   Departing thence upon the even of Saint Peter and Saint Paul, wee entered into the land of the Naymani, who are Pagans.   But upon the very feast day of the saide Apostles, there fel a mightie snowe in that place, and wee had extreame colde weather.   This lande is full of mountaines, and colde beyonde measure, and there is little plaine ground to bee seene.   These two nations last mentioned used not to till their grounde, but, like unto the Tartars, dwelt in tents, which the sayde Tartars had destroyed.   Through this countrey wee were travailing manie dayes.   Then entered wee into the lande of the Mongals, whome wee call Tartars.   Through the Tartars lande wee continued our travaile (as wee suppose) for the space of some three weekes, riding alwayes hastily and with speede, and upon the day of Marie Magdalene we arrived at the court of Cuyne the Emperour elect.   But therefore did we make great haste all this way, because our Tartarian guides were straightly commaunded to bring us unto the court Imperiall with all speede, which court hath beene these many yeeres, ordained for the election of the Emperour.   Wherefore rising earely, wee travailed untill night without eating of any thing, and oftentimes wee

The 22. of July.

came so late unto our lodging, that we had no time to eate
the same night, but that which we should have eaten over
night, was given us in the morning. And often changing
our horses, wee spared no Horse-fleshe, but rode swiftly
and without intermission, as fast as our horses could trot.

How Cuyne enterteined the Minorite Friers.
Chap. 26.

BUt when wee were come unto the court of Cuyne, hee *The curtesie of*
caused (after the Tartars manner) a Tent and all *Cuyne towards*
expenses necessarie to bee provided for us. And his *Ambassadors.*
people entreated us with more regarde and courtesie, then
they did anie other Ambassadours. Howbeeit wee were
not called before his presence, because hee was not as yet
elected, nor admitted unto his empire. Notwithstanding,
the interpretation of the Popes letters, and the message
which we delivered, were sent unto him by the foresaid
Bathy. And having stayed there five or sixe dayes, hee
sent us unto his mother, under whome there was main-
teyned a verie solemne and royall court. And being *The tent roial.*
come thither, we saw an huge tent of fine white cloth
pitched, which was, to our judgement, of so great quantitie,
that more then two thousand men might stand within
it, and round about it there was a wall of planks set up,
painted with divers images. Wee therefore with our *A generall*
Tartars assigned to attende upon us, tooke our journey *assemblie.*
thither, and there were all the Dukes assembled, eche one
of them riding up and downe with his traine over the
hilles and dales. The first day they were all clad in white,
but the second in skarlet robes. Then came Cuyne unto
the saide tent. Moreover, the third day they were all in
blew robes, and the fourth in most rich robes of Baldakin
cloth. In the wall of boardes, about the tent aforesaid,
were two great gates, by one of the which gates, the
Emperour only was to enter, and at that gate there was no
gard of men appointed to stand, although it stood continually open, because none durst go in or come out the
same way : all that were admitted, entred by another gate,

at which there stood watchmen, with bowes, swords, &
arrowes. And whosoever approched unto the tent beyond
the bounds and limit assigned, being caught, was beaten,
but if he fled, he was shot at with arrowes or iron. There
were many that to our judgement, had upon their bridles,
trappers, saddles, and such like furniture, to the value of
20. markes in pure gold. The foresaid Dukes (as we
thinke) communed together within the tent, and consulted
about the election of their Emperor. But all the residue
of the people were placed farre away without the walles of
board, & in this maner they staied almost til noone.

The banquet of
the Nobles.
Then began they to drink mares milk, & so continued
drinking til even tide, and that in so great quantity, as it
was wonderfull. And they called us in unto them, and
gave us of their ale, because we could not drink their
mares milke. And this they did unto us in token of
great honor. But they compelled us to drink so much,
that in regard of our customary diet, wee coulde by no
means endure it. Whereupon, giving them to understand, that it was hurtful unto us, they ceassed to compel

[I. 68.]
Jeroslaus Duke
of Susdal.
us any more. Without the doore stoode Duke Jeroslaus
of Susdal, in Russia, and a great many Dukes of the
Kythayans, and of the Solangi. The two sonnes also of
the king of Georgia, the ligier of the Caliph of Baldach,
who was a Soldan, and (as we thinke) above ten Soldans

Ambassadors
of sundry na-
tions.
of the Saracens beside. And, as it was tolde us by the
agents, there were more then 4000. ambassadors, partly
of such as paide tributes, and such as presented gifts,
and other Soldans, and Dukes, which came to yeeld
themselves, and such as the Tartars had sent for,
and such as were governours of lands. All these were
placed without the lists, and had drinke given unto them.
But almost continually they all of them gave us and
Duke Jeroslaus the upper hand, when we were abroad
in their companie.

How he was exalted to his Empire. Chap. 27.

ANd to our remembrance, we remained there, about the space of foure weekes. The election was to our thinking there celebrated, but it was not published and proclaimed there. And it was greatly suspected so to be, because alwayes when Cuyne came forth out of the tent, he had a noyse of musicke, and was bowed unto, or honoured with faire wands, having purple wooll upon the tops of them, and that, so long as he remained abroad: which service was performed to none of the other Dukes. The foresaid tent or court is called by them Syra Orda. Departing thence, wee all with one accord rode 3. or 4. leagues unto another place, where, in a goodly plaine, by a rivers side, betweene certaine mountaines, there was another tent erected, which was called the golden Orda. For there was Cuyne to be placed in the throne Emperiall, upon the day of the Assumption of our Ladie. But, for the abundance of haile which fell at the same time, as is above said, the matter was deferred. There was also a tent erected upon pillars, which were covered with plates of golde, and were joyned unto other timber with golden nailes. It was covered above with Baldakin cloth, but there was other cloth spread over that, next unto the ayre. Wee abode there unto the feast of Saint Bartholomew, what time there was assembled an huge multitude standing with their faces towards the South. And a certaine number of them beeing a stones cast distant from the residue, making continuall prayers, and kneeling upon their knees, proceeded farther and farther towards the South. Howbeit wee, not knowing whether they used inchantments, or whether they bowed their knees to God or to some other, woulde not kneele upon the grounde with them. And having done so a long time, they returned to the tent, and placed Cuyne in his throne imperiall, and his Dukes bowed their knees before him. Afterwarde the whole multitude kneeled downe in like maner, except our selves, for wee were none of his subjects.

The beginnings of Cuyne his empire.

Syra Orda.

The golden Orda.

The 15. of August.

Wollen cloth.

Of his age and demeanour, and of his seale.
Chap. 28.

THis Emperour, when hee was exalted unto his government, seemed to bee about the age of fourty or fourty five yeeres, He was of a meane stature, very wise and politike, and passing serious and grave in all his demeanour. A rare thing it was, for a man to see him laugh or behave himselfe lightly, as those Christians report, which abode continually with him. Certaine Christians of his familie earnestly and strongly affirmed unto *His inclina-* us, that he himselfe was about to become a Christian. *tion to* A token and argument whereof was, that hee reteined *Christianitie.* divers Cleargie men of the Christians. Hee had likewise at all times a Chappell of Christians, neere unto his great Tent, where the Clearkes (like unto other Christians, and according to the custome of the Græcians) doe sing publiquely and openly, and ring belles at certaine houres, bee there never so great a multitude of Tartars, or of other people in presence. And yet none of their Dukes *His majestie.* doe the like. It is the manner of the Emperour never to talke his owne selfe with a stranger, though he be never so great, but heareth and answeareth by a speaker. And when any of his subjects (howe great soever they bee) are in propounding anie matter of importaunce unto him, or in hearing his answeare, they continue kneeling upon their knees unto the ende of their conference. Neither is it lawfull for any man to speake of any affaires, after they have beene determined of by the Emperour. The sayde Emperour, hath in his affaires both publike and private, an Agent, and Secretary of estate, with Scribes and all other Officials, except advocates. For, without the noyse of pleading, or sentence giving, all things are *A lawlesse* done according to the Emperours will and pleasure. *authoritie.* Other Tartarian princes do the like in those things which belong unto them. But, be it known unto al men, that whilest we remained at the said Emperors court, which hath bin ordained and kept for these many yeeres, the saide Cuyne being Emperor new elect, together with al his princes, erected a flag of defiance against the Church of God, & the Romane empire, and against al Christian kingdomes and nations of the West, unlesse peradventure (which God forbid) they will condescend unto those things, which he hath injoined unto our lord the Pope, & to all potentates and people of the Christians, namely, that they wil become obedient unto him. For, except Christendom, there is no land under heaven, which they stand in feare of, and for that cause they prepare themselves to battel against us. This Emperors father, namely Occoday was poisoned to death, which is the cause why they have for a short space absteined from warre. But their intent and purpose is (as I have above said) to subdue the whole world unto themselves, as they were commanded by Chingis Can. Hence it is that the Emperor in his letters writeth after this maner : The power of God, & Emperour of all men. Also, upon his seale, there is this posie ingraven : God in heaven, and Cuyne Can upon earth, the power of God : the seale of the Emperour of all men.

Warre intended against all Christians.
[I. 69.]

Of the admission of the Friers and Ambassadours unto the Emperour. Chap. 29.

IN the same place where the Emperour was established into his throne, we were summoned before him. And Chingay his chiefe secretary having written downe our names, and the names of them that sent us, with the name of the Duke of Solangi, & of others, cried out with a loude voice, rehearsing the said names before the Emperour, and the assembly of his Dukes. Which beeing done, ech one of us bowed his left knee foure times, & they gave us warning not to touch the threshold. And after they had searched us most diligently for knives, and could not find any about us, we entred in at the doore upon the East side : because no man dare presume to enter at the West doore, but the Emperour onely. In like maner, every Tartarian Duke entreth on the West side into his tent. Howbeit the inferiour sort doe not

Cuyne heareth the Legates.

greatly regard such ceremonies. This therefore was the first time, when we entred into the Emperours tent in his presence, after he was created Emperour. Likewise all other ambassadours were there received by him, but very fewe were admitted into his tent. And there were pre-

Gifts presen-ted unto him. sented unto him such abundance of gifts by the saide Ambassadours, that they seemed to be infinite, namely in Samites, robes of purple, and of Baldakin cloth, silke girdles wrought with golde, and costly skinnes, with other gifts also. Likewise there was a certaine Sun Canopie, or small tent (which was to bee caried over the Emperours head) presented unto him, being set full of precious stones. And a governour of one Province brought unto him a companie of camels covered with Baldakins. They had saddles also upon their backs, with certaine other instruments, within the which were places for men to sitte upon. Also they brought many horses & mules unto him furnished w^t trappers and caparisons, some being made of leather, and some of iron. And we were demanded whether we would bestow any gifts upon him or no? But wee were not of abilitie so to doe, having in a maner spent all our provision. There were also upon an hill standing a good distance from the tents,

500. Carts ful of treasure. more then 500. carts, which were all ful of silver and of gold, and silke garments. And they were all divided be-tweene the Emperour and his Dukes, and every Duke bestowed upon his owne followers what pleased him.

Of the place where the Emperor and his mother tooke their leaves one of another, and of Jeroslaus Duke of Russia. Chap. 30.

A tent of purple. DEparting thence, we came unto another place, where a wonderfull brave tent, all of red purple, given by the Kythayans, was pitched. Wee were admitted into that also, and alwaies when we entred, there was given unto us ale and wine to drinke, & sodden flesh (when we would) to eate. There was also a loftie stage built of boords, where the Emperours throne was placed, being very curiously wrought out of ivorie, wherein also there *A throne of* was golde and precious stones, and (as we remember) *Ivorie.* there were certain degrees or staires to ascend unto it. And it was round upon the top. There were benches placed about the saide throne, whereon the ladies sate towarde the left hand of the Emperour upon stooles, (but none sate aloft on the right hande) and the Dukes sate upon benches below, the said throne being in the midst. Certaine others sate behinde the Dukes, and every day there resorted great companie of Ladies thither. The three tents whereof we spake before, were very large, but the Emperour his wives had other great and faire tentes made of white felt. This was the place where the Emperour parted companie with his mother : for she went into one part of the land, and the Emperour into another to execute justice. For there was taken a certaine Concubine of this Emperour, which had poysoned his father to death, at the same time when the Tartars armie was in Hungarie, which, for the same cause returned home. Moreover, upon the foresaide Concubine, and *The death of* many other of her confederats sentence of judgement was *Occoday re-* pronounced, and they were put to death. At the same *venged.* time Jeroslaus the great Duke of Soldal, which is a part *Or, Susdal.* of Russia, deceased. For being (as it were for honours [I. 70.] sake) invited to eate and drink with the Emperours mother, and immediatly after the banquet, returning unto his lodging, he fel sicke, and within seven dayes, died. And after his death, his body was of a strange blew colour, and it was commonly reported, that the said Duke was poisoned, to the ende that the Tartars might freely and totally possesse his Dukedome.

How the Friers comming at length unto the Emperour, gave, and received letters. Chap. 31.

TO be short, the Tartars brought us unto their *Cuyne dissem-* Emperor, who when he had heard of them, that *bleth with the* we were come unto him, commanded that we should *Legates.*

return, unto his mother. For he was determined the next day, (as it is abovesaid) to set up a flag of defiance against al ye countreis of the West, which he would have us in no case to know. Wherefore returning, we staied some few dayes with his mother, and so returned backe again unto him. With whom we continued for the space of one whole moneth in such extreme hunger and thirst, that we could scarce hold life and soule together. For the provision allowed us for foure dayes, was scantly sufficient for one day. Neither could we buy us any sustenance, because the market was too farre off. How-beit the Lorde provided for us a Russian goldsmith, *Cosmas* named Cosmas, who being greatly in the Emperours *a Russian.* favour, procured us some sustenance. This man shewed unto us the throne of the Emperour, which hee had made, before it was set in the proper place, and his seale, which he also had framed. Afterward the Emperor sent *The message* for us, giving us to understand by Chingay his chief *of Chingay.* Secretary, that wee should write downe our messages & affaires, and should deliver them unto him. Which thing we performed accordingly. After many daies he called for us againe, demanding whether there were any with our Lord the Pope, which understood the Russian, the Sarracen, or the Tartarian language? To whom we answered, that we had none of those letters or languages. Howbeit, that there were certaine Saracens in the land, but inhabiting a great distance from our Lord the Pope. And wee saide, that wee thought it most expedient, that when they had written their mindes in the Tartarian language, and had interpreted the meaning therof unto us, we should diligently translate it into our own tongue, and so deliver both the letter and the translation thereof unto our Lord the Pope. Then departed they from us, and went unto the Emperour. And after the day of S. Martine, we were called for againe. Then Kadac principal agent for the whole empire, and Chingay, and Bala, with divers other Scribes, came unto us, and in-terpreted the letter word for word. And having written it in Latine, they caused us to interprete unto them eche sentence, to wit if we had erred in any word. And when both letters were written, they made us to reade them over twise more, least we should have mistaken ought. For they said unto us : Take heed that ye understand all things throughly, for if you should not understand the whole matter aright, it might breed some inconvenience. They wrote the said letters also in the Saracen tongue, that there might be some found in our dominions which could reade and interprete them, if need should require.

How they were licensed to depart. Chap. 32.

ANd (as our Tartars told us) the Emperour was purposed to send his ambassadors with us. Howbeit, he was desirous (as we thought) that we our selves should crave that favour at his hands. And when one of our Tartars being an ancient man, exhorted us to make the said petition, we thought it not good for us, that the Emperor should send his ambassadours. Wherfore we gave him answere, that it was not for us to make any such petition, but if it pleased the Emperour of his owne accord to send them, we would diligently (by Gods assistance) see them conducted in safetie. Howbeit, we thought it expedient for us, that they should not goe, and that for divers causes. First, because we feared, least they, seeing the dissentions and warres which are among us, should be the more encouraged to make warre against us. Secondly, we feared, that they would be insteade of spies and intelligencers in our dominions. Thirdly, we misdoubted that they would be slaine by the way. For our nations be arrogant and proud. For when as those servants (which at the request of the Cardinall, attended upon us, namely the legates of Almaine) returned unto him in the Tartars attire, they were almost stoned in the way, by the Dutch, and were compelled to put off those garments. And it is the Tartars custome, never to bee reconciled unto such as have slaine their Ambassadours, till they have revenged themselves. Fourthly, least they should bee taken from us

The Legates are loath to have any Ambassadours sent from the Tartars to the Christians.

by mayne force. Fiftly, because there could come no good by their ambassade, for they were to have none other commission, or authoritie, but onely to deliver their Emperours letter unto the Pope, and to the Princes of

[I. 71.] Christendome, which very same letters wee our selves had, and we knew right well, that much harme might ensue thereof. Wherefore, the third day after this, namely,

November 13. upon the feast of Saint Brice, they gave us our passe-port and a Letter sealed with the Emperours owne seale, sending us unto the Emperours mother, who gave unto

They are re- eche of us a gowne made of Foxe-skinnes, with the furre
warded with on the outside, and a piece of purple. And our Tartars
gifts. stole a yarde out of every one of them. And out of that which was given unto our servant, they stole the better halfe. Which false dealing of theirs, we knew well inough, but would make no words thereof.

How they returned homewards. Chap. 33.

The sore jour- THen taking our journey to returne, we travailed all
neys of the Le- Winter long, lying in the deserts oftentimes upon
gates in re- the snow, except with our feete wee made a piece of
turning. ground bare to lye upon. For there were no trees, but the plaine champion field. And oftentimes in the morning, we found our selves all covered with snow driven over us by the winde. And so travailing till the feast of our Lordes Ascension, we arrived at the court of

Bathy. Bathy. Of whom when wee had enquired, what answere he would send unto our Lord the Pope, he said that he had nothing to give us in charge, but onely that we should diligently deliver that which the Emperour had written. And, having received letters for our safe conduct, the thirteenth day after Pentecost, being Saterday, wee were proceeded as farre as Montii, with whome our foresaide associates and servants remained, which were withheld from us, and we caused them to be delivered unto us. From

Corrensa. hence wee travailed unto Corrensa, to whom, requiring gifts the second time at our hands, we gave none, because we had not wherewithall. And hee appointed us two

Comanians, which lived among the common people of
the Tartars, to be our guides unto the citie of Kiow
in Russia. Howbeit one of our Tartars parted not from
us, till we were past the utmost gard of the Tartars.
But the other guides, namely the Comanians, which were
given us by Corrensa, brought us from the last garde unto
the citie of Kiow, in the space of sixe dayes. And there
we arrived fifteene dayes before the feast of Saint John *June 8.*
Baptist. Moreover, the Citizens of Kiow having intelli- *How they*
gence of our approch, came foorth all of them to meete *comed at*
us, with great joy. For they rejoyced over us, as over *their returne.*
men that had bene risen from death to life. So like wise
they did unto us throughout all Russia, Polonia, and
Bohemia. Daniel and his brother Wasilico made us a *Basilius and*
royall feast, and interteined us with them against our *Daniel*
Princes.
willes for the space of eight dayes. In the meane time,
they with their Bishops, and other men of account, being
in consultation together about those matters which we had
propounded unto them in our journey towards the Tartars,
answered us with common consent, saying : that they
would holde the Pope for their speciall Lord and Father,
and the Church of Rome for their Lady & mistresse,
confirming likewise al things which they had sent concerning this matter, before our comming, by their Abbate.
And for the same purpose, they sent their Ambassadours
and letters by us also, unto our Lord the Pope.

Itinerarium fratris Willielmi de Rubruquis de
ordine fratrum Minorum, Galli, Anno gratiæ
1253. ad partes Orientales.

EXcellentissimo Domino & Christianissimo, Lodovico
Dei gratia Regi Francorum illustri, frater Willielmus
de Rubruquis in ordine fratrum Minorum minimus
salutem, & semper triumphare in Christo. Scriptum est
in Ecclesiastico de sapiente, In terram alienarum gentium *Ecclus.* 39.
transibit, bona & mala in omnibus tentabit. Hoc opus, *ver.* 4.
Domine mi Rex, feci : sed utinam ut sapiens & non
stultus. Multi enim faciunt quod facit sapiens, sed non

sapienter, sed magis stultè : de quorum numero timeo me esse. Tamen quocunque modo fecerim; quia dixistis mihi quando recessi à vobis, ut omnia scriberem vobis, quæcunque viderem inter Tartaros, & etiam monuistis ut non timerem vobis scribere longas literas, facio quod injunxistis : Cum timore tamen & verecundia, quia verba congrua mihi non suppetunt, quæ debeam tantæ scribere Majestati. Noverit ergò vestra sancta majestas, quòd anno Domini millessimo ducentessimo, quinquagessimo tertio, nonas Maii ingressi sumus mare Ponti, quod Bulgarici vocant, Majus Mare : & habet mille octo milliaria in longum, ut didici à mercatoribus, & distinguitur quasi in duas partes. Circa medium enim ejus sunt duæ provinciæ terræ, una ad Aquilonem, & alia ad meridiem. Illa quæ est ad meridiem dicitur Synopolis; & est castrum & portus Soldani Turchiæ. Quæ verò ad Aquilonem est, est Provincia quædam, quæ nunc dicitur à Latinis Gasaria, à Græcis verò qui inhabitant eam super littus maris dicitur Cassaria, hoc est Cæsaria. Et sunt promontoria quædam extendentia se in mare, & contra meridiem versus Synopolim. Et sunt trecenta mi'liaria inter Synopolim & Cassariam. Ita quod sint septingenta miliaria ab istis punctis versus Constantinopolim in longum & latum : & septingenta versus Orientem : hoc est, Hiberiam, quæ est provincia Georgiæ. Ad provinciam Gasariæ sive Casariæ applicuimus, quæ est quasi triangularis, ad Occidentem habens civitatem, quæ dicitur Kersova, in qua fuit Sanctus Clemens marterizatus. Et navigantes coram ea vidimus insulam in qua est templum illud quod dicitur Angelicis manibus præparatum. In medio verò quasi in cuspide ad meridiem habet civitatem quæ dicitur Soldaia, quæ ex transverso respicit Synopolim : Et illuc applicant omnes Mercatores venientes de Turchia volentes ire ad terras Aquilonares, & è contrario venientes de Rossia & terris Aquilonaribus, volentes transire in Turchiam. Illi portant varium & grisiam, & alias pelles pretiosas. Alii portant telas de cottone sive bombasio, & pannos sericos & species aromaticas. Ad Orientem verò illius provinciæ est civitas

[I. 72.]

Soldaia.

quæ dicitur Matriga, ubi cadit fluvius Tanais in mare *Matriga* Ponti per orificium habens latitudinem duodecem milli- *civitas.* arium. Ille enim fluvius antequam ingrediatur mare Ponti, facit quoddam mare versus Aquilonem, habens in latitudine & longitudine septinginta milliaria, nusquam habens profunditatem ultra sex passus, unde magna vasa non ingrediuntur illud. Sed mercatores de Constantinopoli applicantes ad prædictam civitatem Matertam, mittunt barcas suas usque ad flumen Tanaim, ut emant pisces siccatos, sturiones, thosas, borbatas, & alios pisces infinitæ multitudinis. Prædicta verò provincia Cassaria cingitur mari in tribus lateribus : ad Occidentem scilicet, ubi est Kersova civitas Clementis, ad meridiem ubi est civitas Soldaia, ad quam applicuimus, quæ est cuspis provinciæ, & ad Orientem Maricandis, ubi est civitas Materta, & orificium Tanais. Ultra illud orificium est Zikia, quæ *Zikia.* non obedit Tartaris : Et Suevi & Hiberi ad Orientem, qui non obediunt Tartaris. Posteà versus meridiem est Trapesunda quæ habet proprium Dominum nomine Guidonem, qui est de genere imperatorum Constantinopolitanorum, qui obedit Tartaris : posteà Synopolis quæ est Soldani Turchiæ qui similiter obedit : posteà terra Vastacii cujus filius dicitur Astar ab avo materno, qui non obedit. Ab orificio Tanais versus Occidentem usque ad Danubium totum est subditum. Etiam ultrà Danubium versus Constantinopolim, Valakia, quæ est terra Assani, & minor Bulgaria usque in Solonomam omnes solvunt eis tributum. Et etiam ultra tributum condictum sumpserunt annis nuper transactis de qualibet domo securim unam, & totum frumentum quod invenerunt in massa. Applicuimus ergò Soldaiæ in 12. Kalendas Junii : & prævenerant nos quidam mercatores de Constantinopoli, qui dixerunt venturos illuc nuncios de terra sancta volentes ire ad Sartach. Ego tamen prædicaveram publicè in Ramis Palmarum apud Sanctam Sophiam, quod non essem nuncius, nec vester, nec alicujus, sed ibam apud illos incredulos secundùm regulam nostram. Tunc cùm applicuissem, monebant me dicti mercatores ut cautè loquerer, quia dixerunt me esse nuncium, & si non dicerem me esse nuncium, quod non præberetur mihi transitus. Tunc loquutus sum hoc modo ad capitaneos civitatis, imò ad vicarios capitaneorum, quia capitanei iverant ad Baatu portantes tributum, & non fuerant adhuc reversi. Nos audivimus, dixi, de Domino vestro Sartach in Terra Sancta quod esset Christianus: & gavisi sunt inde vehementer Christiani, & præcipuè Dominus Rex Francorum Christianissimus, qui ibi peregrinatur, & pugnat contra Saracenos, ut eripiat loca sancta de manibus eorum: unde volo ire ad Sartach, & portare ei literas Domini Regis, in quibus monet eum de utilitate totius Christianitatis. Et ipsi receperunt nos gratanter, & dederunt nobis hospitium in ecclesia Episcopali. Et Episcopus ipsius ecclesiæ fuerat ad Sartach, qui multa bona dixit mihi de Sartach, quæ ego postea non inveni. Tunc dederunt nobis optionem utrum vellemus habere bigas cum bobus ad portandum res nostras vel equos pro summariis. Et mercatores Constantinopolitani consuluerunt mihi quod non acciperem bigas, imò quod emerem proprias bigas coopertas, in quibus apportant Ruteni pelles suas, & in illis includerem res nostras quas vellem quotidiè deponere, quia si acciperem equos, oporteret me in qualibet Herbergia deponere & reponere super alios, & prætereà equitarem lentiori gressu juxta boves. Et tunc acquievi consilio eorum malo, tum quia fui in itinere usque Sarthach duobus mensibus, quod potuissem uno mense fecisse, si ivissem equis. Attuleram mecum de Constantinopoli fructus & vinum muscatum, & biscoctum delicatum de consilio mercatorum ad præsentandum capitaneis primis, ut faciliùs pateret mihi transitus; quia nullus apud eos respicitur rectis oculis, qui venit vacua manu. Quæ omnia posui in una biga, quando non inveni ibi capitaneos civitatis, quia dicebant mihi, quod gratissima forent Sarthach, si possem deferre ea usque ad eum. Arripuimus ergo iter tunc circa Kalend. Junii cum bigis nostris quatuor coopertis & cum aliis duabus quas accepimus ab eis, In quibus portabantur lectisternia ad dormiendum de

nocte, & quinque equos dabant nobis ad equitandum.
Eramus enim quinque personæ. Ego & socius meus [I. 73.]
frater Bartholomeus de Cremona, & Goset lator præsentium, & homo dei Turgemannus, & puer Nicolaus, quem
emeram Constantinopoli de nostra eleemosyna. Dederunt
etiam duos homines qui ducebant bigas & custodiebant
boves & equos. Sunt autem alta promontoria super Mare
à Kersova usque ad orificium Tanais : & sunt quadraginta
castella inter Kersovam & Soldaiam, quorum quodlibet
fere habet proprium idioma : inter quos erant multi Goti,
quorum idioma est Teutonicum. Post illa montana
versus Aquilonem est pulcherrima sylva in planicie, plena
fontibus & rivulis : Et post illam sylvam est planicies
maxima, quæ durat per quinque dietas usque ad extremitatem illius provinciæ ad aquilonem, quæ coarctatur habens
Mare ad Orientem & Occidentem : Ita quod est unum
fossatum magnum ab uno Mari usque ad aliud. In illa
planicie solebant esse Comani antequam venirent Tartari,
& cogebant civitates prædictas & castra ut darent eis
tributum. Et cum venerunt Tartari, tanta multitudo
Comanorum intravit provinciam illam, qui omnes fugerunt
usque ad ripam Maris, quod comedebant se mutuo vivi
morientes : secundum quod narravit mihi quidam mercator, qui hoc vidit : Quod vivi devorabant & lacerabant
dentibus carnes crudas mortuorum, sicut canes cadavera.
Versus extremitatem illius provinciæ sunt lacus multi &
magni : in quorum ripis sunt fontes salmastri, quorum
aqua, quàm cito intrat lacum, efficit salem durum ad
modum glaciei. Et de illis salinis habent Baatu & Sartach
magnos reditus : quia de tota Russia veniunt illuc pro
sale : & de qualibet biga onusta dant duas telas de cottone
valentes dimidiam Ipperperam. Veniunt & per Mare
multæ naves pro sale, quæ omnes dant tributum secundum
sui quantitatem. Postquam ergo recessimus de Soldaia,
tertia die invenimus Tartaros : inter quos cùm intraveram,
visum fuit mihi recte quod ingrederer quoddam aliud
sæculum. Quorum vitam & mores vobis describam prout
possum.

De Tartaris & domibus eorum.

NUsquam habent manentem civitatem, sed futuram ignorant. Inter se diviserunt Scythiam, quæ durat à Danubio usque ad ortum solis. Et quilibet Capitaneus, secundum quod habet plures vel pauciores homines sub se, scit terminos pascuorum suorum, & ubi debet pascere hyeme & æstate, vere & autumno. In hyeme enim descendunt ad calidiores regiones versus meridiem. In æstate ascendunt ad frigidiores versus aquilonem. Loca pascuosa sine aquis pascunt in hyeme quando est ibi nix, quia nivem habent pro aqua. Domum in qua dormiunt fundant super rotam de virgis cancellatis, cujus tigna sunt de virgis, & conveniunt in unam parvulam rotam superius, de qua ascendit collum sursum tanquam fumigatorium, quam cooperiunt filtro albo : & frequentius imbuunt etiam filtrum calce vel terra alba & pulvere ossium, ut albens splendeat, & aliquando nigro. Et filtrum illud circa collum superius decorant pulchra varietate picturæ. Ante ostium similiter suspendunt filtrum opere polimitario variatum. Consumunt enim filtrum coloratum in faciendo vites & arbores, aves & bestias. Et faciunt tales domos ita magnas, quod habent triginta pedes in latitudine. Ego enim mensuravi semel latitudinem inter vestigia rotarum unius bigæ viginti pedum : & quando domus erat super bigam excedebat extra rotas in utroque latere quinque pedibus ad minus. Ego numeravi in una biga viginti duos boves trahentes unam domum : Undecem in uno ordine secundum latitudinem bigæ, & alios undecem ante illos : Axis bigæ erat magnus ad modum arboris navis : Et unus homo stabat in ostio domus super bigam minans boves. Insuper faciunt quadrangulos de virgulis fissis attenuatis ad quantitatem unius arcæ magnæ : & postea de una extremitate ad aliam elevant testudinem de similibus virgis, & ostiolum faciunt in anteriori extremitate : & postea cooperiunt illam cistam sive domunculam filtro nigro imbuto sevo sive lacte ovino, ne possit penetrari pluvia : quod similiter decorant opere polimitario vel plumario. Et in talibus arcis ponunt totam suppellectilem suam & thesaurum : quas ligant fortiter super bigas alteras quas trahunt cameli, ut possint transvadare flumina. Tales arcas nunquam deponunt de bigis. Quando deponunt domus suas mansionarias, semper vertunt portam ad meridiem ; & consequenter collocant bigas cum arcis hinc & inde prope domum ad dimidium jactum lapidis : ita quod domus stat inter duos ordines bigarum quasi inter duos muros. Matronæ faciunt sibi pulcherrimas bigas, quas nescirem vobis [I. 74.] describere nisi per picturam. ‖ Imo omnia depinxissem ‖ *Nota.* vobis si scivissem pingere. Unus dives Moal sive Tartar habet bene tales bigas cum arcis ducentas vel centum. Baatu habet sexdecem uxores : quælibet habet unam magnam domum, exceptis aliis parvis, quas collocant post magnam, quæ sunt quasi cameræ ; in quibus habitant puellæ. Ad quamlibet istarum domorum appendent ducentæ bigæ. Et quando deponunt domus, prima uxor deponit suam curiam in capite occidentali, & postea aliæ secundum ordinem suum : ita quod ultima uxor erit in capite Orientali : & erit spacium inter curiam unius dominæ & alterius, jactus unius lapidis. Unde curia unius divitis Moal apparebit quasi una magna Villa : tunc paucissimi viri erunt in ea. Una muliercula ducet 20. bigas vel 30. Terra enim plana est. Et ligant bigas cum bobus vel camelis unam post aliam : & sedebit muliercula in anteriori minans bovem, & omnes aliæ pari gressu sequentur. Si contingat venire ad aliquem malum passum, solvunt eas & transducunt sigillatim : Vadunt enim lento gressu, sicut agnus vel bos potest ambulare.

De lectis eorum & poculis.

POstquam deposuerint domus versa porta ad meridiem, collocant lectum domini ad partem aquilonarem. Locus mulierum est semper ad latus Orientale hoc est ad sinistrum domini domus cum sedet in lecto suo versa facie ad meridiem : locus verò virorum ad latus occidentale, hoc est ad dextrum. Viri ingredientes domum nullo modo suspenderent pharetram ad partem mulierum. Et

super caput Domini est semper una imago quasi puppa &
statuuncula de filtro, quam vocant fratrem domini : alia
similis super caput dominæ, quam vocant fratrem dominæ,
affixa parieti : & superius inter utramque illarum est una
parvula, macilenta, quæ est quasi custos totius domus.
Domina domus ponit ad latus suum dextrum ad pedes
lecti in eminenti loco pelliculam hœdinam impletam lana
vel alia materia, & juxta illam statuunculam parvulam
respicientem famulas & mulieres. Juxta ostium ad
partem mulieris est iterum alia imago cum ubere vaccino,
pro mulieribus quæ mungunt vaccas. De officio fæmina-
rum est mungere vaccas. Ad aliud latus ostii versus viros est
alia statua cum ubere equæ pro viris qui mungunt equas.
Et cum convenerint ad potandum primo spargunt de potu
illi imagini, quæ est super caput domini : postea aliis
imaginibus per ordinem : postea exit minister domum
cum cipho & potu, & spargit ter ad meridiem, qualibet
vice flectendo genu ; & hoc ad reverentiam ignis : postea
ad Orientem ad reverentiam aeris : postea ad Occidentem
ad reverentiam aquæ : ad aquilonem projiciunt pro
mortuis. Quando tenet dominus ciphum in manu & debet
bibere, tunc primo antequam bibat, infundit terræ partem
suam. Si bibit sedens super equum, infundit antequam
bibat, super collum vel crinem equi. Postquam vero
minister sic sparserit ad quatuor latera mundi, revertitur
in domum & sunt parati duo famuli cum duobus ciphis
& totidem patenis ut deferant potum domino & uxori
sedenti juxta eum sursum in lecto. Et cum habet plures
uxores, illa cum qua dormit in nocte sedet juxta eum in
die : & oportet quod omnes aliæ veniant ad domum illam
illa die ad bibendum : & ibi tenetur curia illa die : &
xenia quæ deferuntur, illa deponuntur in thesauris illius
dominæ. Bancus ibi est cum utre lactis vel cum alio
potu & cum ciphis.

De potibus eorum & qualiter provocant alios ad bibendum.

FAciunt in hyeme optimum potum, de risio, de millio, de melle : claret sicut vinum. Et defertur eis vinum à remotis partibus. In æstate non curant nisi de Cosmos. Stat semper infra domum ad introitum portæ, & juxta illud stat citharista cum citherula sua. Citheras & vielas nostras non vidi ibi, sed multa alia instrumenta, quæ apud nos non habentur. Et cum incipit bibere tunc unus ministrorum exclamat alta voce, HA : & citharista *Similiter in* percutit cicharum. Et quando faciunt festum magnum, *Florida.* tunc omnes plaudunt manibus & saltant ad vocem citharæ, viri coram Domino, & mulieres coram domina. Et postquam dominus biberit, tunc exclamat minister sicut priùs, & tacet citharista : tunc bibunt omnes in circuitu viri & mulieres : & aliquando bibunt certatim valde turpiter & gulose. Et quando volunt aliquem provocare ad potum arripiunt eum per aures & trahunt fortiter ut dilatent ei gulam, & plaudunt & saltant coram eo. Item cum aliqui volunt facere magnum festum & gaudium, unus accipit ciphum plenum, & alii duo sunt ei à dextris & sinistris : & sic illi tres veniunt cantantes usque ad illum cui debent porrigere ciphum, & cantant & saltant coram eo : & cum porrigit manum ad recipiendum ciphum, ipsi subito resiliunt, & iterum sicut prius rever- [I. 75.] tuntur, & sic illudunt ei ter vel quater retrahendo ciphum, donec fuerit bene exhileratus & bonum habeat appetitum, & tunc dant ei ciphum, & cantant & plaudunt manibus & terunt pedibus donec biberit.

De cibariis eorum.

DE cibis & victualibus eorum noveritis, quod in-differenter comedunt omnia morticinia sua. Et inter tot pecora & armenta non potest esse quin multa animalia moriantur. Tamen in æstate quamdiu durat eis cosmos, hoc est lac equinum, non curant de alio cibo. Unde tunc si contingat eis mori bovem vel equum, siccant carnes scindendo per tenues pecias & suspendendo ad solem & ventum, quæ statim sine sale siccantur absque aliquo fætore. De intestinis equorum faciunt andulges meliores quàm de porcis : quas comedunt recentes : reliquas carnes reservant ad hyemem. De pellibus boum faciunt utres magnos, quos mirabiliter siccant ad fumum. De posteriori parte pellis equi faciunt pulcherrimos soculares. De carne unius arietis dant comedere quinquaginta hominibus vel centum. Scindunt enim minutatim in scutella cum sale & aqua, aliam enim salsam non faciunt, & tunc cum puncto cultelli vel furcinula, quas proprias faciunt ad hoc, cum qua solemus comedere pira & poma cocta in vino, porrigunt cuilibet circumstantium buccellam unam vel duas, secundum multitudinem comedentium. Dominus antequam proponitur caro arietis in primo ipse accipit quod placet ei : & etiam si dat alicui partem specialem, oportet quod accipiens comedat eam solus, & nemini licet dare ei. Si non potest totum comedere, asportat secum, vel dat garcioni suo, si est presens, qui custodiat ei : sin aliter, recondit in saptargat suo, hoc est in bursa quadrata, quam portant ad recondendum omnia talia, in qua & ossa recondunt, quando non habent spacium bene rodendi ea, ut postea rodant, ne pereat aliquid de cibo.

Quomodo faciunt Cosmos.

IPsum Cosmos, hoc est lac jumentinum fit hoc modo. Extendunt cordam longam super terram ad duos palos fixos in terra, & ad illam cordam ligant circiter horas tres, pullos equarum quas volunt mungere. Tunc stant matres juxta pullos suos & permittunt se pacifice mungi. Et si aliqua est nimis indomita, tunc accipit unus homo pullum & supponit ei permittens parum sugere, tunc retrahit illum, & emunctor lactis succedit. Congregata ergo multitudine lactis, quod est ita dulce sicut vaccinum, dum est recens, fundunt illud in magnum utrem sive bucellam, & incipiunt illud concutere cum ligno ad hoc aptato, quod grossum est inferius sicut caput hominis & cavatum subtus : & quam cito concutiunt illud, incipit

WILLIAM DE RUBRUQUIS

bullire sicut vinum novum, & acescere sive fermentari, &
excutiunt illud donec extrahant butirum. Tunc gustant
illud ; & quando est temperate pungitivum bibunt :
pungit enim super linguam sicut vinum raspei dum
bibitur. Et postquam homo cessat bibere, relinquit
saporem super linguam lactis amygdalini, & multum
reddit interiora hominis jucunda, & etiam inebriat debilia
capita : multum etiam provocat urinam. Faciunt etiam
Cara-cosmos, hoc est nigrum cosmos ad usum magnorum
dominorum, hoc modo. Lac equinum non coagulatur.
Ratio enim est : quod nullius animalis lac nisi cujus fetet
venter non invenitur coagulum. In ventre pulli equi non
invenitur : unde lac equæ non coagulatur. Concutiunt
ergo lac in tantum, quod omnino quod spissum est in eo
vadat ad fundum rectà, sicut fæces vini, & quod purum
est remanet superius, & est sicut serum, & sicut mustum
album. Fæces sunt albæ multum, & dantur servis, &
faciunt multum dormire. Illud clarum bibunt domini : &
est pro certo valde suavis potus & bonæ efficaciæ. Baatu
habet 30. casalia circa herbergiam suam ad unam dietam,
quorum unumquodque qualibet die servit ei de tali lacte
centum equarum, hoc est, qualibet die lac trium millium
equarum, excepto alio lacte albo, quod deferunt alii.
Sicut enim in Syria rustici dant tertiam partem fructuum,
quam ipsi afferunt ad curias dominorum suorum, ita & isti
lac equarum tertiæ diei. De lacte vaccino primò extrahunt
butyrum & bulliunt illud usque ad perfectam decoctionem, & postea recondunt illud in utribus arietinis
quos ad hoc reservant. Et non ponunt sal in butiro :
tamen propter magnam decoctionem non putrescit : &
reservant illud contra hyemem. Residuum lac quod
remanet post butirum permittunt acescere quantum acrius
fieri potest & bulliunt illud, & coagulatur bulliendo,
& coagulum illud desiccant ad solem, & efficitur durum
sicut scoria ferri. Quod recondunt in saccis contra
hyemem : tempore hyemali quando deficit eis lac, [I. 76.]
ponunt illud acre coagulum, quod ipsi vocant gri-ut, in
utre, & super infundunt aquam calidam, & concutiunt

fortiter donec illud resolvatur in aqua; quæ ex illo efficitur tota acetosa, & illam aquam bibunt loco lactis. Summè cavent ne bibant aquam puram.

De bestiis quas comedunt, & de vestibus, ac de venatione eorum.

MAgni domini habent casalia versus meridiem, de quibus afferunt eis milium & farinam contra hyemem. pauperes procurant sibi pro arietibus & pellibus commutando. Sclavi etiam implent ventrem suum aqua crassa, & hac contenti sunt. Mures cum longis caudis non comedunt & omne genus murium habens curtam caudam. Sunt etiam ibi multæ marmotes, quas ipsi vocant Sogur : quæ conveniunt in una fovea in hyeme 20. vel 30. pariter, & dormiunt sex mensibus : quas capiunt in magna multitudine. Sunt etiam ibi, cuniculi habentes longam caudam sicut cati ; & in summitate caudæ habent pilos nigros & albos. Habent & multas alias bestiolas bonas ad comedendum : quas ipsi valde bene discernunt. Cervos non vidi ibi. lepores paucos vidi, gaselos multos. Asinos sylvestres vidi in magna multitudine, qui sunt quasi muli. Vidi & aliud genus animalis quod dicitur Artak, quod habet recte corpus arietis & cornua torta, sed tantæ quantitatis, quod vix poteram una manu levare duo cornua : & faciunt de cornibus illis ciphos magnos. Habent falcones, gir-falcones, & herodios in magna multitudine : quos omnes portant super manum dexteram : & ponunt semper falconi unam corrigiam parvulam circa collum, quæ pendet ei usque ad medietatem pectoris : per quam cum projiciunt eum ad prædam, inclinant cum sinistra manu caput & pectus falconis, ne verberetur à vento, vel ne feratur sursum. Magnum ergo partem victus sui acquirunt venatione. De vestibus & habitu eorum noveritis, quod de Cataya & aliis regionibus Orientis, & etiam de Perside & aliis regionibus austri veniunt eis panni serici & aurei, & telæ de bambasio, quibus induuntur in æstate. De Russia, de Moxel, & Majore Bulgaria & Pascatir, quæ est

major Hungaria, & Kersis : (quæ omnes sunt regiones ad *Major*
Aquilonem & plenæ sylvis;) & aliis multis regionibus ad *Hungaria.*
latus aquilonare, quæ eis obediunt, adducuntur eis pelles
preciosæ multi generis : quas nunquam vidi in partibus
nostris : Quibus induuntur in hyeme. Et faciunt semper
in hyeme duas pelliceas ad minus : unam, cujus pilus est
ad carnem : aliam cujus pilus est extra contra ventum &
nives, quæ multoties sunt de pellibus lupinis vel vulpibus
vel papionibus. Et dum sedent in domo habent aliam
delicatiorem. Pauperes faciunt illas exteriores de canibus
& capris. Quum volunt venari feras, conveniunt magna
multitudo & circundant regionem in qua sciunt feras esse,
& paulatim appropinquant sibi, donec concludant feras
inter se quasi infra circulum, & tunc sagitant ad eas.
faciunt etiam braccas de pellibus. Divites etiam furrant
vestes suas de stupa setæ, quæ est supra modum mollis, &
levis & calida. Pauperes furrant vestes de tela de bambasio, de delicatiori lana quam possunt extrahere : de gros-
siori faciunt filtrum ad cooperiendum domos suas & cistas,
& ad lectisternia. De lana etiam & tertia parte pilorum
equi admixta, faciunt cordas suas. De filtro etiam faciunt
pavellas sub sellis, & capas contra pluviam. Unde mul- *Nota.*
tum expendunt de lana. Habitum virorum vidistis.

De rasura virorum & ornatu mulierum.

VIri radunt in summitate capitis quadrangulum, & ab
anterioribus angulis ducunt rasuram cristæ capitis
usque ad tempora. Radunt etiam tempora & collum
usque ad summum concavitatis cervicis : & frontem
anterius usque ad frontinellam, super quam relinquunt
manipulum pilorum descendentium usque ad supercilia :
In angulis occipitis relinquunt crines, quibus faciunt tricas,
quas succingunt nodando usque ad aures. Et habitus
puellarum non differt ab habitu virorum, nisi quod aliquantulum est longior. Sed in crastino postquam est
nupta radit calvariam suam à medietate capitis versus
frontem, & habet tunicam latam sicut cucullam monialis,
& per omnia latiorem & longiorem, fissam ante, quam

ligat sub dextro latere. In hoc enim differunt Tartari à
Turcis : quod Turci ligant tunicas suas ad sinistram,
Tartari semper ad dextram. Postea habent ornamentum
capitis, quod vocant botta, quod fit de cortice arboris vel
alia materia, quam possunt invenire, leviore : & est grossum & rotundum, quantum potest duabus manibus com-
plecti; longum vero unius cubiti & plus, quadrum
superius, sicut capitellum unius columnæ. Istud botta
cooperiunt panno serico precioso; & est concavum interius :

& super capitellum in medio vel super quadraturam illam
ponunt virgulam de calamis pennarum vel cannis gracilibus
longitudinis scilicet unius cubiti & plus : & illam sibi
virgulam ornant superius de pennis pavonis, & per longum
in circuitu pennulis caudæ malardi, & etiam lapidibus
præciosis. Divites dominæ istud ornamentum ponunt in
summitate capitis quod stringunt fortiter cum almucia,
quæ foramen habet in summitate ad hoc aptatum, & in
isto recondunt crines suos quos recolligunt à parte posteriori ad summitatem capitis quasi in nodo uno &
reponunt in illo botta, quod postea fortiter ligant sub
gutture. Unde quum equitant plures dominæ simul &
videntur à longe, apparent milites, habentes galeas in
capitibus cum lanceis elevatis. Illud enim botta apparet
galea de super lancea. Et sedent omnes mulieres super
equos sicut viti diversificantes coxas; & ligant cucullas
suas panno serico aerii coloris super renes, & alia fascia
stringunt ad mamillas : & ligant unam peciam albam sub
occulis, quæ descendit usque ad pectus. Et sunt mulieres
miræ pinguedinis, & quæ minus habet de naso pulchrior
reputatur. Deturpant etiam turpiter pinguedine facies
suas : nunquam cubant in lecto pro puerperio.

De officio mulierum, & operibus earum, ac de nuptiis earum.

OFicium fœminarum est ducere bigas, ponere domus
super eas & deponere, mungere vaccas, facere butirum
& griut, parare pelles, & consuere eas, quas consuunt filo
denervis. dividunt enim nervos in minuta fila, & postea illa

contorquent in unum longum filum. Consuunt etiam
soculares & soccos & alias vestes. Vestes vero nunquam
lavant, quia dicunt quod Deus tunc irascitur, & quod fiant
tonitrua si suspendantur ad siccandum : Imo lavantes verberant & eis auferunt. Tonitrua supra modum timent :
tunc omnes extraneos emittunt de domibus suis ; & invol-
vunt se in filtris nigris, in quibus latitant, donec transierit.
Nunquam etiam lavant scutellos, imo carne cocta alveum
in quo debent ponere eam lavant brodio bulliente de
caldaria, & postea refundunt in caldariam. faciunt & filtrum & cooperiunt domos. Viri faciunt solùm arcus &
sagittas, fabricant strepas & fræna, & faciunt cellas, carpen-
tant domos & bigas : custodiunt equos & mungunt equas,
concutiunt ipsum cosmos & lac equinum, faciunt utres in
quibus reconditur : custodiunt etiam camelos, & onerant
eos. Oves & Capras custodiunt mixtim & mungunt aliquando viri, aliquando mulieres. De lacte ovium inspis- *Pellium*
sato & salso parant pelles. Cum volunt manus vel caput *paratio.*
lavare implent os suum aqua & paulatim fundunt de ore
suo super manus, & eadem humectant crines suos, & lavant
caput suum. De nuptiis eorum noveritis, quod nemo
habet ibi uxorem nisi emat eam : unde aliquando sunt
puellæ multum adultæ ante quam nubant : semper enim
tenent eas parentes, donec vendant eas. Servant etiam
gradus consanguinitatis primum & secundum : nullum
autem servant affinitatis. Habent enim simul vel succes-
sive duas sorores. Nulla vidua nubit inter eos, hac ratione ;
quia credunt quod omnes qui serviunt eis in hac vita ser-
vient in futura. Unde de vidua credunt, quod semper
revertitur post mortem ad primum maritum. Unde accidit turpis consuetudo inter eos quod filius scilicet ducit
aliquando omnes uxores patris sui, excepta matre. Curia
enim patris & matris semper accidit juniori filio. Unde
oportet quod ipse provideat omnibus uxoribus patris sui,
quia adveniunt eæ cum curia paterna. Et tunc si vult
utitur eis pro uxoribus, quia non reputat sibi injuriam, si
revertatur ad patrem post mortem. Cum ergo aliquis
fecerit pactum cum aliquo de filia accipienda, facit pater

puellæ convivium, & illa fugit ad consanguineos, ut ibi
lateat : Tunc pater dicit, Ecce filia mea tua est, accipe eam
ubicunque inveneris : Tunc ille quærit eam cum amicis suis,
donec inveniat eam, & oportet, quod vi capiat eam, & ducat
eam quasi violenter ad domum.

De justiciis eorum & judiciis, et de morte ac sepultura eorum.

DE justiciis eorum noveritis, quod quando duo homines
pugnant, nemo audet se intermittere. Etiam pater
non audet juvare filium. Sed qui pejorem partem habet,
appellat ad curiam domini. Et si alius post appellationem
tangat eum, interficitur. Sed oportet quod statim absque
dilatione vadat : Et ille qui passus est injuriam ducit eum
quasi captivum. Neminem puniunt capitali sententia, nisi
deprehensus fuerit in facto, vel confessus. Sed quum diffa-
matus est à pluribus, bene torquent eum, ut confiteatur.
Homicidium puniunt capitali sententia, & etiam coitum
cum non sua. Non suam dico vel uxorem vel famulam :
[I. 78.] Sua enim sclava licet uti prout libet. Item enorme furtum
puniunt morte. Pro levi furto, sicut pro uno ariete, dummodo non fuerit sæpe deprehensus in hoc, verberant
crudeliter. Et si dant centum ictus oportet quod habeant
centum baculos, de illis dico, qui verberantur sententia
curiæ. Item falsos nuncios, quia faciunt se nuncios & non
sunt, interficiunt. Item sacrilegas, de quibus dicam vobis
postea plenius, quia tales reputant veneficas. Quando aliquis moritur plangunt vehementer ululando : & tunc sunt
liberi quod non dant vectigal usque ad annum. Et si quis
interest morti alicujus adulti, non ingreditur domum ipsius
Mangucham usque ad annum. Si parvulus est qui moritur, non ingreditur usque post lunationem. Juxta sepul-
turam defuncti semper relinquunt domum unam. Si est
de nobilibus, hoc est de genere Chingis, qui fuit primus
pater & dominus eorum, illius qui moritur ignoratur sepul-
tura : & semper circa loca illa ubi sepeliunt nobiles suos
est una herbergia hominum custodientium sepulturas. Non
intellexi quod ipsi recondunt thesaurum cum mortuis.

Comani faciunt magnum tumulum super defunctum & erigunt ei statuam versa facie ad orientem, tenentem ciphum
in manu sua ante umbelicum. fabricant & divitibus pyramides, id est domunculas acutas : & alicubi vidi magnas
turres de tegulis coctis : alicubi lapideas domos, quamvis
lapides non inveniantur ibi. Vidi quendam noviter defunctum, cui suspenderant pelles sexdecem equorum, ad
quodlibet latus mundi quatuor inter perticas altas : & appo-
suerunt ei cosmos ut biberet, & carnes ut comederet : &
tamen dicebant de illo quod fuerat baptizatus. Alias vidi
sepulturas versus orientem. Areas scilicet magnas structas
lapidibus, aliquas rotundas, aliquas quadratas, & postea
quatuor lapides longos erectos ad quatuor regiones mundi
circa aream. Et ubi aliquis infirmatur cubat in lecto &
ponit signum super domum suam, quod ibi est infirmus,
& quod nullus ingrediatur : unde nullus visitat infirmum
nisi serviens ejus. Quando etiam aliquis de magnis curiis
infirmatur, ponunt custodes longe circa curiam, qui infra
illos terminos neminem permittunt transire : timent enim
ne mali spiritus vel ventus veniant cum ingredientibus.
Ipsos divinatores vocant tanquam sacerdotes suos.

Qualiter ingressi sunt inter Tartaros, & de ingratitudine eorum.

QUando ergo ingressi sumus inter illos barbaros, visum
fuit mihi, ut dixi superius, quod ingrederer aliud
sæculum. Circumdederunt enim nos in equis postquam
diu fecerant nos expectare sedentes in umbra sub bigis
nigris. Prima quæstio fuit, utrum unquam fuissemus
inter eos. habito quod non : inceperunt impudenter petere
de cibariis nostris, & dedimus de pane biscocto & vino
quod attuleramus nobiscum de villa : & potata una lagena
vini, petierunt aliam, dicentes, quod homo non ingreditur
domum uno pede. non dedimus eis, excusantes nos quod
parum haberemus. Tunc quæsiverunt unde veniremus,
& quo vellemus ire. dixi eis superiora verba, quod audie-
ramus de Sartach, quod esset Christianus, & quod vellem
ire ad eum, quia habebam deferre ei literas vestras. Ipsi

diligenter quæsiverunt, utrum irem de mea voluntate, vel utrum mitterer. Ego respondi quod nemo coegit me ad eundum, nec ivissem nisi voluissem : unde de mea voluntate ibam, & etiam de voluntate superioris mei. Bene cavi, quod nunquam dixi, me esse nuncium vestrum. Tunc quæsiverunt quid esset in bigis, utrum esset aurum vel argentum, vel vestes preciosæ, quas deferrem Sartach. Ego respondi, quod Sartach videret quid deferremus ei, quando perveniremus ad eum ; & quod non intererat eorum ista quærere : sed facerent me deduci usque ad capitaneum suum, & ipse si vellet mihi præbere ducatum usque ad Sartach faceret : sin minus, reverterer. Erat enim in illa provincia unus consanguineus Baatu, nomine Scacatai, cui dominus imperator Constantinopolitanus mittebat literas deprecatorias, quod me permitteret transire. Tunc ipsi acquieverunt, præbentes nobis equos & boves & duos homines, qui deducerent nos. Et alii qui adduxerant nos sunt reversi. Prius tamen antequam prædicta darent, fecerunt nos diu expectare petentes de pane nostro pro parvulis suis : Et omnia quæ videbant super famulos nostros, cultellos, chirothecas, bursas, corrigias, omnia admirantes & volentes habere. Excusabam me, quia longa nobis restabat via, nec debebamus ita cito spoliare nos rebus necessariis ad tantam viam perficiendam. Tunc dicebant quod essem batrator. Verum est quod nihil abstulerint vi : Sed valde importune & impudenter petunt quæ vident. Et si dat homo eis perdit, quia sunt ingrati. Reputant se dominos mundi, & videtur eis, quod nihil debeat eis negari ab aliquo. Si non dat, & postea indigeat servicio eorum, male ministrant ei. Dederunt nobis bibere de lacte suo vaccino, a quo contractum erat butirum, acetoso valde, quod ipsi vocant Apram : & sic recessimus ab eis. Et visum fuit mihi recte, quod evasissem de manibus dæmonum. In crastino pervenimus ad capitaneum. Ex quo recessimus a Soldaia usque ad Sartach in duobus mensibus nunquam jacuimus in domo nec in tentorio, sed semper sub dio, vel sub bigis nostris, nec vidimus aliquam villam, vel vestigium alicujus ædificii ubi

[I. 79.]

WILLIAM DE RUBRUQUIS

fuisset villa, nisi tumbas Comanorum in maxima multitudine. Illo sero dedit nobis garcio qui ducebat nos bibere cosmos ; ad cujus haustum totus sudavi propter horrorem & novitatem, quia nunquam biberam de eo. valde tamen sapidum videbatur mihi, sicut vere est.

De curia Scacatay, & quod Christiani non bibunt cosmos.

MAne ergo obviavimus bigis Scacatay onustis domibus. Et videbatur mihi quod obviaret mihi civitas magna. Mirabar etiam super multitudine armentorum boum & equorum & gregum ovium : paucos videbam homines qui ista gubernarent. unde inquisivi quot homines haberet sub se ? & dictum fuit mihi, quod non plusquam quingentos, quorum medietatem transiveramus in alia herbergia. Tunc incepit mihi dicere garcio qui ducebat nos, quod aliquid oporteret Scacatay dare : & ipse fecit nos stare, & præcessit nuncians adventum nostrum. Jam erat hora plusquam tertia, & deposuerunt domos suas juxta quandam aquam. Et venit ad nos interpres ipsius, qui statim cognito, quod nunquam fueramus inter illos, poposcit de cibis nostris, & dedimus ei, poscebat etiam vestimentum aliquod, quia dicturus erat verbum nostrum ante dominum suum. Excusavimus nos. Quæsivit quid portaremus domino suo ? Accepimus unum flasconem de vino, & implevimus unum veringal de biscocto & platellum unum de pomis & aliis fructibus. Sed non placebat ei, quia non ferebamus aliquem pannum pretiosum. Sic tamen ingressi sumus cum timore & verecundia. Sedebat ipse in lecto suo tenens citharulam in manu, & uxor sua juxta eum : de qua credebam in veritate, quod amputasset sibi nasum inter oculos ut simior esset : nihil enim habebat ibi de naso, & unxerat locum illum quodam unguento nigro, & etiam supercilia : quod erat turpissimum in oculis nostris. Tunc dixi ei verba supradicta. Ubique enim oportebat nos dicere idem verbum. Super hoc enim eramus bene præ- *Nota* moniti ab illis qui fuerant inter illos, quod nunquam *diligenter.* mutaremus verba nostra. Rogavi etiam eum ut dignaretur accipere munusculùm de manu nostra, excusans me, quia monachus eram, nec erat ordinis nostri possidere aurum, vel argentum, vel vestes preciosas. Unde non habebam aliquid talium, quod possem ei dare : sed de cibis nostris acciperet pro benedictione. Tunc fecit recipi, & distribuit statim hominibus suis qui convenerant ad potandum. Dedi etiam ei literas Imperatoris Constantinopolitani : (Hoc fuit in octavis ascensionis) Qui statim eas Soldaiam misit ut ibi interpretarentur : quia erant in Græco, nec habebat secum qui sciret literas Græcas. Quæsivit etiam à nobis, si vellemus bibere cosmos, hoc est, lac jumentinum. Christiani enim Ruteni, Græci, & Alani, qui sunt inter eos, qui volunt stricte custodire legem suam, non bibunt illud : Imo non reputant se Christianos postquam biberunt. Et sacerdotes eorum reconciliant eos, tanquam negassent fidem Christianam. Ego respondi, quod habebamus adhuc sufficienter ad bibendum : & cum ille potus deficeret nobis, oporteret nos bibere illud, quod daretur nobis. Quæsivit etiam quid contineretur in literis nostris, quas mittebatis Sartach. Dixi quod clausæ erant bullæ nostræ : & quod non erant in eis nisi bona verba & amicabilia. Quæsivit & quæ verba diceremus Sartach? Respondi, Verba fidei Christianæ. Quæsivit quæ? Quia libenter vellet audire. Tunc exposui ei prout potui per interpretem meum, qui nullius erat ingenii, nec alicujus eloquentiæ, symbolum fidei. Quo audito, ipse tacuit & movit caput. Tunc assignavit nobis duos homines, qui nos custodirent, & equos & boves : & fecit nos bigare secum, donec reverteretur nuncius, quem ipse miserat pro interpretatione literarum imperatoris ; & ivimus cum eo usque in crastinum Pentecostes.

Qualiter Alani venerunt ad eos in vigilia Pentecostes.

IN vigilia Pentecostes venerunt ad nos quidam Alani,
|| *Vel Akas.*   qui ibi dicuntur || Acias, Christiani secundum ritum Græcorum ; habentes literas Græcas & sacerdotes Græcos : tamen non sunt schismatici sicut Græci ; sed sine accep-

tione personarum venerantur omnem Christianum : &
detulerunt nobis carnes coctas, rogantes ut comederemus
de cibo eorum, & oraremus pro quodam defuncto eorum.
Tunc dixi quod vigilia erat tantæ solennitatis, quod illa die
non comederemus carnes. Et exposui eis de solennitate,
super quo fuerunt multum gavisi ; quia omnia ignorabant
quæ spectant ad ritum Christianum, solo nomine Christi
excepto. Quæsiverunt & ipsi & alii multi Christiani,
Ruteni & Hungari, utrum possent salvari, quia oportebat
eos bibere cosmos, & comedere morticinia & interfecta à
Saracenis & aliis infidelibus : quæ etiam ipsi Græci & [I. 80.]
Ruteni sacerdotes reputant quasi morticinia vel idolis
immolata : quia ignorabant tempora jejunii : nec poterant
custodire etiam si cognovissent. Tunc rectificabar eos
prout potui, docens & confortans in fide. Carnes quas
detulerant reservavimus usque ad diem festum : nihil
enim inveniebamus venale pro auro & argento, nisi pro
telis & aliis ‖ pannis : & illos non habebamus. Quum ‖ *Nota*
famuli nostri offerebant eis ipperpera, ipsi fricabant digitis, *diligentissime.*
& ponebant ad nares, ut odore sentirent, utrum essent
cuprum. Nec dabant nobis cibum nisi lac vaccinum acre
valde & fœtidum. Vinum jam deficiebat nobis. Aqua
ita turbabatur ab equis, quod non erat potabilis. Nisi
fuisset biscoctum quod habebamus, & gratia dei, fortè
fuissemus mortui.

De Saraceno qui dixit se velle baptizari, et de hominibus qui apparent leprosi.

IN die pentecostes venit ad nos quidam Saracenus, qui
cum loqueretur nobiscum, incepimus exponere fidem.
Qui audiens beneficia dei exhibita humano generi in
incarnatione Christi, & resurrectionem mortuorum, &
judicium futurum, & quod ablutio peccatorum esset in
baptismo : dixit se velle baptizari. Et cum pararemus
nos ad baptizandum eum, ipse subito ascendit equum
suum, dicens se iturum domum & habiturum consilium
cum uxore sua. Qui in crastinò loquens nobiscum,
dixit quod nullo modo auderet accipere baptisma, quia

tunc non biberet cosmos. Christiani enim illius loci hoc
dicebant, quod nullus verus Christianus deberet bibere :
& sine potu illo non posset vivere in solitudine illa. A
qua opinione nullo modo potui divertere illum. Unde
noveritis pro certo quod multum elongantur à fide propter
illam opinionem quæ jam viguit inter illos per Rutenos,
quorum maxima multitudo est inter eos. Illa die dedit
nobis ille capitaneus unum hominem, qui nos deduceret
usque ad Sartach : & duos qui ducerent nos usque ad
proximam herbergiam ; quæ inde distabat quinque dietas
prout boves poterant ire. Dederunt etiam nobis unam
capram pro cibo & plures utres lactis vaccini, & de
cosmos parum : quia illud preciosum est inter illos. Et
sic arripientes iter rectè in aquilonem, visum fuit mihi
quod unam portam inferni transissemus. Garciones qui
ducebant nos, incipiebant nobis audacter furari, quia videbant nos parum cautos. Tandem amissis pluribus vexatio
dabat nobis intellectum. Pervenimus tandem ad extremitatem illius provinciæ, quæ clauditur uno fossato ab uno
mari usque ad aliud : extra quam erat herbergia eorum
apud quos intrassemus : videbantur nobis leprosi omnes :
quia erant viles homines ibi collocati, ut reciperent
Salinæ. tributum ab accipientibus sal a salinis superius dictis. Ab
illo loco, ut dicebant, oportebat nos ambulare quindecim
diebus, quibus non inveniremus populum. Cum illis
bibimus cosmos : & dedimus illis unum veringal plenum
fructibus & panem biscoctum. Qui dederunt nobis
octo boves, unam capram pro tanto itinere, & nescio quot
Decem dietæ. utres plenos lacte vaccino. Sic mutatis bobus arripuimus
iter, quod perfecimus decem diebus usque ad aliam
herbergiam : nec invenimus aquam in illa via nisi in fossis
in convallibus factis, exceptis duobus parvis fluminibus.
Et tendebamus rectè in orientem ex quo exivimus prædictam provinciam Gasariæ, habentes mare ad meridiem &
vastam solitudinem ad aquilonem : quæ durat per viginti
dietas alicubi in latitudine : In qua nulla est sylva, nullus
mons, nullus lapis. Herba est optima. In hac solebant
pascere Comani, qui dicuntur Capchat. A Teutonicis

verò dicuntur Valani, & provincia Valania. Ab Isidoro
vero dicitur à flumine Tanai usque ad paludes Meotidis
& Danubium Alania. Et durat ista terra in longitudine a
Danubio usque Tanaim ; qui est terminus Asiæ &
Europæ, itinere duorum mensium velociter equitando
prout equitant Tartari : Quæ tota inhabitabatur à Comanis
Capchat, & etiam ultra à Tanai usque ‖ Etiliam : Inter
quæ flumina sunt decem dietæ magnæ. Ad aquilonem
verò istius provinciæ jacet Russia, quæ ubique sylvas
habet, & protenditur à Polonia & Hungaria usque
Tanaim : quæ tota vastata est à Tartaris, & adhuc
quotidie vastatur. Præponunt enim Rutenis, quia sunt
Christiani, Saracenos : & cum non possunt amplius dare
aurum vel argentum, ducunt eos & parvulos eorum
tanquam greges ad solitudinem ut custodiant animalia
eorum. Ultra Russiam ad aquilonem est Prussia, quam
nuper subjugaverunt totam fratres Teutonici. Et certe
de facili acquierent Russiam, si apponerent manum. Si
enim Tartari audirent, quod magnus sacerdos, hoc est,
Papa faceret cruce signari contra eos, omnes fugerent ad
solitudines suas.

*Comaniæ lon-
gitudo.*

*‖ Etilia quæ
& Volga
flumen.
Russia.*

Prussia.

De tediis quæ patiebantur, & de sepultura Comanorum.

IBamus ergo versus orientem, nihil videntes nisi
cœlum & terram, & aliquando mare ad dextram, quod
dicitur Mare Tanais, & etiam sepulturas Comanorum,
quæ apparebant nobis à duabus leucis secundum quod
solebant parentelæ eorum sepeliri simul. Quam diu
eramus in solitudine bene erat nobis : quòd tædium quod
patiebar quum veniebamus ad mansiones eorum non
possem exprimere verbis. Volebat enim dux noster, quod
ad quoslibet capitaneos ingrederer cum xenio : & ad hoc
non sufficiebant expensæ. Quotidie enim eramus octo
personæ comedentes viaticum nostrum exceptis servientibus, qui omnes volebant comedere nobiscum. Nos enim
eramus quinque, & ipsi tres qui ducebant nos : duo
ducentes bigas, & unus iturus nobiscum usque ad

[I. 81.]

Sartach. Carnes quas dabant non sufficiebant ; nec inveniebamus aliquid venale pro moneta. Et cum sedebamus sub bigis nostris pro umbra, quia calor erat ibi maximus illo tempore, ipsi ita importune ingerebant se nobis, quod conculcabant nos, volentes omnia nostra videre. Si arripiebat eos appetitus purgandi ventrem, non elongabant se a nobis, quam possit faba jactari. Imo juxta nos colloquentes mutuò faciebant immunditias suas : & multa alia faciebant quæ erant supra modum tædiosa. Super omnia gravabat me, quod cum volebam dicere eis aliquod verbum ædificationis, interpres meus dicebat, non facietis me prædicare : quia nescio talia verba dicere. Et verum dicebat. Ego enim perpendi postea, quum incepi aliquantulum intelligere idioma, quod quum dicebam unum, ipse totum aliud dicebat, secundum quod ei occurrebat. Tunc videns periculum loquendi per ipsum, elegi magis tacere. Ambulavimus ergo cum magno labore de mansione in mansionem : ita quod paucis diebus ante festum beatæ Mariæ Magdalenæ veni ad fluvium magnum Tanais : qui dividit Asiam ab Europa, sicut Nilus fluvius Ægypti, Asiam ab Africa. In illo loco quo applicuimus fecerunt Baatu & Sartach fieri quoddam casale de Rutenis in ripa orientali, qui transferunt nuncios & mercatores cum naviculis. Ipsi transtulerunt nos primo & postea bigas ponentes unam rotam in una barca & aliam in alia, ligantes barcas ad invicem ; & sic remigantes transibant. Ibi egit dux noster valde stulte. Ipse enim credebat, quod illi de casali deberent nobis ministrare equos, & dimisit animalia quæ adduxeramus in alia biga, ut redirent ad dominos suos. Et quum postulavimus ab eis animalia, ipsi respondebant quod habebant privilegium à Baatu, quod non tenerentur ad aliud, nisi transferre euntes & redeuntes : etiam à mercatoribus accipiebant magnum tributum. Stetimus ergo ibi in ripa fluminis tribus diebus. Prima die dederunt nobis magnam borbatam recentem : secunda die panem de siligine & parum de carnibus, quas acceperat procurator villæ ostiatim per

WILLIAM DE RUBRUQUIS

diversas domos.   Tertia die pisces siccos, quos habent
ibi in magna multitudine.   Fluvius ille erat ibi tantæ
latitudinis, quantæ est Sequana Parisiis.   Et antequam
pervenissemus ad locum illum, transivimus multas aquas
pulcherrimas & piscosissimas: Sed Tartari nesciunt eos
capere: nec curant de pisce nisi sit ita magnus, quod
possunt comedere carnes ejus, sicut carnes arietinas.
Ille fluvius est terminus Orientalis Russiæ; & oritur
de paludibus quæ pertingunt ad Oceanum ad aquilonem.
Fluvius vero currit ad meridiem in quoddam magnum
Mare septingentorum millium, antequam pertingat ad
Mare Ponti :   Et omnes aquæ quas transivimus vadunt
ad illas partes.   Habet etiam prædictum flumen magnam
sylvam in ripa Occidentali.   Ultra locum illum non
ascendunt Tartari versus Aquilonem : quia tunc temporis
‖ circa introitum Augusti incipiunt redire versus meridiem.   Unde aliud est casale inferius ubi transeunt
nuncii tempore hyemali.   Eramus igitur ibi in magna
angustia, quia nec equos nec boves inveniebamus pro
pecunia.   Tandem postquam ostendi eis, quod laboravi
pro communi utilitate omnium Christianorum, accom-
modaverunt nobis boves & homines: nos autem oportebat ire pedibus.   Tunc temporis metebant siliginem:
triticum non proficiebat ibi bene.   Milium habent in
magna copia.   Mulieres Rutenæ ornant capita sicut
nostræ.   Supertunicalia sua exterius ornant vario vel
grisio a pedibus usque ad genua.   Homines portant
capas sicut Teutonici : sed in capite portant pileos de
filtro acutos in summitate longo acumine.   Ambulavimus
ergo tribus diebus non invenientes populum.   Et cum
essemus valde fatigati & boves similiter, nec sciremus
quorsum possemus Tartaros invenire, accurrerunt subito
duo equi, quos recepimus cum gaudio magno, & as-
cenderunt eos dux noster & interpres, ut specularen-
tur quorsum possemus populum invenire.   Tandem
quarta die inventis hominibus gavisi sumus tanquam
naufragi venientes ad portum.   Tunc acceptis equis
& bobus ivimus de mansione ad mansionem donec per-

Marginalia:

A.D.
1253.

Latitudo Tanais.

Oceanus.

‖*Ad introitum Augusti redeunt ad meridiem.*

venimus usque ad herbergiam Sartach secundo Calendas
Augusti.

De regione Sartach, & de gentibus illius.

REgio ista ultra Tanaim est pulcherrima, habens
flumina & sylvas ad aquilonem. Sunt sylvæ
maximæ, quas inhabitant duo genera hominum : Moxel
scilicet, qui sunt sine lege, puri pagani. Civitatem non
habent sed casulas in sylvis. Dominus eorum & magna
pars eorum fuerunt interfecti in Alemania. Tartari enim
duxerant eos ad introitum Alemaniæ. Unde ipsi multum
commendant Alemanos, sperantes quod adhuc liberabuntur
per eos à servitute Tartarorum. Si mercator veniat ad
eos, oportet quod ille apud quem primo descendit provideat ei quamdiu vult esse inter eos. Si quis dormiat
cum uxore alterius, ille non curat nisi videat propriis
oculis : unde non sunt Zelotypi. Abundant apud eos
porci, mel, & cera, pelles preciosæ, & falcones. Post illos
sunt alii qui dicuntur Merdas, quos latini vocant Merduos,
& sunt Saraceni. Post illos est ‖ Etilia, quæ est major
fluvius, quam unquam viderim : & venit ab Aquilone de
majori Bulgaria tendens ad meridiem : & cadit in quendam lacum habentem spacium quatuor mensium in circuitu,
de quo postea dicam vobis. Ista ergo duo flumina Tanais
& Etilia versus regiones Aquilonis per quas transivimus
non distant ab invicem nisi decem dietis, sed ad meridiem
multum dividuntur ab invicem. Tanais enim descendit
in Mare Ponti : Etilia facit prædictum Mare sive lacum,
cum aliis multis fluminibus, quæ cadunt in illum de Perside. Habebamus autem ad meridiem montes maximos
in quibus habitant in lateribus versus solitudinem illam
Cergis & Alani sive ‖ Acas, qui sunt Christiani & adhuc
pugnant contra Tartaros. Post istos prope Mare sive
lacum Etiliæ sunt quidam Saraceni qui dicuntur Lesgi,
qui similiter obediunt. Post hos est Porta ferrea, quam
fecit Alexander ad excludendas Barbaras gentes de
Perside : de cujus situ dicam vobis postea, ‖ quia transivi
per eam in reditu. Et inter ista duo flumina in illis

[I. 82.]

Merdui Sara-
ceni.
‖ vel Volga
fluvius.

‖ Kerkis.
vel Aas.
Lesgi Sara-
ceni.

‖ Reditus ejus
per Derbent.

terris per quas transivimus habitabant Comani antequam
Tartari occuparent eas.

De Curia Sartach & de gloria ejus.

INvenimus ergo Sartach prope Etiliam per tres dietas:
cujus curia valde magna videbatur nobis: quia habet
sex uxores, & filius ejus primogenitus juxta eum duas vel
tres: & quælibet habet domum magnam & bigas forte
ducentas. Accessit autem ductor noster ad quendam
Nestorinum Coiat nomine, qui est unus de majoribus *Coiat Nestori-*
Curiæ suæ. Ille fecit nos ire valde longe ad domini *nus.*
Januam. Ita vocant illum qui habet officium recipiendi
nuncios. In sero præcepit nobis dictus Coiat, ut
veniremus ad eum. Tunc incepit quærere ductor noster
quid portaremus ei, & cœpit multum scandalizari, quum
vidit quod nihil parabamus ad portandum. Stetimus
coram eo, & ipse sedebat in gloria sua & faciebat sonare
citharam & saltare coram se. Tunc dixi ei verba
prædicta qualiter veniremus ad dominum ejus, rogans
eum ut juvaret nos ut Dominus ejus videret literas
nostras. Excusavi etiam me quia monachus eram, non
habens, nec recipiens, nec tractans aurum vel argentum
vel aliquid preciosum, solis libris & capella in qua
serviebamus deo exceptis: unde nullum xenium affere-
bamus ei nec domino suo. Qui enim propria dimiseram,
non poteram portator esse alienorum. Tunc respondit
satis mansuete, quod bene faciebam ex quo eram
monachus: sic servarem votum meum, & non indigebat
rebus nostris; sed magis daret nobis de suis, si indigere-
mus: & fecit nos sedere & bibere de lacte suo. Et post
pauca rogavit ut diceremus benedictionem pro eo, quod
& fecimus. Quæsivit & quis esset major dominus inter
Francos. Dixi, Imperator, si haberet terram suam in
pace. Non, inquit, sed Rex Franciæ. Audiverat enim
de vobis à domino Baldewyno de Hannonia. Inveni
etiam ibi unum de Sociis domus Dominicæ, qui fuerat
in Cypro, qui narraverat omnia quæ viderat. Tunc
reversi sumus ad hospitium nostrum. In crastino misi

ei unum flasconem de vino Muscato, quod optime se
custodierat in tam longa via; & cophinum plenum
biscocto quod fuit ei gratissimum, & retinuit illo sero
famulos nostros secum. In crastino mandavit mihi quod
venirem ad curiam; afferens literas regis & capellam &
libros mecum, quia dominus suus vellet videre ea: quod
& fecimus, onerantes unam bigam libris & capella, &
aliam pane & vino & fructibus. Tunc fecit omnes libros
& vestes explicari, & circumstabant nos in equis multi
Tartari & Christiani & Saraceni: quibus inspectis,
quæsivit, si vellem ista omnia dare domino suo, quo
audito, expavi, & displicuit mihi verbum, dissimulans
tamen respondi, domine rogamus, quatenus dominus
noster dignetur recipere panem istum, vinum & fructus
non pro xenio quia exiguum quid est, sed pro benedictione, ne vacua manu veniamus coram eo. Ipse
autem videbit literas domini regis, & per eas sciet, qua
de causa venimus ad eum: & tunc stabimus mandato
ejus nos & omnes res nostræ. Vestes enim sanctæ
sunt, & non licet eas contingere nisi sacerdotibus. Tunc
præcepit quod indueremus nos ituri coram domino suo:
quod & fecimus. Ego autem indutus preciosioribus
vestibus accepi in pectore pulvinar, quod erat valde
pulchrum, & biblium quod dederatis mihi, psalterium
pulcherrimum, quod dederat mihi domina regina, in quo
erant picturæ pulchræ. Socius meus accepit missale &
crucem, clericus indutus supercilicio accepit thuribulum:
sic accessimus ante dominum ejus: & levaverunt
[I. 83.]   filtrum quod pendebat ante ostium ut nos posset videre.
Tunc fecerunt flectere genua ter clerico & interpreti:
à nobis non requisiverunt. Tunc monuerunt nos
valde diligenter, ut caveremus ingrediendo & egredi-
endo ne tangeremus limen domus, & ut cantaremus
aliquam benedictionem pro eo. Tunc ingressi sumus
cantando, Salve regina. In introitu autem ostii stabat
bancus cum cosmos & cum ciphis. Et convenerant
omnes uxores ejus: & ipsi Moal. Ingredientes nobiscum
comprimebant nos. Illic Coiac tulit ei thuribulum cum

incenso, quod ipse respexit, tenens in manu diligenter:
postea tulit ei psalterium quod valde respexit, & uxor
ejus sedens juxta eum. Postea tulit biblium, & ipse
quæsivit, si evangelium esset ibi. Dixi, etiam tota
Scriptura Sacra. Accepit etiam crucem in manu sua, &
quæsivit de imagine, utrum esset imago Christi?
Respondi quod sic. Ipsi Nestoriani & Armeni nunquam
faciunt super cruces suas figuram Christi. Unde
videntur male sentire de passione, vel erubescunt eam.
Postea fecit circumstantes nos retrahere se, ut plenius
posset videre ornamenta nostra. Tunc obtuli ei literas
vestras cum transcriptis in Arabico & Syriano. Feceram
enim eas transferri in Acon in utraque litera & lingua.
Et ibi erant sacerdotes Armeni, qui sciebant Turcicum
& Arabicum, & Ille Socius domus Domini qui sciebat
Syrianum, & Turcicum & Arabicum. Tunc exivimus
& deposuimus vestimenta nostra: & venerunt scriptores
& ille Coiac, & fecerunt literas interpretari. Quibus
auditis, fecit recipi panem & vinum & fructus: vesti-
mentà & libros fecit nos reportare ad hospitium. Hoc
actum est in festo Sancti Petri ad vincula.

Qualiter habuerunt in mandatis adire Baatu patrem Sartach.

IN crastino mane venit quidam sacerdos frater ipsius
Coiac postulans vasculum cum chrismate, quia Sartach
volebat illud videre, ut dicebat, & dedimus ei. Hora
vespertina vocavit nos Coiac, dicens nobis: Dominus rex
scripsit bona verba Domino meo: Sed sunt in eis difficilia,
de quibus nihil auderet facere, sine consilio patris sui.
Unde oportet vos ire ad patrem suum, & duas bigas quas
adduxistis heri cum vestimentis & libris dimittetis mihi,
quia Dominus meus vult res diligentius videre. Ego
statim suspicatus sum malum de cupiditate ejus, & dixi
ei. Domine, non solum illas sed etiam duas quas adhuc
habemus relinquemus sub custodia vestra. Non inquit,
illas relinquetis, de aliis facietis velle vestrum. Dixi quod
hoc nullo modo posset fieri. Sed totam dimitteremus ei.

Tunc quæsivit si vellemus morari in terra ? Ego dixi, Si
bene intellexistis literas domini regis, potestis scire, quod
sic. Tunc dixit, quod oporteret nos esse patientes multum, & humiles. Sic discessimus ab eo illo sero. In
crastino mane misit unum sacerdotem Nestorinum pro
bigis, & nos duximus omnes quatuor. Tunc occurrens
nobis frater ipsius Coiacis, seperavit omnia nostra ab ipsis
rebus quas tuleramus pridie ad curiam, & illa accepit
tanquam sua, scilicet libros & vestimenta: & Coiac præ-
ceperat, quod ferremus nobiscum vestimenta quibus induti
fueramus coram Sartach ut illis indueremur coram Baatu
si expediret: quas ille sacerdos abstulit nobisvi, dicens:
Tu attulisti eas ad Sartach, modo vis ferre Baatu ? Et
cum vellem ei reddere rationem, respondit mihi, Ne
loquaris nimis, & vade viam tuam. Tunc necessaria fuit
patientia, quia apud Sartach, non patebat nobis ingressus;
nec aliquis erat, qui nobis exhiberet justiciam. Timebam
etiam de interprete, ne ipse aliquid aliter dixisset, quam
ego dixissem ei : quia ipse bene voluisset, quod de omnibus fecissemus xenium. Unum erat mihi solacium, quia
quum persensi cupiditatem eorum, ego subtraxi de libris
Biblium & sententias, & alios libros quos magis diligebam.
Psalterium dominæ reginæ non fui ausus subtrahere, quia
illud fuerat nimis notatum propter aureas picturas quæ
erant in eo. Sic ergo reversi sumus cum duobus residuis
bigis ad hospitium nostrum. Tunc venit ille, qui debebat
ducere nos ad Baatu, volens cum festinatione arripere iter :
cui dixi quod nulla ratione ducerem bigas. Quod ipse
retulit ad Coiac. Tunc præcepit Coiac quod relinqueremus
eas apud ipsum cum garcione nostro : quod & fecimus.
Sic ergo euntes versus Baatu recta in Orientem, tertia die

*Perveniunt ad
Etiliam vel
Volgam.*

*Tartari volunt
vocari Moal.*

pervenimus ad Etiliam: cujus aquas cum vidi, mirabar
unde ab Aquilone descenderunt tantæ aquæ. Antequam
recederemus à Sartach, dixit nobis supradictus Coiac cum
aliis multis scriptoribus curiæ, Nolite dicere quod dominus
noster sit Christianus, sed Moal. Quia nomen Christianitatis videtur eis nomen cujusdam gentis. In tantam
superbiam sunt erecti, quod quamvis aliquid forte credant

de Christo, tamen nolunt dici Christiani volentes nomen suum, hoc est, Moal exaltare super omne nomen. Nec [I. 84.] volunt vocari Tartari : Tartari enim fuerunt alia gens de quibus sic didici.

Qualiter Sartach, & Mangucham & Kencham faciunt reverentiam Christianis.

TEmpore quo Franci ceperunt Antiochiam tenebat monarchiam in illis lateribus Aquilonis quidam qui vocabatur Concan. Con est proprium nomen : Can *Con can.* nomen dignitatis quod idem est qui divinator. Omnes divinatores vocant Can. Unde principes dicuntur Can, quia penes eos spectat regimen populi per divinationem. Unde legitur in historia Antiochiæ, quod Turci miserunt propter succursum contra Francos ad regnum Con can. De illis enim partibus venerunt omnes Turci. Iste Con *Unde vene-* erat Cara-Catay. Cara idem est quod nigrum. Catai *runt Turci.* nomen gentis. Undè Cara-Catay idem est quod nigri *Caracatay.* Catay. Et hoc dicitur ad differentiam ipsorum Catay qui erant in Oriente super Oceanum de quibus postea *Oceanus.* dicam vobis. Isti Catay erant in quibusdam alpibus per quas transivi. Et in quadam planicie inter illas Alpes erat quidam Nestorinus pastor potens & dominus super popu- lum, qui dicebatur Yayman, qui erant Christiani Nestorini. *Vel Nayman.* Mortuo Con can elevavit se ille Nestorius in regem, & vocabant eum Nestoriani Regem Johannem : & plus *Presbyter Jo-* dicebant de ipso in decuplo quàm veritas esset. Ita enim *hannes.* faciunt Nestoriani venientes de partibus illis. De nihilo enim faciunt magnos rumores. Unde disseminaverunt de Sartach quod esset Christianus, & de Mangu Can & Ken can : quia faciunt majorem reverentiam Christianis, quàm aliis populis, & tamen in veritate Christiani non sunt. Sic ergo exivit magna fama de illo Rege Johanne. Et *Kencham ubi* quando ego transivi per pascua ejus, nullus aliquid sciebat *habitavit.* de eo nisi Nestoriani pauci. In pascuis ejus habitat *Frater And-* Kencam, apud cujus curiam fuit frater Andreas : & ego *reas in Curia* etiam transivi per eam in reditu. Huic Johanni erat *Vut can, vel* frater quidam potens, pastor similiter, nomine Vut : & *Unc.*

I   209   O

ipse erat ultra Alpes ipsorum Caracatay, distans à fratre suo spacium trium hebdomadarum & erat dominus cujusdam Villulæ quæ dicitur Caracarum, populum habens sub se, qui dicebantur Crit, Merkit, qui erant Christiani Nestorini. Sed ipse dominus eorum dimisso cultu Christi, sectabatur idola ; habens sacerdotes idolorum, qui omnes sunt invocatores dæmonum & sortilegi. Ultra pascua istius ad decem vel quindecem dietas erant pascua

Moal : qui erant pauperrimi homines sine capitaneo & sine lege, exceptis sortilegiis & divinationibus, quibus omnes in partibus illis intendunt. Et juxta Moal erant

alii pauperes, qui dicebantur Tartari. Rex Johannes mortuus fuit sine hærede, & ditatus est frater ejus Unc ; & faciebat se vocari Can : & mittebantur armenta greges

ejus usque ad terminos Moal. Tunc temporis Chingis faber quidam erat in populo Moal : & furabatur de animalibus Unc can quod poterat : In tantum quod conquesti sunt pastores Vut domino suo. Tunc congregavit exercitum & equitavit in terram Moal, quærens ipsum Cyngis. Et ille fugit inter Tartaros & latuit ibi. Tunc ipse Vut accepta prædà Moal & à Tartaris reversus est. Tunc ipse Cyngis allocutus est Tartaros & ipsos Moal dicens, Quia sine duce sumus opprimunt nos vicini nostri. Et fecerunt ipsum ducem & capitaneum Tartari & Moal. Tunc latenter congregato exercitu irruit super ipsum Vut, & vicit ipsum, & ipse fugit in Cathaiam. Ibi capta fuit filia ejus, quam Cyngis dedit uni ex filiis in uxorem, ex

quo ipsa suscepit istum qui nunc regnat Mangu. Tunc ipse Cyngis premittebat ubique ipsos Tartaros : & inde exivit nomen eorum, quia ubique clamabatur, Ecce Tartari veniunt. Sed per crebra bella modo omnes fere deleti sunt. Unde isti Moal modo volunt extinguere illud nomen, & suum elevare. Terra illa in qua primo fuerunt, & ubi est adhuc curia Cyngiscan, vocatur Man-

cherule. Sed quia Tartari est regio circa quam fuit acquisitio eorum, illam civitatem habent pro regali, & ibi prope eligunt suum Can.

De Rutenis & Hungaris, & Alanis, & de mari   [I. 85.]
Caspio.

DE Sartach autem utrum credit in Christum vel non
nescio. Hoc scio quod Christianus non vult dici.
Immò magis videtur mihi deridere Christianos. Ipse
enim est in itinere Christianorum, scilicet Rutenorum,
Blacorum, Bulgarorum minoris Bulgariæ, Soldainorum,
Kerkisorum, Alanorum : qui omnes transeunt per eum
quum vadunt ad curiam patris sui deferre ei munera,
unde magis amplectitur eos. Tamen si Saraceni veniant,
& majus afferant, citiùs expediuntur. Habet etiam circa
se Nestorinos sacerdotes, qui pulsant tabulam, & cantant
officium suum.

Est alius qui dicitur Berta super Baatu, qui pascit *Berta vel*
versus Portam ferream, ubi est iter Saracenorum omnium *Berca.*
qui veniunt de Perside & de Turchia, qui euntes ad
Baatu, & transeuntes per eum, deferunt ei munera. Et
ille facit se Saracenum, & non permittit in terra sua
comedi carnes porcinas. Baatu in reditu nostro præce-
perat ei, quod transferret se de illo loco ultra Etiliam ad
Orientem, nolens nuncios Saracenorum transire per eum,
quia videbatur sibi damnosum.

Quatuor autem diebus quibus fuimus in curia Sartach,
nunquam provisum fuit nobis de cibo, nisi semel de modico
cosmos. In via verò inter ipsum & patrem suum habuimus magnum timorem. Ruteni enim & Hungari, &
Alani servi eorum, quorum est magna multitudo inter
eos, associant se viginti vel triginta simul, & fugiunt de
nocte, habentes pharetras & arcus, & quemcunque inveniunt de nocte interficiunt, de die latitantes. Et quando
sunt equi eorum fatigati veniunt de nocte ad multitudinem
equorum in pascuis, & mutant equos, & unum vel duos
ducunt secum, ut comedant quum indiguerint. Occur-
sum ergo talium timebat multum Dux noster. In illa via
fuissemus mortui fame, si non portavissemus nobiscum
modicum de biscocto.

Venimus tandem ad Etiliam maximum flumen. Est

211

enim in quadruplo majus quàm Sequana, & profundissi-
mum : Veniens de majori Bulgaria, quæ est ad Aquilonem, tendens in quendam lacum, sive quoddam mare,
quod modò vocant mare Sircan, à quadam civitate, quæ
est juxta ripam ejus in Perside. Sed Isidorus vocat illud
mare Caspium. Habet enim montes Caspios, & Persidem à meridie : montes verò Musihet, hoc est, Assassi-
norum ad Orientem, qui contiguantur cum montibus
Caspiis : Ad Aquilonem verò habet illam solitudinem, in
qua modò sunt Tartari. Prius verò erant ibi quidam qui

dicebantur Canglæ : Et ex illo latere recipit Etiliam, qui
crescit in æstate sicut Nilus Ægypti. Ad Occidentem
verò habet montes Alanorum & Lesgi ; & Portam feream,
& montes Georgianorum. Habet igitur illud mare tria
latera inter montes, Aquilonare verò habet ad planiciem.

Frater Andreas ipse circumdedit duo latera ejus, meridi-
onale scilicet & Orientale. Ego verò alia duo ; Aquilonare scilicet in eundo à Baatu ad Mangu cham,
Occidentale verò in revertendo de Baatu in Syriam.

Quatuor mensibus potest circumdari. Et non est verum
quod dicit Isidorus, quòd sit sinus exiens ab Oceano :
nusquam enim tangit Oceanum, sed undique circumdatur
terra.

De curia Baatu, & qualiter recepti fuerunt
ab eo.

TOta illa regio à latere Occidentali istius maris, ubi
sunt Porta ferrea Alexandri, & montes Alanorum,
usque ad Oceanum Aquilonarem & paludes Mæotidis ubi
mergitur Tanais, solebat dici Albania : de qua dicit
Isidorus, quòd habet canes ita magnos, tantæque feritatis,
ut tauros premant, leones perimant. Quod verum est,
prout intellexi à narrantibus, quod ibi versus Oceanum
Aquilonarem faciunt canes trahere in bigis sicut boves
propter magnitudinem & fortitudinem eorum. In illo
ergo loco ubi nos applicuimus super Etiliam est casale
novum, quod fecerunt Tartari de Rutenis mixtim, qui
transponunt nuncios euntes, & redeuntes ad curiam Baatu :

WILLIAM DE RUBRUQUIS

quia Baatu est in ulteriori ripa versus Orientem : nec
transit illum locum ubi nos applicuimus ascendendo in
æstate, sed jam incipiebat descendere. De Januario enim
usque ad Augustum ascendit ipse, & omnes alii versus
frigidas regiones, & in Augusto incipiunt redire. De-
scendimus ergo in navi ab illo casali usque ad curiam ejus.
Et ab illo loco usque ad villas majoris Bulgariæ versus
Aquilonem, sunt quinque dietæ. Et miror quis Diabolus
portavit illuc legem Machometi. A Porta enim ferrea,
quæ est exitus Persidis, sunt plusquam triginta dietæ per
transversum, solitudinem ascendendo juxta Etiliam usque
in illam Bulgariam, ubi nulla est civitas, nisi quædam
casalia propè ubi cadit Etilia in mare. Et illi Bulgari sunt
pessimi Saraceni, fortius tenentes legem Machometi, quàm
aliqui alii. Quum ergo vidi curiam Baatu, expavi ; quia
videbantur propè domus ejus, quasi quædam magna
civitas protensa in longum, & populus undique circum-
fusus, usque ad tres vel quatuor leucas. Et sicut populus
Israel sciebat unusquisque, ad quam regionem tabernaculi
deberet figere tentoria : ita ipsi sciunt ad quod latus curiæ
debeant se collocare, quando ipsi deponunt domus. Unde
dicitur curia Orda lingua eorum, quod sonat medium,
quia semper est in medio hominum suorum : hoc excepto,
quod rectà ad meridiem nullus se collocat, quia ad partem
illam aperiuntur portæ Curiæ : Sed à dextris & à sinistris
extendunt se quantum volunt secundum exigentiam
locorum : dummodo rectè ante curiam, vel ex opposito
curiæ non descendunt. Fuimus ergo ducti ad quendam
Saracenum, qui non providebat nobis de aliquo cibo :
sequenti die fuimus ad curiam, & fecerat extendi magnum
tentorium, quia domus non potuisset capere tot homines
& mulieres, quot convenerant. Monuit nos ductor
noster ut non loqueremur, donec Baatu præciperet : &
tunc loqueremur breviter. Quæsivit etiam utrum misissetis nuncios ad eos. Dixi qualiter miseratis ad Kencham,
& quod nec ad ipsum misissetis nuncios, nec ad Sartach
literas, nisi credidissetis eos fuisse Christianos : quia non
pro timore aliquo, sed ex congratulatione, quia audiveratis

Descendit
navi per flu-
men Volga.
Nota.

30 dietæ à
Porta ferrea.

Astracan.

Descriptio cu-
riæ Baatu.

Horda sonat
medium.

Misit rex
Franciæ ad
Kencham
nuncios.

eos esse Christianos, misistis. Tunc duxit nos ad papilio-
nem : & monebamur, ne tangeremus cordas tentorii, quas
ipsi reputant loco liminis domus. Stetimus ibi nudis
pedibus in habitu nostro discoopertis capitibus, & eramus
spectaculum magnum in oculis eorum. Fuerat enim ibi
frater Johannes de Plano carpini, sed ipse mutaverat
habitum ne contemneretur ; quia erat nuncius Domini
Papæ. Tunc inducti fuimus usque ad medium tentorii,
nec requisiverunt ut faceremus aliquam reverentiam genua
flectendo, sicut solent facere nuncii. Stetimus ergo coram
eo quantum possit dici, Miserere mei Deus : & omnes
erant in summo silentio. Ipse verò super solium longum
sedebat & latum sicut lectus, totum deauratum, ad quod
ascendebatur tribus gradibus, & una domina juxta eum.
Viri vero diffusi sedebant à dextris dominæ & à sinistris :
quod non implebant mulieres ex parte una, quia erant ibi
solæ uxores Baatu, implebant viri. Bancus verò cum
cosmos & ciphis maximis aureis & argenteis, ornatis
lapidibus prætiosis erat in introitu tentorii. Respexit ergo
nos diligentius, & nos eum : & videbatur mihi similis in
statura Domino Johanni de Bello monte cujus anima
requiescit in pace. Erat etiam vultus ejus tunc perfusus
gutta rosea. Tandem præcepit ut loquerer. Tunc ductor
noster præcepit ut flecteremus genua, & loqueremur.
Flexi unum genu tanquam homini : tunc innuit quod
ambo flecterem, quod & feci, nolens contendere super hoc.
Tunc præcepit quod loquerer. Et ego cogitans quod
orarem Dominum, quia flexeram ambo genua, Incepi
verba oratione, dicens : Domine, nos oramus Dominum,
à quo bona cuncta procedunt, qui dedit vobis ista terrena,
ut det vobis post hæc cœlestia : quia hæc sine illis vana
sunt. Et ipse diligenter auscultavit, & subjunxi :
Noveritis pro certo quòd cœlestia non habebitis, nisi
fueritis Christianus. Dicit enim Deus, Qui crediderit &
baptizatus fuerit, salvus erit : qui vero non crediderit,
condemnabitur. Ad illud verbum ipse modestè subrisit,
& alii Moal inceperunt plaudere manus deridendo nos.
Et obstupuit interpres meus, quem oportuit me confortare

A.D.
1253.

ne timerem. Tunc facto silentio, dixi : Ego veni ad
filium vestrum, quia audivimus quòd esset Christianus, &
attuli ei literas ex parte Domini Regis Francorum : ipse *Literæ Regis*
misit me huc ad vos. Vos debetis scire qua de causa. *Francorum.*
Tunc fecit me surgere. Et quæsivit nomen vestrum, & [I. 87.]
meum, & socii mei, & interpretis, & fecit omnia scribi.
Quæsivit etiam, quia intellexerat quod exieratis terram
vestram cum exercitu ut haberetis bellum. Respondi,
Contra Saracenos violantes domum Dei Hierusalem.
Quæsivit etiam si unquam misissetis nuncios ad eum.
Ad vos dixi nunquam. Tunc fecit nos sedere, & dari de
lacte suo ad bibendum, quod ipsi valdè magnum reputant,
quando aliquis bibit cosmos cum eo in domo sua. Et
dum sedens respicerem terram, præcepit ut elevarem
vultum, volens adhuc nos amplius respicere, vel fortè pro
sortilegio : quia habent pro malo omine vel signo, vel pro
mala Prognostica, quando aliquis sedet coram eis inclinata
facie quasi tristis, maximè quum appodiat maxillam, vel
mentum super manum. Tunc exivimus, & post pauca,
venit Ductor noster ad nos, & ducens nos ad hospitium,
dixit mihi, Dominus Rex rogat, quod retinearis in terra
ista : & hoc non potest Baatu facere sine conscientia
Mangu cham. Unde oportet quod tu & interpres tuus
eatis ad Mangu cham. Socius verò tuus & alius homo
revertentur ad curiam Sartach ibi expectantes donec
revertatis. Tunc incepit homo DEI Interpres lugere
reputans se perditum : Socius etiam meus contestari, quod
citius amputarent ei caput, quam quod divideretur à me.
Et ego dixi, quod sine socio non possem ire : Et etiam
quod benè indigebamus duobus famulis, quia si contin-
geret unum infirmari, non possem solus remanere. Tunc
ipse reversus ad curiam dixit verba Baatu. Tunc præcepit : vadant duo sacerdotes & interpres : & Clericus
revertatur ad Sartach. Ille reversus dixit nobis summam.
Et quando volebam loqui pro Clerico, quod iret nobiscum, dixit, Non loquamini amplius, quia Baatu definivit,
& eo amplius non audeo redire ad curiam. De eleemosyna habebat Goset clericus viginti sex ipperpera, &

non plus : quorum decem retinuit sibi & puero : & sexdecem dedit homini Dei pro nobis. Et sic divisi sumus cum lachrimis ab invicem : Illo redeunte ad curiam Sartach, & nobis ibi remanentibus.

De itinere fratrum versus curiam Mangu cham.

IN Vigilia Assumptionis pervenit ipse clericus ad Curiam Sartach : & in crastino fuerunt Sacerdotes Nestorini induti vestimentis nostris coram Sartach. Tunc ducti fuimus ad alium hospitem, qui debebat nobis providere de domo & cibo & equis. Sed quia non habuimus quod daremus ei, omnia malè faciebat. Et bigavimus cum Baatu descendendo juxta Etiliam quinque septimanas.

Quinque septimanas juxta Etiliam descendebant.

Aliquando habuit socius meus tantam famem, quod dicebat mihi quasi lachrymando : videbatur mihi quod nunquam comederim. Forum sequitur semper Curiam Baatu. Sed illud erat tam longè à nobis, quod non poteramus ire. Oportebat enim nos ire pedibus pro defectu equorum. Tandem invenerunt nos quidam

Quidam Hungari.

Hungari, qui fuerant Clericuli, quorum unus sciebat adhuc cantare multa corde, & habebatur ab aliis Hungaris quasi Sacerdos, & vocabatur ad exequias suorum defunctorum : Et alius fuerat competenter instructus in Grammatica : qui intelligebat quicquid dicebamus ei literaliter, sed nesciebat respondere : qui fecerunt nobis magnam consolationem, afferentes cosmos ad bibendum, & carnes aliquando ad comedendum : qui quum postulassent à nobis aliquos libros, & non haberem quos possem dare, nullos enim habebam, nisi Biblium & breviarium, dolui multum. Tunc dixi eis, afferte nobis chartas, & ego scribam vobis, quamdiu erimus hîc : quod & fecerunt. Et scripsi utrasque horas Beatæ Virginis & officium defunctorum. Quodam die junxit se nobis quidam

Comanus.

Comanus, salutans nos verbis latinis, dicens, Salvete Domini. Ego mirans, ipso resalutato, quæsivi ab eo, quis eum docuerat illam salutationem. Et ipse dixit quod in Hungaria fuit baptizatus à fratribus nostris qui docuerant illum eam. Dixit etiam quod Baatu quæsiverat ab eo multa de nobis, & quod ipse dixerat ei conditiones ordinis nostri. Ego vidi Baatu equitantem cum turba sua, & omnes patres familias equitantes cum eo, secundùm æstimationem meam non erant quingenti viri. Tandem circa finem exaltationis sanctæ crucis venit ad nos quidam dives Moal, cujus pater erat millenarius, quod magnum est inter eos, dicens, Ego vos debeo ducere ad Mangu cham, & est iter quatuor mensium : & tantum frigus est ibi, quod finduntur ibi lapides & arbores pro frigore : Videatis utrum poteritis sustinere. Cui respondi : Spero in virtute Dei, quod nos sustinebimus, quod alii homines possunt sustinere. Tunc dixit : Si non poteritis sustinere, ego relinquam vos in via. Cui respondi, hoc non esset justum : quia non ivimus pro nobis, nisi missi à Domino vestro : Unde ex quo vobis committimur, non debetis nos dimittere. Tunc dixit, benè erit. Post hoc fecit nos ostendere sibi omnes vestes nostras, & quod sibi videbatur minus necessarium fecit deponere sub custodia hospitis nostri. In crastino attulerunt cuilibet nostrum unam pelliceam villosam arietinam & braccas de eadem, & botas sive bucellos secundùm morem eorum cum soccis de filtro ; & almucias de pellibus secundùm modum eorum. Et secunda die post exaltationem Sanctæ crucis incepimus equitare nos tres habentes signarios : & equitavimus continuè versus Orientem usque ad festum Omnium Sanctorum, per totam illam terram, & adhuc amplius habitabant Cangle, quædam parentela Romanorum. Ad Aquilonem habebamus majorem Bulgariam, & ad meridiem prædictum mare Caspium.

Iter quatuor mensium à Volga. Ingens frigus.

[I. 88.]

26. Septemb.

Cangle populi.

Major Bulgaria.

De flumine Iagag, & de diversis regionibus sive nationibus.

POstquam iveramus duodecim diebus ab Etilia invenimus magnum flumen, quod vocant Iagag : & venit ab Aquilone de terra Pascatir descendens in prædictum mare. Idioma Pascatir & Hungarorum idem est : & sunt pastores sine civitate aliqua. Et con-

Iagag flumen 12. dietis à Volga. Pascatir terra, vel Bascirdorum terra vel Zibier.

217

tiguatur majori Bulgariæ ab Occidente. Ab illa terra versus Orientem in latere illo Aquilonari non est amplius aliqua civitas. Unde Bulgaria major est ultima *Hungari à* regio habens civitatem. De illa regione Pascatir exierunt *Pascatir* Huni, qui posteà dicti sunt Hungari. Unde ipsa est *oriundi.* major Bulgaria. Et dicit Isidorus, quòd pernicibus equis claustra Alexandri rupibus Caucasi feras gentes cohibentia transierunt : ita quod usque in Ægyptum solvebatur eis tributum. Destruxerunt etiam omnes terras usque in Franciam. Unde fuerunt majoris potentiæ, quàm sunt adhuc Tartari. Cum illis occurrerunt Blaci & Bulgari & Vandali. De illa enim majori Bulgaria venerunt illi Bulgari : Et qui sunt ultra Danubium propè Constantinopolin, & juxta Pascatir sunt Ilac, quod idem est quod Blac : sed B. nesciunt *Nota.* Tartari sonare : à quibus venerunt illi qui sunt in terra Assani. Utrosque enim vocant Ilac, & hos & illos lingua Rutenorum & Polonorum, & Boëmorum. Sclavorum est idem idioma cum lingua Vandalorum, quorum omnium manus fuit cum Hunis : & nunc pro majori parte est cum Tartaris quos Deus suscitavit à remotioribus partibus, populum multum, & gentem stultam, *Deut.* 32.21. secundùm quod dicit Dominus, Provocabo eos, id est, non custodientes Legem suam, in eo qui non est populus, & in gente stulta irritabo eos : Hoc completur ad literam super omnes nationes non custodientes Legem Dei. Hoc quod dixi de terra Pascatir scio per fratres Præ- ‖ *Qui fuerunt* dicatores, ‖ qui iverunt illuc ante adventum Tartarorum. *isti fratres?* Et ex tunc erant ipsi subjugati à vicinis Bulgaris Saracenis, & plures eorum facti Saraceni. Alia possunt sciri per Chronica : quia constat quod illæ provinciæ post Constantinopolim, quæ modo dicuntur Bulgaria, Valachia, Sclavonia, fuerunt provinciæ Græcorum. Hungaria fuit *Cangle* Pannonia. Equitavimus ergo per terram Cangle à festo *planicies* Sanctæ crucis usque ad festum Omnium Sanctorum, quo- *ingens.* libet die ferè quantum est à Parisiis usque Aurelianum, secundùm quod possum estimare, & plus aliquando : secundùm quod habebamus copiam equorum. Aliquando

enim mutabamus bis in die vel ter equos. Aliquando
ibamus duobus diebus vel tribus, quibus non inveniebamus populum, & oportebat levius ire. De viginti vel
triginta equis nos semper habebamus pejores, quia extranei eramus. Omnes enim accipiebant ante nos equos
meliores. Mihi semper providebant de forti equo, quia
eram ponderosus valdè: sed utrum suaviter ambularet
vel non, de hoc non auderem facere quæstionem. Nec
etiam audebam conqueri, si durè portaret. Sed fortunam
suam oportebat unumquemque sustinere. Unde oriebatur nobis difficillimus labor: quia multoties fatiga-
bantur equi, antequam possemus pervenire ad populum.
Et tunc oportebat nos percutere & flagellare equos,
ponere etiam vestes super alios saginarios, mutare equos
saginarios; aliquando nos duos ire in uno equo.

De fame & siti, & aliis miseriis quas sustinuerunt in itinere.

DE fame & siti, frigore & fatigatione non est
numerus. Non enim dant cibum nisi in sero. In
mane dant aliquid bibere, vel sorbere milium. In sero
dabant nobis carnes, scapulam arietis cum costis & de
brodio ad mensuram bibere. Quando habebamus de
brodio carnium ad satietatem optimè reficiebamur. Et
videbatur mihi suavissimus potus & maximè nutriens. [I. 89.]
Feria sexta permanebam jejunus usque ad noctem, nihil
hauriens. Tunc oportebat me in tristitia & dolore comedere carnes. Aliquando oportebat nos comedere carnes
semicoctas vel ferè crudas propter defectum materiæ ignis, *Defectus mate-*
quando jacebamus in campis & de nocte descendebamus: *riæ ignis.*
quia tunc non poteramus benè colligere stercora equorum
vel boum: aliam materiam ignis rarò inveniebamus; nisi
forte alicubi aliquas spinas. In ripis etiam aliquorum *Aliqua*
fluminum sunt alicubi sylvæ. Sed hoc rarò. In principio *flumina.*
despiciebat nos multùm Ductor noster, & fastidiebat eum
ducere tam viles homines. Postea tamen quando incepit
nos melius cognoscere, ducebat nos per curias divitum
Moallorum: & oportebat nos orare pro ipsis. Unde si

Vasta solitudo.

‖ *Nota diligenter.*
*Iter versus
meridiem octo
dierum.*

*Asini
velocissimi.*

Montes altissimi.
Terræ cultæ.
*Kenchat villa
Saracenorum.*

*Septimo die
Novembris
ibant super
glaciem.*

*Civitas valdè
parva.*
*Magnus
fluvius.*
*Multæ
paludes.*
Vites.

habuissem bonum interpretem, habebam oportunitatem seminandi multa bona. Ille Chingis primus Cham habuit quatuor filios, de quibus egressi sunt multi, qui omnes habent modo magnas curias: & quotidiè multiplicantur & diffunduntur per illam Vastam solitudinem, quæ est sicut mare. Per multos ergò illorum ducebat nos Ductor noster. Et mirabantur supra modum, quia nolebamus recipere aurum, vel argentum, vel vestes præciosas. Quærebant etiam de magno Papa, si esset ita senex sicut audierant: audierant enim quod esset quingentorum annorum. Quærebant de terris nostris si ibi essent multæ oves, & boves, & equi. De Oceano mari non potuerunt intelligere, quod esset sine termino vel sine ripa. In vigilia omnium Sanctorum dimisimus viam in Orientem, ‖ quia jam populus descenderat multum versus meridiem: Et direximus iter per quasdam Alpes rectè in meridiem continuè per octo dies. In illa solitudine vidi multos asinos, quos vocant Colan, qui magis assimulantur mulis: quos multum prosequuti sunt Dux noste & socii ejus, sed nihil profecerunt propter nimiam velocitatem eorum. Septima die inceperunt nobis apparere ad meridiem montes altissimi: & intravimus planiciem, quæ irrigabatur sicut hortus, & invenimus terras cultas. In octavis omnium Sanctorum intravimus villam quandam Saracenorum nomine Kenchat: cujus capitaneus occurrebat extra villam duci nostro cum cervisia & ciphis. Hic est enim mos eorum; quod de omnibus villis subditis eis, occurratur nunciis Baatu, & Mangu cham cum cibo & potu. Tunc temporis ibant ibi super glaciem. Et prius à festo Sancti Michaelis habueramus gelu in solitudine. Quæsivi de nomine Provinciæ illius: sed quia jam eramus in alio territorio nescierunt mihi dicere, nisi à nomine civitatis, quæ erat valdè parva. Et descendebat magnus fluvius de montibus, qui irrigabat totam regionem, secundùm quod volebant aquam ducere: nec descendebat in aliquod mare, sed absorbebatur à terra: & faciebat etiam multas paludes. Ibi vidi vites, & bibi bis de vino.

WILLIAM DE RUBRUQUIS

De interfectione Ban & habitatione
Teutonicorum.

SEquenti die venimus ad aliud casale propinquius *Casale.*
montibus. Et quæsivi de montibus, de quibus
intellexi, quòd essent montes Caucasi : qui contiguantur *Montes*
ex utraque parte maris ab Occidente usque ad Orientem : *Caucasi con-*
& quod transiveramus mare supradictum, quod intrat *tiguantur mari*
Etilia. Quæsivi etiam de Talas civitate, in qua erant *Talas, vel*
Teutonici servi Buri, de quibus dixerat frater Andreas, de *Chincitalas*
quibus etiam quæsiveram multum in curia Sartach & *civitas.*
Baatu. Sed nihil poteram intelligere, nisi quod Ban *Frater*
dominus eorum fuerat interfectus tali occasione. Ipse *Andreas.*
non erat in bonis pascuis. Et quadam die dum esset
ebrius, loquebatur ita cum hominibus suis. Nonne sum
de genere Chingis can sicut Baatus (Et ipse erat nepos
Baatu vel frater) quare non vadam super ripam Etiliæ,
sicut Baatu, ut pascam ibi ? Quæ verba relata fuerunt
Baatu. Tunc ipse Baatu scripsit hominibus illius, ut
adducerent ei dominum ipsorum vinctum : quod &
fecerunt. Tunc Baatu quæsivit ab eo si dixisset tale *Casale.*
verbum : & ipse confessus est, tamen excusavit se, quia
ebrius erat : (quia solent condonare ebriis :) & Baatu
respondit : Quomodo audebas me nominare in ebrietate
tua ? Et fecit ei amputari caput. De illis Teutonicis
nihil potui cognoscere usque ad curiam Mangu. Sed in
supradicto casali intellexi, quod Talas erat post nos juxta
montes per sex dietas. Quando veni ad curiam Mangu
cham, intellexi quod ipse Mangu transtulerat eos de
licentia Baatu versus Orientem spacio itineris unius
mensis à Talas ad quandam villam quæ dicitur Bolac : *Bolac villa.*
ubi fodiunt aurum, & fabricant arma. Unde non potui *Aurifodinæ.*
ire nec redire per eos. Transivi eundo satis prope, per
tres dietas fortè, civitatem illam : sed ego ignoravi : nec
potuissem etiam declinasse extra viam, si benè scivissem.
A prædicto casali ivimus ad Orientem juxta montes præ- *Intrat*
dictos : & ex tunc intravimus inter homines Mangu *ditionem*
cham, qui ubique cantabant & plaudebant coram ductore *Mangu cham.*

Alpesinquibus habitabant Caracatay.
Magnus fluvius.

Terra culta.
Equius villa bona.
Longissimè à Perside.

Lacus quinde-cem dietarum circuitu.

Cailac magna villa & plena mercatoribus.

Contomanni.

nostro : quia ipse erat nuncius Baatu. Hunc enim honorem exhibent sibi mutuo, ut homines Mangu cham recipiant nuncios Baatu prædicto modo : Et similiter homines Baatu nuncios Mangu. Tamen homines Baatu superiores sunt, nec exequuntur ita diligenter. Paucis diebus post hoc intravimus Alpes, in quibus solebant habitare Cara catay : & invenimus ibi magnum fluvium, quem oportuit nos transire navigio. Post hæc intravimus quandam vallem, ubi vidi castrum quoddam destructum, cujus muri non erant nisi de luto, & terra colebatur ibi. Et pòst invenimus quandam bonam villam quæ dicitur Equius, in qua erant Saraceni loquentes Persicum : longissimè tamen erant à Perside. Sequenti die transgressis illis Alpibus quæ descendebant à magnis montibus ad meridiem, ingressi sumus pulcherrimam planiciem habentem montes altos à dextris, & quoddam mare à sinistris, sive quendam lacum qui durat quindecim dietas in circuitu. Et illa planicies tota irrigabatur ad libitum aquis descendentibus de montibus, quæ omnes recipiuntur in illud mare. In æstate redivimus ad latus Aquilonare illius maris, ubi similiter erant magni montes. In planicie prædicta solebant esse multæ villæ : sed pro majori parte omnes erant destructæ, ut pascerent ibi Tartari : quia optima pascua erant ibi. Unam magnam villam invenimus ibi nomine Cailac, in qua erat forum, & frequentabant eam multi mercatores. In illa quievimus quindecim diebus, expectantes quendam scriptorem Baatu, qui debebat esse socius ducis nostri in negotiis expediendis in curia Mangu. Terra illa solebat dici Organum : & solebant habere proprium idioma, & propriam literam : Sed hæc tota erat occupata à Contomannis. Etiam in literatura illa & idiomate solebant facere Nestorini de partibus illis. Dicuntur Organa, quia solebant esse optimi Organistæ vel Citharistæ, ut dicebatur mihi. Ibi primo vidi Idolatrias, de quibus noveritis, quod sunt multæ sectæ in Oriente.

WILLIAM DE RUBRUQUIS

Quod Nestorini et Saraceni sunt mixti & Idolatræ.

PRimi sunt Jugures, quorum terra contiguatur cum terra prædicta Organum inter montes illos versus Orientem: Et in omnibus civitatibus eorum sunt mixti Nestorini & Saraceni. Et ipsi etiam sunt diffusi versus Persidem in civitatibus Saracenorum. In prædicta civitate Cealac habebant etiam ipsi tres Idolatrias, quarum duas intravi, ut viderem stultitias eorum. In prima inveni quendam, qui habebat cruciculam de atramento super manum suam. Unde credidi quod esset Christianus: quia ad omnia quæ quærebam ab eo, respondebat ut Christianus. Unde quæsivi ab eo: Quare ergo non habetis crucem & imaginem Jesu Christi? Et ipse respondit, non habemus consuetudinem. unde ego credidi quod essent Christiani: sed ex defectu doctrinæ omitterent. Videbam enim ibi post quandam cistam, quæ erat eis loco altaris, super quam ponunt lucernas & oblationes, quandam imaginationem habentem alas quasi Sancti Michaelis: & alias quasi ipsorum tenentes digitos sicut ad benedicendum. Illo sero non potui aliud invenire. Quia Saraceni in tantum invitant eos, quod nec etiam volunt loqui inde eis. Unde quando quærebam a Saracenis de ritu talium, ipsi scandalizabantur. In crastino fuerunt kalendæ & pascha Saracenorum & mutavi hospitium: ita quod fui hospitatus prope aliam Idolatriam. Homines enim colligunt nuncios, quilibet secundum posse suum vel portionem suam. Tunc intrans Idolatriam prædictam inveni sacerdotes Idolorum. In kalendis enim aperiunt templa sua, & ornant se sacerdotes, & offerunt populi oblationes de pane & fructibus. Primò ergo describo vobis ritus communes omnes Idolatrarum: & postea istorum Jugurum; qui sunt quasi secta divisa ab aliis. Omnes adorant ad Aquilonem complosis manibus: & prosternentes se genibus flexis ad terram, ponentes frontem super manus. Unde Nestorini in partibus illis nullo modo jungunt manus orando: sed orant extensis palmis ante pectus.

Porrigunt templa sua ab Oriente in Occidentem : & in
latere Aquilonari faciunt cameram unam quasi eorum
exeuntem : vel aliter, Si est domus quadrata, in medio
domus ad latus aquilonare intercludunt unam cameram
in loco chori. Ibi ergo collocant unam arcam longam
& latam sicut mensam unam. Et post illam arcam
contra meridiem collocant principale idolum : quod ego
vidi apud Caracarum, ita magnum sicut pingitur Sanctus
Christopherus. Et dixit mihi quidam sacerdos Nestorinus, qui venerat ex Cataya, quod in terra illa est
Idolum ita magnum, quod potest videri à duabus dietis.
Et collocant alia idola in circuitu, omnia pulcherrime
deaurata : Super cistam illam, quæ est quasi mensa una,
ponunt lucernas & oblationes. Omnes portæ templorum
sunt apertæ ad meridiem contrario modo Saracenis. Item
habent campanas magnas sicut nos. Ideo credo quod
orientales Christiani noluerunt habere eas. Ruteni tamen
habent & Græci in Gasaria.

fuit apud
Caracarum
frater
Wilhelmus.

[I. 91.] De templis eorum & idolis, & qualiter se habent
in officio deorum suorum.

OMnes sacerdotes eorum rasum habent totum caput
& barbam ; sunt vestiti de croceo, & servant casti-
tatem, ex quo radunt caput : Et vivunt pariter centum
vel ducenti in una congregatione. Diebus quibus intrant
templum, ponunt duo scamna, & sedent è regione chorus
contra chorum habentes libros in manibus, quos aliquando
deponunt super illa scamna : & habent capita discooperta
quamdiu insunt in templo, legentes in silencio, &
tenentes silencium. Unde cùm ingressus fuissem apud
Oratorium quoddam eorum, & invenissem eos ita sedentes, multis modis tentavi eos provocare ad verba, &
nullo modo potui. Habent etiam quocunque vadunt
quendam restem centum vel ducentorum nucleorum,
sicut nos portamus pater noster : Et dicunt semper hæc
verba : Ou mam Hactavi : hoc est, Deus tu nosti ; secundum quod quidem eorum interpretatus est mihi. Et
toties expectant remunerationem à Deo, quoties hoc

dicendo memoratur Dei. Circa templum suum semper
faciunt pulchrum atrium, quod bene includunt muro:
& ad meridiem faciunt portam magnam, in qua sedent
ad colloquendum. Et super illam portam erigunt perticam longam, quæ emineat si possint, super totam villam.
Et per illam perticam potest cognosci, quod domus illa
sit templum Idolorum. Ista communia sunt omnibus
Idolatris. Quando ergo ingressus fui prædictam Idolatriam, inveni sacerdotes sedentes sub porta exteriori. Illi
quos vidi, videbantur mihi fratres Franci esse rasis barbis.
Tyaras habebant in capitibus cartaceas. Istorum Jugu- *Tyaræ*
rum sacerdotes habent talem habitum quocunque vadunt: *cartaceæ.*
semper sunt in tunicis croceis satis strictis accincti desuper
recte sicut Franci: & habent pallium super humerum
sinistrum descendens involutum per pectus & dorsum
ad latus dextrum sicut diaconus portans casulam in quadragesima. Istorum literas acceperunt Tartari. Ipsi in- *Chinenses ita*
cipiunt scribere sursum, & ducunt lineam deorsum, & *etiam scribunt.*
eodem modo ipsi legunt & multiplicant lineas a sinistra
ad dextram. Isti multum utuntur cartis & caracteribus
pro sortilegio. Unde templa sua plena sunt brevibus *Sortilegi.*
suspensis. Et Mangu-cham mittit vobis literas in idiomate Moal & literatura eorum. Isti comburunt mortuos *Combustio*
suos secundum antiquum modum, & recondunt pulverem *mortuorum.*
in summitate pyramidis. Cum ergo sedissem juxta prae-
dictos sacerdotes, postquam ingressus fueram templum
& vidissem idola eorum multa magna & parva: quæsivi
ab eis, quid ipsi crederent de Deo. Qui responderunt,
Non credimus nisi unum Deum. Et ego quæsivi. Creditis quod ipse sit spiritus vel aliquid corporale? Dixerunt, credimus quod sit spiritus. Et ego: Creditis quod
nunquam sumpserit humanam naturam? Dixerunt, minime. Tunc ego: ex quo creditis, quod non sit nisi
unus spiritus, quare facitis ei imagines corporales, & tot
insuper? Et ex quo non creditis quod factus sit homo,
quare facitis ei magis imagines hominum, quàm alterius
animalis? Tunc responderunt, Nos non figuramus istas
imagines Deo. Sed quando aliquis dives moritur ex

nostris, vel filius, vel uxor, vel aliquis charus ejus facit fieri imaginem defuncti, & ponit eam hic: & nos veneramur eam ad memoriam ejus. Quibus ego, Tunc ergo non facitis ista nisi propter adulationem hominum. Immo dixerunt ad memoriam. Tunc quæsiverunt à me quasi deridendo: ubi est Deus? Quibus ego. Ubi est anima vestra? Dixerunt, in corpore nostro. Quibus ego. Nonne est ubique in corpore tuo & totum regit, & tamen non videtur? Ita Deus ubique est, & omnia gubernat, invisibilis tamen, quia intellectus & sapientia est. Tunc cum vellem plura ratiocinari cum illis, interpres meus fatigatus, non valens verba exprimere, fecit me tacere. Istorum sectæ sunt Moal sive Tartari, quantum ad hoc, quod ipsi non credunt nisi unum Deum: tamen faciunt de filtro imagines defunctorum suorum, & induunt eas quinque pannis preciocissimis, & ponunt in una biga vel duabus, & illas bigas nullus audet tangere: & sunt sub custodia divinatorum suorum, qui sunt eorum sacerdotes, de quibus postea narrabo vobis. Isti divinatores semper sunt ante curiam ipsius Mangu & aliorum divitum: pauperes enim non habent eos; nisi illi qui sunt de genere Chingis. Et cum debent bigare, ipsi præcedunt, sicut columna nubis filios Israel, & ipsi considerant locum metandi castra, & post deponunt domos suas; & post eos tota curia. Et tunc cum sit dies festus sive kalendæ ipsi extrahunt prædictas imagines & ponunt eas ordinate per circuitum in domo sua. Tunc veniunt Moal & ingrediuntur domum illam, & inclinant se imaginibus illis & venerantur illas. Et illam domum nemini ingredi extraneo licet: Quadam enim vice volui ingredi & multum durè increpatus fui.

[I. 92.]   De diversis nationibus, & de illis qui comedere solebant parentes suos.

PRædicti vero Jugures, qui sunt mixti cum Christianis & Saracenis, per frequentes disputationes, ut credo, pervenerunt ad hoc, quod non credunt nisi unum deum. Et isti fuerunt habitantes in civitatibus, qui post obedi-

WILLIAM DE RUBRUQUIS

verunt Chingis Cham: unde ipse dedit regi eorum filiam
suam. Et ipsa Caracarum est quasi in territorio eorum :
Et tota terra regis sive presbyteri Johannis & Vut fratris *Patria*
ejus circa terras eorum : Sed isti in pascuis ad aquilonem, *Presbiteri*
illi Jugures inter montes ad meridiem. Inde est quod *Johannis.*
ipsi Moal sumpserunt literas eorum. Et ipsi sunt magni
scriptores eorum : & omnes fere Nestorini sciunt literas
eorum. Post istos sunt ipsi Tangut ad orientem inter *Tangutpopuli,*
montes illos, homines fortissimi, qui ceperunt Chingis in *fortissimi.*
bello. Et pace facta dimissus ab eis, postea subjugavit
eos. Isti habent boves fortissimos habentes caudas plenas *Boves pilosis*
pilis sicut equi, & ventres pilosos & dorsa. Bassiores *caudis : his*
sunt aliis bobus in tibiis, sed ferociores multum. Isti *similes sunt in*
trahunt magnas domos Moallorum : & habent cornua *Quivera*
gracilia, longa, acuosa, acutissima : ita quod oportet *septentrionalis*
semper secare summitates eorum. Vacca non permittit se *provincia.*
injungi nisi cantetur ei. Habent etiam naturam bubali
quia si vident hominem indutum rubeis, insiliunt in
eum volentes interficere. Post illos sunt Tebet homines *Tebet populi.*
solentes comedere parentes suos defunctos, ut causa
pietatis non facerent aliud sepulchrum eis nisi viscera sua.
Modo tamen hoc dimiserunt, quia abominabiles erant
omni nationi. Tamen adhuc faciunt pulchros ciphos de
capitibus parentum, ut illis bibentes habeant memoriam
eorum in jocunditate sua. Hoc dixit mihi qui viderat.
Isti habent multum de auro in terra sua. Unde qui *Auri abun-*
indiget auro, fodit donec reperiat, & accipiat quando in- *dantia.*
diget, residuum condens in terra : quia si reponeret in
arca vel in thesauro, crederet quod Deus auferret ei aliud
quod est in terra. De istis hominibus vidi personas multum deformes. Tangut vidi homines magnos sed fuscos. *Tangut*
Jugures sunt mediocris staturæ sicut nostri. Apud *homines magni*
Jugures est fons & radix ideomatis Turci & Comanici. *sed fusci.*
Post Tebet sunt Langa & Solanga, quorum nuncios *Langa &*
vidi in curia : Qui adduxerant magnas bigas plusquam *Solanga.*
decem, quarum quælibet trahebatur sex bobus. Isti sunt
parvi homines & fusci sicut Hispani : & habent tunicas *Solangi similes*
sicut supertunicale diaconi manicis parum strictioribus : *Hispanis, &*
fusci.

227

& habent in capitibus mitras sicut episcopi. Sed pars
anterior est parum interior quàm posterior, & non ter-
minatur in unum angulum : sed sunt quadræ desuper, &
sunt de stramine rigidato per calorem magnum, & limato
in tantum, quod fulget ad radium solis sicut speculum
vel galea bene burnita. Et circa tempora habent longas
bendas de eadem materia assutas ipsi mitræ ; quæ se
extendunt ad ventum sicut duo cornua egredientia de
temporibus. Et quando ventus nimis jactat eas plicant
eas per medium mitræ superius à tempore in tempus :
& jacent sicut circulus ex transverso capitis. Et princi-
palis nuncius quando veniebat ad curiam, habebat

Tabula de   tabulam de dente elephantino ad longitudinem unius
dente   cubiti, & ad latitudinem unius palmi, rasam multum : Et
elephantino.   quandocunque loquebatur ipsi Cham, vel alicui magno
viro, semper aspiciebat in illam tabulam, ac si inveniret ibi
ea quæ dicebat : nec respiciebat ad dextram vel sinistram,
nec in faciem illius cui loquebatur. Etiam accedens coram
domino & recedens nusquam respicit nisi in tabulam
suam. Ultra istos sunt alii homines, ut intellexi pro vero,

Muc populi.   qui dicuntur Muc, qui habent villas, sed nulla animalia
sibi appropriant : tamen sunt multi greges & multa
armenta in terra ipsorum, & nullus custodit ea. Sed cum
aliquis indiget aliquo, ascendit collem & clamat, & omnia
animalia audientia clamorem accedunt circa illum, &
permittunt se tractari quasi domestica. Et si nuncius vel
aliquis extraneus accedat ad regionem illam, ipsi includunt
eum in domo, & ministrant ei necessaria, donec negocium
ejus fuerit expeditum. Quia si iret extraneus per
regionem, animalia ad odorem ejus fugerent, & efficeren-

Magna   tur sylvestria. Ultra est magna Cathaya, cujus incolæ
Cathaya.   antiquitus ut credo dicebantur Seres. Ab ipsis enim
veniunt optimi panni serici. Et ille populus dicitur Seres
a quodam oppido eorum. Bene intellexi, quod in illa
regione est oppidum habens muros argenteos & pro-
pugnacula aurea. In ista terra sunt multæ provinciæ,
quarum plures adhuc non obediunt Moallis. Et inter *

Aliqua desiderantur.

The journal of frier William de Rubruquis a [I. 93.]
French man of the order of the minorite friers,
unto the East parts of the worlde. An. Dom.
1253.

TO his most Soveraigne, & most Christian
Lord Lewis, by Gods grace the renowmed
king of France, frier William de Rubruk,
the meanest of the Minorites order,
wisheth health & continual triumph in
CHRIST.

It is written in the booke of Ecclesi- *Ecclus. 39.*
asticus concerning the wise man : He shall travell *ver. 4.*
into forren countries, and good and evill shall he trie
in all things. The very same action (my lord and king)
have I atchieved : howbeit I wish that I have done it
like a wise man, and not like a foole. For many there
be, that performe the same action which a wise man doth,
not wisely but more undiscreetly : of which number I
feare my selfe to be one. Notwithstanding howsoever
I have done it, because you commanded mee, when I
departed from your highnes, to write all things unto you,
which I should see among the Tartars, and you wished
me also that I should not feare to write long letters, I have
done as your majestie injoined me : yet with feare and
reverence, because I want wordes and eloquence sufficient
to write unto so great a majestie. Be it knowen therefore unto your sacred Majestie, that in the yeare of our
Lord 1253. about the Nones of May, we entered into the
sea of Pontus, which the Bulgarians call the great sea.
It containeth in length (as I learned of certaine merchants)
1008 miles, and is in a maner, divided into two parts.
About the midst thereof are two provinces, one towards
the North, and another towards the South. The South
province is called Synopolis, and it is the castle and porte
of the Soldan of Turkie : but the North province is
called of the Latines, Gasaria : of the Greeks, which

inhabite upon the sea shore thereof, it is called Cassaria, that is to say Cæsaria. And there are certaine head lands stretching foorth into the sea towards Synopolis. Also, there are 300. miles of distance betweene Synopolis and Cassaria. Insomuch that the distance from those points or places to Constantinople, in length and breadth is about 700. miles : and 700. miles also from thence to the East, namely to the countrey of Hiberia which is a province of

Gasaria. Georgia. At the province of Gasaria or Cassaria we arrived, which province is, in a maner, three square, having a citie on the West part thereof called Kersova, wherein S. Clement suffered martyrdome. And sayling before the said citie, we sawe an island, in which a Church is sayd to be built by the hands of angels. But about the midst of the said province toward the South, as it were, upon a sharpe angle or point, standeth a citie called

Soldaia. Soldaia directly over against Synopolis. And there doe all the Turkie merchants, which traffique into the North countries, in their journey outward, arrive, and as they returne homeward also from Russia, and the said Northerne regions, into Turkie. The foresaid merchants transport thither ermines and gray furres, with other rich and costly skinnes. Others carrie cloathes made of cotton or bombast, and silke, and divers kindes of spices. But upon the East part of the said province standeth a citie

The citie of called Matriga, where the river Tanais dischargeth his
Matriga. streames into the sea of Pontus, the mouth wherof is twelve miles in breadth. For this river, before it entreth into the sea of Pontus, maketh a little sea, which hath in breadth and length seven hundreth miles, & it is in no place thereof above six paces deepe, whereupon great vessels cannot sayle over it. Howbeit the merchants of

‖*Matriga.* Constantinople, arriving at the foresayd citie of ‖ Materta, send their barkes unto the river of Tanais to buy dried fishes, Sturgeons, Thosses, Barbils, and an infinite number of other fishes. The foresayd province of Cassaria is compassed in with the sea on three sides thereof : namely on the West side, where Kersova the citie of Saint

Clement is situate : on the South side the citie of Soldaia whereat we arrived : on the East side Maricandis, and there stands the citie of Matriga upon the mouth of the river Tanais. Beyond the sayd mouth standeth Zikia, *Zikia.* which is not in subjection unto the Tartars : also the people called Suevi and Hiberi towards the East, who likewise are not under the Tartars dominion. Moreover towards the South, standeth the citie of Trapesunda, which hath a governour proper to it selfe, named Guydo, being of the linage of the emperours of Constantinople, and is subject unto the Tartars. Next unto that is Synopolis the citie of the Soldan of Turkie, who likewise is in subjection unto them. Next unto these lyeth the countrey of Vastacius, whose sonne is called Astar, of his grandfather by the mothers side, who is not in subjection. All the land from the mouth of Tanais Westward as farre as Danubius is under their jurisdiction. Yea beyond Danubius also, towards Constantinople, Valakia, which is the land of Assanus, and Bulgaria minor as farre as Solonia, doe all pay tribute unto them. And besides the tribute imposed, they have also, of late yeares, [I. 94.] exacted of every houshold an axe, and all such corne as they found lying on heapes. We arrived therefore at Soldaia the twelfth of the Kalends of June. And divers merchants of Constantinople, which were arrived there before us, reported that certaine messengers were comming thither from the holy land, who were desirous to travell unto Sartach. Notwithstanding I my self had publikely given out upon Palme Sunday within ye Church of Sancta Sophia, that I was not your nor any other mans messenger, but that I travailed unto those infidels according to the rule of our order. And being arrived, the said merchants admonished me to take diligent heede what I spake : because they having reported me to be a messenger, if I should say the contrary, that I were no messenger, I could not have free passage granted unto me. Then I spake after this maner unto the governors of the citie, or rather unto their Lieutenants, because the

governors themselves were gone to pay tribute unto
Baatu, & were not as yet returned. We heard of your
lord Sartach (quoth I) in the holy land, that he was
become a Christian: and the Christians were exceeding
glad therof, & especially the most Christian king of
France, who is there now in pilgrimage, & fighteth against
the Saracens to redeeme the holy places out of their
handes: wherfore I am determined to go unto Sartach,
& to deliver unto him ye letters of my lord the king,
wherein he admonisheth him concerning the good and
commoditie of all Christendome. And they received us
with gladnes, and gave us enterteinement in the cathedrall
Church. The bishop of which Church was with Sartach,
who told me many good things concerning the saide
Sartach, which afterward I found to be nothing so. Then
put they us to our choyce, whither we woulde have cartes
and oxen, or packe horses to transport our cariages. And
the marchants of Constantinople advised me, not to take
cartes of the citizens of Soldaia, but to buy covered cartes
of mine owne, (such as the Russians carrie their skins in)
and to put all our carriages, which I would daylie take
out, into them: because, if I should use horses, I must
be constrained at every baite to take downe my carriages,
and to lift them up againe on sundry horses backs: and
besides, that I should ride a more gentle pace by the oxen
drawing the cartes. Wherfore, contenting my selfe with
their evil counsel, I was traveiling unto Sartach 2.
moneths which I could have done in one, if I had gone
by horse. I brought with me from Constantinople (being
by the marchants advised so to doe) pleasant fruits,
muscadel wine, and delicate bisket bread to present unto
the governours of Soldaia, to the end I might obtaine free
passage: because they looke favourablie upon no man
which commeth with an emptie hand. All which thinges
I bestowed in one of my cartes, (not finding the governours of the citie at home) for they told me, if I could
carrie them to Sartach, that they would be most acceptable
unto him. Wee tooke our journey therefore about the

kalends of June, with fower covered cartes of our owne
and with two other which wee borrowed of them, wherein
we carried our bedding to rest upon in the night, and
they allowed us five horses to ride upon. For there were
just five persons in our company : namely, I my selfe and
mine associate frier Bartholomew of Cremona, and Goset
the bearer of these presents, the man of God Turgemannus, and Nicolas my servant, whome I bought at Constantinople with some part of the almes bestowed upon
me. Moreover, they allowed us two men, which drave
our carts and gave attendance unto our oxen and horses.
There be high promontories on the sea shore from
Kersova unto the mouth of Tanais. Also there are fortie
castles betweene Kersova and Soldaia, every one of which
almost have their proper languages : amongst whome
there were many Gothes, who spake the Dutch tongue.
Beyond the said mountaines towards the North, there is a
most beautifull wood growing on a plaine ful of fountaines
& freshets. And beyond the wood there is a mightie
plaine champion, continuing five dayes journey unto the
very extremitie and borders of the said province northward, and there it is a narrow Isthmus or neck land,
having sea on the East & West sides therof, insomuch
that there is a ditch made from one sea unto the other.
In the same plaine (before the Tartars sprang up) were
the Comanians wont to inhabite, who compelled the
foresayd cities and castles to pay tribute unto them. But
when the Tartars came upon them, the multitude of the
Comanians entred into the foresaid province, and fled all
of them, even unto the sea shore, being in such extreame
famine, that they which were alive, were constrained to
eate up those which were dead : and (as a marchant reported unto me who sawe it with his owne eyes) that the
living men devoured and tore with their teeth, the raw
flesh of the dead, as dogges would gnawe upon carrion.
Towards the borders of the sayd province there be many
great lakes : upon the bankes whereof are salt pits or
fountaines, the water of which so soone as it entereth into

*Frier Bartho-
lomeus de
Cremona.*

*The necke of
Taurica
Chersonesus.*

the lake, becommeth hard salte like unto ice. And out of those salte pittes Baatu and Sartach have great revenues: for they repayre thither out of all Russia for salte: and for each carte loade they give two webbes of cotton amounting to the value of half an Yperpera. There come by sea also many ships for salt, which pay tribute every one of them according to their burden. The third day after wee were departed out of the precincts of Soldaia, we found the Tartars. Amongst whome being entred, me thought I was come into a new world. Whose life and maners I wil describe unto your Highnes as well as I can.

Of the Tartars, and of their houses. Chap. 2.

THey have in no place any setled citie to abide in, neither knowe they of the celestiall citie to come. They have divided all Scythia among themselves, which stretcheth from the river Danubius even unto the rising of the sunne. And every of their captaines, according to the great or small number of his people, knoweth the bounds of his pastures, and where he ought to feed his cattel winter and summer, Spring and autumne. For in the winter they descend unto the warme regions southward. And in the summer they ascend unto the colde regions northward. In winter when snowe lyeth upon the ground, they feede their cattell upon pastures without water, because then they use snow in stead of water. Their houses wherein they sleepe, they ground upon a round foundation of wickers artificially wrought and compacted together: the roofe whereof consisteth (in like sorte) of wickers, meeting above into one little roundell, out of which roundell ascendeth upward a necke like unto a chimney, which they cover with white felte, and oftentimes they lay morter or white earth upon the sayd felt, with the powder of bones, that it may shine white. And sometimes also they cover it with blacke felte. The sayd felte on the necke of their house, they doe garnish over with beautifull varietie of pictures. Before the doore likewise they hang a felt curiously painted over. For they spend all their coloured felt, in painting vines, trees, birds, and beastes thereupon. The sayd houses they make so large, that they conteine thirtie foote in breadth. For measuring once the breadth betweene the wheele-ruts of one of their cartes, I found it to be 20 feete over: and when the house was upon the carte, it stretched over the wheeles on each side five feete at the least. I told 22. oxen in one teame, drawing an house upon a cart, eleven in one order according to the breadth of the carte, and eleven more before them: the axletree of the carte was of an huge bignes like unto the mast of a ship. And a fellow stood in the doore of the house, upon the forestall of the carte driving forth the oxen. Moreover, they make certaine fouresquare baskets of small slender wickers as big as great chestes: and afterward, from one side to another, they frame an hollow lidde or cover of such like wickers, and make a doore in the fore side thereof. And then they cover the sayd chest or little house with black felt rubbed over with tallow or sheeps milke to keepe the raine from soaking through, which they decke likewise with painting or with feathers. And in such chests they put their whole houshold stuffe & treasure. Also the same chests they do strongly bind upon other carts, which are drawen with camels, to ye end they may wade through rivers. Neither do they at any time take down the sayd chests from off their carts. When they take down their dwelling houses, they turne the doores alwayes to the South: & next of all they place the carts laden with their chests, here & there, within half a stones cast of ye house: insomuch that the house standeth between two ranks of carts, as it were, between two wals. The matrons make for themselves most beautiful carts, which I am not able to describe unto your majestie but by pictures onlie: for I would right willingly have painted al things for you, had my skill bin ought in that art. One rich Moal or Tartar hath 200. or 100. such cartes with chests. Duke Baatu hath sixteene wives, every one of which hath one great house, besides other little houses, which they place

The benefite of a painter in strange countreis.

behind the great one, being as it were chambers for their maidens to dwel in. And unto every of the said houses do belong 200. cartes. When they take their houses from off the cartes, the principal wife placeth her court on the West frontier, and so all the rest in their order: so that the last wife dwelleth upon the East frontier: and one of the said ladies courts is distant from another about a stones cast. Whereupon the court of one rich Moal or Tartar will appeare like unto a great village, very few men abiding in the same. One woman will guide 20. or 30. cartes at once, for their countries are very plaine, and they binde the cartes with camels or oxen, one behind another. And there sittes a wench in the foremost carte driving the oxen, and al the residue follow on a like pace. When they chance to come at any bad passage, they let them loose, and guide them over one by one: for they goe a slowe pace, as fast as a lambe or an oxe can walke.

Of their beds, and of their drinking pots.
Chap. 3.

HAving taken downe their houses from off their cartes, and turning the doores Southward, they place the bed of the master of the house, at the North part thereof. The womens place is alwaies on the East side, namely on the left hand of the good man of the house sitting upon his bed with his face Southwards: but the mens place is upon ye West side, namely at the right hand of their master. Men when they enter into the house, wil not in any case hang their quivers on the womens side. Over the masters head there is alwayes an image, like a puppet, made of felte, which they call the masters brother: and another over the head of the good wife or mistresse, which they call her brother being fastened to the wall: and above betweene both of them, there is a little leane one, which is, as it were the keeper of the whole house. The good wife or mistresse of the house placeth aloft at her beds feete, on the right hand, the skinne of a Kidde stuffed with wooll or some other matter, and neare unto

[I. 96.]

that a litle image or puppet looking towards the maidens and women. Next unto the doore also on the womens side, there is another image with a cowes udder, for the women that milke the kine. For it is the duety of their women to milke kine. On the other side of the doore next unto the men, there is another image with the udder of a mare, for the men which milke mares. And when they come together to drinke and make merie, they sprinckle parte of their drinke upon the image which is above the masters head: afterward upon other images in order: then goeth a servant out of the house with a cuppe full of drinke sprinckling it thrise towards the South, and bowing his knee at every time: and this is done for the honour of the fire. Then perfourmeth he the like superstitious idolatrie towards the East, for the honour of the ayre: and then to the West for the honour of the water: & lastly to the North in the behalfe of the dead. When the maister holdeth a cuppe in his hande to drinke, before he tasteth thereof, hee powreth his part upon the ground. If he drinketh sitting on horse backe, hee powreth out part thereof upon the necke or maine of his horse before hee himselfe drinketh. After the servaunt aforesaide hath so discharged his cuppes to the fower quarters of the world, hee returneth into the house: and two other servants stand ready with two cuppes, and two basons, to carrie drinke unto their master and his wife, sitting together upon a bed. And if he hath more wives then one, she with whome hee slept the night before, sitteth by his side the daye following: and all his other wives must that day resorte unto the same house to drinke: and there is the court holden for that day: the giftes also which are presented that daye are layd up in the chests of the sayd wife. And upon a bench stands a vessell of milke or of other drinke and drinking cuppes.

[Of their

Of their drinkes, and how they provoke one another to drinking. Chap. 4.

IN winter time they make excellent drinke of Rise, of Mill, and of honie, being well and high coloured like wine. Also they have wine brought unto them from farre countries. In summer time they care not for any drinke, but Cosmos. And it standeth alwaies within the entrance of his doore, and next unto it stands a minstrell with his fidle. I sawe there no such citerns and vials as ours commonly be, but many other musicall instruments which are not used among us. And when the master of the house begins to drinke, one of his servants cryeth out with a lowde voice HA, and the minstrell playes upon his fidle. And when they make any great solemne feast, they all of them clap their hands & daunce to the noyse of musique, the men before their master and the women before their mistresse. And when the master hath drunke, then cries out his servant as before, and the minstrell stayeth his musique. Then drinke they all around both men and women : and sometimes they carowse for the victory very filthily and drunkenly. Also when they will provoke any man, they pul him by the eares to the drinke, and so lug and draw him strongly to stretch out his throate clapping their handes and dauncing before him. Moreover when some of them will make great feasting and rejoycing, one of the company takes a full cuppe, and two other stand, one on his right hand and another on his left, and so they three come singing to the man who is to have the cuppe reached unto him, still singing and dauncing before him : and when he stretcheth foorth his hand to receive the cuppe, they leape suddenly backe, returning againe as they did before, and so having deluded him thrice or fower times by drawing backe the cuppe untill he be merie, and hath gotten a good appetite, then they give him the cuppe, singing and dauncing and stamping with their feete, untill he hath done drinking.

They use the like custome in Florida.

Of their foode and victuals. Chap. 5.

COncerning their foode and victuals, be it knowen unto
your Highnesse that they do, without al difference or
exception, eat all their dead carrions. And amongst so
many droves it cannot be, but some cattell must needes
die. Howbeit in summer, so long as their Cosmos, that
is, their mares milke lasteth, they care not for any foode.
And if they chance to have an oxe or an horse dye, they
drie the flesh thereof: for cutting it into thin slices and
hanging it up against the Sunne and the wind, it is *Drying of flesh*
presently dried without salt, and also without stenche *in the wind.*
or corruption. They make better puddings of their [I. 97.]
horses then of their hogs, which they eate being new
made: the rest of the flesh they reserve untill winter.
They make of their oxe skins great bladders or bags,
which they doe wonderfully dry in the smoake. Of the
hinder part of their horse hides they make very fine
sandals & pantofles. They give unto 50. or an 100.
men the flesh of one ram to eat. For they mince it in a
bowle with salt and water (other sauce they have none)
and then with the point of a knife, or a litle forke which
they make for the same purpose (such as wee use to take
rosted peares or apples out of wine withal) they reach
unto every one of the company a morsell or twaine,
according to the multitude of guestes. The master of
the house, before the rams flesh be distributed, first of all
himselfe taketh thereof, what he pleaseth. Also, if he
giveth unto any of the company a speciall part, the
receiver therof must eat it alone, and must not impart
ought therof unto any other. Not being able to eate it
up all, he caries it with him, or delivers it unto his
boy, if he be present, to keepe it: if not, he puts it
up into his Saptargat, that is to say, his foure square
buget, which they use to cary about with them for the
saving of all such provision, and wherein they lay up
their bones, when they have not time to gnaw them
throughly, that they may burnish them afterward,

to the end that no whit of their food may come to nought.

How they make their drinke called Cosmos. Chap. 6.

THeir drinke called Cosmos, which is mares milke, is prepared after this maner. They fasten a long line unto 2. posts standing firmely in the ground, & unto the same line they tie the young foles of those mares, which they mean to milke. Then come the dams to stand by their foles gently suffering themselves to be milked. And if any of them be too unruly, then one takes her fole, & puts it under her, letting it suck a while, and presently carying it away againe, there comes another man to milke the said mare. And having gotten a good quantity of this milke together (being as sweet as cowes milke) while it is newe they powre it into a great bladder or bag, and they beat the said bag with a piece of wood made for the purpose, having a club at the lower ende like a mans head, which is hollow within: and so soone as they beat upon it, it begins to boile like newe wine, & to be sower and sharp of taste, and they beate it in that maner till butter come thereof. Then taste they thereof, and being indifferently sharpe they drinke it: for it biteth a mans tongue like the wine of raspes, when it is drunk. After a man hath taken a draught therof, it leaveth behind it a taste like the taste of almon milke, and goeth downe very pleasantly, intoxicating weake braines: also it causeth urine to be avoided in great measure. Likewise Caracosmos, that is to say black Cosmos, for great lords to drink, they make on this maner. First they beat the said milke so long till the thickest part thereof descend right downe to the bottome like the lees of white wine, and that which is thin and pure remaineth above, being like unto whay or white must. The said lees or dregs being very white, are given to servants, and will cause them to sleepe exceedingly. That which is thinne and cleare their masters drinke: and in very deed it is marveilous sweete and holesome liquor. Duke Baatu hath thirty cottages or granges within a daies journey of his abiding place : every one of which serveth him dayly with the Caracosmos of an hundreth mares milk, and so all of them together every day with the milke of 3000. mares, besides white milke which other of his subjects bring. For even as the husbandmen of Syria bestow the third part of their fruicts and carie it unto the courts of their lords, even so doe they their mares milke every third day. Out of their cowes milke they first churne butter, boyling the which butter unto a perfect decoction, they put it into rams skinnes, which they reserve for the same purpose. Neither doe they salte their butter : and yet by reason of the long seething, it putrifieth not : and they keepe it in store for winter. The churnmilke which remaineth of the butter, they let alone till it be as sowre as possibly it may be, then they boile it and in boiling, it is turned all into curdes, which curds they drie in the sun, making them as hard as the drosse of iron : and this kind of food also they store up in sachels against winter. In the winter season when milke faileth them, they put the foresaid curds (which they cal Gry-ut) into a bladder, and powring hot water thereinto, they beat it lustily till they have resolved it into the said water, which is thereby made exceedingly sowre, and that they drinke in stead of milke. They are very scrupulous, and take diligent heed that they drinke not fayre water by it selfe.

Of the beastes which they eat, of their garments, and of their maner of hunting. Chap. 7.

GReat lords have cottages or granges towards the South, from whence their tenants bring them Millet and meale against winter. The poorer sort provide themselves of such necessaries, for ye exchange of rams, & of other beasts skins. The Tartars slaves fil their bellies with thick water, & are therewithall contented. They wil neither eate mise with long tailes,

[I. 98.]

nor any kinde of mise with short tailes. They have
also certaine litle beasts called by them Sogur, which
lie in a cave twenty or thirty of them together, al the
whole winter sleeping there for the space of sixe
moneths: and these they take in great abundance.
There are also a kind of conies having long tayles like
unto cats: & on the outside of their tailes grow blacke
& white haires. They have many other small beasts
good to eat, which they know and discerne right well.
I saw no Deere there, & but a fewe hares, but a great
number of Roes. I saw wild asses in great abundance,
which be like unto Mules. Also I saw another kind
of beast called Artak, having in al resemblance the body
of a ram, & crooked hornes, which are of such bignes,
that I could scarce lift up a paire of them with one
hand: & of these hornes they make great drinking
cups. They have Falcons, Girfalcons, & other haukes

*Our falconers
use the left
fist.
Another
strange cus-
tome, which
I leave to be
scanned by
falconers
themselves.*

in great plenty: all which they cary upon their right
hands: & they put alwaies about their Falcons necks
a string of leather, which hangeth down to ye midst
of their gorges, by the which string, when they cast
them off the fist at their game, with their left hand
they bow downe the heads & breasts of the sayd haukes,
least they should be tossed up & downe, & beaten
with the wind, or least they should soare too high.
Wherefore they get a great part of their victuals, by
hunting & hauking. Concerning their garments and
attire be it knowen unto your Majestie, that out
of Cataya & other regions of the East, out of Persia
also and other countries of the South, there are brought
unto them stuffes of silke, cloth of gold, & cotton
cloth, which they weare in time of summer. But out
of Russia, Moxel, Bulgaria the greater, & Pascatir,
that is Hungaria the greater, and out of Kersis (all
which are Northerne regions & full of woods) & also
out of many other countries of the North, which are
subject unto them, the inhabitants bring them rich and
costly skins of divers sortes (which I never saw in our

countries) wherewithal they are clad in winter. And alwaies against winter they make themselves two gownes, one with the fur inward to their skin, & another with the furre outward, to defend them from wind & snow, which for the most part are made of woolves skins, or Fox skins, or els of Papions. And when they sit within the house, they have a finer gowne to weare. The poorer sort make their upper gowne of dogs or of goats skins. When they goe to hunt for wild beasts, there meets a great company of them together, & invironing the place round about, where they are sure to find some game, by litle & litle they approch on al sides, til they have gotten the wild beasts into the midst, as it were into a circle, & then they discharge their arrowes at them. Also they make themselves breeches of skins. The rich Tartars somtimes fur their gowns with pelluce or silke shag, which is exceeding soft, light, & warme. The poorer sort do line their clothes with cotton cloth which is made of the finest wooll they can pick out, & of the courser part of the said wool, they make felt to cover their houses and their chests, and for their bedding also. Of the same wool, being mixed with one third part of horse haire, they make all their cordage. They make also of the said felt coverings for their stooles, and caps to defende *Great expense* their heads from the weather: for all which purposes *of wooll.* they spend a great quantity of their wooll. And thus much concerning the attyre of the men.

Of the fashion which the Tartars use in cutting their haire, and of the attire of their women. Chap. 8.

THe men shave a plot foure square upon the crownes of their heads, and from the two formost corners they shave, as it were, two seames downe to their temples: they shave also their temples and the hinder part of their head even unto the nape of the necke: likewise they shave the forepart of their scalp downe

to their foreheads, & upon their foreheads they leave
a locke of hayre reaching downe unto their eye browes:
upon the two hindermost corners of their heads, they
have two lockes also, which they twine and braid into
knots and so bind and knit them under each eare one.
Moreover their womens garments differ not from their
mens, saving that they are somwhat longer. But on
the morrowe after one of their women is maried, shee
shaves her scalpe from the middest of her head down
to her forehead, & weares a wide garment like unto
the hood of a Nunne, yea larger and longer in all
parts then a Nuns hood, being open before and girt
unto them under the right side. For herein doe the
Tartars differ from the Turkes: because the Turkes
fasten their garments to their bodies on the left side:
but the Tartars alwaies on the right side. They have
also an ornament for their heads which they call Botta,
being made of the barke of a tree, or of some such
other lighter matter as they can find, which by reason
of the thicknes & roundnes therof cannot be holden
but in both hands together: & it hath a square sharp
spire rising from the top therof, being more then a
cubite in length, & fashioned like unto a pinacle. The
said Botta they cover al over with a piece of rich silke:
& it is hollow within: & upon the midst of the sayd
spire or square toppe, they put a bunch of quils or of
slender canes a cubite long and more: & the sayd
bunch, on the top thereof, they beautifie with Peacocks
feathers, & round about al ye length therof, with the
feathers of a Malards taile, & with precious stones
also. Great ladies weare this kind of ornament upon
their heads binding it strongly with a certain hat or
coyfe, which hath an hole in the crowne, fit for the
[I. 99.] spire to come through it: & under the foresaid ornament
they cover the haires of their heads, which they gather
up round together from the hinder part therof to the
crowne, & so lap them up in a knot or bundel within
the said Botta, which afterward they bind strongly under

their throtes. Hereupon when a great company of such gentlewomen ride together, and are beheld a far off, they seem to be souldiers with helmets on their heads carrying their launces upright: for the said Botta appeareth like an helmet with a launce over it. Al their women sit on horsebacke bestriding their horses like men: & they bind their hoods or gownes about their wastes with a skie coloured silke skarfe, & with another skarfe they girde it above their breasts: & they bind also a piece of white silke like a mufler or maske under their eyes, reaching down unto their breast. These gentlewomen are exceeding fat, & the lesser their noses be, the fairer are they esteemed: they daube over their sweet faces with grease too shamefully: and they never lie in bed for their travel of childbirth.

Of the dueties injoined unto the Tartarian women, and of their labours, and also of their mariages. Chap. 9.

THe duties of women are, to drive carts: to lay their houses upon carts & to take them downe again: to milke kine: to make butter & Gry-ut: to dresse skins & to sow them, which they usually sowe with thread made of sinewes, for they divide sinewes into slender threads, & then twine them into one long thread. They make sandals & socks & other garments. Howbeit they never wash any apparel: for they say that God is then angry, & that dreadful thunder wil ensue, if washed garments be hanged forth to drie: yea, they beat such as wash, & take their garments from them. They are wonderfully afraid of thunder: for in the time of thunder they thrust all strangers out of their houses, & then wrapping themselves in black felt, they lie hidden therein, til the thunder be overpast. They never wash their dishes or bowles: yea, when their flesh is sodden, they wash the platter wherein it must be put, with scalding hot broth out of the pot, & then powre the said broth into the pot againe. They make felte also, & cover their houses therewith. The duties of the men are to make bowes & arrowes, stirrops, bridles, and saddles: to build houses & carts, to keepe horses: to milke mares: to churne Cosmos and mares milke, & to make bags wherein to put it: they keepe camels also & lay burthens upon them. As for sheepe & goates they tend and milke them, aswell the men as the women. With sheeps milke thicked & salted they dresse and tan their hides. When they wil wash their hands or their heads, they fil their mouthes full of water, & spouting it into their hands by little and little, they sprinckle their haire & wash their heades therwith. As touching mariages, your Highnes is to understand, that no man can have a wife among them till he hath bought her: whereupon somtimes their maids are very stale before they be maried, for their parents alwaies keepe them till they can sel them. They keepe the first and second degrees of consanguinitie inviolable, as we do: but they have no regard of the degrees of affinity: for they wil marrie together, or by succession, two sisters. Their widowes marie not at al, for this reason: because they beleeve, that al who have served them in this life, shall do them service in the life to come also. Whereupon they are perswaded, that every widow after death shal returne unto her own husband. And herehence ariseth an abominable & filthy custome among them, namely that the sonne marieth somtimes all his fathers wives except his own mother: For the court or house of the father or mother falleth by inheritance alwaies to the yonger son. Wherupon he is to provide for all his fathers wives, because they are part of his inheritance aswel as his fathers possessions. And then if he will he useth them for his owne wives: for he thinks it no injurie or disparagement unto himselfe, although they returne unto his father after death. Therfore when any man hath bargained with another for a maid, the father of the said damosel makes him a feast: in the meane while she fleeth unto some of her kinsfolks to hide her selfe. Then saith her father unto the bridegrome: Loe, my daughter is yours, take her wheresoever you can find her. Then he and his friends seek for her till they can find her, and having found her hee must take her by force and cary her, as it were, violently unto his owne house.

Of their execution of justice and judgement: and of their deaths and burials. Chap. 10.

COncerning their lawes or their execution of justice, your Majesty is to be advertised, that when two men fight, no third man dare intrude·himself to part them. Yea, the father dare not help his owne sonne. But he that goes by the worst must appeale unto the court of his lord. And whosoever els offereth him any violence after appeale, is put to death. But he must go presently without all delay: and he that hath suffered the injury, carieth him, as it were captive. They punish no man with sentence of death, unles hee bee taken in the deede doing, or confesseth the same. But being accused by the multitude, they put him unto extreame torture to make him confesse the trueth. They punish murther with death, and carnall copulation also with any other besides his owne. By his own, I meane his wife or his maid servant, for he may use his slave as he listeth himself. Heinous theft also or felony they punish with death. For a light theft, as namely for stealing of a ram, the party (not being apprehended in the deed doing, but otherwise detected) is cruelly beaten. And if ye executioner laies on an 100. strokes, he must have an 100. staves, namely for such as are beaten upon sentence given in the court. Also counterfeit messengers, because they feine themselves to be messengers, when as indeed they are none at all, they punish with death. Sacrilegious persons they use in like maner (of which kind of malefactors your Majesty shall understand more fully hereafter) because they esteeme such to be witches. When any man dieth, they lament & howle most pitifully for him: & the said mourners are free from paying any tribute for one whole yeare after. Also whosoever is present at the house

[I. 100.]

where any one growen to mans estate lieth dead, he must
not enter into the court of Mangu-Can til one whole yere
be expired. If it were a child deceased he must not enter
into the said court til the next moneth after. Neere unto
the grave of the partie deceased they alwaies leave one
cottage. If any of their nobles (being of the stock of
Chingis, who was their first lord & father) deceaseth, his
sepulcher is unknowen. And alwayes about those places
where they interre their nobles, there is one house of men
to keep the sepulchers. I could not learn that they use
to hide treasures in the graves of their dead. The Comanians build a great toomb over their dead, & erect the
image of the dead party thereupon, with his face towards
the East, holding a drinking cup in his hand, before his
navel. They erect also upon the monuments of rich
men, Pyramides, that is to say, litle sharpe houses or
pinacles: & in some places I saw mighty towers made of
brick, in other places Pyramides made of stones, albeit
there are no stones to be found thereabout. I saw one
newly buried, in whose behalfe they hanged up 16. horse
hides, unto each quarter of the world 4, betweene certain
high posts: & they set besides his grave Cosmos for him
to drink, & flesh to eat: & yet they sayd that he was
baptized. I beheld other kinds of sepulchers also towards
the East: namely large flowres or pavements made of
stone, some round & some square, & then 4. long stones
pitched upright, about the said pavement towards the 4.
regions of the world. When any man is sicke, he lieth in
his bed, & causeth a signe to be set upon his house, to
signifie that there lieth a sicke person there, to the end
that no man may enter into the sayd house: whereupon
none at all visit any sicke party but his servant only.
Moreover, when any one is sicke in their great courts,
they appoint watchmen to stand round about the said
court, who wil not suffer any person to enter within the
precincts thereof. For they feare least evill spirits or
winds should come together with the parties that enter in.
They esteeme of soothsayers, as of their priests.

Of our first entrance among the Tartars, and of their ingratitude. Chap. 11.

ANd being come amongst those barbarous people, me thought (as I said before) y' 1 was entred into a new world: for they came flocking about us on horse back, after they had made us a long time to awaite for them sitting in the shadow, under their black carts. The first question which they demanded was whether we had ever bin with them heretofore, or no? And giving them answere that we had not, they began impudently to beg our victuals from us. And we gave them some of our bisket & wine, which we had brought with us from the towne of Soldaia. And having drunke off one flagon of our wine they demanded another, saying, that a man goeth not into the house with one foote. Howbeit we gave them no more, excusing our selves that we had but a litle. Then they asked us, whence we came, & whither we were bound? I answered them with the words above mentioned: that we had heard concerning duke Sartach, that he was become a Christian, & that unto him our determination was to travel, having your Majesties letters to deliver unto him. They were very inquisitive to know whether I came of mine own accord, or whether I were sent? I answered that no man compelled me to come, neither had I come, unles I my selfe had bin willing: & that therefore I was come according to mine own wil, & to the will of my superior. I tooke diligent heed never to say that I was your Majesties ambassador. Then they asked what I had in my carts; whether it were gold or silver, or rich garments to carie unto Sartach? I answered that Sartach should see what we had brought, when we were once come unto him, & that they had nothing to do to aske such questions, but rather ought to conduct me unto their captaine, and that he, if he thought good, should cause me to be directed unto Sartach: if not, that I would returne. For there was in the same province one of Baatu his kinsmen called Scacati, unto whom my lord the Emperor of Constantinople had written letters of request, to suffer me to passe through his territory. With this answere of ours they were satisfied, giving us horses & oxen, & two men to conduct us. Howbeit before they would allow us the foresayd necessaries for our journey, they made us to awayt a long while, begging our bread for their yong brats, wondering at all things which they sawe about our servants, as their knives, gloves, purses, & points, and desiring to have them. I excused my self that

we had a long way to travel, & that we must in no wise so soon deprive our selves of things necessary, to finish so long a journey. Then they said that I was a very varlet. True it is, that they tooke nothing by force from me: howbeit they wil beg that which they see very importunatly & shamelesly. And if a man bestow ought upon them, it is but cost lost, for they are thankles wretches. They esteeme themselves lords & think y^t nothing should be denied them by any man. If a man gives them nought, & afterward stands in neede of their service, they will do right nought for him. They gave us of their cowes milke to drink after ye butter was cherned out of it, being very sower, which they cal Apram. And so we departed from them. And in very deed it seemed to me y^t we were escaped out of the hands of divels. On the morrow we were come unto the captain. From the time wherin we departed from Soldaia, till we arrived at the court of Sartach, which was the space of two moneths, we never lay in house or tent, but alwaies under the starry canopy, & in the open aire, or under our carts. Neither yet saw we any village, nor any mention of building where a village had bin, but the graves of the Comanians in great abundance. The same evening our guide which had conducted us, gave us some Cosmos. After I had drunke thereof I sweat most extreamly for the novelty and strangenes, because I never dranke of it before. Notwithstanding me thought it was very savory, as indeed it was.

Of the court of Scacatai: and how the Christians drinke no Cosmos. Chap. 12.

ON the morrowe after we met with the cartes of Sca-catai laden with houses, and me thought that a mighty citie came to meete me. I wondered also at the great multitude of huge droves of oxen, & horses, and at the flockes of sheepe. I could see but a fewe men that guided all these matters: wherupon I inquired how many men he had under him, & they told me that he had not above 500. in all, the one halfe of which number we were come past, as they lay in another lodging. Then the servant which was our guide told me, that I must present somwhat unto Scacatay: & so he caused us to stay, going himselfe before to give notice of our comming. By this time it was past three of the clocke, and they unladed their houses nere unto a certain water: And there came unto us his interpreter, who being advertised by us that wee were never there before, demanded some of our victuals, & we yeelded unto his request. Also he required of us some garment for a reward, because he was to interpret our sayings unto his master. Howbeit we excused our selves as well as wee could. Then he asked us, what we would present unto his Lord? And we tooke a flagon of wine, & filled a maund with bisket, & a platter with apples & other fruits. But he was not contented therewith, because we brought him not some rich garment. Notwithstanding we entred so into his presence with feare and bashfulnes. He sate upon his bed holding a citron in his hand, and his wife sate by him: who (as I verily thinke) had cut and pared her nose betweene the eyes, that she might seeme to be more flat and saddle-nosed: for she had left her selfe no nose at all in that place, having annointed the very same place with a black ointment, and her eye browes also: which sight seemed most ugly in our eies. Then I rehearsed unto him the same wordes, which I had spoken in other places before. For it stoode us in hand to use one and the same speech in all places. For

THE ENGLISH VOYAGES

we were wel forewarned of this circumstance by some which had been amongst the Tartars, that we should never varie in our tale. Then I besought him, that he would vouchsafe to accept that small gifte at our hands, excusing my selfe that I was a Monke, and that it was against our profession to possesse gold, or silver, or precious garments, and therefore that I had not any such thing to give him, howbeit he should receive some part of our victuals in stead of a blessing. Hereupon he caused our present to be received, and immediately distributed the same among his men, who were mette together for the same purpose, to drinke and make merrie. I delivered also unto him the Emperor of Constantinople his letters (this was eight dayes after the feast of Ascension) who sent them forthwith to Soldaia to have them interpreted there: for they were written in Greeke, and he had none about him that was skilfull in the Greeke tongue. He asked us also whether we would drink any Cosmos, that is to say mares milke? (For those that are Christians among them, as namely the Russians, Grecians, and Alanians, who keep their own law very strictly, wil in no case drinke thereof, yea, they accompt themselves no Christians after they have once drunke of it, & their priests reconcile them unto the Church as if they had renounced the Christian faith.) I gave him answere, that we had as yet sufficient of our owne to drinke, and that when our drinke failed us, we must be constrained to drink such as should be given unto us. He enquired also what was contained in our letters, which your Majestie sent unto Sartach? I answered: that they were sealed up, and that there was nothing conteined in them, but good and friendly wordes. And he asked what wordes wee would deliver unto Sartach? I answered: the words of Christian faith. He asked again what these words were? For he was very desirous to heare them.

Then I expounded unto him as well as I could, by mine interpreter, (who had no wit nor any utterance of speech) the Apostles creed. Which after he had heard, holding his peace, he shooke his head. Then hee assigned unto us two men, who shoulde give attendance upon our selves, upon our horses, and upon our Oxen. And hee caused us to ride in his companie, till the messenger whome hee had sent for the interpretation of the Emperours letters, was returned. And so wee traveiled in his companie till the morowe after Pentecost.

Howe the Alanians came unto us on Pentecost or Whitson even. Chap. 13.

UPon the even of Pentecost, there came unto us certaine Alanians, who are there called *Acias, being Christians after the maner of the Grecians, using greeke bookes and Grecian priests: howbeit they are not schismatiques as the Grecians are, but without acception of persons, they honour al Christians. And they brought unto us sodden flesh, requesting us to eat of their meat, and to pray for one of their company being dead. Then I sayd, because it was the even of so great and so solemne a feast day, that we would not eate any flesh for that time. And I expounded unto them the solemnitie of the sayd feast, whereat they greatly rejoyced: for they were ignorant of all things appertayning to Christian religion, except only the name of Christ. They and many other Christians, both Russians, and Hungarians demanded of us, whether they might be saved or no, because they were constrained to drinke Cosmos, & to eate the dead carkases of such things, as were slaine by the Saracens, and other infidels? Which even the Greeke & Russian priests themselves also esteeme as things strangled or offered unto idoles: because they were ignorant of the times of fasting, neither could they have observed them albeit they had knowen them. Then instructed I them aswell as I could and strengthened them in the faith. As for the flesh which they had brought we reserved it untill the feast day. For there was nothing to be sold among the Tartars for gold & silver, but only for cloth and garments, of the which kind of marchandise wee had none at all. When our servants offered them any coine called Yperpera, they

Or, Akas.

Cloth is the chiefe marchandise in Tartarie.

rubbed it with their fingers, and put it unto their noses, to try by the smell whether it were copper or no. Neither did they allow us any foode but cowes milke onely which was very sowre & filthy. There was one thing most necessary greatly wanting unto us. For the water was so foule and muddy by reason of their horses, that it was not meete to be drunk. And but for certaine bisket, which was by the goodnes of God remaining unto us, we had undoubtedly perished.

Of a Saracen which said that he would be baptized: and of certaine men which seemed to be lepers. Chap. 14.

UPon the day of Pentecost there came unto us a certain Saracen, unto whome, as hee talked with us, we expounded the Christian faith. Who (hearing of Gods benefits exhibited unto mankind by the incarnation of our Saviour Christ, and the resurrection of the dead, & the judgement to come, & that in baptisme was a washing away of sinnes) sayd, that hee would be baptized. But when we prepared our selves to the baptizing of him, he suddenly mounted on horsebacke, saying that he would goe home and consult with his wife what were best to be done. And on the morrow after he told us, that he durst in no case receive baptisme, because then he should drinke no more Cosmos. For the Christians of that place affirme that no true Christians ought to drinke thereof: and that without the said liquor he could not live in that desert. From which opinion, I could not for my life remove him. Wherefore be it knowen of a certainty unto your highnes, that they are much estranged from the Christian faith by reason of that opinion which hath bin broached & confirmed among them by the Russians, of whom there is a great multitude in that place. The same day Scacatay the captaine aforesayd gave us one man to conduct us to Sartach, and two other to guide us unto the next lodging, which was distant from that place five dayes journey for oxen to travell. They gave unto us also a goate for victuals, and a great many bladders of cowes milke, & but a little Cosmos, because it is of so great estimation among them. And so taking our journey directly toward the North, me thought that wee had passed through one of hell gates. The servants which conducted us began to play the bold theeves with us, seeing us take so little heed unto our selves. At length having lost much by their theevery, harme taught us wisdome. And then we came unto the extremity of that province, which is fortified with a ditch from one sea unto another: without the bounds wherof their lodging was situate. Into the which, so soone as we had entred, al the inhabitants there seemed unto us to be infected with leprosie: for certain base fellowes were placed there to receive tribute of al such as tooke salt out of the salt *Salt pits.* pits aforesaid. From that place they told us that we [I. 103.] must travel fifteen daies journey, before we shuld find any other people. With them wee dranke Cosmos, and gave unto them a basket full of fruites and of bisket. And they gave unto us eight oxen and one goate, to sustaine us in so great a journey, and I knowe not how many bladders of milke. And so changing our oxen, *Ten dayes* we tooke our journey which we finished in tenne *journey.* dayes, arriving at another lodging: neither found we any water all that way, but onely in certaine ditches made in the valleys, except two small rivers. And from the time wherein wee departed out of the foresaid province of Gasaria, we travailed directly Eastward, having a Sea on the South side of us, and a waste desert on the North, which desert, in some places, reacheth twenty dayes journey in breadth, and there is neither tree, mountaine, nor stone therein. And it is most excellent pasture. Here the Comanians, which were called Capthac, were wont to feede their cattell. Howbeit by the Dutch men they are called Valani, and the province it selfe Valania. But Isidore calleth all that

tract of land stretching from the river of Tanais to the
lake of Mæotis, and so along as farre as Danubius, the
countrey of Alania. And the same land continueth in
length from Danubius unto Tanais (which divideth
Asia from Europe) for the space of two moneths
journey, albeit a man should ride poste as fast as the
Tartars use to ride : and it was all over inhabited by
the Comanians, called Capthac : yea and beyond Tanais,
as farre as the river of Edil or Volga : the space betweene the two which rivers is a great and long
Russia. journey to bee travailed in ten dayes. To the North
of the same province lieth Russia, which is full of
wood in all places, and stretcheth from Polonia and
Hungaria, even to the river of Tanais : and it hath
bene wasted all over by the Tartars, and as yet is
daily wasted by them.

Of our afflictions which we sustained : and of
the Comanians maner of buriall. Chap. 15.

Prussia. THey preferre the Saracens before the Russians,
because they are Christians, and when they are
able to give them no more golde nor silver, they drive
them and their children like flockes of sheepe into the
wildernes, constraining them to keepe their cattell there.
Beyond Russia lieth the countrey of Prussia, which the
Dutch knights of the order of Saint Maries hospitall of
Jerusalem have of late wholly conquered and subdued.
And in very deede they might easily winne Russia, if
they would put to their helping hand. For if the
Tartars should but once know, that the great Priest,
that is to say, the Pope did cause the ensigne of the
crosse to bee displaied against them, they would flee
all into their desert and solitarie places. We therefore
went on towards the East, seeing nothing but heaven
and earth, and sometimes the sea on our right hand,
called the Sea of Tanais, and the sepulchres of the
Comanians, which appeared unto us two leagues off,
in which places they were wont to burie their kinred

altogether. So long as we were travelling through the desert, it went reasonably well with us. For I cannot sufficiently expresse in words the irkesome and tedious troubles which I susteined, when I came at any of their places of abode. For our guide would have us goe in unto every Captaine with a present, and our expenses would not extend so farre. For we were every day eight persons of us spending our waifaring provision, for the Tartars servants would all of them eate of our victuals. We our selves were five in number, and the servants our guides were three, two to drive our carts, and one to conduct us unto Sartach. The flesh which they gave us was not sufficient for us: neither could we finde any thing to be bought for our money. And as we sate under our carts in the coole shadowe, by reason of the extreame and vehement heate which was there at that time, they did so importunately and shamelesly intrude themselves into our companie, that they would even tread upon us, to see whatsoever things we had. Having list at any time to ease themselves, the filthy lozels had not the maners to withdrawe themselves farther from us, then a beane can bee cast. Yea, like vile slovens they would lay their tailes in our presence, while they were yet talking with us: many other things they committed, which were most tedious and loathsome unto us. But above all things it grieved me to the very heart, that when I would utter ought unto them, which might tend to their edification, my foolish interpreter would say: you shall not make me become a Preacher now: I tell you, I cannot nor I will not rehearse any such wordes. And true it was which he saide, For I perceived afterward, when I began to have a litle smattering in the language, that when I spake one thing, he would say quite another, whatsoever came next unto his witlesse tongues end. Then seeing the danger I might incurre in speaking by such an interpreter, I resolved much rather to holde my peace, and thus we traveiled with great toile from lodging to lodging, till at the length,

Extreme heate in Sommer.

a fewe dayes before the feast of Saint Marie Magdalene, we arrived at the banke of the mightie river Tanais which divideth Asia from Europa, even as the river Nilus of Ægypt disjoyneth Asia from Africa. At the same place where wee arrived, Baatu and Sartach did cause a certaine cottage to be built, upon the Easterne banke of the river, for a companie of Russians to dwell in to the ende they might transport Ambassadours and merchants in ferrie-boates over that part of the river. First they ferried us over, and then our carts, putting one wheele into one lyter, and the other wheele into another lyter, having bounde both the lyters together, and so they rowed them over. In this place our guide played the foole most extreamely. For hee imagining that the said Russians, dwelling in the cottage, should have provided us horses, sent home the beasts which we brought with us, in another cart, y^t they might returne unto their owne masters. And when we demanded to have some beasts of them, they answered, that they had a priviledge from Baatu, wherby they were bound to none other service, but only to ferry over goers & commers: and that they received great tribute of marchants in regard therof. We staied therfore by the said rivers side three daies. The first day they gave unto us a great fresh turbut: the second day they bestowed rye bread, and a litle flesh upon us, which the purveyer of the village had taken up at everie house for us: and the third day dried fishes, which they have there in great abundance. The saide river was even as broad in that place, as the river of Sein is at Paris. And before we came there, we passed over many goodly waters, and full of fish: howbeit the barbarous and rude Tartars know not how to take them: neither do they make any reckoning of any fish, except it be so great, that they may pray upon the flesh therof, as upon the flesh of a ram. This river is the limite of the East part of Russia, and it springeth out of the fennes of Mæotis, which fennes stretch unto the North Ocean. And it runneth Southward into a certain great sea 700. miles about, before it falleth into the sea called Pontus Euxinus. And al the rivers, which we passed over, ran with ful stream into those quarters. The foresaid river hath great store of wood also growing upon the West side thereof. Beyond this place the Tartars ascend no farther unto the North : for at that season of the yeere, about the first of August, they begin to returne backe unto the South. And therfore there is another cottage somwhat lower, where passengers are ferried over in Winter time. And in this place wee were driven to great extremitie, by reason that we could get neither horses, nor oxen for any money. At length, after I had declared unto them, that my comming was to labour for the common good of all Christians, they sent us oxen & men ; howbeit we our selves were faine to travel on foote. At this time they were reaping their rye. Wheat prospereth not wel in that soile. They have the seed of Millium in great abundance. The Russian women attire their heads like unto our women. They imbroder their safegards or gowns on the outside, from their feet unto their knees with particoloured or grey stuffe. The Russian men weare caps like unto the Dutch men. Also they weare upon their heads certain sharpe, & high-crowned hats made of felt, much like unto a sugar loafe. Then traveiled we 3. daies together, not finding any people. And when our selves and our oxen were exceeding weary and faint, not knowing how far off we should find any Tartars, on the sudden, there came two horses running towards us, which we tooke with great joy, and our guide and interpreter mounted upon their backes, to see, how far òff they could descry any people. At length upon the fourth day of our journey, having found some inhabitants, we rejoyced like sea-faring men, which had escaped out of a dangerous tempest, and had newly recovered the haven. Then having taken fresh horses, and oxen, we passed on from lodging to lodging, till at the last, upon the

About the beginning of August, the Tartars re- turne South- ward.

second of the Kalends of August, we arrived at the habitation of Duke Sartach himselfe.

Of the dominion of Sartach, and of his Subjects. Chap. 16.

THe region lying beyond Tanais, is a very goodly countrey, having store of rivers and woods toward the North part thereof. There be mighty huge woods *The people of Moxel are Pagans.* which two sorts of people do inhabite. One of them is called Moxel, being meere Pagans, and without law. They have neither townes nor cities, but only cottages in ye woods. Their lord & a great part of themselves were put to the sword in high Germanie. Whereupon they highly commend the brave courage of the Almans, hoping as yet to be delivered out of the bondage of the Tartars, by their meanes. If any merchant come unto them, he must provide things necessary for him, with whom he is first of all enterteined, all the time of his abode among them. If any lieth with another mans wife, her husband, unles he be an eiewitnes therof, regardeth it not: for they are not jelous over their wives. They have abundance of hogs, and great store of hony & waxe, and divers sorts of *The people called Merdui being Saracens.* rich & costly skins, and plentie of falcons. Next unto them are other people called Merclas, which the Latines cal Merdui, and they are Saracens. Beyond them is the river of Etilia or Volga, which is ye mightiest river that ever I saw. And it issueth from the North part of Bulgaria the greater, & so trending along Southward, disimboqueth into a certain lake containing in circuit the space of 4. moneths travel, whereof I will speak *The circuite of the Caspian sea.* hereafter. The two foresaid rivers, namely Tanais & Etilia, otherwise called Volga, towards the Northren *[I. 105.]* regions through the which we traveiled, are not distant asunder above x. daies journey, but Southward they are divided a great space one from another. For Tanais descendeth into the sea of Pontus: Etilia maketh the foresaid sea or lake, with the help of many

260

other rivers which fal therinto out of Persia. And we had to the South of us huge high mountains, upon the sides wherof, towards the said desert, doe the people called Cergis, and the Alani or Acas inhabit, who are as yet Christians, & wage warre against the Tartars. Beyond them, next unto the sea or lake of Etilia, there are certaine Saracens called Lesgi, who are in subjection unto the Tartars. Beyond these is Porta ferrea, or the yron gate, nowe called Derbent, which Alexander built to exclude the barbarous nations out of Persia. Concerning the situation whereof, your majestie shall understand more about the end of this Treatise : for I travailed in my returne by the very same place. Betweene the two foresaid rivers, in the regions through the which we passed did the Comanians of olde time inhabite, before they were overrun by the Tartars.

Of the Court of Sartach, and of the magnificence thereof. Chap. 17.

ANd we found Sartach lying within three daies journey of the river Etilia : whose Court seemed unto us to be very great. For he himselfe had six wives, and his eldest sonne also had three wives : every one of which women hath a great house, & they have ech one of them about 200. cartes. Our guide went unto a certaine Nestorian named Coiat, who is a man of great authoritie in Sartachs Court. He made us to goe very farre unto the Lordes gate. For so they call him, who hath the office of enterteining Ambassadours. In the evening Coiac commanded us to come unto him. Then our guide began to enquire what we would present him withal, & was exceedingly offended, when he saw that we had nothing ready to present. We stoode before him, and he sate majestically, having musicke and dauncing in his presence. Then I spake unto him in the wordes before recited, telling him, for what purpose I was come unto his lorde, and requesting so much favour at his hands, as to bring our letters unto the sight of his Lord. I excused my selfe also, that I was a Monke, not having, nor receiving, nor using any golde, or silver, or any other precious thing, save onely our bookes, and the vestiments wherein wee served God : and that this was the cause why I brought no present unto him, nor unto his Lord. For I that had abandoned mine owne goods, could not be a transporter of things for other men. Then hee answered very courteously, that being a Monke, and so doing, I did well : for so I should observe my vowe : neither did himselfe stand in neede of ought that we had, but rather was readie to bestow upon us such things as we our selves stood in neede of : and he caused us to sit downe, and to drinke of his milke. And presently after he requested us to say our devotions for him : and we did so. He enquired also who was the greatest Prince among the Franckes ? And I saide, the Emperour, if he could injoy his owne dominions in quiet. No (quoth he) but the king of France. For he had heard of your Highnes by lord Baldwine of Henault. I found there also one of the Knights of the Temple, who had bene in Cyprus, and had made report of all things which he sawe there. Then returned wee unto our lodging. And on the morow we sent him a flagon of Muscadel wine (which had lasted very wel in so long a journey) and a boxe full of bisket, which was most acceptable unto him. And he kept our servants with him for that evening. The next morning he commanded me to come unto the Court, and to bring the kings letters and my vestimentes, and bookes with me : because his Lorde was desirous to see them. Which we did accordingly, lading one cart with our bookes and vestiments, and another with bisket, wine, and fruites. Then he caused all our bookes and vestiments to bee laide forth. And there stoode round about us many Tartars, Christians and Saracens on horseback. At the sight whereof, he demanded whether

I would bestow all those things upon his Lord or no?
Which saying made me to tremble, and grieved me full
sore. Howbeit, dissembling our griefe as well as we
could, we shaped him this answere : Sir, our humble
request is, that our Lorde your master would vouchsafe to accept our bread, wine, and fruits, not as a
present, because it is too meane, but as a benediction,
least we should come with an emptie hand before him.
And he shall see the letters of my sovereigne Lord the
king, and by them he shall understand for what cause
we are come unto him, and then both our selves, and
all that we have, shall stand to his curtesie : for our
vestiments be holy, and it is unlawfull for any but
Priests to touch them. Then he commaunded us to
invest our selves in the saide garments, that we might
goe before his Lord : and wee did so. Then I my
selfe putting on our most precious ornaments, tooke in
mine armes a very faire cushion, and the Bible which
your Majesty gave me, and a most beautifull Psalter,
which the Queenes Grace bestowed upon me, wherein
there were goodly pictures. Mine associate tooke a
missal and a crosse : and the clearke having put on his
surplesse, tooke a censer in his hand. And so wee
came unto the presence of his Lord : and they lifted
up the felt hanging before his doore, that hee might
behold us. Then they caused the clearke and the
interpreter thrise to bow the knee : but of us they
required no such submission. And they diligently
admonished us to take heed, that in going in, and in
comming out, we touched not the threshold of the house,
and requested us to sing a benediction for him. Then we
entred in, singing Salve Regina. And within the entrance
of the doore, stood a bench with cosmos, and drinking
cups thereupon. And all his wives were there assembled.
Also the Moals or rich Tartars thrusting in with us
pressed us sore. Then Coiat caried unto his lord the
censer with incense, which he beheld very diligently,
holding it in his hand. Afterward hee caried the Psalter

[I. 106.]

263

unto him, which he looked earnestly upon, and his wife also that sate beside him. After that he caried the Bible: then Sartach asked if the Gospel were contained therein? Yea (said I) and all the holy scriptures besides. He tooke the crosse also in his hand, and demanded concerning the image, whether it were the image of Christ or no? I said it was. The Nestorians & the Armenians do never make the figure of Christ upon their crosses. Wherfore either they seem not to think wel of his passion, or els they are ashamed of it. Then he caused them that stood about us, to stand aside, that he might more fully behold our ornaments. Afterward I delivered unto him your Majesties letters, with the translation therof into the Arabike, & Syriake languages. For I caused them to be translated at Acon into the character, & dialect of both the saide tongues. And there were certain Armenian priests, which had skil in the Turkish & Arabian languages. The aforesaid knight also of the order of the Temple had knowledge in the Syriake, Turkish, & Arabian tongues. Then we departed forth, and put off our vestiments, and there came unto us certaine Scribes together with the foresaid Coiat, & caused our letters to be interpreted. Which letters being heard, he caused our bread, wine and fruits to be received. And he permitted us also to carie our vestiments and bookes unto our owne lodging. This was done upon the feast of S. Peter ad vincula.

No good
consequence.

How they were given in charge to goe unto Baatu the Father of Sartach. Chap. 18.

THe next morning betimes came unto us a certaine Priest, who was brother unto Coiat, requesting to have our boxe of Chrisme, because Sartach (as he said) was desirous to see it: and so we gave it him. About eventide Coiat sent for us, saying: My lord your king wrote good words unto my lord and master Sartach. Howbeit there are certaine matters of difficulty in them concerning which he dare not determine ought, without the advise and counsell of his father. And therfore of necessitie you must depart unto his father, leaving behind you the two carts, which you brought hither yesterday with vestiments and bookes, in my custodie: because my lorde is desirous to take more diligent view thereof. I presently suspecting what mischiefe might ensue by his covetousnes, said unto him: Sir, we will not onely leave those with you, but the two other carts also, which we have in our possession, will we commit unto your custodie. You shall not (quoth he) leave those behinde you, but for the other two carts first named, we will satisfie your request. I saide that this could not conveniently be done: but needes we must leave all with him. Then he asked, whether we meant to tarie in the land? I answered: If you throughly understand the letters of my lorde the king, you know that we are even so determined. Then he replied, that we ought to bee patient and lowly: and so we departed from him that evening. On the morrowe after he sent a Nestorian Priest for the carts, and we caused all the foure carts to be delivered. Then came the foresaid brother of Coiat to meet us, and separated all those things, which we had brought the day before unto the Court, from the rest, namely, the bookes and vestiments, and tooke them away with him. Howbeit Coiat had commanded, that we should carie those vestiments with us, which wee ware in the presence of Sartach, that we might put them on before Baatu, if neede should require: but the said Priest tooke them from us by violence, saying: thou hast brought them unto Sartach, and wouldest thou carie them unto Baatu? And when I would have rendred a reason, he answered: be not too talkative, but goe your wayes. Then I sawe that there was no remedie but patience: for wee could have no accesse unto Sartach himselfe, neither was there any other, that would doe us justice. I was afraide also in regard of the interpreter, least he had spoken other things then I saide unto him: for his will was good that we should have given away all

265

that wee had. There was yet one comfort remaining unto me : for when I once perceived their covetous intent, I conveyed from among our bookes the Bible, and the sentences, and certaine other bookes which I made speciall account of. Howbeit I durst not take away the Psalter of my soveraigne Lady the Queene, because it was too wel known, by reason of the golden pictures therein. And so we returned with the two other carts unto our lodging. Then came he that was appointed to be our guide unto the court of Baatu, willing us to take our journey in all poste-haste : unto whom I said, that I would in no case have the carts to goe with me. Which thing he declared unto Coiat. Then Coiat commaunded, that we should leave them and our servant with him : And we did as he commanded. And so traveling directly Eastward towards Baatu, the third day we came to Etilia or Volga : the streams whereof when I beheld, I wondered from what regions of the North such huge and mighty waters should descend. Before we were departed from Sartach, the foresaid Coiat, with many other Scribes of the court said unto us : doe not make report that our Lord is a Christian, but a Moal. Because the name of a Christian seemeth unto them to be the name of some nation. So great is their pride, that albeit they beleeve perhaps some things concerning Christ, yet will they not bee called Christians, being desirous that their owne name, that is to say, Moal should be exalted above all other names. Neither wil they be called by the name of Tartars. For the Tartars were another nation, as I was informed by them.

[I. 107.]

*They are come
as farre as
Volga.*

*The Tartars
wil be called
Moal.*

*This history of
Presbiter John
in the North-
east, is allead-
ged at large
by Gerardus
Mercator in
his generall
mappe.*

How Sartach, and Mangu-Can, and Ken-Can doe reverence unto Christians. Chap. 19.

AT the same time when the French-men tooke Antioch, a certaine man named Con Can had dominion over the Northren regions, lying thereabouts. Con is a proper name : Can is a name of authority or dignitie, which signifieth a diviner or soothsayer. All diviners are called Can amongst them. Whereupon their princes are called Can, because that unto them belongeth the government of the people by divination. Wee doe reade also in the historie of Antiochia, that the Turkes sent for aide against the French-men, unto the kingdome of Con Can. For out of those parts the whole nation of *From whence* the Turkes first came. The said Con was of the nation *the Turkes first sprang.* of Kara-Catay. Kara signifieth blacke, and Catay is the *first sprang.* name of a countrey. So that Kara-Catay signifieth the blacke Catay. This name was given to make a difference between the foresaid people, and the people of Catay, inhabiting Eastward over against ye Ocean sea: con- *An Ocean sea.* cerning whom your majesty shall understand more here-after. These Catayans dwelt upon certaine Alpes, by the which I travailed. And in a certain plaine countrey within those Alpes, there inhabited a Nestorian shepheard, being a mighty governour over the people called Yayman, *Nayman.* which were Christians, following the sect of Nestorius. After the death of Con Can, the said Nestorian exalted himselfe to the kingdome, and they called him King *Presbiter* John, reporting ten times more of him then was true. *John.* For so the Nestorians which come out of those parts, use to doe. For they blaze abroade great rumors, and reports upon just nothing. Whereupon they gave out concerning Sartach, that he was become a Christian, and the like also they reported concerning Mangu Can, and Ken Can: namely because these Tartars make more account of Christians, then they doe of other people, and yet in very deede, themselves are no Christians. So likewise there went foorth a great report concerning the said king John. Howbeit, when I travailed along by his territories, there was no man that knew any thing of him, but onely a fewe Nestorians. In his pastures *The place of* or territories dwelleth Ken Can, at whose Court Frier *Ken Kan his* Andrew was. And I my selfe passed by it at my *aboade.* returne. This John had a brother, being a mightie man also, and a shepheard like himselfe, called Vut, and *Vut Can, or* he inhabited beyond the Alpes of Cara Catay, being *Unc Can.*

distant from his brother John, the space of three weekes

journey. He was lord over a certain village, called Cara Carum, having people also for his subjects, named Crit, or Merkit, who were Christians of the sect of Nestorius. But their Lorde abandoning the worship of Christ, followed after idoles, reteining with him Priests of the saide idoles, who all of them are worshippers of devils and sorcerers. Beyond his pastures some tenne or

*Moal in olde
time a begger-
ly people.* fifteene dayes journey, were the pastures of Moal, who were a poore and beggerly nation, without governour, and without Lawe, except their soothsayings, and their divinations, unto the which detestable studies, all in

those partes doe apply their mindes. Neere unto Moal were other poore people called Tartars. The foresaid king John died without issue male, and thereupon his brother Vut was greatly inriched, and caused himselfe to be named Can : and his droves and flockes raunged even unto the borders of Moal. About the

same time there was one Cyngis, a blacke smith among the people of Moal. This Cyngis stole as many cattel from Vut Can, as he could possibly get : insomuch that the shepheards of Vut complained unto their Lord. Then provided he an armie, and marched up into the countrey of Moal to seeke for the saide Cyngis. But Cyngis fledde among the Tartars, and hidde himselfe amongest them. And Vut having taken some spoiles both from Moal, and also from the Tartars, returned home. Then spake Cyngis unto the Tartars, and unto the people of Moal, saying : Sirs, because we are destitute of a governour and Captaine, you see howe our neighbours do oppresse us. And the Tartars and Moals appointed him to be their Chieftaine. Then having secretly gathered together an armie, he brake in suddenly upon Vut, and overcame him, and Vut fledde into Cataya. At the same time was the daughter of

Vut taken, which Cyngis married unto one of his sonnes, by whom she conceived, & brought forth the great

Can, which now reigneth, called Mangu-Can. Then

WILLIAM DE RUBRUQUIS

Cyngis sent ye Tartars before him in al places where he came: and thereupon was their name published and spread abroad: for in all places the people woulde crie out: Loe, the Tartars come, the Tartars come. Howbeit, through continuall warres, they are nowe, all of them in a maner, consumed and brought to nought. Whereupon the Moals indevour what they can, to extinguish the name of the Tartars, that they may exalt their owne name. The countrey wherein they first inhabited, and where the Court of Cyngis Can as yet remaineth, is called Mancherule. But because Tartaria *Mancherule.* is the region, about which they have obtained their conquests, they esteeme that as their royall and chiefe citie, and there for the most part doe they elect their great Can.

Of the Russians, Hungarians, and Alanians: and of the Caspian Sea. Chap. 20.

NOw, as concerning Sartach, whether he beleeves in Christ, or no, I knowe not. This I am sure of, that he will not be called a Christian. Yea rather he seemeth unto mee to deride and skoffe at Christians. He lieth in the way of the Christians, as namely of the Russians, the Valachians, the Bulgarians of Bulgaria the lesser, the Soldaianes, the Kerkis, and the Alanians: who all of them passe by him, as they are going to the Court of his father Baatu, to carie giftes: whereupon he is more in league with them. Howbeit, if the Saracens come, and bring greater giftes then they, they are dispatched sooner. He hath about him certaine Nestorian Priestes, who pray upon their beades, and sing their devotions. Also, there is another under Baatu called Berta, who feedeth his cattell toward Porta *Or, Berca.* ferrea, or Derbent, where lieth the passage of all those Saracens, which come out of Persia, and out of Turkie to goe unto Baatu, and passing by, they give rewards unto him. And he professeth himselfe to be a Saracene, and will not permit swines flesh to be eaten in his dominions.

Howbeit, at the time of our returne, Baatu commanded him to remove himselfe from that place, and to inhabite upon the East side of Volga : for hee was unwilling that the Saracens messengers should passe by the saide Berta, because he sawe it was not for his profite. For the space of foure dayes while we remained in the court of Sartach, we had not any victuals at all allowed us, but once onely a litle Cosmos. And in our journey betweene him and his father, wee traveiled in great feare. For certaine Russians, Hungarians, and Alanians being servants unto the Tartars (of whom they have great multitudes among them) assemble themselves twentie or thirtie in a companie, and so secretly in the night conveying themselves from home, they take bowes and arrowes with them, and whomesoever they finde in the night season, they put him to death, hiding themselves in the day time. And having tired their horses, they goe in the night unto a company of other horses feeding in some pasture, and change them for newe, taking with them also one or two horses besides, to eate them when they stand in neede. Our guide therefore was sore afraide, least we should have met with such companions. In this journey wee had died for famine, had we not caried some of our bisket with us. At length we came unto the mighty river of Etilia, or Volga. For it is foure times greater, then the river of Sein, and of a wonderfull depth : and issuing forth of Bulgaria the greater, it runneth into a certaine lake or sea, which of late they cal the Hircan sea, according to the name of a certain citie in Persia, standing upon the shore thereof. Howbeit Isidore calleth it the Caspian sea. For it hath the Caspian mountaines and the land of Persia situate on the South side thereof : and the mountaines of Musihet, that is to say, of the people called Assassini towards the East, which mountaines are conjoyned unto the Caspian mountaines : but on the North side thereof lieth the same desert, wherein the Tartars doe now inhabite. Howbeit heretofore there dwelt certaine

people called Changlæ. And on that side it receiveth *Changlæ.*
the streames of Etilia; which river increaseth in Sommer
time, like unto the river Nilus in Ægypt. Upon the
West part thereof, it hath the mountaines of Alani, and
Lesgi, and Porta ferrea, or Derbent, and the mountaines
of Georgia. This Sea therefore is compassed in on three
sides with the mountaines, but on the North side with
plaine grounde. Frier Andrew, in his journey traveiled *Frier*
round about two sides therof, namely the South and the *Andrew*
East sides: and I my selfe about other two, that is to
say, the North side in going from Baatu to Mangu-Can,
and in returning likewise: and the West side in comming
home from Baatu into Syria. A man may travel round
about it in foure moneths. And it is not true which
Isidore reporteth, namely that this Sea is a bay or gulfe
comming forth of the Ocean: for it doeth, in no part
thereof, joyne with the Ocean, but is invironed on all
sides with lande.

Of the court of Baatu: and howe we were [I. 109.]
interteined by him. Chap. 21.

AL the region extending from the West shore of the
foresaid sea, where Alexanders Iron gate, otherwise called the citie of Derbent, is situate, and from
the mountaines of Alania, all along by the fennes of
Mæotis, whereinto the river of Tanais falleth, and so
forth, to the North Ocean, was wont to be called *The North*
Albania. Of which countrey Isidore reporteth, that *Ocean.*
there be dogs of such an huge stature, and so fierce,
that they are able in fight to match bulles, and to master
lions. Which is true, as I understand by divers, who
tolde me, that there towardes the North Ocean they
make their dogges to draw in carts like oxen, by reason
of their bignesse and strength. Moreover, upon that
part of Etilia where we arrived, there is a new cottage
built, wherein they have placed Tartars and Russians
both together, to ferrie over, and transport messengers
going and comming to and fro the court of Baatu. For

Baatu remaineth upon the farther side towards the East. Neither ascendeth hee in Sommer time more Northward then the foresaide place where we arrived, but was even then descending to the South. From Januarie untill August both he and all other Tartars ascend by the banks of rivers towards cold and Northerly regions, and in August they begin to returne backe againe.

*He descendeth
downe the
river Volga in
a barke.*

We passed downe the streame therefore in a barke, from the foresaid cottage unto his court. From the same place unto the villages of Bulgaria the greater, standing toward the North, it is five dayes journey. I wonder what devill caried the religion of Mahomet thither. For, from Derbent, which is upon the extreame borders of Persia, it is above 30. daies journey to passe overthwart the desert, and so to ascend by the banke of

Astracan.

Etilia, into the foresaid countrey of Bulgaria. All which way there is no citie, but onely certaine cottages neere unto that place where Etilia falleth into the sea. Those Bulgarians are most wicked Saracens, more earnestly professing the damnable religion of Mahomet, then

*The descrip-
tion of Baatu
his court.*

any other nation whatsoever. Moreover, when I first beheld the court of Baatu, I was astonied at the sight thereof : for his houses or tents seemed as though they had bene some huge and mighty citie, stretching out a great way in length, the people ranging up and downe about it for the space of some three or foure leagues. And even as the people of Israel knew every man, on which side of the tabernacle to pitch his tent : even so every one of them knoweth right well, towards what side of the court he ought to place his house when he takes it from off the cart. Wherupon the court

*Horda signifi-
eth the midst.*

is called in their language Horda, which signifieth, the midst : because the governour or chieftaine among them dwels alwaies in the middest of his people : except onely that directly towards the South no subject or inferiour person placeth himselfe, because towards that region the court gates are set open : but unto the right hand, and the left hand they extend themselves as farre as they

will, according to the conveniencie of places, so that they
place not their houses directly opposite against the court.
At our arrivall we were conducted unto a Saracen, who
provided not for us any victuals at all. The day following, we were brought unto the court: and Baatu had
caused a large tent to be erected, because his house or
ordinarie tent could not containe so many men and
women as were assembled. Our guide admonished us
not to speake, till Baatu had given us commandement so
to doe, and that then we should speake our mindes
briefly. Then Baatu demanded whether your Majestie
had sent Ambassadours unto him or no? I answered,
that your Majestie had sent messengers to Ken-Can:
and that you would not have sent messengers unto him,
or letters unto Sartach, had not your Highnes bene
perswaded that they were become Christians: because
you sent not unto them for any feare, but onely for
congratulation, and curtesies sake, in regard that you
heard they were converted to Christianitie. Then led
he us unto his pavilion: and wee were charged not to
touch the cordes of the tent, which they account in stead
of the threshold of the house. There we stoode in our
habite bare-footed, and bare-headed, and were a great
and strange spectacle in their eyes. For indeed Frier *John de Plano*
John de Plano Carpini had byn there before my comming: *Carpini.*
howbeit, because he was the Popes messenger, he changed
his habit that he might not be contemned. Then we
were brought into the very midst of the tent, neither
required they of us to do any reverence by bowing our
knees, as they use to doe of other messengers. Wee
stood therefore before him for the space wherein a man
might have rehearsed the Psalme, Miserere mei Deus:
and there was great silence kept of all men. Baatu
himselfe sate upon a seate long and broad like unto a
bed, guilt all over, with three staires to ascend thereunto,
and one of his ladies sate beside him. The men there
assembled, sate downe scattering, some on the right hand
of the saide Lady, and some on the left. Those places

I 273 S

on the one side which the women filled not up (for there were only the wives of Baatu) were supplied by the men. Also, at the very entrance of the tent, stoode a bench furnished with cosmos, and with stately great cuppes of silver, and golde, beeing richly set with precious stones. Baatu beheld us earnestly, and we him: and he seemed to me to resemble in personage, Monsieur John de beau mont, whose soule resteth in peace. And hee had a fresh ruddie colour in his countenance. At length he commanded us to speake. Then our guide gave us direction, that wee should bow our knees & speak. Wherupon I bowed one knee as unto a man: then he signified that I should kneele upon both knees: and I did so, being loath to contend about such circumstaunces. And again he commanded me to speak. Then I thinking of praier unto God, because I kneeled on both my knees, began to pray on this wise: Sir, we beseech the Lord, from whom all good things doe proceed, and who hath given you these earthly benefites, that it would please him hereafter to make you partaker of his heavenly blessings: because the former without these are but vain and improfitable. And I added further. Be it knowen unto you of a certainty, that you shal not obtain the joyes of heaven, unles you become a Christian: for God saith, Whosoever beleeveth & is baptized, shalbe saved: but he that beleeveth not, shalbe condemned. At this word he modestly smiled: but the other Moals began to clap their hands, and to deride us. And my silly interpreter, of whom especially I should have received comfort in time of need, was himself abashed & utterly dasht out of countenance. Then, after silence made, I said unto him, I came unto your sonne, because we heard that he was become a Christian: and I brought unto him letters on the behalfe of my sovereigne Lord the king of France: and your sonne sent me hither unto you. The cause of my comming therefore is best known unto your selfe. Then he caused me to rise up. And he enquired your majesties name, and my name, and the name of mine

274

associate and interpreter, and caused them all to be put down in writing. He demaunded likewise (because he had bene informed, that you were departed out of your owne countreys with an armie) against whom you waged warre? I answered: against the Saracens, who had defiled the house of God at Jerusalem. He asked also, whether your Highnes had ever before that time sent any messengers unto him, or no? To you sir? (said I) never. Then caused he us to sit downe, and gave us of his milke to drinke, which they account to be a great favour, especially when any man is admitted to drinke Cosmos with him in his own house. And as I sate looking downe upon the ground, he commanded me to lift up my countenance, being desirous as yet to take more diligent view of us, or els perhaps for a kinde of superstitious observation. For they esteeme it a signe of ill lucke, or a prognostication of evill unto them, when any man sits in their presence, holding downe his head, as if he were sad: especially when he leanes his cheeke or chinne upon his hand. Then we departed forth, and immediatly after came our guide unto us, and conducting us unto our lodging, saide unto me: Your master the King requesteth that you may remaine in this land, which request Baatu cannot satisfie without the knowledge and consent of Mangu-Can. Wherefore you, and your interpreter must of necessitie goe unto Mangu-Can. Howbeit your associate, and the other man shall returne unto the court of Sartach, staying there for you, till you come backe. Then began the man of God mine interpreter to lament, esteeming himselfe but a dead man. Mine associate also protested, that they should sooner chop off his head, then withdrawe him out of my companie. Moreover I my selfe saide, that without mine associate I coulde not goe: and that we stood in neede of two servants at the least, to attend upon us, because, if one should chance to fall sicke, we could not be without another. Then returning unto the court, he told these sayings unto Baatu. And Baatu commanded saying: let

the two Priests and the interpreter goe together, but let
the clearke returne unto Sartach. And comming againe
unto us, hee tolde us even so. And when I would
have spoken for the clearke to have had him with
us, he saide: No more words: for Baatu hath resolved,
that so it shall be, and therefore I dare not goe unto
the court any more. Goset the clearke had remaining of the almes money bestowed upon him, 26.
Yperperas, and no more; 10. whereof he kept for himselfe and for the lad, and 16. he gave unto the man of
God for us. And thus were we parted asunder with
teares: he returning unto the court of Sartach, and
our selves remaining still in the same place.

Of our journey towards the Court of Mangu Can. Chap. 22.

UPon Assumption even our clearke arrived at the
court of Sartach. And on the morrow after, the
Nestorian Priestes were adorned with our vestments in
the presence of the saide Sartach. Then wee our selves
were conducted unto another hoste, who was appointed
to provide us houseroome, victualles, and horses. But
because wee had not ought to bestowe upon him, hee did
They travell five weekes by the banke of Etilia. all things untowardly for us. Then wee rode on for-
warde with Baatu, descending along by the banke of Etilia,
for the space of five weekes together: Sometimes mine
associate was so extremelie hungrie, that hee would tell
mee in a manner weeping, that it fared with him as though
hee had never eaten any thing in all his life before.
There is a faire or market following the court of Baatu at
all times: but it was so farre distant from us that we
[I. 111.] could not have recourse thereunto. For wee were constrained to walke on foote for want of horses. At length
Hungarians. certaine Hungarians (who had sometime bene after a sort
Cleargie men) found us out: and one of them could as
yet sing many songs without booke, and was accompted
of other Hungarians as a Priest, and was sent for unto
the funerals of his deceased countrey men. There was

another of them also pretily wel instructed in his Grammer: for hee could understand the meaning of any thing that wee spake, but could not answere us. These Hungarians were a great comfort unto us, bringing us Cosmos to drinke, yea, and sometimes flesh for to eate also: who, when they requested to have some bookes of us, and I had not any to give them (for indeede we had none but onely a Bible, and a breviarie) it grieved mee exceedingly. And I saide unto them: Bring mee some inke and paper, and I will write for you so long as we shall remaine here: and they did so. And I copied out for them Horas beatæ Virginis, and Officium defunctorum. Moreover, upon a certaine day, there was a Comanian *A Comanian.* that accompanied us, saluting us in Latine, and saying: Salvete Domini. Wondering thereat and saluting him againe, I demaunded of him, who had taught him that kinde of salutation? Hee saide that hee was baptized in Hungaria by our Friers, and that of them hee learned it. He saide moreover, that Baatu had enquired many things of him concerning us, and that hee tolde him the estate of our order. Afterwarde I sawe Baatu riding with his companie, and all his subjects that were housholders or masters of families riding with him, and (in mine estimation) they were not five hundred persons in all. At length about the ende of Holy roode, there came a certaine rich Moal unto us (whose father was a Millenarie, which is a great office among them) saying: I am the man that must conduct you unto Mangu-Can, and wee have thither a journey of foure moneths long to travell, and *A journey of* there is such extreame colde in those parts, that stones and *4. moneths* trees doe even rive asunder in regarde thereof. Therefore *from Volga.* I would wish you throughly to advise your selves, whether you be able to indure it or no. Unto whome I answered: I hope by Gods helpe that we shalbe able to brooke that which other men can indure. Then he saide: if you cannot indure it, I wil forsake you by the way. And I answered him: it were not just dealing for you so to doe: for wee goe not thither upon anie businesse of our owne, but by reason that we are sent by your lord. Wherfore sithence we are committed unto your charge, you ought in no wise to forsake us. Then he saide : all shalbe well. Afterward he caused us to shewe him all our garments : and whatsoever hee deemed to be lesse needfull for us, he willed us to leave it behind in the custodie of our hoste. On the morrow they brought unto ech of us a furred gowne, made all of rammes skinnes, with the wool stil upon them, and breeches of the same, and bootes also or buskins according to their fashion, and shooes made of felt, and hoods also made of skinnes after their maner.

The 16. of September.

46. dayes.

Or, Kangittæ.

The second day after Holy rood, we began to set forward on our journey, having three guides to direct us : and we rode continually Eastward, till the feast of All Saints. Throughout all that region, and beyonde also did the people of Changle inhabite, who were by parentage descended from the Romanes. Upon the North side of us, wee had Bulgaria the greater, and on the South, the foresaid Caspian sea.

Or, Iaic.

Of the river of Iagac : and of divers regions or nations. Chap. 23.

Iaic twelve dayes journey from Volga.

Pascatir.

The Hungarians descended from the Bascirdes.

HAving traveiled twelve dayes journey from Etilia, wee found a mightie river called Iagac : which river issuing out of the North, from the land of Pascatir, descendeth into the foresaid sea. The language of Pascatir, and of the Hungarians is all one, and they are all of them shepheards, not having any cities. And their countrey bordereth upon Bulgaria the greater, on the West frontier thereof. From the Northeast part of the said countrey, there is no citie at all. For Bulgaria the greater is the farthest countrey that way, that hath any citie therein. Out of the forenamed region of Pascatir, proceeded the Hunnes of olde time, who afterwarde were called Hungarians. Next unto it is Bulgaria the greater. Isidore reporteth concerning the people of this nation, that with swift horses they traversed the impregnable walles and bounds of Alexander, (which, together with the rocks

278

of Caucasus, served to restraine those barbarous and blood-thirstie people from invading the regions of the South) insomuch that they had tribute paied unto them, as farre as Ægypt. Likewise they wasted all countreis even unto France. Whereupon they were more mightie then the Tartars as yet are. And unto them the Blacians, the *Valachians.* Bulgarians, and the Vandals joyned themselves. For out of Bulgaria the greater, came those Bulgarians. More-over, they which inhabit beyond Danubius, neere unto Constantinople, and not farre from Pascatir, are called Ilac, which (saving the pronunciation) is al one with Blac, (for the Tartars cannot pronounce the letter B) from whom also descended the people which inhabit the land of Assani. For they are both of them called Ilac (both these, & the other) in ye languages of the Russians, ye Polonians, & the Bohemians. The Sclavonians speake all [I. 112.] one language with the Vandals, all which banded them-selves with the Hunnes : and now for the most part, they unite themselves unto the Tartars : whom God hath raised up from the utmost partes of the earth, according to that which the Lord saith : I will provoke them to *Deut. 32. v.* envy (namely such as keepe not his Law) by a people, *21.* which is no people, and by a foolish nation will I anger *Rom. 10. v.* them. This prophecie is fulfilled, according to the literal *19.* sense thereof, upon all nations which observe not the Law of God. All this which I have written concerning the land of Pascatir, was told me by certaine Friers prædicants, which travailed thither before ever the Tartars came abroad. And from that time they were subdued unto their neighbors the Bulgarians being Saracens, whereupon many of them proved Saracens also. Other matters con-cerning this people, may be known out of Chronicles. For it is manifest, that those provinces beyond Con-stantinople, which are now called Bulgaria, Valachia, & Sclavonia, were of old time provinces belonging to the Greekes. Also Hungaria was heretofore called Pannonia. And wee were riding over the land of Cangle, from the *Cangle an huge plaine countrey.* feast of Holy roode, untill the feast of All Saints : traveil- *countrey.*

ing almost every day (according to mine estimation) as farre, as from Paris to Orleans, and sometimes farther, as we were provided of poste horses : for some dayes we had change of horses twise or thrise in a day. Sometimes we travailed two or three daies together, not finding any people, and then we were constrained not to ride so fast. Of 20. or 30. horses we had alwayes the woorst, because wee were strangers. For every one tooke their choice of the best horses before us. They provided mee alwaies of a strong horse, because I was very corpulent & heavy : but whether he ambled a gentle pase or no, I durst not make any question. Neither yet durst I complaine, although he trotted full sore. But every man must be contented with his lot as it fell. Whereupon wee were exceedingly troubled : for oftentimes our horses were tired before we could come at any people. And then wee were constrained to beate and whip on our horses, and to lay our garments upon other emptie horses : yea and sometimes two of us to ride upon one horse.

Of the hunger, and thirst, and other miseries, which wee sustained in our journey. Chap. 24.

OF hunger and thirst, colde and wearinesse, there was no end. For they gave us no victuals, but onely in the evening. In the morning they used to give us a little drinke, or some sodden Millet to sup off. In the evening they bestowed flesh upon us, as namely, a shoulder and breast of rams mutton, and every man a measured quantitie of broath to drinke. When we had sufficient of the flesh-broath, we were marvellously wel refreshed. And it seemed to me most pleasant, and most nourishing drinke. Every Saterday I remained fasting until night, without eating or drinking of ought. And when night came, I was constrained, to my great grief and sorow, to eat flesh. Sometimes we were faine to eate flesh halfe sodden, or almost rawe, and all for want of fewel to seethe it withal : especially when we lay in the fields, or were

benighted before we came at our journeis end : because
we could not then conveniently gather together the doung
of horses or oxen : for other fewel we found but seldome,
except perhaps a few thornes in some places. Likewise *Certaine*
upon the bankes of some rivers, there are woods growing *rivers.*
here and there. Howbeit they are very rare. In the
beginning our guide highly disdained us, and it was
tedious unto him to conduct such base fellowes. Afterward, when he began to know us somewhat better, he
directed us on our way by the courts of rich Moals, and
we were requested to pray for them. Wherefore, had I
caried a good interpreter with me, I should have had
opportunitie to have done much good. The foresaid
Chingis, who was the first great Can or Emperour of the
Tartars, had foure sonnes, of whome proceeded by naturall
descent many children, every one of which doeth at this
day enjoy great possessions : and they are daily multiplied
and dispersed over that huge and waste desert, which is,
in dimensions, like unto the Ocean Sea. Our guide
therefore directed us, as we were going on our journey,
unto many of their habitations. And they marveiled
exceedingly, that we would receive neither gold, nor silver,
nor precious and costly garments at their hands. They
inquired also, concerning the great Pope, whether he was
of so lasting an age as they had heard ? For there had
gone a report among them, that he was 500. yeeres olde.
They inquired likewise of our countreis, whether there
were abundance of sheep, oxen, & horses or no ? Concerning the Ocean sea, they could not conceive of it,
because it was without limits or banks. Upon the even
of ye feast of Al Saints, we forsook the way leading
towards the East, (because the people were now descended
very much South) and we went on our journey by certaine
Alpes, or mountaines directly Southward, for the space of *Eight dayes*
8. dayes together. In the foresaid desert I saw many *journey south-*
asses (which they cal Colan) being rather like unto mules : *ward.*
these did our guide & his companions chase very eagerly : *Asses swift of*
howbeit, they did but lose their labour : for the beastes *foote.*

*High
mountaines.*

[I. 113.]

*Manured
grounds.*

*Kenchat a
village of the
Saracens.*

*The 7. day of
November.*

A great river.

Many lakes.

Vines.

were two swift for them. Upon the 7. day there appeared
to the South of us huge high mountaines, and we entred
into a place which was well watered, and fresh as a garden,
and found land tilled and manured. The eight day after
the feast of All Saints, we arrived at a certain towne of
the Saracens, named Kenchat, the governour whereof met
our guide at the townes end with ale and cups. For it is
their maner at all townes and villages, subject unto them,
to meet the messengers of Baatu and Mangu-Can with
meate and drinke. At the same time of the yere, they
went upon the yce in that countrey. And before the
feast of S. Michael, we had frost in the desert. I
enquired the name of that province : but being now in
a strange territorie, they could not tell mee the name
thereof, but onely the name of a very smal citie in
the same province. And there descended a great river
downe from the mountaines, which watered the whole
region, according as the inhabitants would give it passage,
by making divers chanels and sluces : neither did this
river exonerate it selfe into any sea, but was swallowed
up by an hideous gulfe into the bowels of the earth :
and it caused many fennes or lakes. Also I saw many
vines, and dranke of the wine thereof.

How Ban was put to death : and concerning the
habitation of the Dutch men. Chap. 25.

*A cottage.
The mountains
of Caucasus
are extended
unto the East-
erne Sea.*

*The citie of
Talas, or
Chincitalas.
Frier
Andrew.*

THe day following, we came unto another cottage
neere unto the mountains. And I enquired what
mountains they were, which I understood to be the
mountaines of Caucasus, which are stretched forth, &
continued on both parts to the sea, from the West unto
the East : and on the West part they are conjoyned unto
the foresaid Caspian sea, wherinto the river of Volga
dischargeth his streams. I enquired also of the city of
Talas, wherein were certaine Dutchmen servants unto one
Buri, of whom Frier Andrew made mention. Concerning
whom also I enquired very diligently in the courts of
Sartach & Baatu. Howbeit I could have no intelligence

of them, but onely that their lord & master Ban was put to death upon the occasion following : This Ban was not placed in good and fertile pastures. And upon a certain day being drunken, he spake on this wise unto his men. Am not I of the stocke and kinred of Chingis Can, as well as Baatu ? (for in very deede he was brother or nephew unto Baatu.) Why then doe I not passe and repasse upon the banke of Etilia, to feed my cattel there, as freely as Baatu himselfe doeth ? Which speeches of his were reported unto Baatu. Whereupon Baatu wrote unto his servants to bring their Lorde bound unto him. And they did so. Then Baatu demanded of him whether he had spoken any such words ? And hee confessed that he had. Howbeit, (because it is the Tartars maner to pardon drunken men) he excused himselfe that he was drunken at the same time. Howe durst thou (quoth Baatu) once name mee in thy drunkennesse ? And with that hee caused his head to be chopt off. Concerning the foresaid Dutchmen, I could not understand ought, till I was come unto the court of Mangu-Can. And there I was informed that Mangu-Can had removed them out of the jurisdiction of Baatu, for the space of a moneths journey from Talas Eastward, unto a certaine village, called Bolac : where they are set to dig gold, and to *The village of* make armour. Whereupon I could neither goe nor come *Bolac.* by them. I passed very neere the saide citie in going forth, as namely, within three dayes journey thereof : but I was ignorant that I did so : neither could I have turned out of my way, albeit I had knowen so much. From the foresaide cottage we went directly Eastward, by the mountaines aforesaid. And from that time we travailed *He entreth* among the people of Mangu-Can, who in all places sang *into the* and daunced before our guide, because hee was the *territories of* messenger of Baatu. For this curtesie they doe affoord *Mangu-Can.* eche to other : namely, the people of Mangu-Can receiving the messengers of Baatu in maner aforesaide : and so likewise the people of Baatu intertaining the messengers of Mangu-Can. Notwithstanding the people of Baatu are more surlie and stoute, and shewe not so much curtesie unto the subjectes of Mangu-Can, as they doe unto them. A fewe dayes after, wee entered upon those Alpes where the Cara Catayans were woont to inhabite. And there wee found a mightie river : insomuch that wee were constrained to imbarke our selves, and to saile over it. Afterward we came into a certaine valley, where I saw a castle destroyed, the walles whereof were onely of mudde : and in that place the ground was tilled also. And there wee founde a certaine village, named Equius, wherein were Saracens, speaking the Persian language : howbeit they dwelt an huge distance from Persia. The day following, having passed over the foresaide Alpes which descended from the great mountains Southward, we entred into a most beautiful plaine, having high mountaines on our right hande, and on the left hande of us a certaine Sea or lake, which containeth fifteene dayes journey in circuite. All the foresayde plaine is most commodiously watered with certaine freshets distilling from the said mountaines, all which do fall into the lake. In Sommer time wee returned by the North shore of the saide lake, and there were great mountaines on that side also. Upon the forenamed plaine there were wont to bee great store of villages : but for the most part they were all wasted, in regarde of the fertile pastures, that the Tartars might feede their cattel there. Wee found one great citie there named Cailac, wherein was a mart, and great store of Merchants frequenting it. In this citie wee remained fifteene dayes, staying for a certaine Scribe or Secretarie of Baatu, who ought to have accompanied our guide for the dispatching of certaine affaires in the court of Mangu. All this countrey was wont to be called Organum : and the people thereof had their proper language, and their peculiar kinde of writing. But it was altogether inhabited of the people called Contomanni. The Nestorians likewise in those parts used the very same kinde of language and writing. They are called Organa, because they were wont to be most

Certain Alpes wherein the Cara Catayans inhabited.
A mighty river.

Ground tilled.

Equius.

A lake of fifteene dayes journey in compasse.

[I. 114.]
Cailac a great citie, and full of merchants.

Contomanni.

skilfull in playing upon the Organes or citherne, as it
was reported unto me. Here first did I see worshippers
of idoles, concerning whom, bee it knowen unto your
majestie, that there be many sects of them in the
East countries.

How the Nestorians, Saracens, and Idolaters are joyned together. Chap. 26.

THe first sort of these idolaters are called Jugures :
whose land bordereth upon the foresaid land of
Organum, within the said mountains Eastward : and in
al their cities Nestorians do inhabit together, and they
are dispersed likewise towards Persia in the cities of
the Saracens. The citizens of ye foresaid city of Cailac
had 3. idole-Temples : and I entred into two of them,
to beholde their foolish superstitions. In the first of
which I found a man having a crosse painted with ink
upon his hand, wherupon I supposed him to be a
Christian : for he answered like a Christian unto al
questions which I demanded of him. And I asked
him, Why therefore have you not the crosse with the
image of Jesu Christ therupon ? And he answered :
We have no such custome. Whereupon I conjectured
that they were indeede Christians : but, that for lacke
of instruction they omitted the foresaide ceremonie. For
I saw there behind a certaine chest (which was unto them
in steed of an altar, whereupon they set candles and
oblations) an image having wings like unto the image
of Saint Michael, and other images also, holding their
fingers, as if they would blesse some body. That evening
I could not find any thing els. For the Saracens doe
onely invite men thither, but they will not have them
speake of their religion. And therfore, when I enquired
of the Saracens concerning such ceremonies, they were
offended thereat. On the morrow after were the
Kalends, and the Saracens feast of Passeover. And
changing mine Inne or lodging the same day, I tooke
up mine abode neere unto another idole-Temple. For

*The people
called Jugures
idolaters.*

the citizens of the said citie of Cailac doe curteously invite, & lovingly intertaine all messengers, every man of them according to his abilitie and portion. And entring into the foresaid idole-Temple, I found the Priests of the said idoles there. For alwayes at the Kalends they set open their Temples, and the priests adorne themselves, and offer up the peoples oblations of bread and fruits. First therefore I will describe unto you those rites and ceremonies, which are common unto all their idole-Temples : and then the superstitions of the foresaid Jugures, which be, as it were, a sect distinguished from the rest. They doe all of them worship towards the North, clapping their hands together, and prostrating themselves on their knees upon ye earth, holding also their foreheads in their hands. Wherupon the Nestorians of those parts will in no case joyne their hands together in time of prayer : but they pray, displaying their hands before their breasts. They extend their Temples in length East and West : and upon the North side they build a chamber, in maner of a Vestry for themselves to goe forth into. Or sometimes it is otherwise. If it be a foure square Temple, in the midst of the Temple towards the North side therof, they take in one chamber in that place where the quire should stand. And within the said chamber they place a chest long and broad like unto a table : and behinde the saide chest towardes the South stands their principall idole : which I sawe at Caracarum, and it was as bigge as the idole of Saint Christopher. Also a certaine Nestorian priest, which had bin in Catay, saide that in that countrey there is an idole of so huge a bignes, that it may be seen two daies journey before a man come at it. And so they place other idoles round about the foresaid principal idole, being all of them finely gilt over with pure golde : and upon the saide chest, which is in manner of a table, they set candles and oblations. The doores of their Temples are always opened towards the South, contrary to the custome of the Saracens. They have also great

Frier William was at Caracarum.

belles like unto us. And that is the cause (as I thinke) why the Christians of the East will in no case use great belles. Notwithstanding they are common among the Russians, and Græcians of Gasaria.

Of their Temples and idoles : and howe they behave themselves in worshipping their false gods. Chap. 27.

ALl their Priests had their heads and beards shaven quite over : and they are clad in saffron coloured garments : and being once shaven, they lead an unmaried life from that time forward : and they live an hundreth or two hundreth of them together in one cloister or covent. Upon those dayes when they enter into their temples, they place two long foormes therein : and so sitting upon the sayd foormes like singing men in a quier, namely the one halfe of them directly over against the other, they have certaine books in their hands, which sometimes they lay downe by them upon the foormes : and their heads are bare so long as they remaine in the temple. And there they reade softly unto themselves, not uttering any voice at all. Whereupon comming in amongst them, at the time of their superstitious devotions, and finding them all siting mute in maner aforesayde, I attempted divers waies to provoke them unto speach, and yet could not by any means possible. They have with them also whithersoever they goe, a certaine string with an hundreth or two hundreth nutshels thereupon, much like to our bead-roule which we cary about with us. And they doe alwayes utter these words : *Ou mam Hactani*, God thou knowest : as one of them expounded it unto me. And so often doe they expect a reward at Gods hands, as they pronounce these words in remembrance of God. Round about their temple they doe alwayes make a faire court, like unto a churchyard, which they environ with a good wall : and upon the South part thereof they build a great portal, wherein they sit and conferre together. And upon the top of the said portall they pitch a long pole right up,

[I. 115.]

Bookes.

exalting it, if they can, above all the whole towne besides. And by the same pole all men may knowe, that there stands the temple of their idoles, These rites and ceremonies aforesayd be common unto all idolaters in those parts. Going upon a time towardes the foresayd idoletemple, I found certain priests sitting in the outward portal. And those which I sawe, seemed unto me, by their shaven beards, as if they had bene French men. They wore certaine ornaments upon their heads made of paper. The priestes of the foresaide Jugures doe use such attire whithersoever they goe. They are alwaies in their saffron coloured jackets, which be very straight being laced or buttened from the bosome right downe, after the French fashion. And they have a cloake upon their left shoulder descending before and behind under their right arme, like unto a deacon carying the houssel-boxe in time of lent. Their letters or kind of writing the Tartars did receive. They begin to write at the top of their paper drawing their lines right downe : and so they reade and multiply their lines from the left hand to the right. They doe use certaine papers and characters in their magical practises. Whereupon their temples are full of such short scroules hanged round about them. Also Mangu-Can hath sent letters unto your Majestie written in the language of the Moals or Tartars, and in the foresayd hand or letter of the Jugures. They burne their dead according to the anncient custome, and lay up the ashes in the top of a Pyramis. Now, after I had sit a while by the foresaid priests, and entred into their temple and seene many of their images both great and small, I demanded of them what they beleeved concerning God ? And they answered : We beleeve that there is onely one God. And I demaunded farther : Whether do you beleve that he is a spirit, or some bodily substance ? They saide : We beleeve that he is a spirite. Then said I : Doe you beleeve that God ever tooke mans nature upon him ? They answered : Noe. And againe I said : Sithence ye beleeve that he is a spirit, to what end doe you make so

Paper.
So do the people of China use to write, drawing their lines perpendicularly downward, & not as we doe from the right hand to the lefte.

288

many bodily images to represent him ? Sithence also you beleeve not that hee was made man : why doe you resemble him rather unto the image of a man then of any other creature ? Then they answered saying : we frame not those images whereby to represent God. But when any rich man amongst us, or his sonne, or his wife, or any of his friends deceaseth, hee causeth the image of the dead party to be made, and to be placed here : and we in remembrance of him doe reverence thereunto. Then I replyed : you doe these things onely for the friendship and flatterie of men. Noe (said they) but for their memory. Then they demanded of me, as it were in scoffing wise : Where is God ? To whom I answered : where is your soule ? They said, in our bodies. Then saide I, is it not in every part of your bodie, ruling and guiding the whole bodie, and yet notwithstanding is not seene or perceived ? Even so God is every where and ruleth all things, and yet is he invisible, being understanding and wisedome it selfe. Then being desirous to have had some more conference with them, by reason, that mine interpreter was weary, and not able to expresse my meaning, I was constrained to keepe silence. The Moals or Tartars are in this regard of their sect : namely they beleeve that there is but one God : howbeit they make images of felt, in remembrance of their deceased friends, covering them with five most rich and costly garments, and putting them into one or two carts, which carts no man dare once touch : and they are in the custody of their soothsayers, who are their priests, concerning whom I will give your Highnesse more at large to understand hereafter. These soothsayers or diviners do alwaies attend upon the court of Mangu and of other great personages. As for the poorer or meaner sorte, they have them not, but such onely as are of the stocke and kindred of Chingis. And when they are to remove or to take any journey, the said diviners goe before them, even as the cloudie piller went before the children of Israel. And they appoint ground where the tents must

be pitched, and first of al they take down their owne
houses : & after them the whole court doth the like.
Also upon their festival daies or kalends they take forth
the foresayd images, and place them in order round, or
circle wise within the house. Then come the Moals or
Tartars, and enter into the same house, bowing themselves
before the said images and worship them. Moreover, it
is not lawfull for any stranger to enter into that house.
For upon a certaine time I my selfe would have gone in,
but I was chidden full well for my labour.

Of divers and sundry nations : and of certaine
    people which were wont to eate their owne
    parents.   Chap. 28.

BUt the foresayd Jugures (who live among the
    Christians, and the Saracens) by their sundry dis-
putations, as I suppose, have bene brought unto this, to
beleeve, that there is but one onely God. And they
dwelt in certaine cities, which afterward were brought in
subjection unto Chingis Can : whereupon he gave his
daughter in mariage unto their king. Also the citie of
Caracarum it selfe is in a manner within their territory :
The countrey and the whole countrey of king or Presbyter John, & of
of Presbiter his brother Vut lyeth neere unto their dominions : saving,
John. that they inhabite in certaine pastures Northward, and the
sayde Jugures betweene the mountaines towardes the
South. Whereupon it came to passe, that the Moals
received letters from them. And they are the Tartars
principall scribes : & al the Nestorians almost can skill of
their letters. Next unto them, between the foresaid
Tangut. mountaines Eastward, inhabiteth the nation of Tangut,
who are a most valiant people, and tooke Chingis in
battell. But after the conclusion of a league hee was set
at libertie by them, and afterward subdued them. These
Strange oxen. people of Tangut have oxen of great strength, with tailes
like unto horses, and with long shagge haire upon their
backes and bellyes. They have legges greater then other
oxen have, and they are exceedingly fierce. These oxen

drawe the great houses of the Moals : and their hornes
are slender, long, streight, and most sharpe pointed :
insomuch that their owners are faine to cut off the endes
of them. A cowe will not suffer her selfe to be coupled
unto one of them, unles they whistle or sing unto her.
They have also the qualities of a Buffe : for if they see
a man clothed in red, they run upon him immediately
to kill him. Next unto them are the people of Tebet, *The people of Tebet.*
men which were wont to eate the carkases of their
deceased parents : that for pities sake, they might make
no other sepulchre for them, then their owne bowels.
Howbeit of late they have left off this custome, because
that thereby they became abominable and odious unto al
other nations. Notwithstanding unto this day they make
fine cups of the skuls of their parents, to the ende that
when they drinke out of them, they may amidst all their
jollities and delights call their dead parents to remembrance. This was tolde mee by one that saw it. The *Abundance of golde.*
sayd people of Tebet have great plentie of golde in their
land. Whosoever therefore wanteth golde, diggeth till
he hath found some quantitie, and then taking so much
thereof as will serve his turne, he layeth up the residue
within the earth : because, if he should put it into his
chest or storehouse, hee is of opinion that God would
withholde from him all other gold within the earth. I
sawe some of those people, being very deformed creatures.
In Tangut I saw lusty tall men, but browne and swart in *The stature of*
colour. The Jugures are of a middle stature like unto *the people of Tangut, and*
our French men. Amongst the Jugures is the originall *of the Jugures.*
and roote of the Turkish, and Comanian languages.
Next unto Tebet are the people of Langa and Solanga, *Langa &*
whose messengers I saw in the Tartars court. And they *Solanga.*
had brought more then ten great cartes with them, every
one of which was drawen with sixe oxen. They be little *The people*
browne men like unto Spaniards. Also they have jackets, *of Solanga*
like unto the upper vestment of a deacon, saving that the *Spaniards.*
sleeves are somewhat streighter. And they have miters
upon their heads like bishops. But the fore part of their

miter is not so hollow within as the hinder part: neither
is it sharpe pointed or cornered at the toppe: but there
hang downe certaine square flappes compacted of a kinde
of strawe which is made rough and rugged with extreme
heat, and is so trimmed, that it glittereth in the sunne
beames, like unto a glasse, or an helmet well burnished.
And about their temples they have long bands of the
foresayd matter fastened unto their miters, which hover in
the wind, as if two long hornes grewe out of their heads.
And when the winde tosseth them up and downe too
much, they tie them over the midst of their miter from
one temple to another: and so they lie circle wise overthwart their heads. Moreover their principal messenger
A table of ele- comming unto the Tartars court had a table of elephants
phants tooth. tooth about him of a cubite in length, and a handfull in
breadth, being very smoothe. And whensoever hee spake
unto the Emperor himselfe, or unto any other great
personage, hee alwayes beheld that table, as if hee had
found therein those things which hee spake: neither did
he cast his eyes to the right hand, nor to the lefte, nor
upon his face, with whom he talked. Yea, going too and
fro before his lord, he looketh no where but only upon
The people his table. Beyond them (as I understand of a certainty)
called Muc. there are other people called Muc, having villages, but no
[I. 117.] one particular man of them appropriating any cattell unto
himselfe. Notwithstanding there are many flockes and
droves of cattell in their countrey, & no man appointed to
keepe them. But when any one of them standeth in
neede of any beast, hee ascendeth up unto an hill, and
there maketh a shout, and all the cattell which are within
hearing of the noyse, come flocking about him, and suffer
themselves to be handled and taken, as if they were tame.
And when any messenger or stranger commeth into their
countrie, they shut him up into an house, ministring there
things necessary unto him, untill his businesse be dispatched. For if anie stranger should travell through that
countrie, the cattell would flee away at the very sent of
him, and so would become wilde. Beyond Muc is great

Cathaya, the inhabitants whereof (as I suppose) were of olde time, called Seres. For from them are brought most excellent stuffes of silke. And this people is called Seres of a certain towne in the same countrey. I was crediblie informed, that in the said countrey, there is one towne having walles of silver, and bulwarkes or towers of golde. There be many provinces in that land, the greater part whereof are not as yet subdued unto the Tartars. And amongst *

Somewhat is wanting.

Part of the great Charter granted by king Edward the first to the Barons of the Cinque portes, in the sixt yeere of his reigne 1278. for their good services done unto him by sea: wherein is mention of their former ancient Charters from Edward the Confessor, William the Conqueror, William Rufus, Henry the second, king Richard the first, king John, and Henry the third continued unto them.

Dward by the grace of God king of England, lord of Ireland, & duke of Gascoigne, to all Archbishops, Bishops, Abbots, Priors, Earles, Barons, Justices, Shirifs, Provosts, Officers, & to all Bayliffes and true subjects greeting. You shall knowe that for the faithfull service that our Barons of the five Ports hitherto to our predecessors kings of England, & unto us lately in our armie of Wales have done, and for their good service to us and our heires kings of England, truly to be continued in time to come, we have granted & by this our Charter confirmed for us and our heires, to the same our Barons and to their heires, all their liberties and freedomes. So that they shall be free from all toll, and from all custome; that is to say from all lastage, tallage, passage, cariage,

rivage, asponsage, and from all wrecke, and from all their sale, carying and recarying through all our realme and dominion, with socke and souke, toll and theme. And that they shall have Infangthefe, and that they shall be wreckefree, lastagefree, and lovecopfree. And that they shall have Denne and Strande at great Yarmouth, according as it is contayned in the ordinance by us thereof made perpetually to bee observed. And also that they are free from all shires and hundreds: so that if any person will plead against them, they shall not aunswere nor pleade otherwise then they were wont to plead in the time of the lord, king Henrie our great grandfather: And that they shall have their findelles in the sea and in the land: And that they be free of all their goods and of all their marchandises as our freemen. And that they have their honours in our court, and their liberties throughout all the land wheresoever they shall come. And that they shall be free for ever of all their lands, which in the time of Lord Henrie the king our father they possessed: that is to say in the 44. yere of his reign, from all maner of summonces before our Justices to any maner of pleadings, journeying in what shire soever their lands are. So that they shall not be bound to come before the Justices aforesaid, except any of the same Barons doe implead any man, or if any man be impleaded. And that they shall not pleade in any other place, except where they ought, and where they were wont, that is to say, at Shepeway. And that they have their liberties and freedomes from hencefoorth, as they and their predecessors have had them at any time better, more fully and honourably in the time of the kings of England, Edward, William the first, William the second, Henrie the king our great grandfather, and in the times of king Richard, and king John our grandfathers, and lord king Henrie our father, by their Charters: as the same Charters which the same our Barons thereof have, and which we have seene, doe reasonably testifie. And we forbid that no man unjustly trouble them nor their marchandise upon our

The fishing at great Yarmouth.

Henry the third.

Edward the confessor.

forfeyture of ten pounds. So nevertheless, that when the same Barons shall fayle in doing of Justice or in receiving of Justice, our Warden, and the wardens of our heires of [I. 118.] the Cinque Portes, which for the time shall be, their Ports and liberties may enter for to doe their full Justice. So also that the sayd Barons and their heires, do unto us and to our heirs kings of England by the yeare their full service of 57. shippes at their costs by the space of fifteene *57. Ships of* dayes at our somounce, or at the somounce of our heires. *the Cinque* We have granted also unto them of our speciall grace that *Portes bound* they have Outfangthefe in their lands within the Ports *king 15. dayes* aforesayd, in the same maner that Archbishops, Bishops, *at their owne* Abbots, Earles and Barons, have in their manours in the *costs.* .countie of Kent. And they be not put in any Assises, Juries, or Recognisances by reason of their forreine tenure against their will : and that they be free of all their owne wines for which they do travaile of our right prise, that is to say, of one tunne before the mast, and of another behind the maste. We have granted furthermore unto the said Barons for us and our heires, that they for ever have this liberty, that is to say, That we or our heires shall not have the wardship or mariages of their heires by reason of their landes, which they holde within the liberties and Portes aforesayde, for the which they doe their service aforesayd : and for the which wee and our progenitors had not the wardships and mariages in time past. But we our aforesayd confirmation upon the liberties and freedomes aforesayde, and our grants following to them of our especiall grace, of newe have caused to be made, saving alwaies in al things our kingly dignitie : And saving unto us and to our heires, plea of our crowne, life and member. Wherefore we will and surely command for us and our heires that the aforesaid Barons and their heires for ever have all the aforesaid liberties and freedomes, as the aforesaid Charters do reasonably testifie. And that of our especial grace they have outfangthefe in their lands within the Ports aforesaid after the maner that Archbishops, Bishops,

Abbots, Earles and Barons have in their manours in the county of Kent. And that they be not put in Assises, Juries, or Recognisances by reason of their forreine tenure against their will. And that they bee free of their owne wines for which they travaile of our right price or custome, that is to say of one tunne of wine before the maste, and of another tunne behinde the maste. And that likewise for ever they have the libertie aforesayde: that is to say: That wee and our heires have not the wardships or mariages of their heires by reason of their landes which they holde within the liberties and Portes aforesayd, for which they doe their service aforesaid, and for which wee and our predecessors the wardships and mariages have not had in times past. But our aforesayd confirmation of their liberties and freedomes aforesaid and other grants following to them of our especiall grace of new we have caused to bee made. Saving always and in all things our regall dignity. And saving unto us and our heires the pleas of our crowne of life and member as is aforesayd. These being witnesses, the reverend father Robert of Portuens Cardinall of the holie Church of Rome, frier William of Southhampton Prior povincial of the friers preachers in England, William of Valencia our uncle, Roger of the dead sea, Roger of Clifford, Master Robert Samuel deane of Sarum, Master Robert of Scarborough the Archdeacon of East Riding, Master Robert of Seyton, Bartholomew of Southley, Thomas of Wayland, Walter of Hoptan, Thomas of Normannel, Steven of Pennester, Frances of Bonava, John of Lenetotes, John of Metingham and others. Given by our hand at Westminster the fourteenth day of June, in the sixth yeare of our reigne.

A.D.
c. 1345.

The roll of the huge fleete of Edward the third before Calice, extant in the kings great wardrobe in London, whereby the wonderfull strength of England by sea in those dayes may appeare.

Thomas Walsingham writeth y^t he had once 1100. strong shippes.

The South fleete.

The Kings	Shippes 25. Mariners 419.	Lyme	Ships 4. Mariners 62.	
London	Shippes 25. Mariners 662.	Seton	Ships 2. Mariners 25.	
Aileford	Shippes 2. Mariners 24.	Sydmouth	Ships 3. Mariners 62.	
Hoo	Shippes 2. Mariners 24.	Exmouth	Ships 10. Mariners 193.	
Maydstone	Shippes 2. Mariners 51.	Tegmouth	Ships 7. Mariners 120.	
Hope	Shippes 2. Mariners 59.	Dartmouth	Ships 31. Mariners 757.	
New Hithe	Shippes 5. Mariners 49.	Portsmouth	Ships 5. Mariners 96.	
Margat	Shippes 15. Mariners 160.	Plimouth	Ships 26. Mariners 603.	
‖ Motue	Shippes 2. Mariners 22.	Loo	Ships 20. Mariners 315.	‖ Or, Morne.
Feversham	Shippes 2. Mariners 25.	Yalme	Ships 2. Mariners 47.	[I. 119.]
Sandwich	Ships 22. Mariners 504.	‖ Fowey	Ships 47. Mariners 770.	‖ Or, Foy.
Dover	Ships 16. Mariners 336.	Bristol	Ships 22. Mariners 608.	
Wight	Ships 13. Mariners 220.	Tenmouth	Ships 2. Mariners 25.	
Winchelsey	Ships 21. Mariners 596.	Hasting	Ships 5. Mariners 96.	
Waymouth	Ships 15. Mariners 263.	Romney	Ships 4. Mariners 65.	

Port	Ships	Mariners	Port	Ships	Mariners
Rye	9	156	Swanzey	1	29
Hithe	6	122	Ilfercombe	6	79
Shoreham	20	329	‡ Patricke-stowe	2	27
‡ Soford	5	80	Polerwan	1	60
Newmouth	2	18	Wadworth	1	14
Hamowlhooke	7	117	Kardife	1	51
Hoke	11	208	Bridgwater	1	15
Southhampton	21	576	Kaermarthen	1	16
Leymington	9	159	Cailechesworth	1	12
Poole	4	94	Mulbrooke	1	12
Warham	3	59	Summe of the South fleete.	493	9630

The North fleete.

Port	Ships	Mariners	Port	Ships	Mariners
Bamburgh	1	9	Woodhouse	1	22
Newcastle	17	314	Strokhithe	1	10
Walcrich	1	12	Barton	3	30
Hertilpoole	5	145	Swinefleete	1	11
Hull	16	466	Saltfleet	2	49
Yorke	1	9	Grimesby	11	171
Ravenser	1	27	Waynefleet	2	49

	Ships	Mariners		Ships	Mariners	
Wrangle	1.	8.	Mersey	1.	6.	
‡ Lenne	16.	382.	Brightling-sey	5.	61.	*Now Brickelsey.* ‡ *Or, Linne.*
Blackney	2.	38.	Colchester	5.	90.	
Scarborough	1.	19.	Whitbanes	1.	17.	
Yernmouth	43.	1950. or 1075.	Malden	2.	32.	*Or, Yermouth.*
Donwich	6.	102.	Derwen	1.	15.	
Orford	3.	62.	Boston	17.	361.	
Goford	13.	303.	Swinhumber	1.	32.	
Herwich	14.	283.	Barton	5.	91.	
Ipswich	12.	239.	The Summe of the North fleete.	217.	4521.	

The summe totall of all the English fleete { Ships 700. Mariners 14151.

Estrangers their ships and mariners.

	Ships	Mariners		Ships	Mariners
Bayon	15.	439.	Flanders	14.	133.
Spayne	7.	184.	Gelderland	1.	24.
Ireland	1.	25.			

The summe of all the Estrangers { Ships 38. Mariners 805.

THe summe of expenses aswell of wages, & prests, [I. 121.] as for the expenses of the kings houses, and for other gifts and rewards, shippes and other things necessary to the parties of France and Normandie, and before Calice, during the siege there, as it appeareth in the accompts of William Norwel keeper of the kings Wardrobe, from the 21. day of April in the 18 yeere of the reigne of the said king, unto the foure and twentieth day of November in the one and twentieth yeere of his reigne, is iii. hundreth xxxvii. thousand li. ix.s. iiii.d.

A note out of Thomas Walsingham touching the huge Fleete of eleven hundred well furnished ships wherewith king Edward the third passed over unto Calais in the yeere 1359.

ANno gratiæ 1359. Johannes Rex Franciæ sub umbra pacis, & dolose obtulit Regi Angliæ Flandriam, Picardiam, Aquitaniam, aliasque terras quas equitaverat & vastarat: pro quibus omnibus ratificandis idem Rex Edwardus in Franciam nuncios suos direxit; quibus omnibus Franci contradixerunt. Unde motus Rex Angliæ, celeriter se & suos præparavit ad transfretandum, ducens secum principem Walliæ Edwardum suum primogenitum, ducem Henricum Lancastriæ, & ferè proceres omnes, quos comitabantur vel sequebantur pœne mille currus, habuitque apud Sanwicum instructas optime undecies centum naves, & cum hoc apparatu ad humiliandum Francorum fastum Franciam navigavit, relicto domino Thoma de Woodstock filio suo juniore admodum parvulo, Anglici regni custode, sub tutela tamen.

The same in English.

IN the yeere of our Lord 1359. John the French king craftily, and under pretence of peace, offered unto Edward the third king of England, Flanders, Picardie, Gascoigne, and other territories which he had spoyled and wasted: for the ratifying of which agreement, the foresaid king Edward sent his ambassadors into France, but the Frenchmen gainsaied them in all their articles and

demaunds. Whereupon the king of England being provoked, speedily prepared himselfe and his forces to crosse
the seas, carying with him Edward Prince of Wales his
heire apparant, and Henry duke of Lancaster and almost
all his Nobles, with a thousand wagons and cartes attend-
ing upon them. And the said king had at Sandwich
eleven hundred ships exceedingly well furnished: with
which preparation he passed over the seas, to abate
the Frenchmens arrogancie: leaving his yonger sonne
Thomas of Woodstocke, being very tender of age, as
his vicegerent in the Realme of England; albeit not
without a protectour, &c.

The voyage of Nicholas de Lynna a Franciscan
Frier, and an excellent Mathematician of
Oxford, to all the Regions situate under
the North pole, in the yeere 1360. and in
the raigne of Edward the 3. king of
England.

Uod ad descriptionem partium Septen- *The words of*
trionalium attinet, eam nos accipimus *Gerardus*
ex Itinerario Jacobi Cnoyen Buscodu- *Mercator, in*
censis, qui quædam ex rebus gestis *the foote of his*
Arthuri Britanni citat, majorem autem *general Map,*
partem & potiora, à Sacerdote quodam *upon the de-*
apud Regem Noruegiæ, An. Dom. 1364. *scription of the*
North partes.
didicit.   Descenderat is ex illis quos Arthurus ad has
habitandas insulas miserat, & referebat, An. 1360. Mino-
ritam quendam Anglum Oxoniensem Mathematicum in
eas insulas venisse, ipsisque relictis ad ulteriora arte
Magica profectum descripsisse omnia, & Astrolabio
dimensum esse in hanc subjectam formam ferè, uti ex
Jacobo collegimus.   Euripos illos quatuor dicebat tanto
impetu ad interiorem voraginem rapi, ut naves semel
ingressæ nullo vento retroagi possent, nequè verò unquam tantum ibi ventum esse, ut molæ frumentariæ
circumagendæ sufficiat.   Simillima his habet Giraldus

Cambrensis (qui floruit, An. 1210.) in libro de mirabi-
libus Hyberniæ, sic enim scribit. Non procul ab insulis
Hebridibus, Islandia, &c. ex parte Boreali, est maris
quædam miranda vorago, in quam à remotis partibus
omnes undique fluctus marini tanquam ex condicto
fluunt, & recurrunt, qui in secreta naturæ penetralia se
ibi transfundentes, quasi in Abyssum vorantur. Si verò
navem hâc fortè transire contigerit, tanta rapitur, & attra-
hitur fluctuum violentia, ut eam statim irrevocabiliter vis
voracitatis absorbeat.

Quatuor voragines hujus Oceani, a quatuor oppositis
mundi partibus Philosophi describunt, unde & tam
marinos fluctus, quàm & Æolicos flatus causaliter
pervenire nonnulli conjectant.

[I. 122.] The same in English.

TOuching the description of the North partes, I have
taken the same out of the voyage of James Cnoyen
of Hartzevan Buske, which alleageth certaine conquests
of Arthur king of Britaine: and the most part, and
chiefest things among the rest, he learned of a certaine
priest in the king of Norwayes court, in the yeere 1364.
This priest was descended from them which king Arthur
had sent to inhabite these Islands, and he reported that in
the yeere 1360, a certaine English Frier, a Franciscan,
and a Mathematician of Oxford, came into those Islands,
who leaving them, and passing further by his Magicall
Arte, described all those places that he sawe, and tooke
the height of them with his Astrolabe, according to the
forme that I (Gerard Mercator) have set downe in my
mappe, and as I have taken it out of the aforesaid James
Cnoyen. Hee sayd that those foure Indraughts were
drawne into an inward gulfe or whirlepoole, with so great
a force, that the ships which once entred therein, could
by no meanes be driven backe againe, and that there is
never in those parts so much winde blowing, as might be
sufficient to drive a Corne mill.

Giraldus Cambrensis (who florished in the yeere 1210,

under king John) in his booke of the miracles of Ireland, hath certaine words altogether alike with these. *videlicet*: Not farre from these Islands (namely the Hebrides, Island &c.) towards the North there is a certaine woonderful whirlpoole of the sea, whereinto all the waves of the sea from farre have their course and recourse, as it were without stoppe: which, there conveying themselves into the secret receptacles of nature, are swallowed up, as it were, into a bottomlesse pit, and if it chance that any shippe doe passe this way, it is pulled, and drawen with such a violence of the waves, that eftsoones without remedy, the force of the whirlepoole devoureth the same.

There is a notable whirlepoole on the coast of Norway, called Malestrande, about the latitude of 68.

The Philosophers describe foure indraughts of this Ocean sea, in the foure opposite quarters of the world, from whence many doe conjecture that as well the flowing of the sea, as the blasts of the winde, have their first originall.

A Testimonie of the learned Mathematician master John Dee, touching the foresaid voyage of Nicholas De Linna.

Nno 1360. (that is to wit, in the 34. yeere of the reigne of the triumphant king Edward the third) a frier of Oxford, being a good Astronomer, went in companie with others to the most Northren Islands of the world, and there leaving his company together, hee travailed alone, and purposely described all the Northerne Islands, with the indrawing seas: and the record thereof at his returne he delivered to the king of England. The name of which booke is Inventio Fortunata (aliter fortunæ) qui liber incipit a gradu 54. usque ad polum. Which frier for sundry purposes after that did five times passe from England thither, and home againe.

Inventio Fortunata.

It is to be noted, that from the haven of Linne in Norfolke (whereof the foresaid Francisan frier tooke his

name) to Island, it is not above a fortnights sailing with
an ordinarie winde, and hath bene of many yeeres a
very common and usuall trade: which further appeareth
by the privileges granted to the Fishermen of the towne

An. 2. *&* 4.
& 31.
Edwardi
tertii.

of Blacknie in the said Countie of Norfolke, by king
Edward the third, for their exemption and freedome from
his ordinary service, in respect of their trade to Island.

The voyage of Henry Earle of Derbie, after
Duke of Hereford, and lastly king of Eng-
land, by the name of Henry the fourth,
An. Dom. 1390. into Prussia and Lettowe,
against the infidels, recorded by Thomas of
Walsingham.

An. Dom.
1390.

Ominus Henricus Comes de Derbie per
idem tempus profectus est in le Pruys,
ubi cum adjutorio marescalli dictæ patriæ,
& cujusdam Regis vocati Wytot devicit
exercitum Regis de Lettowe, captis quatuor ducibus, & tribus peremptis, &
amplius quam trecentis, de valentioribus
exercitus supradicti pariter interemptis. Civitas quoque

‖ *Alias Vilna.*

vocatur ‖ Will, in cujus castellum Rex de Lettowe nomine
Skirgalle confugerat, potenti virtute dicti Comitis maximè,

[I. 123.]

atque suorum capta est. Namque qui fuerunt de familia
sua primi murum ascenderant, & vexillum ejus super
muros, cæteris vel torpentibus vel ignorantibus, posuerunt.
Captaque sunt ibi vel occisa quatuor millia plebanorum,
fratre Regis de Poleyn inter cæteros ibi perempto, qui
adversarius nostri fuit. Obsessumque fuit castrum dictæ
Civitatis per quinque hebdomadas: Sed propter infirmi-
tates, quibus vexabatur exercitus magistri de Pruys & de
Lifland noluerunt diutiùs expectare. Facti sunt Christiani
de gente de Lettowe octo. Et magister de Lifland duxit
secum in suam patriam tria millia captivorum.

The same in English.

ABout the same time L. Henry the Earle of Derbie
travailed into Prussia, where, with the helpe of the
Marshall of the same Province, and of a certaine king
called Wytot, hee vanquished the armie of the king of
Lettowe, with the captivitie of foure Lithuanian Dukes,
and the slaughter of three, besides more then three
hundred of the principall common souldiers of the sayd
armie which were slaine. The Citie also which is called
Wil or Vilna, into the castle whereof the king of Lettow
named Skirgalle fled for his savegard, was, by the valour
of the sayd Earle especially and of his followers, surprised and taken. For certaine of the chiefe men of his
familie, while others were slouthfull or at least ignorant of
their intent, skaling the walles, advanced his colours thereupon. And there were taken and slaine foure thousand
of the common souldiers, and amongst others was slaine
the king of Poland his brother, who was our professed
enemie. And the castle of the foresaid Citie was besieged
for the space of five weekes: but by reason of the infir-
mities and inconveniences wherewith the whole armie was
annoyed, the great masters of Prussia and of Lifland
would not stay any longer. There were converted of the
nation of Lettowe eight persons unto the Christian faith.
And the master of Lifland carried home with him into his
countrey three thousand captives.

[The voyage

The voyage of Thomas of Woodstocke Duke of Glocester into Prussia, in the yeere 1391. written by Thomas Walsingham.

|| Filius natu minimus Edwardi 3.

Odem tempore dux Gloverniæ Dominus || Thomas de Woodstock, multis mœrentibus, iter apparavit versùs le Pruys: quem non Londinensium gemitus, non communis vulgi moeror retinere poterant, quin proficisci vellet. Nam plebs communis tàm Urbana quàm rustica metuebant quòd eo absente aliquod novum detrimentum succresceret, quo præsente nihil tale timebant. Siquidèm in eo spes & solatium totius patriæ reposita videbantur. Ipse verò mòx, ut fines patriæ suæ transiit, illicò adversa agitatus fortuna, nunc hàc nunc illàc turbinibus procellosis circumfertur; & in tantum destituitur, ut de vita etiam desperaret. Tandem post Daciam, post Norwagiam, post Scoticam barbariem non sine mortis pavore transcursam, pervenit Northumbriam, & ad castellum se contulit de Tinnemutha velùt assylum antiquitùs notum sibi: ubi per aliquot dies recreatus, iter assumpsit versus manerium suum de Plashy, magnum apportans gaudium toti regno, tam de ejus evasione, quàm de adventu suo.

Reditus.

The same in English.

AT the same time the Duke of Glocester Lord Thomas of Woodstock (the yongest sonne of Edward the third) to the great griefe of many, tooke his journey towards Prussia: whom neither the Londoners mones nor yet the lamentation of the communaltie could restraine from his intended expedition. For the common people both of the Citie and of the countrey feared lest in his absence some newe calamitie might happen; which they feared not while he was present. For in him the whole nation seemed to repose their hope and comfort. Howbeit having skarce passed as yet the bounds of his owne

countrey, he was immediatly by hard fortune tossed up
and downe with dangerous stormes and tempests, and was
brought into such distresse, that he despaired even of his
owne life. At length, having not without danger of
death, sailed along the coastes of Denmarke, Norway, and
Scotland, he returned into Northumberland, and went to
the castle of Tinmouth as unto a place of refuge knowen
of olde unto him : where, after hee had refreshed himselfe
a fewe dayes, hee tooke his journey toward his Mannour
of Plashy, bringing great joy unto the whole kingdome,
aswell in regard of his safetie as of his returne.

The verses of Geofrey Chaucer in the knights [I. 124.]
    Prologue, who living in the yeere 1402. (as
    hee writeth himselfe in his Epistle of Cupide)
    shewed that the English Knights after the
    losse of Acon, were wont in his time to
    travaile into Prussia and Lettowe, and other
    heathen lands, to advance the Christian faith
    against Infidels and miscreants, and to seeke
    honour by feats of armes.

The English Knights Prologue.

Knight there was, and that a worthie man,
that from the time that he first began
to riden out, he loved Chevalrie,
trouth, honour, freedome, and Curtesie.
full worthy was he in his lords warre :
and thereto had hee ridden no man farre,
As well in Christendome as in Heathennesse,   *Long travaile.*
and ever had honour for his worthinesse.
    At Alisandre hee was, when it was wonne :   *Alexandria.*
full oft time hee had the bourd begon
aboven all nations in Pruce,
In Lettowe had hee riden, and in Ruce,   *Lettowe,Ruce.*
no Christen man so oft of his degree :
In Granade at the siege had he bee

A.D.
1402.
*Algezer in
Granado.
Layas in
Armenia.
Froysart. lib.
3. cap. 40.
Satalie in the
mayne of Asia
neere Rhods.
Tremisen is in
Barbarie.
|| Or, Palice
Froysart lib.
3. cap. 40.
Turkie.
The time
when Chaucer
wrote, is thus
mentioned in
the end of
his letter of
Cupide.*

At Algezer: and ridden in Belmarye:
At Leyes was hee, and also at Satalye,
When they were wonne: and in the great see
at many a Noble armie had hee bee.
At mortall battailes had he bin fifteene,
And foughten for our faith at Tramissen,
in listes thries, and aye slayne his foe:
   This ilke worthie Knight had bin also,
sometime with the lord of || Palathye
ayenst another Heathen in Turkie.

Written in the lustie moneth of May
in our Palace, where many a million
of lovers true have habitation,
The yeere of grace joyfull and jocond,
a thousand, foure hundred and second.

The original, proceedings and successe of the Northren domestical and forren trades and traffiques of this Isle of Britain from the time of Nero the Emperour, who deceased in the yeere of our Lord 70. under the Romans, Britons, Saxons, and Danes, till the conquest: and from the conquest, untill this present time, gathered out of the most authenticall histories and records of this nation.

A testimonie out of the fourteenth Booke of the Annales of Cornelius Tacitus, prooving London to have bene a famous Mart Towne in the reigne of Nero the Emperour, which died in the yeere of Christ 70.

AT Suetonius mira constantia medios inter hostes Londinium perrexit, cognomento quidem coloniæ non insigne, sed copia negociatorum & commeatu maxime celebre.

The same in English.

BUt Suetonius with wonderfull constancie passed through the middest of his enemies, unto London, which though it were not honoured with the name and title of a Romane Colonie, yet was it most famous for multitude of Marchants and concourse of people.

[I. 125.]

A testimonie out of Venerable Beda (which died in the yeere of our Lord 734.) prooving London to have bene a Citie of great traffike and Marchandize not long after the beginning of the Saxons reigne.

Beda Ecclesiasticæ historiæ Gentis Anglorum lib. 2. cap. 3.

ANno Dominicæ incarnationis sexcentesimo quarto Augustinus Britanniarum Archiepiscopus ordinavit duos Episcopos, Mellitum videlicet & Justum : Mellitum quidem ad prædicandum provinciæ Orientalium Saxonum, qui Tamesi fluvio dirimuntur à Cantia, & ipsi Orientali Mari contigui, quorum Metropolis Londonia Civitas est, super ripam præfati fluminis posita, & ipsa multorum emporium populorum, terra marique venientium.

The same in English.

IN the yeere of the incarnation of Christ 604. Augustine Archbishop of Britaine consecrated two Bishops, to wit Mellitus and Justus. He appoynted Mellitus to preach to the East Saxons, which are divided from Kent by the river of Thames, and border upon the Easterne sea, whose chiefe and Metropolitane Citie is London, seated upon the banke of the aforesayd river, which is also a Marte Towne of many nations, which repayre thither by sea and by land.

[The league

The league betweene Carolus Magnus and Offa
King of Mercia concerning safe trade of the
English Marchants in all the Emperours
Dominion. This Offa died in the yeere of
our Lord 795.

Malmsbur. de
gestis Regum
Anglorum lib.
1. cap. 4.

Ffa interea Carolum magnum Regem
Francorum frequentibus legationibus
amicum paravit: quamvis non facile quod
suis artibus conduceret in Caroli animo
invenerit. Discordarunt antea, adeo ut
magnis motibus utrobique concurrentibus,
etiam negociatorum commeatus prohiber-
entur. Est Epistola Albini hujusce rei index, cujus
partem hic apponam.

Nesico quid de nobis venturum sit. Aliquid enim
dissentionis diabolico fomento inflammante, nuper inter
Regem Carolum & Regem Offam exortum est: ita ut
Navigatio utrinque navigatio interdicta negociantibus cesset. Sunt
interdicta. qui dicant nos pro pace in illas partes mittendos. Et
nonnullis interpositis, Nunc, inquit, ex verbis Caroli
fœdus firmum inter eum & Offam compactum subjiciam.
Carolus gratia Dei Rex Francorum, & Longobardorum,
& patricius Romanorum, viro venerando & fratri
charissimo Offæ Regi Merciorum salutem. Primo
gratias agimus omnipotenti deo, de salute animarum, de
Catholicæ fidei sinceritate, quam in vestris laudabiliter
paginis reperimus exaratam. De peregrinis vero qui pro
amore Dei, & salute animarum suarum beatorum Apostolorum limina desiderant adire, cum pace sine omni
perturbatione vadant. Sed si aliqui, non religioni servientes, sed lucra sectantes, inveniantur inter eos, locis
Negociatorum opportunis statuta solvant telonia. Negociatores quoque
Anglicanorum volumus ut ex mandato nostro patrocinium habeant in
patrocinium. Regno nostro legitime. Et si aliquo loco injusta
affligantur oppressione, reclament ad nos vel nostros
judices, & plenam videbimus justitiam fieri.

The same in English.

IN the meane season Offa by often legacies solicited
Charles le maigne the king of France, to be his friend:
albeit he could not easily finde king Charles any whit
enclined to further and promote his craftie attempts.
Their mindes were so alienated before, that, bearing hauty
stomacks on both parts, even the mutuall traffique of *Traffique*
their Marchants was prohibited. The Epistle of Albinus *prohibited.*
is a sufficient testimony of this matter: part whereof I
will here put downe.

I know not (quoth he) what will become of us. For
there is of late, by the instigation of the devill, some
discord and variance sprung up betweene king Charles
and king Offa: insomuch that sailing to and fro is [I. 126.]
forbidden unto the Marchants of both their dominions. *Navigation*
Some say that we are to be sent, for the obtaining of a *forbidden.*
peace, into those partes. And againe, after a fewe lines.
Nowe (quoth he) out of Charles his owne words, I will *A league be-*
make report of the league concluded betweene him and *tweene Carol.*
Offa. *Mag. and K.*
Offa.

Charles by the grace of God king of the Franks and
Lombards and Senatour of the Romanes, unto the reverend
and his most deare brother Offa king of the Mercians
sendeth greeting. First we doe render unto almightie
God most humble thankes for the salvation of soules, and
the sinceritie of the Catholique faith, which we, to your
great commendation, have found signified in your letters.
As touching those pilgrimes, who for the love of God
and their owne soules health, are desirous to resort unto
the Churches of the holy Apostles, let them goe in peace
without all disturbance. But if any be found amongst
them not honouring religion, but following their owne
gaine, they are to pay their ordinarie customes at places
convenient. It is our pleasure also and commandement, *Protection of*
that your marchants shall have lawfull patronage and *the English*
protection in our dominions. Who, if in any place they *Marchants.*
chance to be afflicted with any injust oppression, let them

make their supplication unto us, or unto our Judges, and
we will see justice executed to the full.

An ancient testimonie translated out of the olde
Saxon lawes, containing among other things
the advancement of Marchants for their thrise
crossing the wide seas, set downe by the
learned Gentleman Master William Lambert
pagina 500. of his perambulation of Kent.

IT was sometime in English lawes, that the people and
the lawes were in reputation: and then were the
wisest of the people worship-worthy, every one after
his degree: Earle, and Churle, Thein, and under-Thein.
And if a churle thrived so, that hee had fully five hides
of his owne land, a Church and a Kitchin, a Belhouse,
and a gate, a seate, and a severall office in the Kings
hall, then was he thenceforth the Theins right worthy.
And if a Thein so thrived, that he served the king, and
on his message rid in his houshold, if he then had a
Thein that followed him, the which to the kings journey
five hides had, and in the kings seate his Lord served,
and thrise with his errand had gone to the king, he
might afterward with his foreoth his lords part play at
any great neede. And if a Thein did thrive so, that
he became an Earle; then was he afterward an Earles
right worthie. And if a Marchant so thrived, that he
passed thrise over the wide seas, of his owne craft, he
was thencefoorth a Theins right worthie. And if a
scholar so prospered thorow learning that he degree
had, and served Christ, he was then afterward of dignitie and peace so much worthie, as thereunto belonged:
unlesse he forfaited so, that he the use of his degree
use ne might.

A.D.
c. 1027.

A testimonie of certaine priviledges obtained for *William of* the English and Danish Marchants of Con- *Malmsb. lib.* radus the Emperour and John the Bishop *2. cap. 9. de* of Rome by Canutus the King of England *Anglorum.* in his journey to Rome, extracted out of a letter of his written unto the Cleargie of England.

It vobis notum quia magna congregatio nobilum in ipsa solemnitate Pascali, Romæ cum Domino Papa Joanne, & imperatore Conrado erat, scilicet omnes principes gentium a monte Gargano, usque ad istum proximum Mare : qui omnes me & honorifice suscepere, & magnificis donis honoravere. Maxime autem ab imperatore donis variis & muneribus pretiosis honoratus sum, tam in vasis aureis & argenteis, quam in palliis & vestibus valde pretiosis. Locutus sum igitur cum ipso imperatore, & Domino Papa, & principibus qui ibi erant, de necessitatibus totius populi mei, tam Angli quam Dani, ut eis concederetur lex æquior, & pax securior in via Romam adeundi, & ne tot clausuris per viam arcerentur, & propter injustum teloneum fatigarentur. Annuitque postulatis Imperator, & Rodulphus Rex, qui maxime ipsarum clausurarum dominatur, cunctique principes edictis firmarunt, ut homines mei tam Mercatores, quàm alii orandi gratia viatores, absque omni anguria clausurarum & teloneariorum, cum firma pace Romam eant & redeant.

The same in English.

[I. 127.]

YOu are to understand, that at the feast of Easter, there was a great company of Nobles with Pope John and Conradus the Emperour assembled at Rome, namely all the Princes of the nations from mount Garganus unto the West Ocean sea. Who all of them

Garganus a mountaine of Apulia in Italie.

honourably interteined me, and welcomed mee with rich
and magnificent gifts : but especially the Emperour
bestowed divers costly presents and rewards upon mee,
both in vessels of golde and silver, and also in cloakes
and garments of great value. Wherefore I conferred
with the Emperour himselfe and the Pope, and with
the other Princes who were there present, concerning the
necessities of all my subjects both Englishmen and
Danes ; that a more favourable law & secure peace in
their way to Rome might bee graunted unto them, and
that they might not bee hindered by so many stops
& impediments in their journey, and wearied by reason
of injust exactions. And the Emperour condescended
unto my request, and King Rodulphus also, who hath
greatest authoritie over the foresaid stops and streights,
and all the other princes confirmed by their Edicts,
that my subjects, as well Marchants, as others who
travailed for devotions sake, should without all hinderance and restraint of the foresaid stops and customers,
goe unto Rome in peace, and returne from thence in
safetie.

The flourishing state of Marchandise in the Citie
    of London in the dayes of Willielmus Mal-
    mesburiensis, which died in the yeere 1142.
    in the reigne of K. Stephen.

Guliel.
Malmesb. de
gestis pont.
Anglorum lib.
2.

Aud longe a Rofa quasi viginti quinque milliariis
est Londonia Civitas nobilis, opima civium
divitiis, constipata negociatorum ex omni terra,
& maxime ex Germania venientium, commerciis. Unde
fit ut cum ubique in Anglia caritas victualium pro sterili
proventu messium sit, ibi necessaria distrahantur & eman-
tur minore, quàm alibi, vel vendentium compendio,
vel ementium dispendio. Peregrinas invehit merces
Civitatis finibus Tamesis fluvius famosus, qui citra urbem
ad 80. milliaria fonticulo fusus, ultra plus 70. nomen
profert.

The same in English.

NOt farre from Rochester, about the distance of
five and twenty miles, standeth the Noble Citie
of London, abounding with the riches of the inhabitants, and being frequented with the traffique of Marchants resorting thither out of all nations, and especially
out of Germanie. Whereupon it commeth to passe, that *Germanie.*
when any generall dearth of victuals falleth out in England, by reason of the scarcitie of corne, things necessary
may there be provided and bought with lesse gaine unto
the sellers, and with lesse hinderance and losse unto the
buyers, then in any other place of the Realme. Outlandish wares are conveighed into the same Citie by the
famous river of Thames: which river springing out of
a fountaine 80. miles beyond the Citie, is called by one
and the selfe same name. 70. miles beneath it.

The aforesaid William of Malmesburie writeth of
    traffike in his time to Bristowe in his fourth
    booke de gestis pontificum Anglorum, after
    this maner.

IN eadem valle est vicus celeberrimus Bristow
nomine, in quo est navium portus ab Hiber-
nia & Norwegia & cæteris transmarinis terris
venientium receptaculum, ne scilicet genitalibus divitiis
tam fortunata regio peregrinarum opum frauderetur
commercio.

The same in English.

IN the same valley stands the famous Towne of
Bristow, with an Haven belonging thereunto, which
is a commodious and safe receptacle for all ships directing
their course for the same, from Ireland, Norway, and *Norway.*
other outlandish and foren countreys: namely that a
region so fortunate and blessed with the riches that
nature hath vouchsafed thereupon should not bee destitute of the wealth and commodities of other lands.

[I. 128.] The league betweene Henry the second and Fredericke Barbarossa Emperour of Germanie, wherein is mention of friendly traffike betweene the Marchants of the Empire and England, confirmed in the yeere of our Lord 1157. recorded in the first Booke and seventeenth Chapter of Radevicus Canonicus Frisingensis, being an appendix to Otto Frisingensis.

Bidem tunc affuere etiam Henrici Regis Angliæ missi, varia & preciosa donaria multo lepore verborum adornata præstantes. Inter quæ papilionem unum quantitate maximum, qualitate optimum perspeximus. Cujus si quantitatem requiris, non nisi machinis & instrumentorum genere & adminiculo levari poterat : si qualitatem, nec materia nec opere ipsum putem aliquando ab aliquo hujusce apparatu superatum iri. Literas quoque mellito sermone plenas pariter direxerat, quarum hic tenor fuit. Præcordiali amico suo, Frederico Dei gratia Romanorum imperatori invictissimo, Henricus Rex Angliæ, dux Normanniæ, & Aquitaniæ, & Comes Andegavensis, salutem, & veræ dilectionis concordiam. Excellentiæ vestræ quantas possumus referimus grates, dominantium optime, quod nos nunciis vestris visitare, salutare literis, muneribus prævenire, & quod his charius amplectimur, pacis & amoris invicem dignatus estis fœdera inchoare. Exultavimus, & quodammodo animum nobis crescere, & in majus sensimus evehi dum vestra promissio, in qua nobis spem dedistis, in disponendis Regni nostri negociis, alacriores nos reddidit, & promptiores. Exultavimus inquam, & tota mente magnificentiæ vestræ assurreximus, id vobis in sincero cordis affectu respondentes, quod quicquid ad honorem vestrum spectare noverimus, pro posse nostro effectui mancipare

parati sumus. Regnum nostrum, & quicquid ubique nostræ subjicitur ditioni vobis exponimus & vestræ committimus potestati, ut ad vestrum nutum omnia disponantur, & in omnibus vestri fiat voluntas imperii. Sit igitur inter nos & populos nostros dilectionis & *Commercia* pacis unitas indivisa, commercia tuta : Ita tamen ut *inter Germa-* vobis, qui dignitate præminetis, imperandi cedat authori- *nos & Anglos.* tas, nobis non deerit voluntas obsequendi. Et sicut vestræ Serenitatis memoriam vestrorum excitat in nobis munerum largitio, sic vos nostri quoque reminisci præoptamus, mittentes quæ pulchriora penes nos erant, & vobis magis placitura. Attendite itaque dantis affectum, non data, & eo animo quo dantur accipite. De manu beati Jacobi, super qua nobis scripsistis, in ore magistri Hereberti & Guilielmi Clerici nostri verbum posuimus. Teste Thoma Cancellario apud Northanton.

The same in English.

THere were present also the same time, the messengers of Henry king of England presenting divers rich and precious gifts, and that with great learning & eloquence of speech. Amongst the which we saw a pavilion, most large in quantity, & most excellent in quality. For if you desire to know the quantitie therof, it could not be erected without engines and a kinde of instruments, and maine force : if the qualitie, I thinke there was never any furniture of the same kinde, that surpassed the same either in stuffe or workemanship. The said king directed his letters also, full of sugred speeches, the tenour whereof was this that followeth.

To his entirely beloved friend Frederick by the grace of God Emperour of the Romanes most invincible, Henry king of England, duke of Normandie and Aquitaine, Earle of Anjou wisheth health and concord of sincere amitie. We doe render unto your highnes (most renowmed and peerelesse Prince) exceeding great thanks for that you have so graciously vouchsafed by your messengers to visite us, in your letters to salute us, with your gifts to prevent us, and (which wee doe more highly esteeme of then all the rest) to beginne a league of peace and friendship betweene us. We rejoyced, and in a maner sensibly felt our selves to bee greatly emboldened, and our courage to encrease, whilest your promise, whereby you put us in good comfort, did make us more cheerefull and resolute, in managing the affaires of our kingdome. We rejoyced (I say) & in our secret cogitations did humble obeisance unto your Majestie, giving you at this time to understand from the sincere & unfained affection of our heart, that whatsoever we shal know to tend unto your honour, we are, to our power most ready to put in practise. Our kingdome, and whatsoever is under our juris-diction we doe offer unto you, and commit the same unto your highnesse, that all matters may be disposed according to your direction, and that your pleasure may in all things be fulfilled. Let there be therefore betweene our selves and our subjects, an indivisible unitie of friendship and peace, and safe trade of Marchandize: yet so, as that unto you (who excell in dignitie) authoritie in commanding may bee ascribed, and diligence in obey-ing shall not want in us. And as the liberalitie of your rewards doeth often put us in remembrance of your Majestie, even so in like maner sending unto

[I. 129.] your Highnesse the most rare things in our custodie, and which we thought should be most acceptable unto you, wee doe most heartily wish that your selfe also would not altogether bee unmindefull of us. Have respect therefore not unto the gifts, but unto the affection of the giver, and accept of them with that minde, where-with they are offered unto you.

Concerning the hand of S. James, about which you wrote unto us, we have sent you word by M. Herbert, and by William the Clerke. Witnes Thomas our Chancelour at Northanton.

A generall safe conduct graunted to all forreine
Marchants by king John in the ‖ first yeere ‖ 1199.
of his reigne, as appeareth in the Records of
the Tower, Anno 1. Regis Joannis.

Oannes Dei gratia &c. Majori & Com-
munitati Londinensi salutem. Sciatis
voluntatem esse nostram, quod omnes
Mercatores de quacunque fuerint terra
salvum habeant conductum ire & redire
cum mercibus suis in Angliam. Volu- *Solitæ merca-*
mus etiam quod eandem habeant pacem *torum consue-*
tudines.
in Anglia, quam Mercatores de Anglia habent in terris
illis unde fuerunt egressi. Et ideo vobis præcipimus,
quod hoc faciatis denunciari in Balliva vestra, & firmiter
teneri ; permittentes eos ire & redire sine impedimento
per debitas & rectas & solitas consuetudines in Balliva
vestra. Teste Galfredo filio Petri comite Essexiæ apud
Kinefard 5. die Aprilis.

In eadem forma scribitur vicecomiti Sudsex, Majori &
communitati Civitatis Winton, Ballivo de Southampton,
Ballivo de Lenne, Ballivo Kent, Vicecomiti Norffolciæ &
Suffolciæ, Vicecomiti dorset & Sommerset, Baronibus de
quinque portubus, Vicecomiti de Southampton sire, Vicecomiti de Herteford & Essex, Vicecomiti Cornubiæ &
Devon.

The same in English.

JOhn by the grace of God &c. to the Maior and
communaltie of London, greeting. You are to
understand, that it is our pleasure, that all Marchants
of what nation soever, shall have safe conduct to passe
and repasse with their Marchandize into England. It
is our will also, that they be vouchsafed the same favour
in England, which is granted unto the English Marchants
in those places from whence they come. And therefore
we give you in charge, that you cause this to be pub-

lished, and proclaimed in your bailiwicke, & firmely to
be observed, permitting them to goe & come, without
impediment, according to the due, right and ancient
customes used in your said Bailiwicke. Witnesse
Geofry Fitz-Peter Earle of Essex at Kinefard the 5.
day of April.

The same forme of writing was sent to the sherife of
Sudsex, to the Maior and communaltie of the Citie of
Winchester, to the Baily of Southampton, the Baily
Lenne, the Baily of Kent, the sherife of Norfolke and
Suffolke, the sherife of Dorset and Sommerset, the
Barons of the Cinque-ports, the sherife of Southampton-
shire, the sherife of Hertford and Essex, the sherife
of Cornewal and Devon.

Literæ regis Henrici tertii ad Haquinum Regem
     Norwegiæ de pacis fœdere & intercursu mer-
candisandi ‖ Anno 1. Henrici 3.

Enricus Dei gratia &c. Haquino eadem
gratia Regi Norwegiæ salutem. Immensas
nobilitati vestræ referimus gratiarum
actiones de his quæ per literas vestras &
prudentem virum Abbatem de Lisa, nobis
significastis, volentes & desiderantes fœdus
pacis & dilectionis libenter nobiscum inire,
& nobiscum confœderari. Bene autem placet & placebit
nobis quod terræ nostræ communes sint, & Mercatores &
homines qui sunt de potestate vestra libere & sine
impedimento terram nostram adire possint, & homines &
Mercatores nostri similiter terram vestram. Dum tamen
literas vestras patentes super hoc nobis destinetis, & nos
vobis nostras transmittemus. Interim autem bene
volumus & concedimus, quod Mercatores tam de terra
vestra quàm nostra eant, veniant, & recedant per terras
nostras. Et si quid vestræ sederit voluntati, quod facere
valeamus, id securè nobis significetis. Detinuimus autem
adhuc Abbatem prædictum, ut de navi vestra & rebus in

ea contentis pro posse nostro restitutionem fieri faceremus : per quem de statu nostro & Regni nostri vos
certificare curabimus, & quàm citius &c.   Teste me ipso
apud Lamhithe decimo die Octobris.

Eodem modo scribitur S. Duci Norwegiæ ibidem &
eodem die.

The letters of King Henry the third unto [I. 130.]
   Haquinus King of Norway concerning a
   treatie of peace and mutuall traffique of
   marchandize, &c.

HEnry by the grace of God, &c. unto Haquinus by
the same grace King of Norway, sendeth greeting.
Wee render unto your highnesse unspeakeable thanks
for those things which by your letters, and by your
discreete subject the Abbat of Lisa, you have signified
unto us, and also for that you are right willing and desirous to begin and to conclude betweene us both, a league
of peace and amitie.   And wee for our part both nowe
are, and hereafter shalbe well contented, that both our
lands be common, to the ende that the Marchants and
people of your dominions may freely and without
impediment resort unto our land, and our people and
Marchants may likewise have recourse unto your territories.   Provided, that for the confirmation of this
matter, you send unto us your letters patents, and wee
will send ours also unto you.   Howbeit in the meane
while wee doe will and freely graunt, that the Marchants
both of our and your lands, may goe, come, and returne
to and from both our Dominions.   And if there be ought
in your minde, whereby we might stand you in any
stead, you may boldly signifie the same unto us.   Wee
have as yet deteined the foresaid Abbat, that wee might,
to our abilitie, cause restitution to be made for your ship,
and for the things therein contained : by whome wee will
certifie you of our owne estate, and of the estate of our

kingdome so soone, &c.   Witnesse our selfe at Lamhith the tenth of October.

Another letter in the same forme and to the same effect was there and then sent unto S. Duke of Norway.

Mandatum pro Coga Regis Norwegiæ Anno 13. Henrici 3.

Andatum est omnibus Ballivis portuum in quos ventura est Coga de Norwegia, in qua venerint in Angliam milites Regis Norwegiæ & Mercatores Saxoniæ, quod cum prædictam Cogam in portus suos venire contigerit, salvò permittant ipsam Cogam in portubus suis morari, quamdiu necesse habuerit, & libere sine impedimento inde recedere quando voluerint.   Teste Rege.

The same in English.
A Mandate for the King of Norway his Ship called the Cog.

WEe will and commaund all bailifes of Portes, at the which the Cog of Norway (wherein certaine of the king of Norwaie his souldiers, and certaine Marchants of Saxonie are comming for England) shall touch, that, when the foresaid Cog shall chance to arrive at any of their Havens, they doe permit the said Cog safely to remaine in their said Havens so long as neede shall require, and without impediment also freely to depart thence, whensoever the governours of the sayd ship shall thinke it expedient.   Witnesse the King.

Carta pro Mercatoribus de Colonia anno 20. Henrici 3. Confirmata per Regem Edwardum primum 8. Julii Anno Regni 18. prout extat in rotulo cartarum de Anno 18. Regis Edwardi primi.

|| Antiqua consuetudo Gildhallæ Coloniensium Londini.

Ex Archiepiscopis &c. salutem.   Sciatis nos quietos clamasse pro nobis & hæredibus nostris dilectos nostros, Cives de Colonia, & mercandisam suam de illis duobus solidis, || quos solebant dare de Gildhalla sua

KING HENRY III.'S CHARTER

London, & de omnibus aliis consuetudinibus & demandis,
quæ pertinent ad nos in London, & per totam terram
nostram ; & quod liberè possunt ire ad ferias, per totam
terram nostram & emere & vendere in villa London &
alibi, salva libertate Civitatis nostræ London. Quare
volumus & firmiter præcipimus pro nobis & hæredibus
nostris, quod prædicti cives de Colonia prænominatas
libertates & liberas consuetudines habeant per totam
terram nostram Angliæ sicut prædictum est. His testibus,
venerabili patre Waltero Caerleolensi Episcopo, Willielmo
de Ferariis, Gilberto Basset, Waltero de Bello campo,
Hugone Disspenser, Waltero Marescallo, Galfrido Dis-
penser, Bartholomæo Pech, Bartholomæo de Saukevill, &
aliis. Data per manum venerabilis patris Radulphi Cicis-
trensis Episcopi, Cancellarii nostri apud Davintre Octavo
die Novembris, Anno Regni nostri vicesimo.

The same in English.

A Charter graunted for the behalfe of the Marchants of Colen in the twentieth yeere of
Henry the third, confirmed by King Edward
the first, as it is extant in the roule of Charters, in the eighteenth yeere of King Edward
the first.

THe King unto Archbishops &c. greeting. Be it
knowen unto you, that wee have quite claimed, and
for us and our heires released our welbeloved the Citizens
of Colen and their marchandize, from the payment of
those two shillings which they were wont to pay out of
their Gildhall at London, and from all other customes and
demaunds, which perteine unto us, either in London, or
in any other place of our Dominions : and that they may
safely resort unto Fayers throughout our whole Kingdome,
and buy and sell in the Citie of London. Wherefore we
will and firmely command for us and our heires, that the
forenamed Marchants of Colen may enjoy the liberties
and free priviledges above-mentioned, throughout our

The ancient custome of the Coloners Gildhall in London.

whole kingdome of England as is aforesaid. Witnesses, the reverend father Walter Bishop of Carlil, William de Ferariis, Gilbert Basset, Walter de Beau-champ, Hugh Disspenser, Walter Marescal, Geofrie Disspensser, Bartholomew Peach, Bartholomew de Saukevill and others. Given by the hand of the reverend father Ralph Bishop of Chichester and our Chauncellour at Davintre, the eight day of November, in the twentieth yeere of our reigne.

Carta Lubecensibus ad septennium concessa.
Anno 41. Henrici 3.

Ricardus Comes Cornubiæ Rex Romanorum.

Enricus dei gracia Rex Angliæ, dominus Hiberniæ, dux Normanniæ, Aquitaniæ, & Comes Andegaviæ, omnibus Ballivis suis salutem. Sciatis nos ad instantiam dilecti & fidelis fratris nostri Ricardi Comitis Cornubiæ in Regem Romanorum electi, suscepisse in protectionem & defensionem nostram & salvum & securum conductum nostrum Burgenses de Lubek in Alemania cum omnibus rebus & mercandisis quas in Regnum nostrum deferent, vel facient deferri. Et eis concessimus, quod de omnibus rebus & mercandisis suis nihil capiatur ad opus nostrum vel alterius contra voluntatem eorundem ; sed libere vendant & negocientur inde in Regno prædicto, prout sibi viderint expedire. Et ideo vobis mandamus, quod dictis Burgensibus vel eorum nunciis in veniendo in terram nostram cum rebus & mercandisis suis, ibidem morando, & inde recedendo, nullum inferatis, aut ab aliis inferri permittatis impedimentum aut gravamen. Nec eos contra quietantiam prædictam vexetis, aut ab aliis vexari permittatis. In cujus rei testimonium has literas nostras fieri fecimus patentes per septennium durantes : Dum tamen iidem Burgenses interim bene & fideliter se habuerint erga præfatum electum fratrem nostrum. Teste meipso apud Westmonasterium undecimo die Maii Anno Regni nostri quadragesimo primo. Hæc litera duplicata est, pro Burgensibus & mercatoribus Dacis, Brunswig, & Lubek.

Carta conditionalis.

The same in English.

The charter of Lubek granted for seven yeeres, obtained in the one and fortieth yeere of Henry the third.

HEnry by the grace of God King of England, Lord of Ireland, Duke of Normandie and Aquitaine, and Earle of Anjou, to all his Bailifs sendeth greeting. Know ye that at the instant request of our welbeloved and trusty brother Richard Earle of Cornewal being of late elected king of the Romanes, we have received under our protection and defence, and under our safe and secure conduct, the citizens of Lubek in Alemain, with all their goods and wares, which they shall bring or cause to be brought into our kingdome. We have also granted unto them, that of all their goods and merchandize, nothing shal be seized unto the use of our selves, or of any other without their owne consent, but that they may freely sell and exercise traffike therewith, according as they shall thinke expedient. And therefore we straightly command you, that neither your selves do offer, nor that you permit any other to offer any impediment or molestation unto the said Burgers or unto their messengers, either at their comming into our land, with their goods and marchandize, in the time of their abode there, or at their departure from thence, and that yee neither molest them your selves, nor yet suffer them by others to be molested, contrary to the aforesaid Charter. In testimonie whereof, we have caused these our Letters to be made Patents, during the space of seven yeeres next following.

Provided, that the sayd Burghers doe in the meane time behave themselves well and faithfully towards our foresaid elected brother. Witnesse our selves at Westminster the eleventh day of March, in the one and fortieth yeere of our reigne.

This Letter was doubled, namely for the Burghers, and the Marchants of Denmarke, of Brunswig, and of Lubecke.

Carta pro Mercatoribus Alemanniæ, qui habent
domum in London, quæ Gildhalla Teutonicorum vulgariter nuncupatur Anno 44.
Henrici tertii, & Anno primo & 29.
Edwardi primi renovata & confirmata.

D instantiam Serenissimi principis Rich-
ardi Romanorum Regis charissimi fratris nostri concedimus mercatoribus
Alemanniæ, illis videlicet qui habent
domum in Civitate nostra London,
quæ Gildhalla Teutonicorum vulgariter
nuncupatur, quod eos universos manu-
tenebimus per totum Regnum nostrum in omnibus
iisdem libertatibus & liberis consuetudinibus, quibus
ipsi nostris & ‖ progenitorum nostrorum temporibus
usi sunt & gavisi. Ipsosque extra hujusmodi libertates & liberas consuetudines non trahemus, nec trahi
aliquatenus permittemus. In cujus rei testimonium has
literas nostras fieri fecimus patentes.

‖ *Nota anti-
quitatem.*

The same in English.

A charter for the Marchants of Almaine, who
have an house at London commonly called
‡ the Guild hall of the Dutch, graunted in
the 44. yeere of Henry the third, renued
and confirmed in the 1. & 29. yeere of
Edward the first.

‡ *The Stiliard.*

AT the instant request of the most gracious Prince
Richard king of the Romanes our most deare
brother, wee doe graunt unto the Marchants of Alemain
(namely unto those that have an house in our citie of
London, commonly called the Guildhall of the Dutch
Merchants) that we will, throughout our whole Realme,
maintaine all and every of them, in all those liberties
and free customes, which both in our times, and in the

times of our progenitors, they have used and enjoyed.
Neither will we inforce them beyond these liberties and
free customes, nor in any wise permit them to be inforced. In witnesse whereof, wee have caused these
our letters to be made patents.

Mandatum regis Edwardi primi de mercatoribus [I. 133.]
alienigenis.

MErcatores extranei vendant mercimonia sua in
civitate London &c. infra quadraginta dies post
ingressum suum, anno 3. Edwardi primi.

The same in English.

A mandate of king Edward the first concerning
outlandish marchants.

WE will and command that outlandish marchants
doe sel their wares in the citie of London &c.
within forty dayes of their arrivall.

The great Charter granted unto forreine marchants by king Edward the first, in the 31
yeare of his reigne commonly called Carta
mercatoria, Anno Domini 1303.

Dwardus Dei gratia Rex Angliæ, Dominus
Hiberniæ, dux Aquitaniæ, Archiepiscopis,
Episcopis, Abbatibus, Prioribus, Comiti-
bus, Baronibus, Justitiariis, Vicecomiti-
bus, præpositis, ministris, & omnibus
ballivis & fidelibus suis salutem. Circa
bonum statum omnium mercatorum sub-
scriptorum regnorum, terrarum, & provinciarum, videlicet Alemanniæ, Franciæ, Hispaniæ, Portugalliæ,
Navarræ, Lombardiæ, Thusciæ, Provinciæ, Cataloniæ,
ducatus nostri Aquitaniæ, Tholosaniæ, Caturluni, Flandriæ, Brabantiæ, & omnium aliarum terrarum &
locorum extraneorum, quocunque nomine censeantur,
venientium in regnum nostrum Angliæ & ibidem

conversantium nos præcipua cura sollicitat, qualiter
sub nostro dominio tranquillitatis & plenæ securitatis
immunitas eisdem mercatoribus futuris temporibus
præparetur. Ut itaque vota ipsorum reddantur ad
nostra & regni nostri servitia promptiora, ipsorum
petitionibus favorabiliter annuentes, & pro statu eorundem plenius assecurando, in forma quæ sequitur ordin-
antes, pro nobis & hæredibus nostris in perpetuum
subscripta dictis mercatoribus duximus concedenda.

1. Inprimis videlicet quod omnes mercatores dictorum
regnorum & terrarum salvè & secure sub tuitione
& protectione nostra in dictum regnum nostrum
Angliæ, & ubique infra potestatem nostram alibi
veniant cum mercandisis suis quibuscunque, de mura-
gio, pontagio & pannagio liberi & quieti. Quodque
infra idem regnum & potestatem nostram in civitatibus,
burgis, & villis mercatoriis possunt mercari duntaxat
in grosso tam cum indigenis seu incolis ejusdem regni
& potestatis nostræ prædictæ, quàm cum alienigenis,
extraneis, vel privatis. Ita tamen quod merces, quæ
vulgariter merceriæ vocantur, ac species, minutatim
vendi possint, prout antea fieri consuevit. Et quod
omnes prædicti mercatores mercandisas suas, quas ipsos
ad prædictum regnum & potestatem nostram adducere,
seu infra idem regnum & potestatem nostram emere,
vel aliàs acquirere contigerit, possint quo voluerint tam
infra regnum & potestatem nostram prædictam, quàm
Exceptio extra ducere vel portare facere, præterquam ad terras
contra notorios manifestorum & notoriorum hostium regni nostri, sol-
regni hostes. vendo consuetudines quas debebunt: vinis duntaxat
exceptis, quæ de eodem regno seu potestate nostra,
postquam infra idem regnum seu potestatem nostram
ducta fuerint, sine voluntate & licentia speciali non
liceat eis educere quoquo modo.

2. Item quod prædicti mercatores in civitatibus, burgis,
& villis prædictis pro voluntate sua hospitari valeant,
& morari cum bonis suis ad gratiam ipsorum, quorum
sunt hospitia sive domus.

EDWARD I.'S GREAT CHARTER

Item quod quilibet contractus per ipsos mercatores 3.
cum quibuscunque personis undecunque fuerint super
quocunque genere mercandisæ initus, firmus sit &
stabilis, ita quod neuter mercatorum ab illo contractu
possit recedere, vel resilire, postquam denarius Dei inter
principales personas contrahentes datus fuerit & receptus.
Et si forsan super contractu ejusmodi contentio oriatur,
fiat inde probatio aut inquisitio secundum usus & consuetudines feriarum & villarum, ubi dictum contractum [I. 134.]
fieri contigerit & iniri.

Item promittimus præfatis mercatoribus pro nobis & 4.
hæredibus nostris in perpetuum concedentes, quod
nullam prisam vel arrestationem, seu dilationem occasione prisæ de cætero de mercimoniis, mercandisis seu
aliis bonis suis per nos vel alium seu alios pro aliqua
necessitate vel casu contra voluntatem ipsorum mercatorum aliquatenus faciemus, aut fieri patiemur, nisi
statim soluto precio pro quo ipsi mercatores aliis ejusmodi mercimonia vendere possint, vel eis aliter satisfacto,
ita quod reputent se contentos: Et quod super mercimonia, mercandisas, seu bona ipsorum per nos vel ministros nostros nulla appreciatio aut estimatio imponetur.

Item volumus quod omnes ballivi & ministri feriarum, 5.
civitatum, burgorum, & villarum mercatoriarum mercatoribus antedictis conquerentibus coram iis celerem
justitiam faciant de die in diem sine dilatione secundum
legem mercatoriam, de universis & singulis quæ per *Lex*
eandem legem poterunt terminari. Et si forte inveni- *mercatoria.*
atur defectus in aliquo ballivorum vel ministrorum prædictorum, unde iidem mercatores vel eorum aliquis
dilationis incommoda sustinuerint vel sustineant, licet
mercator versus partem in principali recuperaverit damna
sua, nihilominus ballivus vel minister alius versus nos,
prout delictum exigit puniatur. Et punitionem istam
concedimus in favorem mercatorum prædictorum pro
eorum justitia maturanda.

Item quod in omnibus generibus placitorum, salvo 6.
casu criminis pro quo infligenda est pœna mortis, ubi

mercator implacitatus fuerit, vel alium implacitaverit, cujuscunque conditionis idem implacitatus extiterit, extraneus vel privatus, in nundinis, civitatibus, sive Burgis, ubi fuerit sufficiens copia mercatorum prædictarum terrarum, & inquisitio fieri debeat, sit medietas inquisitionis de eiisdem mercatoribus, & medietas altera de probis & legalibus hominibus loci illius ubi placitum illud esse contigerit. Et si de mercatoribus dictarum terrarum numerus non inveniatur sufficiens, ponentur in inquisitione illi qui idonei invenientur ibidem, & residii sint de aliis bonis hominibus & idoneis de locis in quibus placitum illud erit.

7. Item volumus, ordinamus, & statuimus, quod in qualibet villa mercatoria & feria regni nostri prædicti & alibi infra potestatem nostram pondus nostrum in certo loco ponatur, & ante ponderationem statera in præsentia emptoris & venditoris vacua videatur, & quod brachia sint equalia : & ex tunc ponderator ponderet in æquali. Et cum stateram posuerit in æquali statim amoveat manus suas, ita quod remaneat in æquali : quodque per totum regnum & potestatem nostram sit unum pondus & una mensura : & signo standardi nostri signentur : Et quod quilibet possit habere stateram unius quaternionis, & infra, ubi contra domini loci, aut libertatem per nos & antecessores nostros concessam illud non fuerit, sive contra villarum & feriarum consuetudinem hactenus observatam.

8. Item volumus & concedimus, quod aliquis certus homo fidelis & discretus Londini residens assignetur justitiarius mercatoribus memoratis, coram quo valeant specialiter placitare, & debita sua recuperare celeriter, si Vicecomites & Majores eis non facerent de die in diem celeris justitiæ complementum : Et inde fiat Commissio extra Cartam præsentem concessa mercatoribus antedictis : scilicet de his quæ sunt inter mercatores & mercatores secundum legem mercatoriam deducenda.

Lex mercatoria quæ ?

9. Item ordinamus & statuimus, & ordinationem illam statutumque pro nobis & hæredibus nostris in perpetuum

volumus firmiter observari, quod pro quacunque libertate, quam nos vel hæredes nostri de cætero concedemus, præfati mercatores supradictas libertates vel earum aliquam non amittant. Pro prædictis autem libertatibus & liberis consuetudinibus obtinendis, & prisis nostris remittendis iidem supradicti mercatores universi & singuli pro se & omnibus aliis de partibus suis nobis concorditer & unanimiter concesserunt, quod de quolibet dolio vini, quod adducent vel adduci facient infra regnum & potestatem nostram, & unde marinariis fretum solvere tenebuntur, solvent nobis & hæredibus nostris nomine Custumæ duos *Antiquæ* solidos ultra antiquas custumas debitas & in denariis solvi *Custumæ.* consuetas nobis, aut alias infra quadraginta dies, postquam extra naves ad terram posita fuerint dicta vina. Item de quolibet sacco lanarum, quem dicti mercatores, aut alii nomine ipsorum ement & è regno educent, aut emi & educi facient, solvent quadraginta denarios de incremento ultra custumam antiquam dimidiæ marcæ, quæ prius fuerat persoluta. Et pro lasta coriorum extra regnum & potestatem nostram vehendorum dimidiam marcam supra id quod ex antiqua custuma ante solvebatur. Et similiter de trecentis pellibus lanitis extra regnum & potestatem nostram ducendis quadraginta denarios ultra certum illud, quod de antiqua custuma fuerat prius datum. Item duos [I. 135.] solidos de quolibet scarlato & panno tincto in grano. Item decem & octo denarios de quolibet panno, in quo pars grani fuerit intermixta. Item duodecim denarios de quolibet panno alio sine grano. Item duodecim denarios de qualibet æris quintalla.

Cumque de præfatis mercatoribus nonnulli eorum alias   10. exercere soleant mercandisas, ut de Averio ponderis, & de aliis rebus subtilibus, sicut de pannis Tarsensibus, de serico, & cindallis, de seta & aliis diversis mercibus, & de equis etiam & aliis animalibus, blado & aliis rebus & mercandisis multimodis, quæ ad certam custumam facile poni non poterunt, iidem mercatores concesserunt dare nobis & hæredibus nostris de qualibet libra argenti estimationis seu valoris rerum & mercandisarum hujus-

modi, quocunque nomine censeantur, tres denarios de
libra in introitu rerum & mercandisarum ipsarum in
regnum & potestatem nostram prædictam infra viginti
dies postquam hujusmodi res & mercandisæ in regnum &
potestatem nostram adductæ & etiam ibidem exoneratæ
seu venditæ fuerint. Et similiter tres denarios de qualibet
libra argenti in eductione quarumcunque rerum & mercandisarum hujusmodi emptarum in regno & potestate
nostris prædictis ultra custumas nobis aut aliis ante datas.
Et super valore & estimatione rerum & mercandisarum
hujusmodi de quibus tres denarii de qualibet libra argenti
sicut prædicitur sunt solvendi, credatur eis per literas,
quas de Dominis aut sociis suis ostendere poterunt : Et
si literas non habeant stetur in hac parte prædictorum
mercatorum, si præsentes fuerint, vel valetorum suorum
in eorundem mercatorum absentia, juramentis.

11. Liceat insuper sociis de societate prædictorum mercatorum infra regnum & potestatem nostram prædictas,
lanas vendere aliis suis sociis, & similiter emere ab iisdem
absque custuma solvenda. Ita tamen quod dictæ lanæ ad
tales manus non deveniant, quod de custuma nobis debita
defraudemur. Et præterea est sciendum, quod postquam
supradicti mercatores semel in uno loco infra regnum &
potestatem nostram custumam nobis concessam superius
pro mercandisis suis in forma solverint supradicta, &
suum habeant inde warantum, sive hujusmodi mercandisæ
infra regnum & potestatem nostram remaneant, sive
exterius deferantur, (exceptis vinis, quæ de regno &
potestate nostris prædictis sine voluntate & licentia nostra
sicut prædictum est, nullatenus educantur :) Volumus, ac
pro nobis, ac hæredibus nostris concedimus, quod nulla
exactio, prisa, vel præstatio, aut aliquod onus super
personas mercatorum prædictorum, mercandisas seu bona
eorundem aliquatenus imponatur contra formam expressam
superius & concessam. His testibus veracibus principali-
bus, Roberto Cantuariensi Archiepiscopo totius Angliæ
primate, Waltero Coventriæ & Lichfildiæ episcopo,
Henrico de Lacy Lincolniense, Humfredo de Bohum

comite Herfordiense & Essexiæ & Constabulo magno
Angliæ, Adomaro de Valentia, Galfrido de Gaymal,
Hugone de Lespensor, Waltero de Bello campo, senescallo
hospitii nostri, Roberto de Buriis, & aliis. Datum per
manum nostram apud Windesore, primo die Februarii,
anno regni nostri xxxi.

The aforesaid generall Charter in English.

EDward by the grace of God king of England, lord of
Ireland, duke of Aquitaine, to Archbishops, Bishops,
Abbots, Priors, Earles, Barons, Justices, Vicounts, governours, officers, and all bayliffes, and his faithfull people
sendeth greeting. Wee have speciall care for the good
estate of all marchants of the kingdomes, lands, and
countreis following : to wit of Almaine, France, Spaine,
Portugal, Navarre, Lombardie, Florence, Provence,
Catalonia, of our duchie of Aquitaine, Tholosa, Catur-
lune, Flanders, Brabant, and of all other forreine countreis
and places by what name soever they be called, which
come into our kingdome of England, and there remayne,
that the sayd marchants may live in quiet and full
securitie under our dominion in time to come. Wherefore that their hearts desires may bee more readily inclined
to our service and the service of our kingdome, wee
favourably agreeing to their petitions, for the fuller asring
of their estate, have thought good to graunt to the sayd
marchants for us and our heires for ever these priviledges
under written, ordaining in forme as followeth.

First, that all marchants of the sayd kingdomes and   1.
countreys may come into our kingdome of England, and
any where else into our dominion with their marchandises
whatsoever safely and securely under our defence and
protection without paying wharfage, pontage, or pannage.
And that in Cities, Boroughs, and market townes of the
sayd kingdome and dominion they may traffique onely by
the great as well with the naturall subjects and inhabitantes of our aforesayde kingdome and dominion, as with
forreiners, straungers, or private persons. Yet so, that

[I. 136.]

marchandises which are commonly called mercerie wares, and spices, may be sold by the small, as heretofore hath bin accustomed. And that all the aforesaid marchants may cary or cause to be caried whither they will, aswell within our realme or dominion, as out of the same ; *An exception for traficking with ye known enemies of the kingdome.* saving unto the countreis of the manifest and knowne enemies of our kingdome, those marchandises which they shall bring into our foresayd realme and dominion, or buy, or otherwise purchase in our sayd realme and dominion, paying such customes as they ought to doe : except onely wines, which it shall not be any wayes lawfull for them to cary out of our sayd realme and dominion without our speciall favour and licence, after they be once brought into our realme and dominion.

2.   Item that the aforesayd marchants may at their pleasure lodge & remaine with their goods in the cities, boroughs, and townes aforesaid, with the good liking of those which are owners of their lodgings.

3.   Item that every bargaine made by the said marchants with any maner of persons, of what places soever they be, for any kind of marchandise whatsoever, shalbe firme & stable, so that none of both the marchants shall shrinke or give backe from that bargaine, after that the earnest penie be once given and taken betweene the principall bargayners.   And if peradventure any strife arise about the same bargaine, the triall and inquirie thereof shall be made according to the uses and customes of the fayres and townes where it chanced that the said bargaine was made and contracted.

4.   Item, we promise the aforesaid marchants granting for ever for us and our heires, that from hence foorth we will not in any wise make nor cause to be made any stay or arrest, or any delay by reason of arrest of their wares, marchandises or other goods, by our selves, or by any other or others for any neede or accident against the will of the sayd marchants, without present payment of such a price as the marchants would have sold those marchandises for to other men, or without making of them other

satisfaction, so that they shall hold themselves well contented : and that no price or valuation shalbe set upon their wares, marchandises, & goods by us or by any officer of ours.

Item, we will that all bayliffes and officers of fayres, cities, boroughs, and market townes shall doe speedie justice from day to day without delay according to the lawe of Marchants to the aforesayd marchants when they shall complaine before them, touching all and singuler causes, which may be determined by the same law. And if default be found in any of the bayliffes or officers aforesayd, whereby the sayd marchants or any of them have sustained, or do sustaine any damage through delay, though the marchant recover his losses against the partie principall, yet the bayliffe or other officer shall be punished to us ward, according to the qualitie of the default. And wee doe grant this punishment in favour of the aforesayd marchants in regard of the hastening of their justice.

Item, that in al maner of pleas, saving in case where punishment of death is to be inflicted, where a marchant is impleaded, or sueth another, of what condition soever hee bee which is sued, whether stranger or home borne, in fayres, cities, or boroughs, where sufficient numbers of marchants of the foresayd countreis are, and where the triall ought to bee made, let the one halfe of the Jurie be of the sayd marchants, and the other halfe of good and lawfull men of the place where the suite shall fall out to bee : and if sufficient number of marchants of the sayd countries cannot bee found, those which shall be found fit in that place shall be put upon the jurie, and the rest shall be chosen of good and fit men of the places where such suit shall chance to be.

Item we will, we ordaine, and wee appoint, that in every market towne and fayre of our realme aforesayd and elsewhere within our dominion our weight shall bee set in some certaine place; and that before the weighing

5.
Where is this law now become ?

6.

7.

the balance shall bee seene emptie in the presence of the buyer and of the seller, and that the skales bee equall: and that afterward the weigher weigh in the equall balance. And when hee hath set the balances even, let him straightway remoove his hands, so that the balance way remayne even: And that throughout all our kingdome and dominion there be one weight and one measure, and that they be marked with the marke of our standard. And that every man may have a weight of one quarter of an hundred, and under, where the same hath not bin contrary to the liberty of the lord of the place, and contrary to the libertie granted by us and our predecessors, or contrary to the custome of townes and fayres which hath hitherto beene observed.

8.   Item we will and we grant that some certaine faythfull and discreete man resident in London be appointed to doe Justice to the aforesayd marchants, before whome they may have their sutes decided, and may speedilie recover their debts, if the Shiriffes and Maior should not from day to day give them speedy justice. And hereof let a Commission be made: which we grant unto the aforesaid marchants besides this present Charter: to wit of such things as betweene marchant and marchant are to be decided according to the lawe of marchants.

9.   Item we ordayne and appoynt, and wee will that this ordinance and statute shall firmely bee observed for ever for us and our heires, that the aforesayd marchants shal

[I. 137.]

not loose the aforesayd liberties nor any of them, for any liberty whatsoever, which wee or our heires hereafter shall grant. And for the obtayning of the aforesayd liberties and free customes, and for remission of our arresting of their goods, the aforesayd marchants all and every of them for themselves and all other of their parties with one accorde and one consent have granted unto us, that of every tunne of wine, which they shall bring or cause to be brought into our realme and dominion, for which they shall bee bound to pay

freight unto the mariners, besides the olde customes
which are due and were woont to bee payd unto us, they
will pay unto us and to our heires in the name of a
custome two shillings in money, either out of hande, or
else within fortie dayes after the sayd wines shall bee
brought on land out of the shippes. Item for every
sacke of wooll, which the sayd marchants or others in
their name shall buy and carie out of the realme, or
cause to bee brought and caried out, they will pay forty
pence above the old custome of halfe a marke, which
was payed heretofore: And for a last of hides to bee
caryed out of our realme and dominion halfe a marke
above that which heretofore was payed by the olde
custome. And likewise for three hundreth Felles with
the wooll on them to bee transported out of our realme
and dominion fortie pence, above that certaine rate which
before was payed by the olde custome: Also two
shillings upon every scarlate and every cloth died in
graine. Item eighteene pence for every cloth wherein
any kind of graine is mingled. Item twelve pence upon
every cloth dyed without graine. Item twelve pence
upon everie quintall of copper.

And whereas sundrie of the aforesayd marchants are
woont to exercise other marchandises, as of Haver de
pois, and other fine wares, as sarcenets, lawnes, cindalles,
and silke, and divers other marchandises, and to sell
horses and other beastes, corne, and sundrie other things
and marchandises, which cannot easily bee reduced unto
a certaine custome: the sayd marchants have granted to
give unto us, and to our heires of every pound of silver
of the estemation and value of these kinde of goods
and marchandises, by what name soever they be called,
three pence in the pound in the bringing in of these
goods into our realme and dominion aforesaid, within
twentie dayes after these goods and marchandises shall
be brought into our realme and dominion, and shall be
there unladen and solde. And likewise three pence upon
every pound of silver in the carying out of any such

goods and marchandises which are bought in our realme
and dominion aforesayd above the customes beforetime
payd unto us or any of our progenitors. And touching
the value and estimation of these goods and marchandises, whereof three pence of every pound of silver, as
is aforesayd, is to be payd, credite shalbe given unto
them upon the letters which they are able to shewe
from their masters or parteners. And if they have no
letters in this behalfe, we will stand to the othe of the
foresayd marchants if they bee present, or in their
absence to the othes of their servants.

Moreover, it shall be lawfull for such as be of the
company of the aforesayd marchants within our realme
and dominion aforesayd, to sell woolles to other of their
company, and likewise to buy of them without paying
of custome. Yet so, that the said wools come not to
such hands, that wee be defrauded of the custome due
unto us. And furthermore it is to be understood, that
after that the aforesaid marchants have once payed in
one place within our realme and dominion, the custome
above granted unto us in forme aforesayd for their
marchandises, & have their warrant therof, whether
these marchandises remayne within our kingdome or be
caried out (excepting wines, which in no wise shalbe carried
forth of our realme and dominion aforesayd, without
our favour & licence as is aforesayd) we wil and we grant
for us and our heires, that no execution, attachment, or
loane, or any other burthen be layd upon the persons
of the aforesayd marchants, upon their marchandises or
goods in any case, contrary to the forme before mentioned and granted. The faithfull & principall witnesses
of these presents are these, Robert Archbishop of Canter-
bury, Primate of all England, Walter bishop of Coven-
trey and Lichfield, Henry Lacie of Lincolne, Humfrey
de Bohume, Earle of Herford and Essex, high Constable
of England, Adomare of Valentia, Geofrey of Gaymal,
Hugh Spenser, Walter Beauchampe Seneschall of our
house, Robert of Bures, and others. Given by our

owne hand at Windesore the first day of February, in
the yere of our reigne xxxi.

De mercatoribus Angliæ in Norwegia arestatis, &
  eorum mercimoniis de arrestandis literæ Edwardi
  secundi anno sexto regni sui, Haquino regi
  Norwegiæ.

Agnifico principi domino Haquino Dei gratia regi
Norwegiæ illustri, amico suo charissimo Edwardus
eadem Dei gratia rex Angliæ, Dom. Hiberniæ, &
dux Aquitaniæ salutem cum dilectione sincera. Miramur
non modicum & in intimis conturbamur de gravaminibus
& oppressionibus quæ subditis nostris infra regnum [I. 138.]
vestrum causa negociandi venientibus his diebus plus
solito absque causa rationabili, sicut ex gravi querela
didicimus, inferuntur. Nuper siquidem Willihelmus
filius Laurentii de Waynfleete, Simon filius Alani de
eadem, Guido filius Mathei & eorum socii mercatores
nostri nobis conquerendo monstrarunt, quod cum ipsi
quosdam homines & servientes suos cum tribus navibus
suis ad partes regni vestri, ad negotiandum ibidem
transmisissent : & naves illæ in portu villæ vestræ de *Villa de*
Tonnesbergh halece & aliis bonis diversis usque ad *Tonnesbergh.*
magnam summam oneratæ fuissent : Et licet nautis
navium prædictarum hominibusque & servientibus prædictis à regno vestro liberè cum navibus & bonis prædictis
ad partes Angliæ redeundi vestras fieri feceritis de conductu, postmodum tamen antequam naves illæ propter
venti contrarietatem portum prædictum exire potuerunt,
quidam ballivi vestri naves prædictas cum hominibus &
bonis omnibus tunc existentibus in eisdem, occasione
mortis cujusdam militis nuper ballivi vestri in Vikia per
malefactores & piratas, dum naves prædictæ in portu
supradicto sicut præmittitur remanserunt supra mare ut
dicitur interfecti, de mandato vestro ut dicebant arrest-
arunt, & diu sub aresto hujusmodi detinebant, quousque
videlicet homines & marinarii prædicti de quadraginta

libris sterlingorum certo die statuto ad opus vestrum pro qualibet navi prædictarum solvendis inviti & coacti securitatem invenissent : Et similiter de eisdem navibus cum hominibus prædictis infra portum prædictum citra festum nativitatis Sancti Joannis Baptistæ proximo futuro ad standum tunc ibidem de personis & navibus suis vestræ gratiæ seu voluntatis arbitrio reducendis tres obsides ulterius liberassent : quod ipsis valde grave censetur, & auditu mirabile auribus audientium non immerito reputatur. Et quia contra rationem & æquitatem, omnemque justitiam fore dinoscitur, atque legem, quòd delinquentium culpæ seu demerita in personis vel rebus illorum qui criminis rei conscii vel participes, seu de hujusmodi delinquentium societate non fuerunt, aliqualiter ulciscantur, vestram amicitiam affectuose requirimus & rogamus, quatenus præmissa diligenti meditatione zelo justitiæ ponderantes, obsides prædictos jubere velitis ab hostagiamento hujusmodi liberari, dictamque securitatem relaxari penitus & resolvi. Scientes pro certo, quod si malefactores prædicti, qui dictum militem vestrum, ut dicitur, occiderunt, alicubi infra regnum seu potestatem nostram poterunt inveniri, de ipsis justitiam & judicium secundum legem & consuetudinem ejusdem regni fieri faciemus. Non enim possumus his diebus æquanimiter tolerare, quod naves prædictæ seu aliæ de regno nostro, quæ semper promptæ ad nostrum servitium esse debent, extra idem regnum ad partes remotas se divertant sine nostra licentia speciali. Quid autem ad hanc nostram instantiam faciendum decreveritis in præmissis, nobis si placeat rescribatis per præsentium portatorem. Datæ apud Windesore decimo sexto die Aprilis.

The same in English.

The letters of Edward the second unto Haquinus
king of Norway, concerning the English marchants arrested in Norway, and their goods
to be freed from arrest.

O the mighty Prince, lord Haquinus, by
the grace of God the famous king of
Norway his most deare friend, Edward
by the same grace of God, king of
England, lord of Ireland, duke of Aquitaine, greeting and sincere love. We
marvell not a little, and are much dis-
quieted in our cogitations, considering the greevances and
oppressions, which (as wee have beene informed by
pitifull complaints) are at this present, more then in times
past, without any reasonable cause inflicted upon our
subjects, which doe usually resort unto your kingdome
for traffiques sake. For of late one William the sonne of
Laurence of Wainfleete, and one Simon the sonne of Alan
of the same towne, and Guido the sonne of Mathew, and
their associates our marchants, in complayning wise
declared unto us : that having sent certaine of their factors
and servants, with three shippes into your dominions,
there to exercise traffique, and the sayd ships being laden
in the haven of your towne of Tonnesbergh, with Her- *The towne of*
rings and other commodities, to a great value : and also *Tonesbergh.*
the said mariners, men, and servants of the foresayd
shippes, being licenced by vertue of the safe conduct
which you had granted them, freely to returne from your
kingdome unto the parts of England with their ships and
goods aforesayd, but afterward not being able to depart
out of your haven by reason of contrary windes : certaine
of your bayliffes upon occasion of the slaughter of a
knight being himselfe also of late your bayliffe of Vikia,
committed by malefactors and Pirates upon the sea,
whilest the sayd shippes remained in the haven aforesayd,

did at your commandement (as they say) arrest, and for a long season also deteined under that arrest, the foresaid ships, with all the men and goods that were in them : namely untill such time, as the men and mariners aforesaide (beeing driven perforce, and constrained thereunto) should lay in sufficient securitie for the payment of fortie pounds sterling, upon a certain day appointed, unto your use, for every of the foresaide ships : and also untill they had moreover delivered three pledges, for the bringing of the saide ships and men backe againe into the foresaid haven, before the feast of the nativitie of S. John the Baptist next ensuing, then and there to stand unto your favour and curtesie, as touching the said persons, and those ships of theirs : which dealing, the parties themselves take very grievously, yea, and all others that heare thereof thinke it to be a strange and unwonted course. And because it is most undoubtedly contrary to all reason, equitie, justice, and lawe, that the faults or demerits of offenders should in any sort be punished in such persons, or in their goods, as neither have bene accessory nor partakers in the crime, nor have had any society with the saide offenders : we doe heartily intreat and request your Highnes, that weighing and pondering the matter in the balance of justice, you would of your love and friendship, command the foresaid pledges to be set at libertie, and the said securitie utterly to bee released and acquited. And know you this for a certaintie, that if the foresaide malefactors, who (as it is reported) slewe your Knight aforesaide, shall any where within our realme and dominions be found, we wil cause justice and judgement to bee executed upon them, according to the Lawe and custome of our sayde Realme. For we cannot in these times conveniently and well indure, that the ships aforesaide, or any other ships of our kingdome (which ought alwayes to be in a readinesse for our service) should without speciall licence, depart out of our saide kingdome, unto forreine dominions. Nowe, what you shall think good at this our request to performe in the premisses, may it please you by the bearer of these presents to returne an answere unto us. Geven at Windsore the 16. of April.

Another Letter of Edward the second, to Haqui- nus King of Norway, in the behalfe of cer- taine English Marchants.

MAgnifico Principi Dom. Haquino Dei gratia regi Norwegiæ illustri, amico suo charissimo, Edwardus eadem Dei gratia Rex Angliæ, dominus Hyberniæ, & dux Aquitaniæ, salutem cum dilectione sincera. Querelam dilectorum Mercatorum nostrorum Thomæ de Swyn de Waynfleete, & Simonis filii Alani de eadem recepimus, continentem, Quod cùm ipsi nuper quosdam servientes suos infrà regnum vestrum pro suis ibidem exercendis mercimoniis transmisissent, Thesaurarius vester bona & mercimonia prædictorum Thomæ & Simonis ad valenciam quadraginta librarum, quæ servientes prædicti in villa de Northberne in sua custodia habuerunt, die Sancti Michaelis ultimò præterita fecit absque causa rationabili arestari, & ea adhuc taliter arestata detinet injustè, in ipsorum Thomæ & Simonis damnum non modicum & depauperationem manifestam. Et quia eisdem mercatori- bus nostris subvenire volumus, quatenus suadente justitia poterimus in hac parte, vestram amicitiam requirimus cum affectu, quatenus audita querela prædictorum Thomæ & Simonis, vel ipsorum atturnatorum super restitutione bonorum & mercimoniorum prædictorum impendere velitis eisdem celeris justitiæ complementum : Ita quod pro defectu exhibitionis justitiæ super arestatione prædicta non oporteat nos pro mercatoribus nostris prædictis de alio remedio providere. Nobis autem quid ad hanc nos- tram instantiam duxeritis faciendum, rescribere velitis per præsentium portitorem. Datæ ut suprà.

Northbernæ villa.

The same in English.

TO the mightie Prince Lord Haquinus, by the grace of God the famous King of Norway, his most deare friend Edward by the same grace of God king of

England, Lorde of Ireland, and Duke of Aquitaine, greeting and sincere love. Wee received the complaint of our welbeloved Merchants Thomas de Swyn of Waynfleet, and Simon the sonne of Alanus of the same towne: the contents whereof are, that whereas of late, the saide parties sent certaine of their servants to traffike in your kingdome, your Treasurer upon the feast of S. Michael last past, without any just or reasonable occasion, caused the goods and merchandise of the foresaide Thomas and Simon, to the value of fortie pound, which their said servants had under their custodie at the towne of Northberne, to be arrested, and as yet also injuriously deteineth the same under the same arrest, to the great damage and impoverishing of the sayd Thomas and Simon. And forasmuch as our desire is to succour these our marchants so far foorth as we can, Justice requiring no lesse in this behalfe, we doe right earnestly request you, that having hearde the complaint and supplication of the foresayde Thomas and Simon, or of their Atturneyes, you woulde of your love and friendship, vouchsafe them speedie administration of Justice, about the restitution of their goods and marchandise aforesaide: least that for want of the exhibiting of Justice about the foresaid arrest, we be constrained to provide some other remedie for our marchants aforesaid. Our request is, that you would by the bearer of these presents, returne an answere unto us, what you are determined to doe, at this our instant motion. Given as above.

[I. 140.]

A third letter of King Edward the second, to Haquinus King of Norway in the behalfe of certaine English Marchants.

MAgnifico Principi Domino Haquino Dei gratia Regi Norwegiæ illustri, amico suo charissimo, Edwardus eadem Dei gratia Rex Angliæ, dominus Hyberniæ, & dux Aquitaniæ, salutem cum dilectione sincera. Pro mercatoribus nostris Lennæ, & partium vicinarum, quos Ballivus & Officiarii vestri civitatis vestræ Bergen dudum ceperunt, & stricto carceri manciparunt, quorum multi ut jam intelleximus, propter alimentorum subtractionem & duritiam, ac asperitatem carceris perierunt, ut ipsorum & bonorum suorum deliberationem præcipere curaretis, vestræ serenitati Regiæ nostras nuper transmisimus literas speciales. Sed vos, retentis adhuc in carcere nostris mercatoribus sicut prius, nobis per literas vestras quas audivimus & intelleximus diligenter, inter cætera rescripsistis, quod quidam mercatores de regno vestro de injuriis, violentiis & arrestationibus, quibus in regno nostro his diebus sunt, ut asserunt, contra justitiam aggravati, multipliciter conqueruntur, adjiciendo in vestris literis memoratis, quod quidam iniquitatis filii in villa Lennæ, ad piscandum ut dicebant halecia venientes, quendam militem Ballivum vestrum, in Vikia unà cum decem aliis subditis vestris, in vestris & regni vestri negotiis existentibus crudeliter occiderunt. Super quibus mens nostra gravatur quàmplurimum & turbatur, præsertim quum nunquam nostræ fuerit voluntatis, quod injuriæ, violentiæ, seu arrestationes aliquæ mercatoribus, vel aliis de regno vestro per aliquos de regno & potestate nostris fierent indebitè vel injustè : nec adhuc intelligere possumus, quod mercatoribus vestris per aliquem vel aliquos de subditis nostris huc usque aliter factum fuerit : Scientes pro certo quod si nobis per inquisitiones legitimas constare poterit hujusmodi gravamina subditis vestris infra regnum nostrum illata fuisse, nos sufficientes emendas, & satisfactiones debitas super illis, celerísque justitiæ complementum fieri faciemus. Et insuper si malefactores prædicti, qui præfatum militem, & alios secum existentes, ut præmittitur, occiderunt, de regno, seu potestate nostra sint, vel infrà idem regnum vel potestatem poterunt inveniri, de ipsis judicium & justitiam fieri præcipiemus, secundùm Leges & consuetudines regni nostri. Et quia inter nos & vos, nostròsque & vestros subditos hinc inde foveri desideramus mutuam concordiam & amorem ; ita quod mercatores nostri & vestri mercandisas suas in nostris &

A.D.
1313.
*Antiquitas
commercii in-
ter Angliam
& Norwe-
giam.*

THE ENGLISH VOYAGES

vestris regnis & dominiis liberè, & absque impedimento valeant exercere, prout temporibus progenitorum nostrorum fieri consuevit, & ex dictarum literarum vestrarum serie collegimus evidenter vos promptos esse similiter, & paratos ad omnia & singula, quæ pro vobis & vestris subditis super discordiis, contentionibus, aut gravaminibus inter nostros & vestros subditos qualitercunque suscitatis pro bono pacis & justitiæ fuerint æquanimiter facienda : Nos consimilia pro nobis & nostris, quantum ad nos & ad ipsos attinet, illius amore, qui pacis author fore dinoscitur, & pro quiete & commodo populi utriusque regnorum nostrorum, quatenus jus & ratio dictitaverint, promittimus nos facturos : Vestram amicitiam requirentes obnixius & rogantes, quatenus mercatores nostros prædictos, qui adhuc superstites relinquuntur, quos etiam tempore, quo dicta felonia committi dicebatur, interclusos tenebat custodia carceralis, jubere velitis nostri contemplatione, zelóque justitiæ ab hujusmodi custodia liberari, bona ab ipsis capta eis prout justum fuerit restitui faciendo. Et ut deliberatio mercatorum nostrorum prædictorum, & bonorum suorum eò facilius concedatur, placeat vobis cum diligentia debita ponderare, quod Galfridus Drewe, & quidam alii mercatores nostri de Lenne, quibusdam mercatoribus de regno vestro occasione ejusdem gravaminis ipsis mercatoribus vestris,

ad sectam Tidemanni Lippe infrà regnum nostrum, ut dicebatur, illati, centum libras sterlingorum persolverunt, sicut in quodam scripto indentato inter Ingelramum Lende de Thorenden, & quosdam alios mercatores vestros ex parte una, & præfatum Galfridum, & quosdam alios de regno nostro similiter ex altera confecto, vidimus contineri. Si qui verò de subditis vestris de aliquibus subditis nostris, de aliqua injuria ipsis facta querelas in curia nostra deponere voluerint, & prosequi cum effectu, ipsorum subditorum vestrorum petitiones admitti, & eis super querelis hujusmodi plenam & celerem justitiam fieri faciemus. Ita quod iidem subditi vestri exinde reputare debebunt meritò se contentos.

Et interim de excessibus & gravaminibus subditis vestris
infrà regnum nostrum qualitercunque illatis inquiri faciemus cum diligentia veritatem. Vestræ igitur voluntatis
beneplacitum in præmissis nobis rescribere velitis per
præsentium portitorem. Datæ apud Westminster tertio
die Aprilis.

The same in English.

TO the mightie Prince king Haquinus, by the grace
of God the famous king of Norway, his most
deare friend Edward by the same grace of God, king
of England, lord of Ireland, Duke of Aquitaine, greeting
and sincere love. We sent of late unto your royall
majestie our special letters, for the behalfe of our late
marchants of Lenne, and of the coast adjoyning (whome
your baily and officers of the citie of Bergen lately
apprehended, committing them to close prison, many
of whome, as we understand, are, for want of due
nourishment, and by reason of the extremitie & loath-
somnesse of the prison, quite perished) that you would
cause them and their goods to bee released. Howbeit,
you reteining as yet our marchants in durance as before,
in your letters, which we have diligently heard, and
throughly understood, have, amongst other matters,
returned this answere unto us : that certaine marchants
of your kingdome doe make sundrie complaints of
injuries, violences and arrests, whereby they have lately
(as themselves avouch) contrary to justice bene aggrieved
and oppressed in our dominions : adding moreover in
your sayde letters, that certaine sonnes of iniquitie of
the towne of Lenne, comming, as they saide, to fish
for herrings, cruelly murthered a certaine Knight, who
was in times past your bayliffe of Vikia, together with
ten others of your subjects, being imployed about the
affaires of your kingdome. In consideration whereof
our minde is exceedingly and above measure grieved
and troubled, especially sithence it was never any part
of our intent, that any injuries, violences, or arrests

should unjustly be inflicted upon any marchants, or
any others of your realme by any of our kingdomes:
neither can we as yet have any intelligence, that any
such hard measure hath bene offered unto any of your
marchants, by any one or moe of our subjects: giving
you for a certaintie to understand, that if upon lawfull
inquisition we shalbe advertised of any such grievances,
which have bene offered unto your subjects within our
realme, we will cause speedie justice to be administred,
and sufficient recompence, and due satisfaction to be
made in regarde thereof. And moreover, if the saide
malefactors, which, as it is aforesaid, slewe the forenamed Knight, and others of his companie, either be
appertaining unto our kingdome and dominion, or may
at any time be found within our saide kingdome or
dominion, we will command justice and judgement to
be executed upon them, according to the lawes and
customes of our realme. And forasmuch as our desire
is, that mutuall concord and amitie should be mainteined
and cherished between your and our subjects on both

*The antiquity
of traffique
betweene Eng-
land and Nor-
way.*

parts: so that our and your marchants may, in both
our Realmes and dominions, freely and without impediment exercise their traffique, as in the times of our
progenitors it hath bene accustomed: Whereas also we
evidently gathered out of the contents of your letter,
that you are in like sort readie and willing to put all
things in practise, which are by you and your subjects
(for the taking away of discords, contentions, and moles-
tations howsoever occasioned, and sprung up betweene
your and our subjects) lovingly to be performed: we
also doe promise for our selves, and our subjects, so
much as in us and them lieth, for his sake who is
knowen to be the author of peace, and for the benefite
& tranquilitie of both our Realmes (as justice and
reason shall move us) to doe the like. Desiring and
earnestly requesting at your hands, that of your love
and friendship, having regard of us, and consideration
of justice, you would commaund that our foresaide

marchants, who as yet remaine alive, and who also at
the time of the saide felonie committed, were shut
up in close prison, be delivered out of the saide
thraldome, causing their goods which have bene taken
from them, to bee, according unto justice, restored to
them again. And that the deliverie of our foresaide
marchants and goods, may be the more easily yeelded
unto, may it please you with diligent observation to
consider, that Gefferey Drew, and certaine other of our
marchants of Lenne, upon occasion of the greivances
offered unto your marchants within our Realme, (as
the report goeth) at the suite of Tidman Lippe, paide
unto the same your marchants an hundreth pound
sterling : even as in a certain Indenture made betweene
Ingelram Lende of Thorenden, and some other of your
marchants on the one part, and betweene the foresaide
Geffrey, and certaine of our marchants on the other
part, wee sawe conteined. Moreover, if any of your
subjects be minded to exhibite, and effectually to
prosecute their complaints in our Court, concerning any
of our subjects, or of any injury done unto them, we
will cause the petitions of those your subjects to be
admitted, and also full and speedie justice to be
administred, upon any such like complaints of theirs.
Insomuch, that those your subjects shal thinke themselves right well and sufficiently contented therewithall.
And in the meane space we will cause diligent inquisition of the trueth to be made, of all excesses and
grievances howsoever offered unto your subjects within
our dominions. May it please you therfore, by the
bearer of these presents, to returne an answere unto
us, what you are determined to doe in the premisses.
Given at Westminster, the third day of April.

[I. 142.]

[De Stapula

De Stapula tenenda in certo loco ordinatio,
Anno 13. Edwardi secundi.

REx collectoribus custumæ lanarum & pellium
lanutarum in portu London salutem. Cùm nos
vicesimo die Maii anno regni nostri sexto attendentes
damna & gravamina, quæ mercatoribus de regno nostro
diversimodè evenerunt, ex eo quod mercatores tam
indigenæ quàm alienigenæ lanas & pelles lanutas infrà
regnum & potestatem nostram ementes, & se cum
eisdem lanis & pellibus ad vendendum eas ad diversa
loca infrà terras Brabantiæ, Flandriæ, & de Artoys
eorum libito voluntatis transtulerint : & volentes etiam
hujusmodi damnis & gravaminibus quatenus bono modo
possemus providere, de consilio nostro ordinaverimus,
quod mercatores indigenæ & alienigenæ lanas & pelles
hujusmodi infrà regnum & potestatem prædictam ementes,
& ad terras prædictas ibidem vendendas ducere volentes,
lanas illas & pelles ad certam stapulam infrà aliquam
earundem terrarum, per Majorem & Communitatem
eorundem mercatorum, de regno nostro ordinandam
assignari, ac prout & quando expedire viderint mutan-
dum, & non ad alia loca in terris illis ducant, seu duci
faciant ullo modo : & inter cætera concesserimus
mercatoribus de regno nostro supradicto pro nobis &
hæredibus nostris, quòd ipsi Major & consilium
dictorum mercatorum, qui pro tempore fuerint, quibuscunque mercatoribus indigenis seu alienigenis, qui
contra dictam ordinationem venerint, & modo rationabili convicti fuerint, certas pecuniæ summas pro delictis
illis imponant, & quod illæ hujusmodi summæ de
bonis & mercimoniis mercatorum sic delinquentium,
ubicunque ea infrà regnum & potestatem prædictam
inveniri contigerit, per ministros nostros ad opus
nostrum leventur : prout in Charta nostra inde confecta
plenius continetur : quam quidem Chartam per singulos
comitatus regni nostri super costeras maris fecimus
publicari, & firmiter inhiberi, ne qui mercatores indigenæ

Major &
Communitas
stapulæ.

Charta anno
regni sexto
confecta.

ORDINANCE OF THE STAPLE

seu alienigenæ contra tenorem Chartæ prædictæ sub
pœnis contentis in eadem venerint ullo modo : Ac
postmodum dato nobis intelligi, quod quàmplures
mercatores tam indigenæ quàm alienigenæ, lanas &
pelles lanutas infrà regnum & potestatem prædictas
ementes, & se cum eisdem lanis & pellibus ad
vendendum eas ad alia loca in dictis terris, quàm ad
Stapulam juxta concessionem nostram prædictam per
Majorem & communitatem dictorum mercatorum de
regno nostro in aliqua terrarum illarum ordinatam &
assignatam transtulerint in nostri contemptum, & contra
Chartam ordinationis, publicationis & inhibitionis prædictarum assignaverimus quosdam fideles nostros in
diversis partibus regni ad inquirendum de lanis &
pellibus lanutis ad dictas terras alibi quàm ad Stapulam
illam ductis, ita quod emendæ inde ad nos pertinentes,
ad opus nostrum leventur ; etiam intellexerimus, quod
quasi omnes mercatores tam indigenæ quàm alienigenæ
hujusmodi mercimonia in dicto regno nostro exercentes
sunt culpabiles de præmissis : & quod plures inde
indictati, ac alii timentes inde indictari, lanas suas ac
pelles lanutas sub nominibus aliorum non culpabilium
faciunt advocari, & extra regnum nostrum transmitti
quibusdam alienigenis, sic culpabilibus in dictum regnum
forsitan non reversuris, ut sic forisfacturas prædictas
effugiant, & nos de emenda ad nos sic pertinente
illudant : quæ si permitterentur sic transire in nostri
damnum non modicum redundarent. Nos volentes
hujusmodi fraudibus obviare, & nostris damnis quatenus
bono modo poterimus præcavere, vobis præcipimus
firmiter injungentes, quod à singulis mercatoribus lanas
seu pelles lanutas per portum prædictum ad partes
exteras ducere volentibus corporale sacramentum ad
sancta Dei Evangelia recipiatis, quod ipsi lanas seu
pelles lanutas sub nomine ipsius, cujus propriæ sunt,
& non alterius advocabunt. & tunc recepta ab illo cujus
lanæ & pelles hujusmodi erunt, vel nomine suo
sufficiente securitate pro qua respondere volueritis, de

351

respondendo & faciendo nobis id quod ad nos pertinet de lanis & pellibus lanutis per ipsum ductis seu missis ad aliquam dictarum terrarum Flandriæ & Brabantiæ, & de Artoys contra formam Chartæ, proclamationis, & inhibitionis supradictarum, si ipsum super hoc convinci contingat, lanas & pelles illas lanutas extra portum prædictum, recepta prius custuma debita de eisdem, ad partes exteras transire permittatis. Teste Rege apud Doveram decimo octavo die Junii, per ipsum Regem & Consilium.

Et postmodum per breve de privato sigillo eodem modo mandatum est collectoribus custumæ prædictæ in portubus subscriptis : Videlicet,

In portu villæ Southhampton.
In portu villæ Weymouth.
In portu villæ Sancti Botolphi.
In portu villæ de Kingtone super Hull.
In portu villæ de novo Castro.
In portu villæ de magna Iernemutha.
In portu villæ de Lenne.
In portu villæ de Gypwico.

The same in English.
An Ordinance of the Staple to bee holden at one certaine place.

THe King unto his Collectors of custome, for wooll and woollen fels, in his port of London, greeting. Whereas we upon the 20. of May, in the sixt yeere of our reigne, considering the damages and grievances that have diversly happened unto the marchants of our realme, upon occasion that the marchants both of our owne, & of other countreis, buying up wooll and woollen fels within our kingdome and dominions, have, for the better sale thereof, at their pleasure conveyed themselves, and trasported the said wooll & fels into sundry places within the provinces of Brabant, Flanders and Artoys : and being desirous also, to our power, to provide a remedie against such damages and inconveniences, have ordained by our counsel, that all marchants, both homeborne and aliens, buying up such wools and fels, within our kingdome and dominion aforesaid, and being desirous to transport them into the foresaid provinces, there to bee solde, may carrie the saide wools and fels, or cause them to be caried to some certaine staple, within any of the saide Provinces, by the Maior and Communaltie of the said marchants of our realme, to be appointed and assigned, and when they shall thinke it expedient, to be changed and removed, and not unto any other place within the saide Provinces whatsoever : and whereas also, amongst other things, we have granted unto the marchants of our foresaid realme, for us and our heires, that the Maior and Councel of the saide marchants for the time being, may impose upon all marchants, homeborne or aliens whatsoever, that shall transgresse the foresaid ordination, and shall thereof lawfully be convicted, certaine summes of money to be paid for their offences, and that such summes must by our ministers and officers, to our use, be levied out of the goods and wares of the marchants so offending, wheresoever they shall chance to be found within our kingdome and dominions aforesaid, as in our Charter made for the *A Charter made in the sixt yeere of his reigne.* same purpose, it is more plainly expressed, (which Charter we have caused to be published upon the Seacoasts, throughout all the countreys of our realme, and a strong prohibition to be proclaimed, that no marchants, neither home-borne, nor strangers, may in any wise transgresse the tenour of the foresaide Charter, under the penalties therein contained) and whereas afterward it beeing given us to understand, that divers marchants both home-borne, and aliens, bought up such woolles and woollen felles within our saide Realme and dominions, and conveyed themselves with the saide wools and felles for the sale thereof, unto other places within the foresaide Provinces, besides the saide Staple, which was, according to our graunt aforesaide, appointed and ordained by the Maior and communaltie of the said marchants of our Realme, in some one of those Provinces, to the contempt of our authoritie, and contrary to the Charter of the ordination, publication, and inhibition aforesaide, wee assigned certaine of our faithfull subjects, in divers parts of our Realme, to make inquisition for such wools and woollen felles, as were conveyed unto any other place of the saide Provinces, then unto the Staple, so that by these meanes, the penalties due unto us might bee levied unto our use : and having intelligence also, that in a maner all marchants both home-borne, and strangers bartering such wares in our kingdome, are culpable of the premisses, and that many being indicted thereupon, and others fearing to bee indicted, doe cause their wools and woollen felles to bee avouched under the

[I. 144.] names of persons not culpable, and to be sent over unto certaine strangers being also culpable, and not minding perhaps to return any more into our realme, that they may so escape the foresaid forfeitures, and defraud us of the penaltie, appertaining of right unto us, (which abuses, if they were suffered so to goe unpunished woulde redound unto our extreame hinderance :) and beeing likewise desirous to withstand such deceitefull dealing, and so farre forth as wee can, to prevent our owne losses, we firmely command, and streightly charge you, that you doe receive of every particular marchant, desirous to convey any wools, or woollen fels out of the foresaid port, into any forrein dominions, a corporal oath upon Gods holy Evangelists : that they shall avouch all those wools and woollen fels under his name unto whom they doe properly belong, & under the name of none other : and then taking sufficient security from the owner of those wools and fels, or in his name, in regard whereof you wil undertake to warrantize, and make good unto us those penalties and forfaitures which shal unto us appertaine, for all wools, and woollen fels conveied or sent by any of the foresaid merchants unto any of the

ORDINANCE OF THE STAPLE

said provinces of Flanders, Brabant, and Artoys, contrary to the Charter of the Proclamation and inhibition above mentioned (if they shal chance to be convinced hereof) that first, our due custome being received, you doe permit the said wools and woollen fels to passe out of the foresaid port into forrein countries. Witnes the king at Dover the 18. day of June. By the king himselfe and his Councell.

And afterwarde by a Writte under the Kings privie Seale there was a like commandement given unto the Collectors of the custome aforesayde in the portes underwritten.

That is to say:

In the port
of the
Towne of

{
Weymouth.
Southhampton.
Saint Botulphs towne, now called Boston.
Kingtone upon Hull.
Newcastle.
Iernemouth magna, or Yermouth.
Lenne.
Gypwick or Ipswich.
}

END OF VOLUME I.

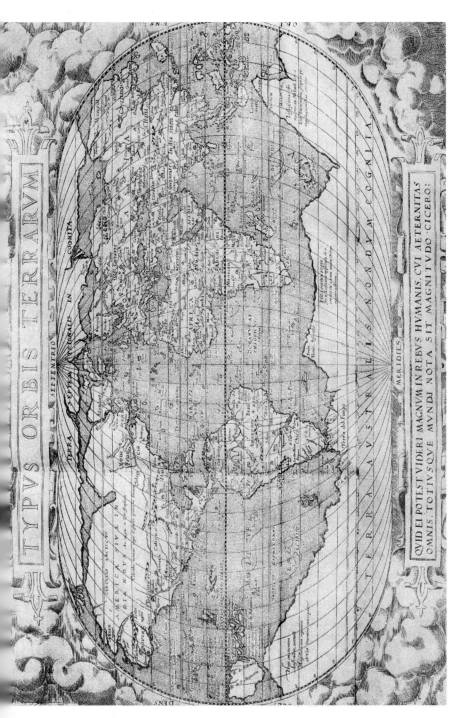

The material originally positioned here is too large for reproduction in this reissue. A PDF can be downloaded from the web address given on page iv of this book, by clicking on 'Resources Available'.

CPSIA information can be obtained at www.ICGtesting.com
Printed in the USA
LVOW13s0648060414

380405LV00001BA/53/P